YEAR TO SUCCESS

Written By

BO BENNETT

www.YearToSuccess.com

For my mother, Sandy Bennett
who is without doubt,
running around Heaven showing
everyone her little boys book.

Archieboy Holdings, LLC.
365 Boston Post Road, #311
Sudbury, MA 01776

First printing in April of 2004

publisher@archieboy.com
http://www.yeartosuccess.com

Contents

Acknowledgements

I would like to thank Deborah Ali and Kimberly Bennett for their hard work and dedication in helping me correct my careless typos, the spelling errors that my spell checker missed, and my grammatical mistakes that would otherwise make me look like a third grader. A special thanks to Marci O'Daffer and other Year To Success members who have also brought several written blunders to my attention.

I would like to thank my mother, Sandy Bennett, who was a great salesperson and a loving and caring individual. I would like to thank my father, Bob Bennett, for allowing me to work beside him while growing up. I would like to thank my brother, Stephen Bennett, for showing me how even drastic changes in people are possible, and my sister, Debbie Lancsc, for teaching me so many of life's valuable lessons.

I would like to give thanks and recognition to the many success authors who have inspired me throughout the years. The authors who have most influenced my own success philosophy outlined in this book are (in alphabetical order) *Dale Carnegie, Napoleon Hill, Anthony Robbins, Donald Trump, Denis Waitley, Dr. Andrew Weil,* and *Zig Ziglar.* I strongly recommend books and/or audio programs by any of these authors.

Most of all, I would like to thank my wife, Kimberly Bennett, and my two children, Annabelle and Trebor, for their support, encouragement, and inspiration. Thank you.

Introduction

The meaning of this book.

Have you been promised success if you follow a few quick and dirty "rules" or "secrets" of success? Are you tired of irrelevant analogies that do nothing for you but make you feel inadequate? Have you had enough of highly metaphysical concepts and not enough practical solutions? Have you had your fill of grossly exaggerated claims that try to trick you into thinking success is easy? Are you all "affirmationed" out? You are not alone.

Think of success as a game of chance in which you have control over the odds. As you begin to master concepts in personal achievement, you are increasing your odds of achieving success. *Year To Success* is a full year course in success, designed to be a practical guide to achieving your definition of success. Each day of this course will, through practical application, increase your odds of achieving success. It has been said that one line of wisdom can change your life more than volumes of books. Imagine what hundreds of pages of wisdom can do.

Why this book is different.

Year To Success is perhaps the most complete book on success ever written. It uses my "formula" for success: ***education + inspiration + action = success***. *Education:* each week starts off with two educational articles and ends with two more educational articles. *Inspiration:* the third day of the week is a success biography on someone I believe is one of the most successful people in history. These success biographies are full of inspiration to help keep your flame for success burning on high. *Action:* each of the educational articles has one or more action steps associated with it. Taking action is what this book is all about. It is doing the action steps that bring you closer to success.

How to use this book.

This book can be read from cover to cover, or by jumping around from topic to topic, depending on what interests you most on a particular day. However, *Year To Success* was created as a one-year course in success with a total of 366 days (just to make sure we are covered with leap year). Most people start Day 1 on a Monday, so the two days of "R&R" (review and reflection) fall on the weekend. However, you can start on any day of the year you wish. You may choose to read through the book the first time as you would any other book, skipping the action steps, then beginning the course by reading one article a day and completing the action steps. To get the most out of this book, just be sure to actually do the action steps associated with each educational article.

It is suggested you get yourself a "success journal" for this course. This can be any notebook where you keep all of your written action steps organized and centralized.

Why I wrote this book.

Since age 10, I have been fascinated with success and personal achievement. What makes some people achieve so much and others so little? This question continued to burn inside of me until I decided to commit my full attention to organizing my 20 years of research and experience into one complete collection that offered individuals a realistic approach to achieving success.

As a father, I wanted to put what I have learned in writing for my kids, for a time when they are old enough to understand the meaning behind the words. We never know when our time is up on this earth and I may not be around to share this essential information with them.

Why I waited 21 years to write this book.

The last thing I wanted to be was a successful author who became successful by selling books on success. Although I achieved financial success many years ago, it was not until recently that I began to discover how important personal development and personal achievement is in true success. I needed to first put my theories to the test before I shared these ideas with others.

My writing style.

When it comes to the English language, perfection is in the eye of the beholder, and it also depends on what century you're living in. I don't use words like "thither" and I don't mind ending a sentence with a preposition now and then (I paraphrase Sir Winston Churchill when I say that not ending a sentence with a preposition "is a rule up with which I will not put"). Even God ends sentences with prepositions: "Have you eaten from the tree that I commanded you not to eat from?" Genesis 3:10–12.

I have a casual style of writing that is meant to be more like I am speaking directly to you. My goal is to reach as many people as possible, not to impress a select few with my perfect grammar (which I don't have anyway). My professionalism should be apparent in the content itself. Communication is about being effective, not always about being proper.

Religion / God.

I feel religion is very personal to everyone. Having faith in a higher power is another way of increasing one's odds of success. I believe that the level of faith one has in the higher power is directly related to the increase in the odds. However, I do my best to tiptoe around this area when possible so as to not offend or alienate those with strong personal beliefs.

The whole he/she/his/hers issue.

I really wish someone of authority, like Mr. Webster or one of his offspring, would come up with a singular pronoun that was gender independent like "shis" for his or her. Until that time, we writers must play the "do not offend anyone" game and use crappy grammar by writing "they", play switch-aroo and change genders, and/or use the "s/he" slash thing which you will never see me do.

I resort to both the poor grammar solution and the switching of genders just because this is what helps my writing flow. So I apologize in advance for offending the males when I use a feminine pronoun, the females when I use a masculine pronoun, and my fifth grade English teacher when using plural pronouns when a singular should be used.

Why I chose the people I did for the success biographies.

The 52 success biographies in this course were chosen based on a number of factors.

- they all have very inspiring stories
- they are/were all tremendously successful at what they set out to do
- information could be confirmed by several sources
- they are people who have touched the lives of the majority of Y2S readers in some way
- they are "heroes" of mine

I would be the first to admit, that none of these people are perfect. After all, who is? I am sure anyone can dig up dirt on any one of these people. My success biographies focus on the positive contributions the person made to the world, not their faults. Get inspiration from how they mastered principles of success, and leave the dirt behind.

Offending material.

With over 250 articles, I would be surprised if you didn't get offended by at least something I've written! If I attempted to make each article neutral and not offend anyone, I would have to leave out all humor, and I would not be able to communicate the true message. Trying to please everyone all the time is a recipe for failure. I apologize if you are offended in any way by one of my ideas, beliefs, or attempts at humor. Please accept my apology, and continue with the next day. I certainly do not ask that you accept all of my beliefs, but I ask that you accept my opinion (I hope that didn't offend you!).

YEAR TO SUCCESS

Day 1: Why Success?

As humans, we are all driven by an inner desire to feel important. That is, we all want to know that our lives make a difference in a positive way. We want to know that in some way, the world is a better place because we are part of it. Success is another way of saying that we are doing just that.

Many people aspire to nothing more than going through a day's work and catching the game on the sports channel before passing out on the couch, while others spend 18 hour days in the E.R. saving lives, create works of art that touch the lives of millions, or donate hospitals to cities. Those who do not desire success will never get it. You must be ready for it and pursue it with a passion.

The definition of success is personal to each one of us. However, most people include the following in their definition of success:

- living your dream
- living every day with passion
- having true wealth; that is, knowing you have more than you need
- learning appreciation and gratitude
- positively influencing the lives of others in some way
- true happiness
- having loved ones with whom to share it all

If you are only interested in financial gain, and that alone is your definition of success, that is fine. No matter what your definition and ultimate goal, if you pursue it with passion and determination you will ultimately get what you want. However, with the pursuit of money alone you will find that once you have it, there is still very much missing in your life.

Today **is** the first day of the rest of your life and more important, day one of a series of 366 days that will have a dramatically positive influence on your life. Mark this day as the day you made a commitment to change your life for the better and start living your dreams.

ACTION STEP(S):

---

1) Take time to write down your definition of success. Be specific. Do not use phrases like "lots of money"... instead say "annual income of X and total net worth of Y". You must be able to know for certain when you reach your definition of success, at least your definition at the start of this program. Write this down and save it somewhere where you can access it one year from now.

"Nothing in this world can take the place of persistence. Talent will not; nothing is more common than unsuccessful people with talent. Genius will not; unrewarded genius is almost a proverb. Education will not; the world is full of educated derelicts. Persistence and determination alone are omnipotent."

- Calvin Coolidge (1872–1933)

Day 2: Remembering and Using People's Names

It has been said that a person's name is the most important word in the world to that person. Using a person's name in conversation is one of the best ways to build rapport. Sounds good, but if you are like most people, the names of people you meet go in one ear and out the other. So step one is remembering the name.

Many memory experts believe that we all have perfect memories. We are capable of remembering just about any detail from our lives no matter how far back and how specific. The challenge is **recalling** the information from our memory.

There are dozens of techniques for remembering names; some work for some people and some do not. For this reason, I am listing many of them for you to choose the one that works best for you. You may want to adapt a few techniques rather than just one. For example, use a visual technique for those you meet face to face, and when they tell you the names of their children, use an association technique to associate the person you met with their children's names. The key again is to use what works best for you.

Here are some steps that should all be followed each time you meet someone:

1) **LISTEN AND PAY ATTENTION TO THE NAME.** This may seem so obvious, yet it is so overlooked. Pay attention to the name when it is given to you and make sure you can recall it 5 seconds later. If you can, you are halfway to putting this name in your long-term memory.

2) **Repeat immediately.** The first sentence out of your mouth after hearing a name should include that name. "It is a pleasure to meet you, Jennie". Use this instead of "Jennie, it is nice to meet you" because saying the person's name right after they say it is

often a mindless automated response that does very little, if anything, toward helping you remember the name.

3) **Repeat often.** Be careful with this one. You do not want to sound like a psycho, or worse a pushy salesperson, by overdoing it. However, people love to hear their own name and this technique will keep your listener interested in what you have to say.

4) **End the conversation with their name.** This is the best way to end any conversation. "Jennie, it was great meeting you". This not only once more sinks their name into your memory, but says to the person that you have cared enough to remember their name.

5) **Comment on and/or ask questions about the name.** "Jennie, have you always been called Jennie or do people call you Jen as well?" or "Do you spell Jennie with a 'y' or 'ie'?" If it is a unique name, ask about its origin or say that it is a beautiful name (if you really think it is).

6) **Review.** After the conversation is over with the person, review their name and face in your mind several times. Do this frequently over the next 24 hours. As you get better with steps 1-5, this step will become less important.

Memory is linked to your senses and emotions. As you incorporate more emotion and more of your senses into remembering a name, the name will become more difficult to forget.

Now here are some techniques used to remember names:

1) **Face association.** Examine a person's face discreetly when you are introduced. Try to find an unusual feature, whether ears, hairline, forehead, eyebrows, eyes, nose, mouth, chin, complexion, etc. Create an association between that characteristic, the face, and the name in your mind. The association may be to associate the person with someone you know with the same name, or may be to associate a rhyme or image from the name with the person's face or defining feature.

2) **Substitution.** Take a person's name and substitute objects that you can visualize with that name. Then associate those objects with the person somehow. For example, "Murphy" can be substituted with "Murphy's oil soap". Visualize the person pouring the soap all over them while dancing the jig. Why dancing the jig? The more outrageous you make the visualization, the better it will stick to memory. Just try not to laugh when making the association, especially if the person is in the process of telling you they have just been fired.

3) **Paint their name on their forehead.** OK, not literally, but in your imagination. Use your favorite color paint and clearly see each letter as you paint it. If you are standing closer than a few feet from the person, do not look directly at their forehead but rather between their eyes.

4) **Association with someone you know.** Associate the person you meet with someone you know or know of with the same name. Then visualize the person you know in the same situation as the person you have met. For example, if you meet a "Will" picture your Uncle Will (assuming you have an Uncle Will) standing there, in that same spot. To make the association stronger, visualize your uncle Will doing something that he is known for doing—like his loud drunken laugh.

If you forget the person's name at anytime during the conversation, THIS IS THE TIME TO ASK. Do not be embarrassed to say something like, "Forgive me but I've forgotten your name..." or "I am sorry, what was your name again?" Remember that most people forget names. Those who make it a point to humble themselves and ask for a name again are seen as someone who cares about learning the name.

The more you do this, the more second nature it will become and remembering names will be an automatic process for you. Using names in conversation will take you a long way in building and maintaining rapport, as well as helping others to both remember you and like you. You will soon find that remembering names becomes a game and it is really quite fun, not to mention one of the best skills that anyone can posses!

ACTION STEP(S):

---

1) Go through a magazine and learn the names of all the people for which there are photos and names. It is best to use a magazine that does not have many movie stars or famous people whose names you already know. Or if you prefer go through your friend's/spouse's high school yearbook and do the same. Remember the names (first name only is fine) of at least 50 people.

2) Commit yourself to remembering the names of all the characters introduced in movies you watch.

3) Make your best effort to remember the name of every new person you meet, simply because it makes the other person feel special and important.

"The secret of a good memory is attention, and attention to a subject depends upon our interest in it. We rarely forget that which has made a deep impression on our minds."

- Tryon Edwards (1809–1894)

Day 3: Inspiration from Henry Ford

Henry Ford (1863–1947) was the founder, vice-president, and chief engineer of the Ford Motor Company.

Success is age independent. Henry Ford constructed his first steam engine at the age of 15.

Success is not formal education. Ford's formal education was limited to what is rumored to be about three years.

Success is fueled by failure. After two unsuccessful attempts to establish a company to manufacture automobiles, the Ford Motor Company was incorporated in 1903 with Henry Ford as vice-president and chief engineer.

Success is problem solving. By early 1914, Ford's innovative assembly line had resulted in a monthly labor turnover of 40 to 60 percent in his factory, largely because of the unpleasant monotony of assembly-line work and repeated increases in the production quotas assigned to workers. Ford met this difficulty by doubling the daily wage to $5 and shaving one hour off the workday.

Success is overcoming competition. In 1905, there were 50 start-up companies a year trying to get into the auto business, and Ford succeeded.

Success is doing what you feel in your gut is right, despite public opinion. The Wall Street Journal called Ford's daily wage increase plan "an economic crime," and critics everywhere heaped "Fordism" with equal scorn.

Success is seeking out those who can help you with your goals. In 1903, Ford found twelve people willing to invest a total of

$28,000 in another motor company. Ford was then able to begin production of the Model A car. The car sold well and the company flourished and by 1907 the profits reached $1,100,000 In 1909, Ford made the decision to manufacture only one type of car, the Model T, which changed automotive history forever.

[Sources: http://www.hfmgv.org, http://www.biography.com]

"If you think you can do a thing or think you can't do a thing, you're right."

- Henry Ford (1863–1947)

Day 4: General Life Purpose

What is your general purpose here on the earth? Does your existence make the world a better place? Consider the statements below and think about where you currently fit in. There is no right or wrong answer.

1) I am here to live the highest quality life I can. This includes working toward constant self-improvement and engaging in leisure activities such as golf and fishing. My time on this earth is limited and I will do what I can to get the most self-gratification possible.

2) It is my purpose to provide for my family and give my family the highest quality of life possible. My "free" time should be spent with my family, for my family.

3) My purpose on this earth is to do as much good for as many people as possible within my lifetime. I realize that there is a world beyond myself and my family that needs something that I can provide.

Don't confuse general life purpose with just "life purpose". General life purpose is a starting point for determining your life purpose that helps you decide who and what is most important in your life right now.

See this as a scale with your typical self-centered individual on one end and someone like Mother Teresa or Gandhi on the other end. Where do you now see yourself on this scale? Would you like to be somewhere else on the scale? Before you blurt out an answer somewhere near a Gandhi, be realistic and consider the sacrifices and lifestyle of each step in the scale. Consider what is "socially acceptable" and if you are willing to defy social boundaries by living your life differently than most. If you are a family-oriented person and you wish to shift more to #1 or #3, how will your family react? Will they support you? What if they don't?

This exercise in finding your general life purpose is one of the many very important first steps to success. You must be at peace with yourself and feel no guilt as to what you desire from life. Once you have this confidence, the pursuit of your goals becomes easier and more enjoyable.

ACTION STEP(S):

1) Decide what people or groups of people you want to spend your life (or at least this part of your life) benefiting. Be honest with yourself. Write down in a paragraph who will benefit from your life purpose.

2) Now write down the reasons why you are focusing where you are on the scale. For example, if you are 16 years old and your current life purpose is to have fun and do all you can while you are young, then add that as a reason. If you are just starting a family and your focus is on your family, you might put down that your family needs you most at this time in your life. Or if you have been there, done that, and feel it is time to give back to the world, list that as a reason. The goal is to remove any guilt you might otherwise feel by not focusing on your own needs, your family's, or those less fortunate.

3) If you have a significant other in your life, be sure to discuss this with them. A relationship is a partnership and both parties must be in agreement on expectations. After your discussion, alter your purpose if necessary and/or your relationship.

"Many persons have a wrong idea of what constitutes true happiness. It is not attained through self-gratification but through fidelity to a worthy purpose."

- Helen Keller (1880–1968)

Day 5: Positive Mental Attitude

One of the few things we have complete control over is our thoughts. When faced with adversity, we can choose to focus on the negative in the situation or the positive. A positive mental attitude, or PMA, is something everyone can adopt with a little practice. The benefits of a PMA are beyond comprehension, and according to many achievers, the number one reason for their success.

A positive mental attitude is seeing the benefits, opportunities, and good in situations rather than the setbacks, problems, and bad. More important, it is focusing on this positive and using it to your advantage. PMA is asking how something can be done rather than saying it can't be done. It is the driving force behind persistence and perseverance.

There is a belief that nothing in this world is "good" or "bad", but rather everything is balanced and it is only our perception that makes good and bad. Whether you believe that to be true or not, it is hard to debate that perception and attitude have much to do with how we view the world.

Shortly after adopting a positive mental attitude you will find more opportunities, successes, and "good luck" in your life than ever before. The main reason for this is the universal principle that like attracts like. PMA is a snowball effect that, once begun, builds and grows stronger with each positive event in your life. Conversely, negative thought does the same, which is why it can be very difficult for negative people to change.

The list of benefits of adopting a positive mental attitude goes on, however, the most compelling reason for adopting a PMA is that it is the major part of having an attractive personality. Most people do not like to be around negative people. A positive mental attitude shows in everything you say and do from casual conversation to your performance at work. A PMA will help you in just about anything you do including increasing your income, being promoted at work, getting a new job, and in strengthening your relationships. With those kinds of benefits, why would anyone choose negativity?

Developing a positive mental attitude is not difficult, but like everything else it just takes a little practice to master. Here are some suggestions to help you build your PMA.

- Scrutinize every event in your life that appears negative and look for the positive. Make a written list if you have to of all the good that resulted from the negative event or situation. Do NOT give up until your list of positives is equal to or greater than the negative. After forcing yourself to do this for a while, this thought process will happen instantaneously. It really is almost miraculous the difference it will make in your life.
- Surround yourself with positive people. Negativity is even more contagious than the common cold. It spreads like a wildfire that is out of control and the best way to avoid it is to stay out of its path. However, I am not a believer in ditching those you spend time with, unless necessary. Instead, be extra positive when around these people and watch it "rub off" onto them. Send those you know that could use some help with their PMA this article (e-mail feature below). You can also start spending more time with positive people and less time with those whom you find negative. The right online communities, such as the YearToSuccess.com discussion board and chat room are excellent places to meet those who share the same positive mental attitude goals.
- Read and listen to positive, motivational and inspirational material. Bookstores and libraries have a wide selection; you just need to know where to look.
- Avoid the morning news and news before bedtime. It is almost always morbid and depressing. Instead start and end your day with inspirational music or just good conversation (even if with yourself!)

- If you catch yourself thinking negatively or especially projecting a negative attitude STOP IMMEDIATELY, take a deep breath, and do everything in the first suggestion.

With a positive mental attitude on your side you will find yourself a magnet to a never-ending stream of positive events that will improve your quality of life and the lives of those around you. A PMA will certainly bring you one giant leap closer to success.

ACTION STEP(S):

1) Write down all the negative events surrounding your life right now, one negative event at the top of each page. Then do your best to fill the page with positives that come from the negative. Remember that everything has perfect balance. It is up to you to use your PMA to find that balance.

2) Commit to making an effort not to give in to the negativity of others. Do not feed their negativity with negativity of your own. When you are around a negative person, use your PMA and watch hope and inspiration begin to show on that person. If you find they are in too deep and you cannot help them, excuse yourself and walk away.

Days 6 and 7 are for "R&R"—review and reflection. Spend these days reviewing the last five articles and reflecting on the information and how it relates to your life. Now is also a good time to make sure all the action steps for the previous days have been completed.

Day 8: Using Humor Effectively

Laughter is said to be the best medicine known to man. With that in mind, the development of a good sense of humor and the ability to make people laugh can do more good for those you come into contact with than an entire pharmacy of drugs.

Besides just making other people happy and feel good, humor can be used to make light of an otherwise awkward situation, and ease both tension and ill feelings while building rapport. In a speaking or writing situation, humor can keep an audience interested in what you have to say, thus helping you become a better communicator. If popularity is one of your goals, then humor is a very effective tool. It is difficult not to like someone who makes you laugh.

People have different senses of humor; this is why not all people find all the same comedians funny. This is also why some people (such as myself) just about lose control of bodily functions when watching movies like *The Naked Gun*, while others just roll their eyes. Despite these differences, humor is recognized and the effects of humor remain.

Here are some different kinds of humor that you can use. You may find that you are better at delivering some kinds of humor than others. If you have a natural talent at one kind of humor, work on developing it. You may find a good backup career. :)

- **The Joke.** This is a fictitious story or question that has most likely been told to you. Jokes are most appropriate when the content relates to your current discussion or the situation you are in. However, joke tellers are like delivery boys who just carry the message and don't write it, and most people recognize that.
- **The Funny Story.** This is a true story (or one you believe to be true) about something that has happened to you or someone close to you. Try to avoid funny stories that happened to a "friend of a friend" because most times they

are just not believable. Use the universal "humor license" and just say "friend"—the close the relationship to the person or persons in the story, the funnier the story.

- **The Impersonation.** Impersonations are only funny when you are impersonating someone or something that your audience knows. Impersonations are also a bit risky especially when you do not want to offend the person you are impersonating.

- **Physical Comedy.** If you have ever seen Chris Farley, Chevy Chase or Steve Martin in action, you have seen great examples of physical comedy. Physical comedy usually involves an exaggeration of the body and deliberate clumsiness to make others laugh. It is important with physical comedy to be deliberate enough so others see you as funny, rather than just clumsy.

- **What Ifs.** What if after reading the above paragraph on physical comedy, you got up to use the restroom and tripped? The thought of that is funny (unless of course you are at the fragile age where a trip means trip to the hospital—in which case you should avoid physical comedy all together). "What Ifs" are great for a chuckle and to lighten situations.

- **Sarcasm.** If you have ever seen David Spade in a movie or TV show you have seen sarcasm at its best. Or someone like Rita Ruder who says, "I love being married. It's so great to find that one special person you want to annoy for the rest of your life." It is important to note, however, that sarcasm should be used carefully with those you know who can take such comments lightheartedly. Sarcasm is not generally seen as a positive quality and very often it is used to express negative emotions.

- **Slapstick Comedy.** My favorite example of a classic slapstick comedy is _The Naked Gun_ series with Frank Drebbin, or just about any movie where Leslie Nielsen is the star. An example of slapstick comedy is when Frank is searching through an office for clues, opens a drawer and says "BINGO" then pulls out a Bingo game card. Slapstick is also known as excessive silliness, but I admire slapstick for its inherent genius.

Here are my ten "Rules of Humor". Follow them and humor will serve you well. Break them, and you will be the subject of other people's humor.

1. **NEVER EVER take credit for someone else's joke.** Not only is it just wrong, but if you try to pass a joke or funny comment off as your own and someone hears you that knows it is not yours, it will make for a very awkward situation that even the best sense of humor may not be able to get you out of. If you repeat something funny that someone else has said, start with "As _____ would say..." or somehow otherwise make it clear that the joke is not your original thought. You can still use humor and maintain your integrity.

2. **Make sure if you tell a joke or say something funny it is to a new audience.** Learn a lesson from your over-intoxicated relatives at parties. A joke may be funny once, but try to pass it off again to the same audience and you will be on your way to comedic purgatory.

3. **Be appropriate.** There is a time and place for everything and humor is no exception. For example, humor can be very effective at a funeral to make others feel better but telling jokes at the guest of honor's expense may not be a good idea.

4. **Keep it short.** Long-winded jokes and stories do more damage than good.

5. **Be smooth.** Often the delivery is more important than content. Stuttering and messing up words can really make a mess of humor. My favorite example of this is Chris Farley in *Tommy Boy* when he is attempting to repeat his father's "Bull and T-bone" joke (if you have not seen the movie, rent it!)

6. **Timing.** Even the funniest joke delivered at the wrong time (too late, too early) can flop.

7. **Relevancy.** Make sure the humor is relevant to the conversation or situation. Starting an insurance speech with a joke about getting a haircut just does not flow.

8. **Do not make jokes at other people's expense.** This can be very tempting at times, especially with "easy targets".

Hold your tongue and use your creativity to redirect your humor elsewhere.

9. **Don't overdo it.** Be funny, have a good sense of humor, but do not be a comedian. This is true for everyone except comedians who make a living by making people laugh. In everyday life, and especially business, you want people to take you seriously. Know when to be serious.

10. **Don't be corny.** Unless the members of your audience are frequent patrons of "Chuck E. Cheese", stay away from the corny jokes. If you want to know what I mean by corny, pick up a package of kids' Dixie cups—the ones with the "jokes"—and read the cups.

Realize that even professional comedians deliver jokes that fail. We often do not see these because their televised jokes are collections of their best jokes that have been proven. If you know how to properly respond to a failed joke, you can end up with a situation more humorous than if the joke had succeeded. Here are some things you can do when people fail to find humor in your joke:

- Pretend you are holding a microphone in one hand, and while tapping the hand with your other hand's two fingers, say, "Hello, is this thing on?"
- Quickly cover up by asking a question.
- Don't laugh at your own jokes and people may not think you were trying to be funny.

Using humor effectively requires practice and self-confidence. Remember, with every joke that does not go over well, your art of humor will improve.

ACTION STEP(S):

---

1) Do one of the following in front of an audience in the next 24 hours (audience can be business associates, a group of friends, or just your spouse). a) Tell a joke. If you do not know one, use the Internet to find one, b) tell someone a funny story, c) do your best impersonation, or d) pretend you hit your head on the door when you open it, using your hand to make the bang sound, then hold your head and do your best groaning.

"A sense of humor is part of the art of leadership, of getting along with people, of getting things done."

- Dwight D. Eisenhower (1890–1969)

Day 9: Perseverance, Persistence and Determination

If the "how to" for achieving success had to be summed up in just one single word, that word would be **perseverance**. It is the one characteristic shared by all successful people throughout history. Perseverance is the true essence of success.

There are three words in the English language that are often used synonymously, yet have slightly different meanings when referring to success. They are:

Persistence. The act of holding firmly and steadfastly to a purpose, state, goal, or undertaking despite obstacles, warnings, or setbacks.

Determination. The quality of mind which reaches definite conclusions; decision of character; resoluteness.

Perseverance. Persistent determination.

Einstein said that the definition of insanity included doing something repeatedly despite the same results. At first this made complete sense to me, picturing a guy in a straight-jacket banging his head against the wall, or Jack Nicholson in _The Shining_ banging out on his typewriter "All work no play makes Jack a dull boy" over and over. Then, I thought about how ironic it was seeing the similarity of the words persistence and insanity and how the two can be easily confused.

There is a story about Walter P. Chrysler who, in 1905, bought his first car, which he immediately took apart in order to see how it worked. After putting it back together again, he repeated the process—rumor has it several times. Chrysler's friends and family thought he had lost his mind. Needless to say, Chrysler's persistence allowed him to create one of the largest automobile manufacturing companies in the world and realize success beyond his dreams.

Persistence is NOT insanity. Giving up your purpose or goal due to obstacles—that's insanity! In the case of Chrysler, although assembling the car over and over did produce the same apparent results, there was a learning and thought process going on in Chrysler's head. As for Jack in *The Shining*... well, he was just plain insane.

The key to determination is the word "decision". You must decide what you want before you can get it. Despite the sanity and perfectly legitimate reasoning behind back up plans, I always admired those who refused to even think of a backup plan because they were so determined that their plan was going to work. Determination takes great self-confidence and decisiveness. You must be willing to completely disregard all alternatives to your decision and set it clear in your mind that you MUST and you WILL.

Perseverance is a great word that is defined by persistent determination. It is such a powerful word that once you experience true perseverance, simply reading, saying or hearing the word will energize you.

ACTION STEP(S):

---

1) Take time to think about your own life and where you are today. If you are not where you want to be, why? Think back to your goals, dreams and any obstacles that may have gotten in the way. Did you persist in spite of the obstacles or did you use those obstacles as excuses not to persist?

Day 10: Inspiration from Benjamin Franklin

Benjamin Franklin (1706–1790) was perhaps the most famous American in history who was best known for being an American statesman and inventor.

Success is not limiting yourself. Franklin became famous for being a scientist, an inventor, a statesman, a printer, a philosopher, a musician, and an economist.

Success is turning frustration into opportunities. Franklin had poor vision and needed glasses to read. He became tired of constantly taking his glasses off and putting them back on again. Franklin used this frustration to create a way to see both near and far without the need for taking off his glasses. He had two pairs of spectacles cut in half and put half of each lens in a single frame. Today, we call them bifocals.

After Franklin's "retirement", he spent much time reading books. However, he found he had great difficulty reaching for books high on his shelves. He created a long wooden arm with a claw on the end to assist him with this task and ease his frustration.

Success is doing what you feel is right in your heart despite public opinion. After both physical and mental abuse by one of Ben's older brothers, Ben decided to run away to Philadelphia in 1723, even though running away was illegal at the time.

Success is work. Franklin had a simple formula for success. He believed that successful people worked just a little harder than other people.

Success is knowing when to move on. In 1748, Franklin's business was flourishing so he retired, turning it over to his foreman in return for a regular stipend. He did this so he would have more time for his scientific pursuits.

Success is spawned from the desire to help others. Ben's older brother, John, suffered from kidney stones and Ben wanted to help him feel better. Ben developed a flexible urinary catheter that appears to have been the first one produced in America.

Success is not about being an only child or about getting attention from parents. Ben was one of 17 siblings!

Success is living usefully. Franklin had a strong belief that good citizenship included an obligation of public service and served his state and country for most of his life. To Benjamin Franklin, there was no greater purpose in life than to "live usefully."

[Sources: http://www.ushistory.org, http://www.lucidcafe.com, http://www.biography.com]

"Early to bed and early to rise, makes a man healthy, wealthy, and wise."

- Benjamin Franklin

Day 11: Specific Purpose

In the movie _The Jerk_, starring my all time favorite actor/comedian, Steve Martin, Nathan (Steve) set off to discover his "special purpose". Once he knew what it was, or thought he knew what it was, his life had meaning and direction. In real life, the same holds true. However, to avoid laughing every time I say "special purpose" (if you have seen _The Jerk_, you understand why) I prefer to refer to one's ultimate life goal as "specific purpose".

A few days ago, we contemplated our general purpose in life, which answered the general question, "who will benefit from our existence?" Now with our specific purpose, we answer the question, "what are we going to do with our lives?" with more detail and thought.

Before you start breaking a sweat with anxiety over this question, let me preface the remainder of this topic with these words: very often people never set goals for the same reason some people never find true love—they are "waiting" for that perfect someone (or perfect whatever in the case of goals). Rarely do people know exactly what they want and it is even less common for people to know their ultimate goal in life. No sweat. Just be as specific as you can. If the most specific you can be is "I wanna be rich!" then I would ask you to define what "rich" means to you. The more specific you can be the better.

A specific purpose is like a personal "mission statement". It's funny how businesses realize the importance of this structure and purpose, yet individuals do not. Make your personal mission statement as detailed and descriptive as possible. When writing it, use the present tense with statements like "I am a commander in the air force leading over 100 soldiers, traveling all over the world while meeting new people". While you are writing this all down, visualize it as well. Visualization is an important part of success, one that will be referred to many times in this program, so now is a good time to start putting it to use.

Once you have your specific purpose, you are free to add to it, alter it and even completely change it. Identifying a specific purpose is a very good starting point, but be forewarned that it should not control your destiny. Life is full of changes and these changes may bring new opportunity and desires to you. Keep an open mind. If after spending years pursuing a career as an astronaut, you decide you really want to be a ballerina, then change your specific purpose. Just make sure changes made to your specific purpose are not due to failure or frustration, but rather a true desire in your heart.

ACTION STEP(S):

1) Write down your specific purpose with as much detail as possible. Use a whole page if you can. Be sure to write as if you have already achieved your special purpose; "I am...", "I have...", etc.

"Thoughts lead on to purposes; purposes go forth in action; actions form habits; habits decide character; and character fixes our destiny."

- Tyron Edwards

Day 12: The Power of Choice

Where we are today is a result of choices we have made in our past. Choices as minor as what to have for breakfast to choosing what we want to do for a living. Each of us were born with the gift of free will and we have the right to choose our destiny by a series of lifelong decisions. Accept responsibility for who you are and where you are today and understand that with the exception of some external forces, you are where you are because of the choices you have made.

What about choices like going to work? You may be saying, "I have a family to support and I cannot choose to skip work. If I skip work, I get fired." Although that may true, you choose not to skip work and keep your job. The choice of skipping work is yours and you must accept the consequences of each of your decisions. Even in the extreme situation that someone has a gun to your head, you have the choice to do what they request, or get shot. Choice is always present and always yours.

What about the person who gets hit by a bus? He obviously did not choose to get hit by a bus, but providing he is still alive, he can certainly choose how he responds to the situation. He can spend the rest of his days focusing on "why me?" and how unfortunate he is, or make millions writing the best seller, *Life After Being Hit by a Bus*, and help other victims of tragic bus accidents. Although we cannot always choose what happens to us or around us, we can choose how we deal with it.

A successful person understands this concept well and understands that her choices make her who she is today. She does not use the negative statement "I HAVE to" but rather "I WANT to". Having to do something makes you subconsciously believe that you have no choice in the situation, which is rarely ever true. Once you truly understand that you choose to do something rather than have to do it, your attitude becomes positive and you see the benefits rather than focusing on the negative.

Other people will respect you for your candor when being more truthful with a statement like "I prefer to". The words "I have to" are often used as a defense mechanism and used as an excuse not to do something. An extreme example is Marcia Brady on "The Brady Bunch" who uses the excuse "I have to wash my hair tonight" to get out of a date. What Marcia is really saying is that she would rather wash her hair tonight than go on a date with that boy. Understanding that Marcia has choice in the matter and if she were savvy enough to avoid the words "I have to", she would have ultimately told the boy the truthful reason why she did not want to go out with him since "I would rather wash my hair" is just plain mean. However, if the cast members followed my advice rather than the script, "The Brady Bunch" probably wouldn't have made it past the pilot episode.

ACTION STEP(S):

---

1) Commit to avoiding the words "I have to" from now on. Instead, substitute the words with something like "I want to" or "I prefer to". If you catch yourself saying, "I have to", think about what you REALLY meant to say and do your best to say what you really mean the next time.

Days 13 and 14 are for "R&R"—review and reflection. Spend these days reviewing the last five articles and reflecting on the information and how it relates to your life. Now is also a good time to make sure all the action steps for the previous days have been completed.

Day 15: Making Excuses

By definition, an excuse is an explanation offered to justify or obtain forgiveness. In its true meaning then, an excuse is really nothing more than a reason. An excuse becomes an obstacle in your journey to success when it is made in place of your best effort or when it is used as the object of the blame.

It's three o'clock on a rainy afternoon. While Jim is on his way to an important four o'clock meeting, his car starts to smoke and stalls on the freeway. After cursing the radiator, the car, and his Maker, Jim calls AAA and gets his car towed to the nearest garage. He then takes a taxi to the meeting and shows up at 4:45, 15 minutes before the meeting is over. When asked why he is so late, he proceeds to blame his car for breaking down, AAA for showing up late, the garage for requiring him to fill out so much paperwork, and the taxi for taking him "the long way". After Jim's sob story is finished, his boss responds with, "Would you like some cheese with that whine?" Needless to say, Jim's name will not be coming up for promotion any time soon.

Jim, like most people, realized that his car breaking down was out of his immediate control and that it was certainly a good excuse to use for missing the meeting. He figured that even by showing up after such an ordeal, his boss would be impressed. Knowing that, he did what most "normal" people would do in the same situation.

Remember that a successful person is not "normal". He or she is part of that 2% of the population and tends to raise the eyebrows of others. Now given the same situation, "successful" Jim knows that no excuses are good excuses, and that the best excuses are those never made. With that in mind, besides calling AAA he calls his sister, whom he persuades to drive her car over to him and sit in his broken down car, while he takes her car to the meeting, which he makes right on time. *(Authors note: If Jim's sister is anything like mine, the persuasion probably consisted of a pretty large dollar amount.)*

Despite your best efforts, at times you will be asked for an excuse. In another scenario, successful Jim, despite his best efforts, misses the first 45 minutes of the meeting. When asked by his boss why he is late he responds, "Car trouble. Next time when I hear my car making funny noises, I will get it checked and not let it break down. I really do apologize." His boss responds with, "Well your car broke down, there was nothing you could do about it. Don't worry, it happens to us all."

Note how Jim in the last scenario took responsibility for missing the meeting and did not put the blame on someone or something else. Nor did Jim douse himself with blame. Jim realized that he made an error by not taking adequate care of his car and forgave himself.

Next time you are asked for an excuse for something, think about the other person and spare them the details that are only important to you. Better yet, use your creative mind to avoid the need for excuses altogether and you will find people will treat you with the respect you deserve.

ACTION STEP(S):

---

1) Write down the top ten reasons why you feel you are not at your optimum level of success today. Do this now before reading action step #2.

2) Look at your list of ten excuses... I mean reasons :) How many of those are really poor excuses? Are you putting blame on someone else or circumstances? Do your best to rewrite each reason following the principles outlined in this article.

3) Commit to doing your best to avoid having to make excuses. If excuses are necessary, do not blame others or external events.

Day 16: Enthusiasm!

The source of the word "enthusiasm" comes from the Greek word *enthousiasmos*, which ultimately comes from the adjective *entheos*, "having the god within," formed from *en*, "in, within," and *theos*, "god." Since its introduction in the English language in the early fifteenth century, its meaning has become disassociated with religion and god (the word god is "a god" and not "the God", because of its Greek origin) and now means great excitement for, or interest in, a subject or cause. It is this excitement, or the feeling of having a god (or the God) within oneself, which is the fuel by which success is powered.

I generally do not think the modern day definition of the word does it justice. Enthusiasm is NOT the same as just being excited. Being enthusiastic about something is very much like being inspired by a supreme being. One gets excited about going on a roller coaster. One becomes enthusiastic about building a roller coaster. Enthusiasm is excitement with inspiration, motivation, and a pinch of creativity.

Enthusiasm will empower you to do just about anything you want, but most of all it will help you do it exceptionally well. The feeling of enthusiasm has amazing effects on the physical body as well. Voice, posture, heart rate and energy, to name a few, are all positively affected when one is filled with enthusiasm. Those around you easily detect this enthusiasm. When another finds you enthusiastic about something, it is difficult for that person not to share some of your enthusiasm. This is incredibly important when selling a product, service, or idea to others. With enthusiasm, your success rate increases phenomenally.

Enthusiasm springs from desire and passion. It is difficult to become enthusiastic about something like taking out the garbage, but certainly possible. For example, an inventor on his quest to automate the taking-out-garbage process could enthusiastically take out the garbage over and over—the source of his enthusiasm being the idea of revolutionizing the garbage industry. A great way to become enthusiastic is to visualize a time when you were enthusiastic about something. Think about what you were feeling, what you were seeing, and what you were hearing. Replay the "scene" in your head until you begin to start feeling the enthusiasm once more.

Use words, body language, and visual aids to share your ideas. Use enthusiasm to share your feelings. The ability to allow others to share your passion, even if temporarily, is priceless.

ACTION STEP(S):

1) Practice calling on your enthusiasm. Visualize a time when you were enthusiastic about something. Think about what you were feeling, what you were seeing, and what you were hearing. Replay the "scene" in your head until you begin to start feeling the enthusiasm once more.

"Nothing great was ever achieved without enthusiasm."

- Ralph Waldo Emerson

Day 17: Inspiration from Bill Gates

William H. Gates (1955–) is the Chairman and Chief Software Architect of Microsoft Corporation.

Success is creating jobs and opportunity. Gates' company, Microsoft, employs more than 50,000 people in 72 countries and regions.

Success is sharing. Bill and his wife, Melinda, have endowed a foundation with more than **$24 billion** to support philanthropic initiatives in the areas of global health and learning.

Success is passion for knowledge. Gates became inseparable from the computer. In his youth, he would stay in the computer room all day and night, writing programs, reading computer literature and anything else he could to learn about computing.

Success is following your heart's desire. Bill did well at Harvard, but just as in high school, his heart was not in his studies. After locating the school's computer center, he lost himself in the world of computers once again. In his junior year, Gates left Harvard to devote his energies to Microsoft, a company he had begun in 1975 with his childhood friend Paul Allen.

Success is vision. When Gates first saw the cover of Popular Electronics with a picture of the Altair 8080 and the headline "World's First Microcomputer Kit to Rival Commercial Models", he knew that the home computer market was about to explode and that someone would need to make software for the new machines.

Success is unwavering commitment. Within a few days of being introduced to the Altair, Gates had called MITS (Micro

Instrumentation and Telemetry Systems), the makers of the Altair. He told the company that he and Paul Allen (now the CEO of Microsoft) had developed a version of the computing language "BASIC" that could be used on the Altair. This was not entirely true. The fact was, they had not even written a line of code. With that statement however, Gates totally committed himself.

Success is not always about innovation.

- Microsoft's first product was a version of the programming language BASIC for the Altair 8080. BASIC, invented by John Kemeny and Thomas Kurtz in 1964, was someone else's idea. So was the Altair. Gates used the two to fill a need that was not currently being met.
- IBM hired Microsoft to build its operating system. Microsoft bought Q-DOS from a company called Seattle Computer Products and "repackaged" it for the PC once again making PC history.
- In May 1990, Microsoft introduced its own version of Apple windows and called it Microsoft Windows 3.0, which, of course, made computer history.
- Microsoft's first browser, Internet Explorer 1.0, was not even their product. It was licensed from a company called Spyglass. Today, the Internet Explorer is by far the most widely used Web browser.

[Sources: http://www.biography.com, http://www.microsoft.com]

"Your most unhappy customers are your greatest source of learning."

- Bill Gates, Business @ The Speed of Thought

Day 18: Avoid Exaggeration

Exaggerating, or taking a truth out of proportion, is one of the evils of communication. Here are some of the top reasons why people feel the need to exaggerate:

1) they want to sound more interesting
2) they want more sympathy from the listener
3) they want to embellish their point and make it more convincing
4) they want to use the power of numbers to get the point across, even if it means lying about the numbers

The fact is exaggerating is lying, or "stretching the truth". No good ever comes from lying.

Here are some forms of exaggeration that you should avoid.

Obvious Exaggeration. This is where the listener knows immediately the speaker is exaggerating because the statement is impossible. Example, "There's like a million people downstairs waiting for you." This is a somewhat childish statement that does not give the listener a true idea of the actual number and often leads to the follow-up question, "How many...really?"

Absolute Exaggeration. This is where the speaker uses words like "all", "everybody" or "always". These statements are often made out of desperation or anger and do not give the listener a true sense of the situation. For example, "Everybody is upset about today's meeting". Chances are all 68 staff members are not upset, just a few are. What the speaker is doing is making assumptions based on a few samples, or in many cases, her own opinion.

Indirect Exaggeration. This is where the speaker will answer a question or make a statement in an attempt to lean the listener to an idea or way of thinking. For example, if a husband and wife are talking about going out or staying in for the evening and the wife says, "Well, it is almost six o'clock so we will have to wait anywhere we go." This indirectly tells the husband that she does not want to go out. Why? For one thing, the wife is using absolute exaggeration by stating there will be a wait "anywhere". In addition, the time is actually 5:35, not quite "almost six o'clock". People tend to "bend time" on their side when they want to indirectly make a statement or prove a point.

The one area where exaggeration is appropriate is in comedy. Comedians, writers, and others who are looking to use humor, find exaggeration a useful tool. If you do use exaggeration for this reason, just be sure it is obvious to your audience and not deceptive.

Avoiding exaggerating will keep your statements honest and people will respect you more for it. In addition, it is better communication to say what you mean and avoid follow-up questions. Knowing when others are exaggerating and seeing through their statements to the real meaning will also help you to be a better communicator.

ACTION STEP(S):

1) Commit to actively listening for exaggeration when others speak. In your mind, rephrase their statement to a more honest and accurate one that does not use exaggeration.

2) Commit to avoiding exaggeration. When you do catch yourself, immediately correct yourself by rephrasing your statement.

" 'Tis a rule of manners to avoid exaggeration."

- Ralph Waldo Emerson (1803–1882)

Day 19: Remembering Numbers

In today's computerized, handheld PC, and pen recorder filled world, there seems little need to remember numbers. The truth is, despite all the gadgets available there are still times when accessing a gadget to jot down or record numbers is just inconvenient or simply not possible. For these times, we rely on "ol' unreliable" (our memory).

All recent theories in mind development agree that, like the universe, there is no known limit to one's memory. Remembering people, faces, sounds, smells, sights and other more "interesting" things than numbers seems to be much easier for most people. Why is that?

Numbers, unlike most concrete objects, cannot be visualized well. They do not make a strong enough impression in the mind for us to be able to recall the numbers at will. Unlike trying to remember a vivid image, numbers just do not do well in our memories.

There IS a solution to this, and a very good one at that. It is referred to by many as the "Peg System". With the Peg System, you associate numbers 0–9 with sounds while creating words with the sounds made from the numbers you are trying to remember. Once the word is created, you vividly picture the words and associate them in a strange and memorable way. With this system, you only need to "memorize" ten general sounds associated with the ten numbers 0 thorough 9. Once you have those memorized, you will be able to memorize and recall a number of any length, forward and backward for as long as you wish to keep the number in your memory.

First, here is what you need to memorize: there is a non-vowel sound or sounds associated with each of the ten numbers. **These sounds have nothing to do with the sounds of pronouncing the numbers.** If there are multiple sounds associated with a single number, you will notice that the sounds are almost the same, as in the case of number 9 with the hard "p" and "b" sound. Here are the ten numbers and their associated sounds that need to be memorized:

1 = t,d,th
2 = n
3 = m
4 = r
5 = l
6 = ch,sh,j,cz
7 = k,g,qu
8 = f,v
9 = p,b
0 = s,z,tz

Therefore, to remember the number 1, we can use the word "tie" and visualize a crazy looking, colorful tie. Even though the word "tie" also has a long "i" sound, the long "i" is not one of our 10 non-vowel sounds so is ignored. These ignored sounds help us to construct words easily. Technically, because of the other sounds associated with the number 1, we can also use the word "die" or even the word "the" remember the number 1, but the word "tie" is much easier to visualize.

In a more practical example, let us assume our gym membership number is "4268" and we need to present this number each time we check in. As we read the number, we make the sounds and start constructing the words as we can make them up. The numbers 42 can be the word "rain" (4 is the "r" sound and 2 is the "n" sound) and the numbers 68 could be the word "chef". When we create the first word, we need to associate the first word with something that will help us to remember what the numbers are for. Better yet, if you can create a single "scene" that will reveal the number to you, then do it. My image would be rain falling from the ceiling right over the sign-in counter at the gym, and then the rain turns to chefs. This is a hard image to forget and an easy one to picture. Now each time I come to gym I see the mental picture and get the number 4268 from r-n-ch-f or rain chef.

It is referred to as the Peg System because like hanging a hat on a peg, we are "hanging" our first image (hat) on the item that is associated with the number (peg). This first association is vital because otherwise you will have a bunch of demented images floating around in your head with no home.

Remembering numbers can not only be a great party trick to impress your friends, but it can come in handy when the need arises to remember important phone numbers. Train your memory. Practicing this technique will not only help with your memory recall, but it will help with your creative visualization as well.

ACTION STEP(S):

1) Commit this number to memory by using the technique in this article: 154957266456395030583720095

2) Set on your calendar to recall this number one week from now.

Days 20 and 21 are for "R&R"—review and reflection. Spend these days reviewing the last five articles and reflecting on the information and how it relates to your life. Now is also a good time to make sure all the action steps for the previous days have been completed.

Day 22: The Words You Use Make All the Difference

The words that come out of your mouth and go through your head have an incredible effect on your actions and behavior. The subconscious mind is known for gravitating toward what you focus on. The same effect holds true for simply saying or thinking of words and expressions. For example, "It can't be done" is a very powerful statement that stops your mind from presenting you with a solution of how it can be done. The results of rephrasing that statement to "How can it be done?" are nothing short of amazing.

The words you choose make all the difference when it comes to the way others perceive you. Radiate a positive mental attitude and an optimistic personality. Your boss does not want to hear "That's impossible". What she wants to hear is "If you assign one more person to assist me, I can not only have this ready by Friday, but I can even have it delivered to the prospect's office". If you are in a leadership role, saying, "This will never work" is setting a very poor example. Instead say, "How can we make this work?" and allow the creative juices to start flowing!

Here are just some examples of phrases you should avoid, along with their possible substitutions:

- I can't do it *should be* **How can it be done?**
- It will never work *should be* **How can I make it work?**
- That's impossible *should be* **Anything is possible**
- Someday I... *should be* **Today (on Tuesday, June 12, or any specific date) I...**
- I should have *should be* **Next time I will**
- I'll try *should be* **I will do my best**
- I'm no good at... *should be* **I will get better at...**

Once you start making a conscious effort to avoiding saying these phrases and limiting yourself, you will no longer think this way either—and vice-versa. The power of using the right words, or perhaps more important avoiding the wrong words, is astonishing. Put this concept into practice and experience the positive results for yourself.

ACTION STEP(S):

---

1) Everyone has their own limiting phrases they use on a regular basis. Take some time to write down yours. Then, write down possible alternatives for each one that make a positive statement.

"Always and never are two words you should always remember never to use."

- Wendell Johnson

Day 23: You ARE a Salesperson

If you are a parent, student, teacher, musician, actor, doctor, laborer, or currently doing nothing for work, you are a salesperson. Everyone sells something. Everyone is in business for him or herself. You are in the business of marketing or selling your services and skills. Even when already employed, you are constantly selling others ideas, reasons for promotion, comfort, etc. In this respect, everyone should have a good understanding of the key concepts of both sales and marketing to attract success.

Selling does not necessarily have to involve the exchange of money. People sell something to somebody just about every day and rarely realize they are selling nor even fully understand the sales process. Sales is an important, frequent, and necessary part of life. The better we are at it, the more often we will get the things we want.

- The salesperson sells goods or services to customers
- The parent sells values and wisdom to their children
- The teacher sells knowledge to students
- The student sells desire for knowledge to teachers (and sometimes excuses)
- The doctor sells skills, advice, and comfort to patients
- The actor sells entertainment to the audience

Since you are a salesperson, why not be a great salesperson? All too often I hear, "I hate sales" or worse, "I hate salespeople". What these people really mean to say is "I dislike pushy salespeople who annoy me" (to me, the word "hate" is worse than any other 4 letter word I know). Do not be prejudiced against salespeople, or any group for that matter. If you are one of these anti-salesperson people, think back to all the times you bought anything where someone knowledgeable and friendly helped you by educating you on the product or service and perhaps even saving you money in the process. The more you can appreciate the value of the salesperson, the more you will do to improve your own sales skills.

I like to think of sales as the ability to gracefully persuade, not manipulate, a person or persons into a win-win situation. Sales skills are large part of success in anything you do. Learn to embrace them and enjoy their benefits.

ACTION STEP(S):

1) Write down how your life would benefit if you were a "master salesperson". Think about as many situations as you can in your past where you were selling something to someone, whether it be a product, service, or idea.

2) Promise yourself to show more respect to salespeople, even if they happen to annoy or interrupt you. Remember that they are people just like you, with feelings and emotions, who are just doing their job.

"I love to go shopping. I love to freak out salespeople. They ask me if they can help me, and I say, 'Have you got anything I'd like?' Then they ask me what size I need, and I say, 'Extra medium.'"

- Steven Wright

Day 24: Inspiration from Donald Trump

Donald Trump (1946–) is a real estate billionaire, best-selling author, and most recently, executive producer of a hit TV show.

Success is dealing with change, both positive and negative. The Donald Trump story is one of the most amazing stories of financial roller coaster rides there is. He went from real estate billionaire, to being close to $900 million dollars in debt, back to billionaire in a relatively short period of time.

Success is making your own mark, regardless of your upbringing. Donald was raised in a well-to-do family and had many opportunities and advantages in his youth. Despite his privileged upbringing, he did not inherit anything and went on to fame and fortune through his own business accomplishments.

Success is making the right connections. When Donald first moved to Manhattan, he was practically broke. Regardless, he squandered what money he did have to join one of the city's most exclusive clubs and met some very influential people.

Success is having an attractive personality. Donald Trump is funny, smart and honest. He is a very likeable person who knows the value of honest admiration.

Success is handling pressure. In 1991 when Trump was about $900 million in debt, it was his ability to deal with pressure that allowed him to stay in the game and eventually pull off one of the largest financial comebacks in history.

Success is self-promotion. Donald Trump is a very public figure who uses his popularity to fuel his success. He has appeared on dozens of movies, commercials and TV shows and currently stars in a reality-based TV series. It is reported that 98% of Americans surveyed know who Donald Trump is.

Success is doing great things for others. There is a story about an unemployed mechanic who once helped Donald Trump get his limo working again after it stalled on the highway. The mechanic did not accept anything for his services besides a "thank you". Trump was so impressed with the mechanic's generosity that the next day he sent flowers to the man's wife, and a letter certifying that the man's mortgage had been paid off in full.

[Sources: http://www.askmen.com, http://www.nbc.com, http://www.biography.com]

"Money was never a big motivation for me, except as a way to keep score. The real excitement is playing the game."

- Donald Trump, "Trump: Art of the Deal"

Day 25: Time Mastery: Part 1

The successful individual understands and appreciates the value of time. Time is one of our precious resources that is rarely valued as it should be. Time management is having control over our time. We can't stop time or reverse it, but we can use it to our advantage.

There are thousands of resources on time management available; however, most I have come across seem to be written by employers wanting to maximize their profits by getting more work out of their employees. I believe to be a true master of time you must realize how valuable this skill is in the achievement of your own success. Mastering your time, not just managing it, will bring you the following benefits:

Increase your personal productivity. Imagine getting twice as much done each day as you do now without working any harder or longer. How much would that be worth to you? This is not only possible, but it can be expected when you become a true master of your time.

Relieve stress. One of the main reasons so many people suffer stress is that they feel their lives are disorganized. They often feel "under the gun" and like they have too much to do and too little time to do it. People often feel like they are constantly playing catch-up rather than forging ahead. They feel like they are just "spinning their wheels" while not getting anywhere. Does any of this sound familiar? With any of these feelings, how could one not be stressed? Once you master your time, these feelings, and the associated stresses, will be history.

Forge ahead. This is the main benefit that most time management books, lecturers, and resources fail to get across to their audiences. When you master your time, you have time needed to work on your life purpose. You can no longer make excuses (by this time you should not be making excuses anyway) that "you have not got the time". You have the same 24 hours in a day as Bill Gates has—the difference is how you choose to spend your time. Forging ahead is making the time for what you are passionate about doing while still doing the things you need to do to pay the bills. This is something that all successful people must do.

There are many benefits associated with traditional time management, however, they are beyond the scope of this article. Forging ahead alone should be enough motivation for you to reevaluate how you spend your time.

Here are some good time management techniques that act as the foundation of time mastery.

- **Catalog your time**. Make a log of what you do in the average day. Do this for about a week.
- **Eliminate wastage from your day.** Stop doing the things that bring you no benefit whatsoever. You will be surprised how many you will find in your day.
- **Make "to do" lists.** Prioritize your activities and assign a time to each as to how long it will take. This will help you begin the activities you know you have time to finish.
- **Schedule calls.** Set aside time for both incoming and outgoing calls. Phone calls can interrupt your workflow. Once you are interrupted from a productive mental state of mind, it is often difficult to get back into that state of mind and productivity suffers.
- **Learn to say "no".** Saying no in advance to extra work is much easier than having to apologize later for not being able to complete something on time. Refuse excessive workloads.
- **Do not neglect long-term projects.** Just because they may not be due soon, they will be due eventually. Working on these projects often will save you from the last minute crunch that causes stress.
- **Be decisive.** Make decisions quickly. It is important to have enough information to make an informed decision, however, too often people do not know what "enough" is and hold off on making decisions. Most of the time, a poor decision is better than no decision.

- **Deal with e-mail effectively.** Make use of spam filters to stop from having to read the garbage that comes to your inbox. Create sub-folders to organize your incoming e-mail, but be sure to keep the things that need your attention in the short term in your inbox. Once you file it away, it is often neglected.
- **Don't procrastinate.** Procrastination is putting off until tomorrow what you should be doing today. This is so important that I have devoted a whole day to it later in this course. For now, just do your best not to put things off.

Time management skills are the foundation for time mastery. They are to be used in conjunction with time mastery skills for maximum benefit. Tomorrow, we will discuss the techniques and practices of time mastery.

ACTION STEP(S):

---

1) Starting on your next "average" day, keep a written log of how your time is spent. For example it may look something like this:

6:05–6:15: got up, used bathroom, did a few stretches
6:15–6:45: read the morning paper
6:45–8:00: watched TV
...

If your days vary greatly, you many want to do this for a few days to get a true sense of how you spend your time.

2) Make a "to do" list of everything you need to do. These lists are liberating. Once you put down on paper the things racing through your mind, you can focus on more positive and productive things like your life purpose and goals.

Day 26: Time Mastery: Part 2

Yesterday we introduced the concept of time mastery and focused on time management. Today, we will explore time mastery techniques used by those who want to do more than squeeze an extra hour out of their day. Making use of these techniques and principles will allow you the time for pursuit of your life purpose and other goals.

Here are the six techniques and principles that take over where most traditional time management skills leave off.

Get assistance. How much is your time worth? Can you be paying an assistant or delegating authority to someone else on some of your activities? The successful individual knows that others' labor is one of the best investments that can be made.

Do multiple things at once. The mind is much more powerful and capable than most people think. It is possible to overlap some of your activities and get twice as much done in the same period of time. For example, you can listen to educational material or enjoy a good book on tape (or CD) while either driving to work or exercising. Look at your day's schedule and get creative.

Get up earlier. You can read 100 medical papers on sleep and the human body written by 100 top scientists and doctors and you will come to the same conclusion... nobody has any idea how much sleep the "average person" needs. The consensus is, our own bodies will let us know. So get up an hour earlier each day and see how your body responds. That's an extra 45 eight-hour work days a year or 365 more hours you can spend on your hobby, family, goals, and/or life purpose.

Don't confuse relaxing with wasting time. If you get relaxation from spinning in your chair then trying to walk a straight line, playing a game or two of Solitaire, or blowing spit bubbles, then do it! The body and mind need relaxing activities throughout the day. However, make sure these activities are for relaxation and not for procrastination.

Get exercise. While a good workout schedule may take about three hours of your week, it will allow you to be much more productive. It is like a racecar stopping for fuel and a tire change; if it kept going, it would go farther in the short run but very soon slow down or just stop. Like a racecar, your body is a complex machine that needs to be fueled and properly maintained for peak performance.

Push yourself. The reason most people fail to reach even a fraction of their potential is that they do not push themselves hard enough. We end conversations with "Don't work too hard!" or "Take it easy!" and this is exactly what the average person does. The average person goes on frequent coffee breaks, socializes when they should be working and "takes it easy". The other two percent of the population (those who consider themselves successful) get their high not by caffeine, but by accomplishment. They save social banter for more appropriate times and don't "take it easy". They work harder and smarter than the rest of the population and are rewarded for it.

Here is the big secret of time mastery: once your life purpose activities begin to replace your daily "have to" activities, your motivation increases, your work becomes your play, relaxation is obtained from your work, and productivity will increase exponentially! Don't just be a manager of time, be a master of time.

ACTION STEP(S):

1) Read over the six techniques and principles in this article and write down if and how you can make use of them.

"Time is the most valuable thing a man can spend."

- **Theophrastus (300 BC–287 BC)**

Days 27 and 28 are for "R&R"—review and reflection. Spend these days reviewing the last five articles and reflecting on the information and how it relates to your life. Now is also a good time to make sure all the action steps for the previous days have been completed.

Day 29: Separating Performance from Performer

How often do you say to yourself something like "I can't believe how stupid I am" when you find yourself doing something... well, stupid. How often do you find yourself telling others, like your kids, spouse, or friends that they are stupid? In either case, you are verbally reinforcing a negative belief that will interfere with your success and the success of those you care about.

When you do something dumb, idiotic or stupid, realize that it was your performance, or what you did, that deserves the criticism and not you. Perhaps more important, use your positive mental attitude and criticize your action by telling yourself "That didn't work. Now I know better for next time". An action you take is just one of the millions of actions you will take in your lifetime. Is it fair to put a label on yourself just because of one, or even several of your actions? Successful people radiate self-esteem, not self-disgust.

Criticizing others is an art in itself, and one that will be explored in this program. For now, the most important aspect of criticism, especially when criticizing others, is to separate the performance from the performer. Do not criticize the doer but criticize the deed. Nothing does more to hurt the self-esteem of a person, or knock them off their path to success, than poorly delivered criticism like name-calling. Sticks and stones may break bones, but for most people, names will do even worse. You see, bones will heal by themselves.

If you want to be successful in parenting and raise kids with high self-esteem, be a successful coach with a confident team, a respected manager with confident employees or if you want success yourself, remember and practice this one simple rule of criticism: always separate the performance from the performer.

ACTION STEP(S):

---

1) Make a promise to yourself to never again engage in name calling. When criticizing, always be conscious of the need to criticize a person's actions, not the person.

"Never criticize a man until you've walked a mile in his moccasins."

- American Indian Proverb

Day 30: The Subconscious Mind

At one time or another, we have all heard of the subconscious mind yet very few people understand how to use it. Many people even disregard its existence because they cannot see it, touch it, hear it, smell it, or taste it. The successful individual not only knows of its existence, but knows how to "program" the subconscious mind for success.

Our mind, as we know it, consists of two levels of activity: the conscious and the subconscious. Your conscious mind is the logical, reasoning portion of your mind. It uses the five senses to gather information and come to logical conclusions by both deductive and inductive reasoning. To be brief, just about everything we know of as "thinking" is done with the conscious mind.

Here is the really interesting part—over 90 percent of your mental activity is subconscious. This is the "work done" that you are not even aware of. The subconscious works 24 hours a day with no breaks. It is the part of the mind that controls your autonomic bodily functions such as breathing, digestion, and the beating of your heart. It is the same part of the mind that takes over activities once they become "second nature" to you, like riding a bike or doing simple math.

In terms of success, the subconscious mind is like a computer program that controls our thoughts, habits, beliefs, and convictions. Most people do not like the fact that they can be "programmed" like a computer or a robot, nor do they like the fact that the subconscious mind can control their actions and thoughts. However, we ultimately control our subconscious mind and we have the ability to reprogram it for success.

Our programming started early in life when our parents, friends, teachers, siblings, TV and media wrote our initial program. These same influences continue to program most people today because most people are not aware of their powerful influence. Advertisers certainly are. A perfect example is beer commercials. They begin with beautiful people frolicking in slow motion on a white sandy beach on a perfect day. The people all appear happy, healthy, successful, and sexy. Then the name of the beer is displayed on screen. Now almost everyone who watches these commercials are reasonable enough to know that drinking beer is not going to bring them all of those things seen in the commercial. So why do they work so well? **The subconscious mind cannot reason. It interprets images, words, and feelings literally.** The commercials do exactly what the advertisers want them to do— associate a positive feelings and images with their products. This is mind programming.

We can program our own subconscious minds for success simply by doing the same things: associate great feelings with all of the things you want from life. Use positive, successful statements when talking and thinking while avoiding negative talk and thought.

The subconscious acts like an unlimited size hard drive that stores every image, sound, feeling, taste, and smell we have ever encountered. This is how hypnotism allows us to recall memories in such detail from the past. It is important to know that you don't really forget things; you are just unable to recall them. This fact alone will improve your confidence and help significantly with recalling details from memory. Once you believe you've forgotten something, you are right.

Throughout this course we will be discussing detailed techniques for programming your subconscious mind for success. Understand the power of the subconscious mind, and you will be an expert "programmer" before you know it.

ACTION STEP(S):

---

1) Choose one of your bad habits (come on... we all have at least one). How did this become a habit? Think back to why you started

doing this. Was it something you saw someone do, like a friend or parent? What was your reason for starting this? Was it a good reason or do you think it could be a negative program in your subconscious mind? (sorry... not at the point in the course where we are correcting bad habits yet!)

"The power to move the world is in the subconscious mind."

- William James, the father of American psychology

Day 31: Inspiration from Oprah Winfrey

Oprah Winfrey (1954–) is one of the most important figures in popular culture, most well known as the talkshow host on her TV show, "Oprah".

Success is putting the past behind you no matter how terrible. Despite suffering abuse and molestation as a child, Oprah Winfrey found it in herself to be the best she knew she could be, and eventually become one of the most influential people in history (Forbes Top 100).

Success is helping others. In 1994, President Clinton signed the "Oprah Bill," a law designed to protect children from abuse.

Success is doing it better. In 1986, her show, "The Oprah Winfrey Show" took over Donahue as the nation's top-rated talk show, even though Donahue pioneered the talk show format.

Success is holding tight to your morals and values, even at the expense of your career. In 1994, when talk shows started to become increasingly trashy and exploitative, Winfrey pledged to keep her show free of tabloid topics. Although her show's ratings initially fell, Oprah earned the respect of her viewers. This earned respect did more for her career in the long run than by giving in to the public's demand for daytime TV trash ever will.

Success is having the power to influence. Any book she promotes on her show becomes an instant best seller. Any charity she supports on air sees phenomenal increases in donations. Any industry she condemns on air suffers serious financial losses (beef industry).

Success is diversification. In addition to her huge success with her television show, Oprah owns several businesses, has written several books, made several movies, and publishes her own magazine.

Success is reaching people on a personal level. Oprah is known for her empathy for others. When a guest's story moves her, she cries and offers the guest a warm embrace.

[Sources: http://www.oprah.com, http://www.biography.com]

"My philosophy is that not only are you responsible for your life, but doing the best at this moment puts you in the best place for the next moment."

- Oprah Winfrey

Day 32: Self-Esteem

It was a snowy winter night when George Bailey stood on the bridge of Bedford Falls and convinced himself that he was more valuable dead than alive. George made a very common mistake on that cold, fictional night when he determined his worth based purely on his finances. It took a second-class angel named Clarence to restore his self-esteem and show him vividly how valuable his life really was. Although Frank Capra's _It's a Wonderful Life_ is just a movie (and a great one at that), it a great example of true self-esteem.

Self-esteem is value or worth that one bestows on oneself. It is the inner feeling one has about oneself. High self-esteem is a character trait of a healthy individual. One can never have too much self-esteem. Self-esteem is _loving_ oneself, whereas over-confidence and narcissism are being _in love_ with oneself.

Our current level of self-esteem is low, high, or somewhere in between and is always changing. For many people, they go through life with low self-esteem and never do much to improve their situation in life because they feel deep inside they are just not worth it. Many of these feelings of inadequacy come from childhood and the school system. Adolescents have a seemingly natural ability to be able to lower the self-esteem of just about any individual. Unfortunately, despite their age, some people never mature mentally past adolescence and the destructive criticism and mental abuse continues to be dished out to their children, employees, and/or students.

As adults, we often give ourselves low self-esteem by associating our self-worth with our bank accounts. We see rejection and failure as permanent, and give into a negative mental attitude like "why not smoke, we're all going to die eventually anyway".

The best thing you can do for yourself is love yourself. For those of you who think that sounds too mushy, I will rephrase that to: the best thing you can do for yourself is build your self-esteem. Individuals with high-self esteem:

- are self-motivated
- accept responsibility for their actions
- take pride in their accomplishments
- are loving and lovable
- are capable of handling criticism
- take command and control of their lives
- are focused on goals
- have tolerance and respect for others
- have integrity
- are willing to take risks

It is amazing how much time and money people will spend on temporary feel-good-about-themselves solutions, yet not do a thing to create lasting self-esteem. A new suit will make one look and feel sharp, but that feeling will quickly wear off with the novelty of the suit. The outside-in approach to building self-esteem is about looking your best to feel your best and works well in the short-term, but should be used in conjunction with, and not in place of, the inside-out approach of building lasting self-esteem.

Success without high self-esteem is not likely. People detect low self-esteem in others and will treat them accordingly. Fortunately, building self-esteem is quite easy, especially for those with a positive mental attitude. Here are several ways you can build your self-esteem from both the outside in and the inside out.

<u>Outside In</u>

- **Carry yourself well.** Keep your head up, shoulders back and chest out. Don't be a sloucher.
- **Dress for success.** Look nice when going out in public. A simple rule is to dress just a bit better than the others you come across. Take care of your personal hygiene as well.
- **Speak clearly and confidently.** Do not slur your words or mumble. Make eye contact when speaking with someone.
- **Stay in shape.** Take care of your physical body.

Inside Out

- **Realize your importance to others.** Think about all the lives that have been and are being touched by your life.
- **Self-worth is based on what you are capable of doing, not what you have done.** Since human potential is limitless, thus your potential is limitless; your self-worth is limitless as well.
- **"No one can make you feel inferior without your consent"** is one of the wisest truisms of our time said by the very bright Eleanor Roosevelt. The feelings of emotion like inferiority are something we generate within and over which we have complete control. Do not allow others' perceptions or comments to negatively affect your self-esteem.
- **Engage in positive self-talk.** Your subconscious mind has much to do with your self-esteem. Be careful what you say to yourself because your subconscious mind is always listening.
- **Invest in yourself.** Books, tapes, classes, on-line courses, and anything that will feed your mind with knowledge and positive information are all great investments in you. Work on specialized skills that will make you more marketable in the workplace.
- **Realize that rejection and failure made you stronger and smarter.** Rejection and failure and rejection are not always "bad" things. Rumor has it, Colonel Sanders was rejected over 1000 times before he sold his chicken recipe. Rejection and failure and rejection are a part of life and two things successful people encounter more often than those who are afraid to try.

Healthy self-esteem is an important part of happiness in life and high self-esteem is vital to success. You are a unique individual and have it within yourself to accomplish such wonderful things. The moment you realize this, you will possess the gift of high self-esteem.

ACTION STEP(S):

---

1) Write down where you see yourself on the self-esteem scale. On the left side of the page write "low self-esteem" and on the right side write "high self-esteem". Put a big "x" where you feel you are on this scale.

2) Follow the steps for building self-esteem in today's lesson. Commit to doing this on a regular basis until you have the high self-esteem that you deserve to have.

"Self-esteem is the reputation we acquire with ourselves."

- Nathaniel Branden

Day 33: What Do You Want?

Achievement begins with knowing what you want. Like your specific purpose, you must clearly identify what you really want out of life. Unlike your specific purpose, we are not talking about just one large major goal. What you want from life can be a list of a couple things or pages and pages of material, emotional and spiritual desires. It's your list.

How can you possibly pursue what you want in life if you don't really know what you want? You may think you know what you want, but often when you get it, you realize that you either didn't really want it, or having the thing you wanted takes away more enjoyment of life than it brings. So how do you find out what you really want?

STEP 1: Brainstorm. Sit in a quiet place and write down everything you THINK you want in life from material wealth to relationships. Include things like spare time for hobbies, spiritual goals, where you want to live, travel to, friends you want to have, family, health, and anything else you can possibly want out of life. You do not have to be too specific here, for example, if you really do want the latest BMW every year just write "latest BMW"—no need for model numbers, colors, etc. This does not have to be done in one sitting; it could be done over several hours or several days. Don't continue with step 2 until you are satisfied with what is on the list.

STEP 2: Prioritize. Circle what is most important to you on the list. Let's trim our watermelon vine so the watermelon we keep can grow to full size.

STEP 3: Eliminate. Elimination of wants and desires is not as tough as it seems. As soon as you realize that there are more reasons NOT to want something than to want something, you no longer want it. Carefully look at each item on your list and think about all that you would need to give up to have and enjoy that item on your list. For example, realize along with home ownership comes taxes, mortgages, and upkeep—so this may cause you to reconsider your "one home in each state" goal. Before you start crossing things off your list, remember that life is not two dimensional; your wants exist in time. So if your list has both being a Hugh Hefner (the Playboy mansion guy) and a family man, the former can take place early in life while the family life can come later. Look out for contradictions that exist like spending more time with kids/grandkids and sailing around the world alone for two years.

STEP 4: Visualize. Create a vivid motion picture in your mind of your ideal life. Play this "movie" often and write it down like a story that is already happening. From this point, everything you do in your life should bring you closer to this ideal life you have created for yourself.

If you have a life-long partner, it is important that you do this exercise together. Or you may choose to each do the exercise, then compare notes and make sure that both of your life plans are consistent with each other's.

The main reason people do not get what they want out of life is because they do not want it badly enough. "It would be nice to have three months vacation a year" is often heard but those who passionately desire this usually go as far to take a teaching job to have the summers off to pursue other interests. If your list is full of things that would just be "nice" to have, chances are you will not get them.   If you do have these items on your list, either create a desire for having them by visualization or just cross them off and focus on what you are passionate about and you will get it.

ACTION STEP(S):

---

1) Begin the exercise in this article. It may take you several days to complete it.

"In the world there are only two tragedies. One is not getting what one wants, and the other is getting it."

- Oscar Wilde (1854–1900), Lady Windermere's Fan, 1892, Act III

Days 34 and 35 are for "R&R"—review and reflection. Spend these days reviewing the last five articles and reflecting on the information and how it relates to your life. Now is also a good time to make sure all the action steps for the previous days have been completed.

Day 36: Think HUGE

It is not enough to think big. The world is full of big thinkers. You must think HUGE.

By thinking "huge", you are no longer limited by thought. Everything starts with thought and since thought is limitless why create mental limits? Most people would answer, "just being realistic". Was Henry Ford being "realistic"? Here was a guy, who had next to no education, who started and ran one of the largest companies of his time. Was that a realistic expectation? Often people are doomed to mediocrity by thinking they can only expect what is "realistic" or "normal" for most people. Don't make this same mistake. You are not like most people.

Thinking huge paints a mental picture that will remain in your subconscious mind. Every thing you do, both consciously and subconsciously will attempt to bring you closer to that picture. For example, when I started Archieboy Holdings, LLC., I did not want to create a 20 million dollar hosting company—I had already done that. I wanted to create a 100 million dollar hosting empire. As a result of this "huge thought" the software and systems we have built are capable of reaching and surpassing those kinds of numbers. Had I thought of just creating another company like the last one I created, we would not be as far along as we are today due to marketing and software limitations.

By thinking huge you will be much better off when having to compromise as well. Not only compromises with others, but when your huge thoughts do not materialize (as they often won't— otherwise they were not huge enough) you will find that you have still achieved considerable success.

Remember, thought is without limits. Get inspiration from people like Henry Ford, Ben Franklin, and Bill Gates whose successes all began with huge ideas.

ACTION STEP(S):

1) Make a conscious effort to think without limits. Only the average person limits their thinking, the successful person does not.

"A man is not idle because he is absorbed in thought. There is a visible labor and there is an invisible labor."

- Victor Hugo (1802–1885)

Day 37: Responding vs. Reacting

During my high school and college years, I was, at times, what we called a real "hot head". I was very easily angered and often expressed it. What I did not realize at the time is that my anger and hostility would almost always be misdirected due to my initial reactions. I reacted first, then thought later rather than thinking first. Responding, on the other hand, is reaction with thought.

In martial arts, we teach kids and adults the importance of controlling anger and using their brain to avoid conflict before resorting to physical contact. This is done with practice, and lots of it. Stopping yourself from reacting to situations is not easy, since it seems almost natural (thus the expression "natural reaction"). However, this concept is so important that every effort should be made to avoid reacting to situations and start responding to them.

Here are some reasons why your response to situations can be vital to your success:

- Many business deals include emotion and emotion causes reactions. Doing or saying something in a business dealing out of pure emotion is never a good idea, and it often causes you to make a poor decision.
- Success begins with self-esteem or how you feel about yourself. Have you ever felt good about yourself after "barking" at a co-worker, friend, or loved one?
- Responding to a potentially life-threatening situation could save your life. You can't be successful if you are dead! (I guess you could be successfully dead...)

Responding is reaction with thought. As we already know, your mind is an amazing tool that is capable of generating appropriate responses to situations in a mere fraction of a second if you let it. The key is to work on holding back initial reactions until your brain has a chance to present you with the proper response. Some people refer to this as "getting composure". Have you ever seen a person get all emotional when rebuking a statement someone had just made then in the middle of their yelling just stop, take a deep breath with their eyes closed and calmly say something like "Listen, I am sorry for getting so upset, but..." This is a perfect example of response taking over a reaction and a great first step. As you consciously work on responding to situations, the time between the stimuli and response will lessen until it is almost instant. Once you master this, responding will be a task handled by your subconscious mind and it will be done without any conscious effort.

ACTION STEP(S):

1) From this point on, stop yourself from reacting to situations the moment you realize it. This does not mean keeping your hand on a hot stove until you can think about the best thing to do. This means not yelling "*$&@!#!!" in front of your kids after you pull your hand off. Use the "get composure" technique if needed and take a deep breath, then respond.

"A life of reaction is a life of slavery, intellectually and spiritually. One must fight for a life of action, not reaction."

- Rita Mae Brown

Day 38: Inspiration from George Burns

George Burns (1896-1996) was one of the greatest comedians/entertainers of several generations.

Success is having high self-esteem. "I can't afford to die; I'd lose too much money."

Success is loving what you do. "Fall in love with what you do for a living. I don't care what it is. It works." George also said, "Retire? I'm gonna stay in show business until I'm the only one left."

Success is sharing your wealth. In 1985, George Burns made a generous gift to establish the George Burns Intensive Care Unit at the Motion Picture & Television Hospital.

Success is motivation. "Don't stay in bed, unless you can make money in bed."

Success is knowing what happiness means to you. "Happiness is having a large, loving, caring close-knit family... in another city."

Success is appreciation. "Nice to be here? At my age it's nice to be anywhere."

Success is making keen observations. "Too bad that all the people who know how to run the country are busy driving taxicabs and cutting hair."

Success is making a contribution to society. In remembrance of George Burns, President Bill Clinton summed it up best saying, "He enabled us to see humor in the toughest of times and laugh together as a nation. We will miss him greatly."

[Sources: http://www.workinghumor.com, http://www.biography.com, http://entertainment.msn.com]

"By the time you're eighty years old you've learned everything. You only have to remember it."

- George Burns (1896-1996)

Day 39: Fear of Success

"How could someone fear something so great like success?" you may be asking yourself. The fact is, most people do, and it is this fear that keeps them from achieving it. Fear comes from the lack of understanding. It is clear to see that those who have not taken the time to explore success will not understand it and thus fear it. Having limiting beliefs about success also contributes to our fear of success.

Let's look at some of the most common fears or limiting beliefs about success.

"It's lonely at the top". It certainly is not crowded at the top considering only about 2% feel they are successful. However, "lonely" is not the right word. Olympians who stand on the winner's platform when receiving their medals certainly are not lonely. There are times going it alone is much better than being held back by others. The top is reserved for those with enough perseverance to make it there.

"With success comes responsibility". There is no debating this. Success often brings great responsibility as it does great wealth. Successful people use their wealth to hire people to take care of their responsibilities. Lawyers, accountants, brokers, assistants, housekeepers, gardeners... the list goes on. Life at the top does not have to be difficult.

"When you are at the top, there is only one way to go". This is one of those silly pessimistic statements. First of all, what is "the top"? There is no limit to success, wealth, or happiness so you can really never get to the top. Even if you were at the top, why couldn't you just spend the rest of your days there?

"People resent successful people." In actuality, resentful people resent successful people. You cannot change everyone else's thoughts so why bother trying. For every person who resents a successful person, there is a person who resents a failure. So why not just be successful?

"Successful people are conceited". Conceit is not a characteristic of success. Those who are successful do possess high self-esteem as well as high self-confidence. These traits are often misinterpreted as conceit or narcissism but are very different.

"To be successful, you must cut corners, cheat, or act immorally". This can't be further from the truth. Unless you act with honesty and integrity, and have high moral standards you will never have lasting success. Do not be misled by the press with their interpretations of tycoons like Donald Trump and Bill Gates. The media knows that scandals sell. People would rather hear rumors and fabricated "facts" than how people like Donald and Bill donate fortunes to charitable efforts.

"I would rather devote myself to love and/or my family than the pursuit of success". This is my favorite one. Someone, sometime got it in their mind that one has to choose between love and success. It seems like Hollywood is a big believer in this one as well. Do you know the movie about the guy who is very successful in his work, but then has to choose between love and work, then chooses love and lives happily ever after? There are HUNDREDS of movies with this exact same theme. Success does not come at the expense of love and family. Love and family are actually a huge part of success. Problems arise when one neglects love and family in order to achieve something besides success, like riches or fame. Success is about finding balance, not abandoning your goals.

Fearing success will hold you back. Identify your fears and limiting beliefs and just as we did above, realize that they are without merit. Once you do, you will be yet another giant step closer to your success.

ACTION STEP(S):

---

1) Write down all the reasons why you think success would be a bad thing. Then, next to each reason, put on your success cap and write down why that really is not a good reason. If you cannot seem to do that, post your reason on the discussion board and let other members help you!

"No passion so effectually robs the mind of all its powers of acting and reasoning as fear."

- Edmund Burke

Day 40: Fitness Basics

"Please don't tell me I have to do sit-ups to be successful!" you may be saying after reading the title. Short answer, no. Crunches, leg-lifts, and other ab exercises will do just fine. :) For the long answer, read on.

The mind, body, and spirit are all connected. This is a fact that is widely recognized by both doctors and scientists around the globe. It is said that your outside (body) is a reflection of your inside (mind). By no means must you become an Arnold Schwarzenegger or Jane Fonda to be fit. Although being fit can mean something different to everyone, I like to define fitness as the state in which your body and mind function at your optimal levels. Being fit is not difficult. It can take as little as 20 minutes a day, three days a week.

Here are my top reasons to commit to a regular exercise program and commit to be fit.

- **More energy.** Expending energy creates more energy. Morning workouts allow you to go through your day with a natural high, caffeine-free energy, and alertness.
- **Reduce your risk of getting heart disease.** Heart disease is the number one "cause" of death in the USA (actually heart disease is the result of a lack of exercise, a poor diet, bad genes, and other unknowns—so these are the actual cause of death).
- **Manage stress effectively.** Exercise is perhaps the #1 doctor recommended stress management tool. Regular workouts make it difficult to build up stress and tension.
- **Longevity.** Live a longer, healthier life by protecting your body against many forms of disease, which would otherwise severely lower your quality and/or duration of life.
- **Improved brain function.** Get that extra advantage by thinking more clearly.

- **Better social life.** People are attracted to fit people for the same reason people are attracted to positive people. Being fit is just an attractive quality.
- **Improved self-esteem.** If you are one of those people who look in the mirror with disgust, realize that 1) you are probably being too hard on yourself and 2) you can do something about your appearance. Fitness is one of the ways to improve your self-esteem from the outside in.
- **Reduced sickness.** Strengthen your immune system by keeping fit and avoid spreading sickness to your loved ones. Reduce the time spent sick in bed and increase the time spent doing what you really want.

General fitness can be divided into three categories: **resistance training**, **cardio training**, and **nutrition**. For the purpose of this article, just realize that a combination of the three is what is needed for ideal fitness.

There are many ways to get fit, some are free and others can cost big money. Depending on your budget and schedule, you can begin by joining a local gym or spending about $10 on a fitness book that contains home exercises you can do without purchasing any equipment.

If you are currently in a physically demanding job, you still need a well-balanced fitness program. Generally jobs that are physically demanding may address your cardiovascular needs, but not muscular and certainly not nutritional. Likewise, a job lifting heavy objects may focus on just one or a few muscles and result in an unbalanced physique.

Your mind cannot survive without your body. Take care of your body, and in return your body will take care of you.

ACTION STEP(S):

1) If you are not currently 100% committed to a fitness program, write down all the reasons why you are not. Then carefully think about each answer and use your creative mind to counter each objection to your commitment. If you cannot think of a convincing counter, post your reason(s) for not committing on the members' discussion board for feedback and ideas.

"Physical fitness is not only one of the most important keys to a healthy body, it is the basis of dynamic and creative intellectual activity."

- John F. Kennedy

Days 41 and 42 are for "R&R"—review and reflection. Spend these days reviewing the last five articles and reflecting on the information and how it relates to your life. Now is also a good time to make sure all the action steps for the previous days have been completed.

Day 43: Livin' the High Life

I can honestly say that as a 32-year-old man, by my own free will, I have never in my life taken a puff of a cigarette, tried any illegal drug or narcodic, or drank an alcoholic beverage or even a cup of coffee. The fact that I had quite an active social life in both high school and college, yet never took a sip of alcohol in those eight years is almost Oprah-worthy. There are many reasons for this such as upbringing, health, and self-esteem. But my main for reason for abstaining from such depressants and stimulants is the natural high I already have just going through life. Before you say "Oh, please.... give me a break", read on.

Life is full of natural highs that are brought on both internally and externally. Unlike natural highs, artificial highs brought on by drugs (including alcohol and caffeine) come with **equal or greater unnatural lows**. Read that last line again. You can control your natural highs and lows but you cannot control artificial or unnatural ones—they control you. I have learned to spend most of my time in a natural high state. Trust me, if I could bottle this, I would put the liquor stores and drug lords out of business (and probably be assassinated). It is this concept of not being in control of my feelings that has kept me away from drugs these last 32 years and will no doubt continue to keep me away.

In addition to the enormous list of side effects that come with the use of drugs, there is one major side effect that seems to be ignored—tolerance. The body has the ability to build a tolerance to foreign substances. This is very similar to inflation where you keep paying more and more for the same item. Your mind begins to "tolerate" the stimulant or depressant and you require more of it to give you the same high your mind and body now desire. Do you know people who start their day craving several cups of coffee, go through their day with several "coffee breaks" then end their day with "unwinding" alcoholic beverages, while smoking several packs of cigarettes throughout the day? I would be willing to wager they were not always like this. That kind of "daily fix" takes time to build up.

There is no negative tolerance build up to a natural high. Natural highs are brought on by positive events that don't have negative side effects and no equal or greater low that ultimately follows. A tolerance, if one exists, will cause you to just do more of a positive thing to bring on the high. Here is a partial list of my "drugs" that keep me high on life. Yours may be different.

- creating something of value
- helping others
- being enthusiastic
- being motivated
- exercise
- having fun
- making love (which includes all of the above as well)
- creating wealth
- spending quality time with my family
- having appreciation and gratitude

Herein lies another "secret" of success. **The body and mind crave and need highs. If you deny them artificial highs, you will be forced to do the positive things needed to create natural highs.** Buying a high that you can drink, snort, or inject is easier than spending the energy it takes to create a natural high. Successful individuals do what's best not what's easiest.

Best of all, natural highs are completely legal and mostly free! Being in complete control of your body, emotions, and feelings will allow you to experience natural highs that work for the achievement of success, not against it, and you will reach your goals in life faster and more consistently.

ACTION STEP(S):

1) Spend a few minutes thinking about your use of artificial stimulants and depressants. Are you substituting those highs for natural highs?

"Tobacco, coffee, alcohol, hashish, prussic acid, strychnine, are weak dilutions; the surest poison is time."

- Ralph Waldo Emerson

Day 44: Failure is the Seed to Success

One of the more limiting factors in the achievement of success is the fear of failure. Why? People all too often internalize failure and say "I failed" or "I am a failure" as a general statement rather then seeing failure for what it really is—a single attempt at a specific goal that did not produce the desired results.

Think of an airline that fails to keep one of their planes in the air. The plane crashes killing over 200 people instantly. Does the airline give up and go out of business? Not likely. They pay the price for failure, learn from it, and move on. How do your failures in life compare with killing 200+ people? Think about this next time you are faced with failure and it will certainly help put things in perspective.

Just about all successful people have more failures behind them than their unsuccessful or even "average" counterpart. It is the act of persevering when others give up that makes winners stand out and whiners stand down. Failure is a positive force when seen as a necessary step to success. Failure becomes a negative force when seen as final or seen as a defeat.

Realize that from each failure, you can often harvest an equal or greater future success and you will never look at failure the same way again. In most cases, if you make the effort to learn from your mistakes, the wisdom you get will be of far greater benefit to you. For example, if you fail to get that big account and your competitor succeeds, ask the would-be customer why? She will most likely give you priceless information that will allow you to close many more sales in the future. In this case, the failure (the one lost sale) resulted in future success (several sales) of much greater value.

Remember that the smartest, richest, most powerful, most influential, and most honorable individuals throughout history have failed more times than those who "played it safe" in life.

Successful individuals welcome failure and learn to fail successfully.

ACTION STEP(S):

---

1) Never again say "I failed" or "I am a failure". Replace those self-destructive statements with something like "this attempt failed" or "this plan failed".

2) Write down all your recent and/or "large" failures. Next to each, write down all you have learned from the failure. Also write down all the positives that came as a result of the failure. When you are done, look over your list of "failures" again... is it really that bad?

"You always pass failure on the way to success."

- Mickey Rooney (1920–)

Day 45: Inspiration from J.K. Rowling

J.K. Rowling (1965–) is the best-selling author of the Harry Potter book series.

Success is doing what you are passionate about. "I am an extraordinarily lucky person, doing what I love best in the world. I'm sure that I will always be a writer."

Success is bringing about enthusiasm in others. Rowling has said that her greatest reward is the enthusiasm of her readers.

Success is believing in yourself. In America, there are nearly 80 million Harry Potter books in print, and each title has been on The New York Times, USA Today, and Wall Street Journal bestseller lists. Several publishers turned down her finished manuscript before one took interest, each offering many reasons why her book would never do well.

Success is having faith. Publishers kept turning down the Harry Potter book mainly because "it was too long". However, J.K. Rowling had enough faith in her creation to persist until it was published.

Success is often about rough beginnings. The first reading J.K. Rowling did for her book was to about four people. The bookshop staff felt so sorry for her that they stood around and listened as well.

Success is dealing with criticism. The Harry Potter series, which Christian groups have attacked because of its themes of witchcraft and wizardry, was removed from a public school in Bridgeport Township, Michigan.

Success is brought on by inspiration. Rowling first thought of Harry while riding a train back in 1990. "Harry just strolled into my head fully formed."

Success is patience. It was one year from the time Rowling finished her first book to the time a publisher bought it.

[Sources: http://www.biography.com, http://www.scholastic.com, http://www.infoplease.com]

"I was very low, and I had to achieve something. Without the challenge, I would have gone stark raving mad."

- J.K. Rowling

Day 46: Write it Down!

How many times have you had a great idea or answer to a question or problem pop into your mind, only to forget it shortly after? Chances are that many of these times you have even forgotten that you had the idea or answer, so you don't even remember forgetting! How many times has a task, or something you needed to do, occupied your thoughts all day long until you got it done? To keep ideas or answers from slipping away, or to clear to mind so you can be more focused, write things down.

When ideas or answers just come to you, the subconscious mind released some information into your conscious mind. Most of the time, this is information you have been seeking whether you knew it or not. This occurs more frequently when you are sleeping since this is the time your conscious mind is most receptive to your subconscious mind. It is these times of "enlightenment" when some of your best ideas come about. Write them down or record them immediately. With today's technology, digital recorders are as small as a pen and cost very little. This is often a better solution than a pen and paper since there are times like driving a car when writing is not possible or just dangerous. Do not let these valuable ideas slip away. Brilliant ideas that lead to success are not always born in the boardroom, classroom, or office; they come to us at inconvenient times and in inconvenient places. These brilliant ideas stem from the genius within all of us. When it speaks to us, we should not only listen but be prepared to write it down as well.

Perhaps an even more important reason for writing things down is so your conscious mind can be free for more productive or relevant thought. All too often we dwell on something we need to do at some future time. We dwell on it because we do not want to forget about it. Doing this inhibits both our concentration and attention. Add the item on your daily planner or to do list and allow yourself to forget about it. Your time will be spent more productively and without the anxiety of a "to do" task following you around like a dark cloud.

Don't let your "million dollar idea" be forgotten moments after it comes to you. Don't allow your days to be spent thinking about what needs to be done at some future time. Whether you choose the old-fashioned pen and paper or one of the high-tech recorders, recording ideas, answers, and things to do is a great habit of successful individuals.

ACTION STEP(S):

1) Get yourself either a small notebook and pen or recorder to have near you at all times—or at the very least just by your bed, since this is where the majority of "record-worthy" ideas and answers come to you.

"I write down everything I want to remember. That way, instead of spending a lot of time trying to remember what it is I wrote down, I spend the time looking for the paper I wrote it down on."

- Beryl Pfizer

Day 47: Analogies, Similes, and Anecdotes

"Success is a butterfly, beautiful and flowing."
"Leadership is like a bear, always protecting its young."

What do these two statements mean? Did some great philosopher say these immortal words? The truth is, they are gibberish and I, just now, made them up. However, chances are you read them as mystical puzzles and if asked, you would search your mind for the underlying meaning. I did not mean to trick you; I was just proving a point that we are all guilty of interpreting analogies, similes, and anecdotes as truth rather than what they often are: just catchy phrases that sound good.

Lawyers use these powerful tools very often in court to make a point and win a jury to their way of thinking. Debaters use these tools as well because they know the power of such statements. Authors use these tools to reinforce their point. These are very powerful tools used for both persuasion and manipulation. Use them for persuasion, but never let yourself be manipulated by them.

Analogies, similes, and anecdotes all have one major thing in common: they are not meant to be taken literally. Here are the definitions of these figures of speech and some examples.

Analogy - Similarity in some respects between things that are otherwise dissimilar. Example: "Success is a journey, not a destination."

Simile - A figure of speech in which two essentially unlike things are compared, often in a phrase introduced by like or as. Example: "The future is like heaven, everyone exalts it, but no one wants to go there now." - James A. Baldwin

Anecdote - A short account of an interesting or humorous incident. Example: "My father did that once and got fired for it."

Any statement that does not have a literal meaning is up for interpretation. Acceptance of such statements without really understanding the meaning is like being brainwashed and should be avoided. Statements such as, "Money is the root of all evil" or "It is lonely at the top" have gained much popularity over the years and are automatically accepted as truths to many, much to their own financial detriment. Who said these things? What did they mean? Some of these statements date back to before Christ and have been translated so many times that the intended meaning has been lost long ago. Other statements have been made by bitter individuals from whom none of us should be taking advice. In some cases, the time and circumstances surrounding such statements are beyond our comprehension. It is possible that the statement may have been true only for the speaker of the "immortal" words, but not anyone else.

Similes and analogies are great for avoiding jargon to explain something to someone to help them to understand. Anecdotes are great for making or reinforcing a point. You can adopt these techniques to be a more effective communicator. More important, now that you understand these techniques, use your common sense when encountering one of these parts of speech and do not automatically believe everything you read or hear.

ACTION STEP(S):

---

1) Think about how you can use analogies, similes, and anecdotes in your daily life.

2) Commit to listening for analogies, similes, and anecdotes. Once you recognize their use, you will be more consciously aware of them, thus not automatically accepting them as truth.

"All perception of truth is the detection of an analogy."

- Henry David Thoreau (1817–1862)

Days 48 and 49 are for "R&R"—review and reflection. Spend these days reviewing the last five articles and reflecting on the information and how it relates to your life. Now is also a good time to make sure all the action steps for the previous days have been completed.

Day 50: Customer Service

Everyone should be an expert in customer service. Customer service skills are used in just about every job and career there is. People often do not feel the need to learn customer service skills because they do not deal with "customers". They may not deal with a group that is referred to as "customers", but they do deal with customers. For example,

- Doctors have patients
- Lawyers have clients
- Teachers have students
- Police have citizens [to protect]
- Writers have readers
- Babysitters have kids
- YearToSuccess.com has members

Take for example the high school janitor (or custodial technician to be P.C.). He can go about his day mopping floors and keeping to himself. However, he can also have a very positive influence on students by greeting students, learning their names, smiling and getting them to smile back, helping new students find their way around, personally returning lost items to students, etc.

Success in any industry begins with the use of exceptional customer service skills. Do not assume that just because your "customers" have nowhere else to go for your services, like in the case of a police officer protecting her citizens, that treatment of customers is any less important. People are people—in any industry—and should be treated as valued customers. It is just the right thing to do. If you have just your own self-interest in mind, then realize how you treat customers will ultimately reflect on you and your performance on the job. Likeability is a major factor in salary increases and promotions. Building positive relationships with your customers also makes your job a whole lot easier, more enjoyable and more rewarding. In business especially, exceptional customer service is a must.

Throughout this program I will be sharing ideas on customer service. It is important to realize that this does apply to you. Even if the job you are currently in requires no customer service skills whatsoever (a job where you only deal with co-workers), if you are striving for success, whatever you do to get there will require customer service skills. Become an expert in customer service and both your "customers" and superiors will appreciate you more for it.

ACTION STEP(S):

1) To think about: Who are your customers in life? If they are paying customers with a choice to go elsewhere, would they?

"The great thing is the start—to see an opportunity for service, and to start doing it, even though in the beginning you serve but a single customer—and him for nothing."

- Robert Collier

Day 51: Gratitude and Appreciation

It is the typical Hollywood story that we all have heard: someone we know of on the big screen or TV appears to have it all. He or she has the admiration of millions of fans, beautiful companions, and all the money one can possibly need in a lifetime. Yet this superstar lives in misery and carries out a self-destruct sequence that sometimes even leads to taking his or her own life. The superstar had everything; everything except gratitude.

Gratitude is the state of being grateful or thankful. It is the continual reflection of what's *right* with your life rather than the constant dwelling on what's wrong. Back here in the real world (us non-Hollywood people) gratitude is just as important. Success is often realized with the expression of the internal feeling of gratitude. One who feels true success does not sink into depression or begin to self-destruct.

Why do most people find it so difficult to have gratitude? It has to do with how our brains function. We can only focus on one thing at a time. While our attention and concentration is in one place, everything else is shut out by our minds. Take a moment right now to look around you and listen to all the sounds. All of this, just a moment ago, was filtered out by your mind as something that was not important to your current thought. Our focus shifts with change. For example, if it started to thunder and lightning outside right now (and you can see or hear it) you would most likely notice. However, after about an hour of continual thunder and lightning, your brain would filter it out as it would background noise. Gratitude is difficult to find because the things we should be most grateful for in our lives rarely change enough to get our attention.

Here are a few gratitude-building steps:

1) Write down all the things in your life for which you should be grateful. It is OK to be general with statements like "being alive",

rather than making statements like "breathing, my heart beating, white blood cells, etc.". However, the more specific you are, the more gratitude you will have.

2) Really think about NOT having each item on your list above, and what your life would be like. If it really does not matter to you, then the item on the list should be removed or categorized under a more general category.

3) Consider some of the things we often take for granted. Depending on where you are in the country or world, you may or may not have some of these things:

- freedom
- opportunity
- public libraries
- clean air to breathe
- clean water to drink
- abundance of food
- electricity
- protection

4) Think of those less fortunate than you.

5) Help those less fortunate than you. This does not always involve giving away money. Be creative. There are many ways you can help others by sharing some of the things you possess, including knowledge.

It is important to your success to have gratitude and it is important to your character to show it. The act of showing gratitude is known as appreciation. Appreciation is the externalization of gratitude usually in the form of words, writing, a gesture, or even just a look. Expressing your appreciation for others and other's actions will strengthen your personal and business relationships.

Here are a few ways you can show appreciation

- a warm embrace
- a firm handshake with a gentle smile
- a sincere "thank you"
- a passionate kiss
- a hand-written card with a sincere message of appreciation

Gratitude is humbling and will keep you likable once you are rich and/or famous. It will keep you motivated and positive; it will help you to stay on track in pursuit of your life purpose. Show your appreciation for others frequently and emphatically, and in return, you will be appreciated more for it. You will be amazed at the results.

ACTION STEP(S):

---

1) Follow the gratitude building steps in the today's lesson. Commit to doing this once per month, or when you find yourself in an unappreciative state of mind.

2) Pick up a small object nearby. Take a few minutes to study it, feel it, taste it, and smell it. Think about all of the work that went into creating the object. Learn to appreciate that object.

3) Start showing at least twice as much appreciation for others and others' actions as you have been showing. "Double the dosage".

"Gratitude is not only the greatest of virtues, but the parent of all others."

- Cicero (106 BC–43 BC)

Day 52: Inspiration from Jack La Lanne

Jack La Lanne (1914–) is known to many as America's number one physical fitness expert and guru, often called, "The Godfather of Fitness".

Success is achieved through frustration. Jack was picked on and made fun of as a child. He was addicted to sugar and had suffered poor health. It was with this frustration he set out to transform his mind and body into the "Godfather of Fitness" he is today.

Success is desiring knowledge. Jack says he became a voracious reader and absorbed everything that would help him to improve himself.

Success is not being satisfied with helping only yourself, but doing all you can to help others. Jack was determined to share his newly found secrets (remember, back in 1936 they were secrets) of health and fitness with others. In 1936, at age 21, he opened the first modern health studio.

Success is acquiring specialized knowledge. In just a few short years, Jack had learned more about the workings of the muscles in the body than most doctors.

Success is doing what you know is right despite "professional" criticism. "People thought I was a charlatan and a nut," Jack says. "The doctors were against me—they said that working out with weights would give people heart attacks and they would lose their sex drive; women would look like men. Even the coaches predicted that athletes would get muscle bound and didn't want them to work out with weights."

Success is innovation. Jack developed the first models of the exercise equipment that is standard in the health spas of today.

Success is overcoming adversity. Jack was forced to give up golf many years back due to a serious automobile accident. Despite doctors telling him his golfing days were over, Jack proved he could overcome adversity by not only golfing once again, but shooting considerably better at age 82 than he did at age 50.

Success is the constant pursuit of doing what you love doing best. Even at the mature age of 88, Jack continues to tour the world with his wife, giving motivational lectures on exercise and nutrition.

[Sources: http://www.jacklalanne.com]

"If the mind can conceive, the body can achieve."

- Jack La Lanne

Day 53: Trying New Things

The world is full of new and exciting things to try. There is a certain kind of freedom, or renegade quality, to living by the words "variety is the spice of life" or "try everything once; go back and do the things you like again", but this kind of advice can be dangerous to living a successful lifestyle.

One of the biggest mistakes we make is by taking the "if it feels good now, then do it" approach to trying new things. We spend so much time and effort preaching to our youth about the dangers of alcohol and smoking, and we expect them to put off this need for immediate pleasure in favor of long-term wellness. Yet as post-pubescent adults full of "wisdom", we choose to try new things in quite the same way as a 13 year old would. We may not have our co-workers next to us egging us on ("Go! Go! Go!"), but we choose to try new things based purely on immediate gratification.

The best way to "quit" any destructive habit is never to start in the first place. Quitting something we get pleasure out of is very difficult, especially when it comes to substances that are chemically addictive. According to a recent HBO Family special on teenage smoking, 7 out of 10 high school seniors who smoke wish they'd never started. Don't live in regret and be a "woulda, coulda, shoulda" type of person; be smart enough to think before you act, and avoid more serious longer-term consequences to your short-term pleasures.

In our continual efforts to better ourselves and improve our lifestyle, we want to try new things. But before we do, we should consider the consequences of our actions. This is done by asking yourself, "Will trying this put me closer to my goals and my life purpose?" For example, trying a new dish for dinner made up of pasta and fresh vegetables to replace a Big-Mac™ meal, would be a good choice whereas trying cigarettes that will lead to all kinds of social and physical problems, would clearly not be a good choice.

So perhaps it would be wiser for us to adopt the credo, "Try anything once, *providing it is consistent with your life's goals*; go back and do the things you like again". I admit, it may not sound as "smooth" or catchy, but it sure makes a lot of sense.

ACTION STEP(S):

---

1) Think about the last few things you have tried for the first time recently. In retrospect, were these good choices?

2) Commit to trying new things only if they fit in with your life's goals. Do not risk a destructive addiction, habit, or activity that will take you further from your goals and thus further from success.

"We keep moving forward, opening new doors, and doing new things, because we're curious and curiosity keeps leading us down new paths."

- Walt Disney

Day 54: The Pain and Pleasure Principle

One of the most complex questions we can ask, "Why do we do the things we do?", actually does have a very simple answer. The answer is to avoid pain and/or to gain pleasure. This age-old concept recently popularized by success author Anthony Robbins, is just as true today as it was thousands of years ago. Does this concept sound too simplistic? At first I thought so, but after years of putting this "theory" to the test I have yet to come up with an ultimate motivator other than avoiding pain or gaining pleasure. Understanding this principle is like unlocking the secrets to human behavior, and will allow you to take complete control over your own life and help others to regain control over theirs.

Why do people smoke cigarettes? As a non-smoker, you may even go as far as seeing smokers as "less than human". I mean, how could human beings do that to themselves? The fact is, smokers are every bit as human as the rest of us; smokers just associate more pleasure with smoking than they do pain and/or associate more pain to not smoking than they do pleasure. It is that simple. Understanding this principle will allow you to be more empathetic to others' actions and behaviors.

Understanding this principle is only the first step. To change a behavior, we just need to associate more pain with the behavior and more pleasure with changing the behavior. Once that is done, without question or exception, the behavior will change. Your desire to avoid pain and gain pleasure is even stronger than any chemical addiction you may have. It is that powerful. Think of it as an old-fashioned scale, where we have the reasons for change on one side and reasons not to change on the other. Even though it is always better to think in positive terms, the need to avoid pain is generally a greater motivator than the need to gain pleasure. So in order to change the behavior, we need to tip our scale to the reasons for change.

At this point, you may be saying to yourself that it can't be that easy. Well it is, and it isn't. The key is to make the associations strong enough in your mind so you are convinced, without question, the behavior must change. Let's go through this process with the example of biting fingernails.

1) Identify the behavior you wish to change. We did that— biting (hopefully, just our own) fingernails.

2) Decide to change the behavior. You know you want to stop biting your fingernails but you continue to bite them. The reason is (and this is *always* the case), that you associate more pleasure with biting your fingernails than you do pain. Remember, when a successful person makes a decision, they eliminate all other options.

3) Get the facts. In the old days, like before 1995, you would need to go to the library and spend hours researching. Today, we use the Internet and get all the facts we can possibly handle in minutes (I prefer Google.com because of the lack of intrusive ads). Be sure to check the reliability of your sources. "Jim's fingernail-biting heaven" may not be the best source for facts. This step allows you to gather reasons for changing the behavior.

4) Make a cons and pros list. Notice I wrote "cons and pros" and not "pros and cons". This is because the cons list should be first, that is, in this case, the reasons for NOT changing the behavior. Be completely honest with yourself and list all of the reasons why you do not want to change the behavior. Your list may look something like this:

Reasons NOT to change behavior (cons)

- biting my fingernails helps me to relieve stress and tension
- I can't stand having long fingernails
- gives me something to do
- I would rather bite my fingernails than be snacking on food or smoking

Now for the reasons to change (pros), do more than just write them down. Vividly imagine each reason with your eyes closed if needed. You can't just read and write the words, you have to paint a clear mental picture.

Reasons TO change behavior (pros)

- well manicured nails on both males and females are attractive and often admired by others
- the millions of germs and microscopic organisms that live under my fingernails should stay there, and not be relocated to my mouth
- nails that are not bitten will not bleed or cause pain
- an attractive member of the opposite sex would be more likely to want to kiss me without fingernails in my mouth
- biting fingernails is a viewed as a sign of weakness and reflects poorly on my character

5) Revisit and Rebuke. Now revisit your cons list and rebuke your own statements with positive, behavior changing reasons and alternatives when possible.

- biting my fingernails helps me to relieve stress and tension - *biting my fingernails actually adds to stress since I only do this when I am stressed. Nail biting is not good form of releasing stress. Instead, I will use one of the squeeze balls or grippers and build up my forearm muscles as well as relieve stress!*
- I can't stand having long fingernails - *I will then make sure I use a nail clipper to cut my nails to an acceptable length to me. I will also be sure that the nail clipper is nearby at all times.*
- gives me something to do - *I have enough to do. Do I really want to spend my energy and time biting my nails that just grow back every day?*
- I would rather bite my fingernails than be snacking on food or smoking - *Why not snack on something low in calories and nutritious like carrots or celery? Heck, after writing*

*the pros of not biting fingernails, even snacking on
Twinkies would be better than biting my fingernails!*

At this point, you should be convinced without question that
changing the behavior is a MUST. If not, go back to step 3 and get
more facts. Talk to people who have changed the behavior and
add their successful reasons for change to your pros list. If you
ever "fall off the wagon", there is only one reason: you still
associate more pleasure with the behavior than pain, or more pain
to quitting than pleasure.

The pain and pleasure principle is simple yet so powerful. It is
more powerful than any drug, chemical, or addiction.
Understanding this principle makes it clear that not only is
changing of a behavior possible, but with enough reasons on your
side, change of the behavior is inevitable.

ACTION STEP(S):

1) Put this principle to use right away! Which of your behaviors do
you want to change? Start small to see the power of this principle
then move on to bigger things. Follow the steps above for
accomplishing this.

2) Use this principle and the steps above to convince yourself
without question, that you MUST be successful. Associate pain
with not being successful and extreme pleasure of being
successful.

"The happiest is the person who suffers the least pain; the most miserable who enjoys the least pleasure."

- Jean Jacques Rousseau (1712–1778)

Days 55 and 56 are for "R&R"—review and reflection. Spend these days reviewing the last five articles and reflecting on the information and how it relates to your life. Now is also a good time to make sure all the action steps for the previous days have been completed.

Day 57: Create a Win-Win Situation

There is only one kind of successful negotiation; it is the kind where both parties come out ahead. I really do not like using the word "win" because that implies a game of some sort where there are winners and losers. Negotiation occurs everywhere in life and life is not a game. To be a successful negotiator, you must have the other person's interests in mind as well as your own.

People negotiate with their spouses, family members and friends as well as in business. Consider this all to common negotiation session between my 4-year-old daughter and me.

My Daughter: *"Daddy? Can I have some ice-cream?"*
Me: *"You have barely eaten your dinner. If you want dessert, you need to finish your dinner."*
My Daughter: *"But I am not hungry. My tummy says 'No more food!'"*
Me: *"Then your tummy does not want dessert either"*
My Daughter: *"No, there is room in there for ice-cream only."*
Me: *"OK, then just finish your chicken."*
My Daughter: *"How about 3 more bites?".*
Me: *(assuming there is 5 bites left) "7 bites!"*
My Daughter: *"4 bites!"*
Me: *"5 BIG bites and finish your milk."*
My Daughter: *"OK, Daddy".*

You can see, in this negotiation session both parties came out ahead. My daughter got her dessert, and I made sure she had eaten most of her meal, which she would otherwise not have eaten. This was a successful negotiation.

If you are the type that went "for the jugular" and got as much as you could from a negotiation, you may THINK you have "won", but almost always you will end up losing in the long run. Here are a few reasons why this is true.

- **Resentment.** This is especially important to avoid in a negotiation with someone with whom you are in regular contact. When you have the upper hand in a negotiation, and you abuse that power by forcing a win-lose outcome, ill feelings and resentment ultimately follow resulting in a poor relationship. These "grudges" are often very damaging later on in the relationship.

- **Short-lived victory.** When one is pressured to give away more than one can actually afford, disaster ultimately follows. For example, you may one day be in a negotiation with a poor negotiator who does not think well under pressure. This person may agree to give you all you are asking for, only later not being able to deliver on the promise. A good example of this is a partner in business who negotiates a much larger share of the business than deserved. The "losing" partner later realizes that she cannot make it with such a small share, and is forced to quit. The business then collapses and both parties lose big because of the greed of the other.

- **What goes around, comes around.** You may be able to get away with taking advantage of someone once, maybe even a few times, but eventually it will come right back to you.

The key is to approach each negotiation as a partnership rather than a competition. Treat those you are negotiating with as partners and not adversaries. Remember that you are interested in the same common goal—a mutually beneficial arrangement or a win-win situation.

ACTION STEP(S):

1) Keep this very important key negotiating principle in mind from now on and commit to using it in your next negotiation, personal or business.

Day 58: Project a Positive Personality

Did you ever meet someone whom you thought was extremely pleasant and had a great personality, and then later talked to someone else who met the same person on a different occasion and felt the exact opposite about the person? For example, "Hi Cindy. Boy, that Phil is great guy. What a pleasant and polite guy he is!" Cindy responds, "Are you kidding? I met that jerk last week and I found him to be rude and arrogant!" It is possible that Phil was in a bad mood when he met Cindy. However, the more likely reason is as follows: **the people we meet often reflect our own personality**.

Imagine that. It is like walking up to a mirror and introducing and chatting with yourself. Our initial reactions are to mirror the facial expressions like frown and smile, energy levels or enthusiasm, speech patterns, and even attitude of the people we meet.

This works both in the short-term and long-term. The short-term effect is the projection of almost a carbon copy of the personality you project. This effect is most noticeable when you first meet someone in the first 5 minutes or so of the conversation. But what if the two people who meet project opposite personalities? Generally, in this case there is one dominant personality, and it is almost always the more positive one. Be that person with the more positive personality.

Have you ever heard someone say, "They bring out the best in me"? What an amazing power to have—bringing out the best in others. This is actually the long-term effect of projecting a positive personality. When you continually "lift" others up by projecting a positive personality they are subconsciously becoming more positive and feeling good about themselves.

Here are five things you can do to project a positive personality when meeting new people.

1) Do your best to be in a positive state of mind when meeting new people. First impressions are most important.

2) Smile. A warm smile when first meeting someone, and while speaking with them, is almost always returned.

3) Think of new people you meet as your best friends and treat them with the same friendliness.

4) Be enthusiastic! Be excited to meet the person and show it.

5) Speak clearly and address the person with the same level of respect as you wish to be addressed. For example "Nice to meet you, Sir", or more casually, "Nice to meet you, Ed".

More important, project the qualities you would like the person to show you in return. I recently had a wall-to-wall carpet installed in a room we use as the gym. The day prior to the installers arriving, we received a very stern phone call from the carpet place reminding us that everything must be removed from the room before they arrive—their installers are not responsible for removing the gym equipment. When the installers showed up early, I met them at the door and offered to help them carry the large rug into the house. Although they graciously refused my help, I could not stop them from helping me clear out the gym.

Project a positive personality. When you do this you will find that the people you meet are more helpful and polite. This will give you a better attitude toward new people you meet and just people in general. By bringing out the best in others, you will be bringing out the best in yourself.

ACTION STEP(S):

1) Become aware of the kind of personality you are projecting in your personal and business relationships. Commit to projecting a

more positive image in your relationships and witness for yourself the change in the other person's personality.

"The art of being yourself at your best is the art of unfolding your personality into the person you want to be. . . . Be gentle with yourself, learn to love yourself, to forgive yourself, for only as we have the right attitude toward ourselves can we have the right attitude toward others."

- Wilfred Peterson

Day 59: Inspiration from Arnold Schwarzenegger

Arnold Schwarzenegger (1947–) made his mark first in the field of professional bodybuilding, then in Hollywood.

Success is having goals, even if your goals change. Young Arnold had a goal as a boy in Austria: to get on the local soccer team. In order to reach his goal he started working out with weights. In a very short period of time, Arnold found a new passion that would lead him to success.

Success is extreme determination. As a teenager back in Austria, Schwarzenegger was so determined to become the greatest bodybuilder in history that he would break into the gym to train on Sundays. It is said that he would train until he collapsed from exhaustion.

Success is having controlled obsessions. Schwarzenegger was said to have been "obsessed with money" early in his life, and he took the steps he felt were necessary to attain wealth, including studying business and economics at the University of Wisconsin.

Success is having a dream. Arnold had a dream: to become the best bodybuilder in the world. He did not slow down until his dream became a reality in 1975 when he won his sixth consecutive Mr. Olympia title.

Success is compassion. Arnold temporarily stopped competing because he felt he "wasn't giving others a chance to win."

Success is lifestyle. Although Arnold reached his dream in 1975, he continued to have more dreams and more goals including acting, politics, business ownership, real estate, family, sharing, and more. In just about all areas, Arnold has become a huge success.

Success is helping others less fortunate. In 1990, Schwarzenegger was named chairman of President George Bush's Council on Physical Fitness. For many years, he has supported sports programs for underprivileged children, including the Inner-City Games and the Special Olympics.

Success is not avoiding failure. Despite Arnold's successful acting career, he has produced several "disappointing" films over the years, but never ceases to keep turning out the blockbusters.

Success is sharing knowledge with others. Arnold has literally shaped the bodybuilding community by writing several books on the subjects of fitness and nutrition. His experiences, knowledge and beliefs have been an inspiration to millions of people around the world who strive to live a fit lifestyle.

[Sources: http://www.biography.com, http://www.schwarzenegger.com]

"I'll be back."

- Arnold Schwarzenegger

Day 60: How Success Works

I remember when I listened to my first success program; it was called "The Seeds of Greatness" by Denis Waitley. At age 10, I did not understand that much but I enjoyed every word of the program. I was, however, waiting for him to tell me exactly how to become successful. Was there a certain widget I needed to create or sell? Who would I sell it to? How exactly was I going to make my million dollars? I anxiously waited to hear these answers.

By the end of the program, I realized that none of my questions would be answered. I became a bit discouraged and turned to the classified section in magazines such as *Success* and *Entrepreneur*. "Ahhh! I found it!" Here, hidden in the back of these well-known periodicals were hundreds of people with the answers I was looking for and willing to give me exact details on how to make a million dollars for only a few hundred dollars! What a bargain! Well, after many years and several thousand dollars I finally understood how success really works and learned several valuable lessons.

1) The pursuit of quick riches only leads to cons, scams and shady sales jobs. Anyone promising instant fortune with little or no effort really means that only they will become instantly rich off people who send them money.

2) Nobody can tell you exactly how to become successful. Lasting success must be achieved through passion, and only you know what you are passionate about. Following someone else's exact steps to success may lead you to their idea of success, but not yours.

3) Many people who sell "how to get rich" ideas only became rich themselves by selling their own books, tapes and seminars on how to get rich! These are authors that usually hide their professional background from their readers.

Since age 10, I have purchased hundreds of books and tapes on all aspects of success, as well as attended seminars by some of my favorite speakers. These have been the driving force that helped me find the exact way to achieve success. The key word is "find". It was up to me to use the information I had gathered to define my own goals and pursue them with passion. Success is very personal to each individual. Anyone who wants to sell you overnight success or wealth is not interested in your success, they are interested in your money.

ACTION STEP(S):

1) Commit to completing this course! There is nothing better than a daily dosage of educational, inspirational, motivational, and positive-ational ;) material to drive you closer to achieving your meaning of success.

"Instead of thinking about where you are, think about where you want to be. It takes twenty years of hard work to become an overnight success."

- Diana Rankin

Day 61: Abraham Maslow's Hierarchy of Needs

Success is about fulfilling the needs of others. Successful companies and organizations generally do this by offering products or services that others desire. Individuals can fulfill needs of others in many different ways. Before an organization or individual can meet the needs of others, they must first understand how one is motivated by unsatisfied needs, then identify and satisfy those needs.

Abraham Maslow, a mid-twentieth century psychologist, is known for establishing the theory of a hierarchy of needs, writing that human beings are motivated by unsatisfied needs, and that certain lower needs must be satisfied before higher needs can be satisfied. Unlike others before him, rather than building this theory from the study of the mentally ill, he studied exemplary people such as Albert Einstein, Frederick Douglas, and Eleanor Roosevelt to name just a few. His theory helps millions of people live fulfilled lives as well as helps managers, business people, and entrepreneurs satisfy the needs others.

Abraham Maslow's Hierarchy of Needs

Physiological Needs. Physiological needs are the very basic needs such as air, water, food, sleep, etc. If these needs are not satisfied, it could lead to serious mental and physical illness and even death. Fulfilling these needs allows us to live in a state of homeostasis. If these needs are not satisfied completely, it is difficult for our minds to focus on the fulfillment of the other needs below.

Safety Needs. There are essentially two parts to this category of needs—safety and security. Safety needs is the physical and psychological desire to be safe from physical harm. This need is a big motivator for learning the martial arts, buying a Volvo, or buying a house in a safe neighborhood. Security needs are more related to fear of change or loss, as in the case of job security.

Security is almost all psychological, and despite the resources available to some people, this is a need that they can never seem to meet. This is mostly due to low self-esteem or the inability to control fear.

Love Needs. Love and the feeling of belonging follow in the hierarchy. Love, in this sense, is non-sexual and could refer to a marriage, friendship, support group, membership (like YearToSuccess.com!), congregation, and even a not-so-positive inner city gang.

Esteem Needs. This is the need for high self-esteem, which is one's self-worth or value. Self-esteem can easily be built internally in many positive ways. However, self-esteem can also easily be both built up and destroyed by others or external events.

Self-Actualization Needs. The need for self-actualization is pursuing the heart's desire and becoming the best one can be. This is the need for living in harmony with others, making a difference in the world, having faith in a higher power, philanthropy, and more.

Self-actualization is the need that is so often never fulfilled by most people because they are so caught up in their attempts to fulfill the first four basic needs. Yet this is where success in life is found. It is no coincidence that the fulfillment of this need often leads to the helping of others.

There are many ways you can put Maslow's theory to practical use in your pursuit of success. Here are some ideas

- understand and fulfill your own needs and live a satisfied life
- make better decisions based on your true needs rather than just financial needs
- learn to identify and offer ideas on how to satisfy the needs of those with whom you "negotiate"
- satisfy the needs of employees, contractors, or students
- satisfy the needs of friends or family

- identify new markets for a product or service
- have more empathy for others

Abraham Maslow's hierarchy of needs does indeed have many useful purposes in both business and one's personal life. It also reveals what I believe to be a major key to success: helping others fulfill their own needs. Keep these motivators in mind next time you are in a negotiation, being asked for a raise, or even just deciding what you really want out of life.

ACTION STEP(S):

---

1) Go through your needs. Are they being met? Where on the hierarchy are you being "held up"? What can you do about it?

"A musician must make music, an artist must paint, a poet must write, if he is to be ultimately at peace."

- Abraham H. Maslow

Days 62 and 63 are for "R&R"—review and reflection. Spend these days reviewing the last five articles and reflecting on the information and how it relates to your life. Now is also a good time to make sure all the action steps for the previous days have been completed.

Day 64: Building Another's Esteem

We have already discussed the value of self-esteem: how important it is in success as well as how it is one of the top motivators. We have discussed ways to build our self-esteem and we have discussed ways that others can deliberately or indeliberately lower our self-esteem. There is another very powerful way to control esteem, and that is by giving it to others.

Giving away esteem is one of those crazy things like love and smiles in that the more you give away, the more you get in return. However, building another's esteem or self-image is not about what you get, it is about helping others to achieve their full potential and to break any mental limitations they have imposed on themselves. Too many cynical people in this world do nothing but criticize, condemn, complain, and destroy other people's self-images. As one of the successful people in this world, do your part to restore balance: be a builder of esteem and not a destroyer.

Here are some ways you can build esteem in others.

- If you need to criticize, criticize the person's actions and not the person. Never saying something like, "You are stupid." Say, "I know you can do so much better if you apply yourself." Young people in general are more likely to believe the words they hear rather than the intended meaning. Even with adults, our subconscious minds process what is said and do not interpret or analyze statements. Repeated hearing of these kinds of negative statements creates a self-fulfilling prophecy.
- Compliment others. Learn to look for the good in others rather than the faults. Once you do this, it is easy to find things to compliment others on. Be sure that the compliment is sincere. For example, if you like their hat, tell them. If you don't like their hat, say nothing about it.
- Treat others respectfully. Ask their views and opinions, take their views and opinions seriously, and give them

meaningful and realistic feedback. This caters to a person's need for importance and does wonders for their self-esteem.

- Remind others of their importance to you often. Tell your family members how much you love them. Tell your friends how much you appreciate their friendship. Tell employees how much you appreciate the work they do for you.
- Remind others of their importance in general. From the guy who mops the floors to the President of the United States, everyone is important in some way. Remind people of their importance and how they make a difference, even if in a small way.
- Share knowledge. By sharing motivational, inspirational, and educational material with others, you are helping them to build their own self-esteem. This is perhaps the best way to build a loved one's or close friend's self-esteem.

You can help loved ones, friends, co-workers, and even strangers build their self-esteem. It can be as simple as sharing a sincere compliment. Get in the habit of building up others and being a positive influence on those in your life.

ACTION STEP(S):

1) Take some time to think about the relationships you have in your life. Are you an esteem builder or destroyer? If the latter, use one or more of the esteem building steps to make amends.

"What we obtain too cheap, we esteem too lightly; it is dearness only that gives everything its value."

- Thomas Paine

Day 65: Success is a Lifestyle

People generally want instant results with as little work as possible. They buy diet pills hoping to reach their ideal weight within days. They buy exercise gadgets from infomercials hoping to get that washboard stomach in 10 days with just minutes a day. They buy audio programs on success hoping to have what it takes to be successful after a few hours of listening. Things just do not work this way.

Health, fitness, education, and success are admired by so many because of the dedication and commitment they take to achieve. Success is not found in a bottle, pill, gadget, book or audio program. Success is created inside your mind using the information you get from education, experiences, and wisdom. There is not one secret to success, nor just a few "magic" principles. There are thousands of ideas, beliefs, concepts, and skills which when put into action, result in success.

Too many people get discouraged from reaching their goals and are turned off by motivational or educational material because they read one book and claim, "it didn't work". There are many rungs on the ladder of success. Sticking with this analogy, visualize a very tall ladder that takes you to the top of a very tall building where you will find ultimate success. If one action takes you one rung higher on the ladder of success, then perhaps 1000 actions of same importance will bring you all the way to the top. Your definition of success determines how high your ladder is.

All actions are not equal. For example, I believe that mastering perseverance is far more valuable to success than say remembering numbers. However, every single idea, belief, concept, and skill you possess and convert into action will take you closer to success. It is these small, gradual changes that stick and become part of your lifestyle. There is even more good news: the law of increasing returns is in effect here as well. This is also referred to as, 1+1=3, momentum, snowball effect, good things happen to good people, the rich get richer, etc. As you condition yourself for success, you will find success becomes easier to achieve.

One of the biggest mistakes people make in the pursuit of success is giving up on single ideas, beliefs, skills, and concepts because they see little or no change from them. They change to a successful behavior, notice no change, and revert back to old behavior. This is like taking a step up your ladder, not being able to see the top any better, then stepping back down. With this pattern, you can easily see why so many never reach success.

Some people reach success early in the process and either just stop progressing or worse revert back to old unsuccessful behaviors. Success must be maintained just like taking care of your body. This is why success is a lifestyle. You can diet and reach your ideal weight but unless you eat right from that point on you will put the weight back on. If you work out and build a buff hard body, then stop exercising, the flabbiness will very quickly return. Success is no different. You never know it all and when you think you do, life can kick you in the groin and send you back to where you started.

Success is a lifestyle. Live every day of your life with success in mind and allow your success skills to build up each and every day by replacing your old negative, limiting beliefs and behaviors. Don't get discouraged and never, ever, give up your dreams. Very soon, your success will be inevitable.

ACTION STEP(S):

---

1) Take 5 minutes to think about this fact. Every good idea, belief, concept, and skill you adopt will bring you closer to success.

Day 66: Inspiration from Helen Keller

Helen Keller (1880-1968) was a writer, lecturer, and advocate for the deaf and blind.

Success is overcoming adversity. Miss Keller managed to develop admirable powers of intellectual and emotional achievement, despite losing both her hearing and sight before the age of two. She traveled to over 40 countries and became a leading figure who publicly campaigned on behalf of civil rights, human dignity, women's suffrage, and world peace.

Success is continual education. Although Miss Keller's formal education ended when she received her B.A. degree, throughout her life she continued to study and stayed informed on all matters of importance to modern people.

Success is being optimistic. Miss Keller was an optimist. In fact, one of her well-known essays was on the subject, appropriately entitled "Optimism".

Success is sharing and caring. Since Miss Keller was a young woman, she was always willing to help others by writing articles, essays and books, giving lectures, and most of all sharing her own personal story of how a severely disadvantaged person can accomplish so many great things.

Success stems from frustration. In her book *Midstream*, Miss Keller wrote of her frustrations with learning, specifically the pace. It was with this frustration that she pushed herself to new limits that allowed her to excel mentally beyond a level to which most non-disadvantaged, educated people aspire.

Success is learning. In addition to English, Miss Keller learned to read French, German, Greek, and Latin... in braille!

Success is inspiring others. Miss Keller has been an inspiration to millions of people around the world and will continue to inspire millions more though her legacy.

Success is having character. Miss Keller devoted most of her life to helping others. Many noted her kindness, generosity and enthusiasm. She thought the best of people and typically brought out the best in others she met.

Success is not using age as an excuse to call it quits. In 1955, when she was 75 years old, she embarked on one of her longest and most grueling journeys, a 40,000-mile, five-month-long tour through Asia.

Success is making a difference in the world. In his eulogy, Senator Lister Hill of Alabama expressed the feelings of the whole world when he said of Helen Keller, "She will live on, one of the few, the immortal names not born to die. Her spirit will endure as long as man can read and stories can be told of the woman who showed the world there are no boundaries to courage and faith."

[Sources: http://www.biography.com, www.afb.org, http://www.helenkeller.org]

Day 67: Create a Stressless Lifestyle

Some estimates say that about 80% of diseases are stress related. This means that if we learn to manage our stress and avoid unnecessary stress we can greatly improve our chances of avoiding disease and illness. Another result of stress that is often overlooked is its effect on the mind's performance. Any time the mind is forced to focus on negative forces (stress), it is difficult to stay positive and pursue your goals. Since stress in life is inevitable, the key is to create a stressless lifestyle.

Stress is defined as "a mentally or emotionally disruptive or upsetting condition occurring in response to adverse external influences and capable of affecting physical health; usually characterized by increased heart rate, a rise in blood pressure, muscular tension, irritability, and depression." It is clear that stress, by definition, is negative and destructive. **However, it is not the adverse external influences that cause the stress, it is the response that causes the mentally or emotionally disruptive or upsetting condition**. As we already know, we cannot control external influences, but we do have complete control over our responses.

To me, managing stress is a wasteful activity that I would much rather not have to spend time and energy dealing with. In medical terms, managing stress is like treating the symptoms and not treating the disease. To create a stressless lifestyle we must focus on avoiding stress altogether, and then managing the stress we do have.

Avoiding Stress. If you only remember one thing from this article, remember that stress is our response to adverse external influences. In most simplistic terms, we can train our minds to respond positively to these adverse external influences that would otherwise cause stress. This concept is amazing because it works. The ability to respond positively to such influences is one that comes in time, and one that you will no doubt possess by the end of this course. It is all part of your positive mental attitude.

Here are some ways you can condition your body and mind to deal with adverse external influences positively.

- Make sure you are getting enough sleep. Your body will let you know how much is enough.
- Eat a balanced, nutritious diet. Good nutrition can improve your ability to handle stress by keeping your immune system strong.
- Exercise. Cardiovascular (aerobic) activity is the best-known stress prevention activity there is. As little as 20 minutes a day, three days a week can work wonders in more than one way.

In addition to the above, you can also avoid stress by avoiding adverse external influences that trigger the responses that then cause stress. Here are some ways to do just that.

- Don't procrastinate. If you are like most people who get stressed by doing things "last minute", then don't.
- Be organized. A neat desk and a manageable schedule can help you sail through the workday.
- Delegate responsibilities – don't try to do too much, and learn to say no.
- Be willing to resolve disputes; don't hold on to anger and never hold grudges.
- Like what you do. The more you spend your day doing things you do not enjoy, the more stress you will have. If you are not willing to change how you spend your day, then at least change your attitude.

Managing stress. So you have done your best to avoid stress yet some stress is still present in your life. Here are some ways to effectively manage these stresses.

- Identify the "stress factors" in your life. Consider each stress factor a problem that needs resolution. Solve the problem or manage it.
- Manage "bad" stress with "good" stress. Exercise is the most common example of putting your body and/or mind under deliberate strain to manage stress. You also may want to try playing sports, riding roller-coasters, watching action movies, or anything else that gets your heart pumping and adrenaline flowing.
- Avoid using caffeine, cigarettes, or alcohol as a way of dealing with stress. Taking artificial stimulants and depressants to manage stress is like pouring gasoline on a fire.
- Relax. Take deep breaths and clear your head.
- Laugh. The old saying that laughter is the best medicine is very true. When you laugh your internal organs are being massaged. Laughter has a very positive healing effect on your body, mind, and spirit.

Don't "fight" or "battle" stress, manage it. When we work with our bodies we get things done much more effectively than when we work against them. Respond to adverse external influences in your life positively and with humor when possible. Master this, and managing stress won't even be necessary.

ACTION STEP(S):

---

1) Identify and write down each of the "stress factors" in your life. Consider each stress factor a problem that needs resolution. Realize that it is your reaction to these problems that is causing stress and once you have a plan for resolving the problem or managing it, there is no need to be stressed over it.

Day 68: Your Dream Collage

The majority of us are visual people; that is, we rely on our sense of sight more than any other sense for learning. Visualization is the act of vividly imagining something as if it were happening and believing your visualization as if it were true. Although this level of visualization takes practice and time, the "dream collage" can help get you there much quicker.

The dream collage is your own personal collection of photographs, magazine clippings or other images that visually define your idea of success. It is made up of images that really move you and ignite the desire within you. Building your dream collage is a great way for you to find out what you really want. A dream collage is pictures of your goals. It is both motivational and inspirational, but more important, it is personal. It is personal in the sense that the images must inspire you, otherwise they are just images. For example, a photograph of a black Porsche may be nice, but if your dream car is a red Ferrari, then get a photo of a red Ferrari.

Here are some ideas of images you can add to your dream collage.

- an attractive person
- a person of the same sex with the ideal body you'd like to have—underwear ads are great for this
- a person dressed like you would like to dress
- a person with hair you admire
- your dream house
- your dream kitchen, family room, or any room in the house
- family, kids
- car
- vacation images (exotic destinations, images of "paradise", etc.)
- money

Your dream collage can be a large poster board on your wall with images glued to it, or just a folder hidden in your desk with the images in the pocket. If it is not in a place where you can see it, be sure to take it out often. I personally use a glue stick and glue the images to a page in my success notebook and keep my favorite photos on my desk. Use whatever method works best for you.

Your dream collage is like your future photo album. This is an extremely powerful way to train your mind in visualization and belief, as well as to get the things you want out of life. Review your dream collage often and fill yourself with instant motivation.

ACTION STEP(S):

1) Start your collage today with at least one image. If you have no magazines around, search the Internet. Just start with one image that really inspires you to reach your goals.

"Go confidently in the direction of your dreams. Live the life you have imagined."

- Henry David Thoreau (1817–1862)

Days 69 and 70 are for "R&R"—review and reflection. Spend these days reviewing the last five articles and reflecting on the information and how it relates to your life. Now is also a good time to make sure all the action steps for the previous days have been completed.

Day 71: Today is a New Day

I have always enjoyed the saying, "Today is the first day of the rest of your life", and not just because of its irony, but also because of how true it is. Behind that somewhat comedic statement is a meaning so important to your success; you should memorize it and repeat it to yourself on a regular basis. Understanding the meaning of this statement is what turns losers into winners and failures into successes.

Today is the first day of the rest of your life. Your life is different today than it was yesterday. You are a different person today than you were yesterday. You are a better person today. The mistakes you have made in the past do not have to haunt you in the present or the future. Just because you failed yesterday, does not mean, in any way, that you will fail today. Today is a new day.

I know so many people who have given up trying to better themselves because they have read motivational books before, listened to "all" the tapes, been to the seminars, and they "didn't work" or they were not inspired by the content. They have made up their minds that it is pointless to pursue personal achievement. This decision is justified by their claim to have "learned from experience", which can be, in many circumstances, a very valid reason. However, when "learning from experience" is used as an excuse to give up on doing something great for yourself or others, it is no longer valid.

People who come from dysfunctional families are not destined for a dysfunctional life. People who have a criminal history can and do move on to legitimate and productive careers. If you were born and raised in a low-income neighborhood, it certainly does not mean that you must spend the rest of your life there. Your past does not have to equal your future. Change in this world is inevitable; make it work to your advantage.

Yesterday's failure brings you one step closer to today's success. The loser of yesterday's race will, with persistence and determination, become the winner of today's race. Your failures in life bring you closer to success. Never give up because of your past. Today is the first day of the rest of your life. How are you going to choose to live it?

ACTION STEP(S):

---

1) Why are you not exactly where you want to be today? Does it have anything to do with events in your past? Are you using your past as an excuse for not being exactly where you want to be? Think about this.

2) Do you know another person who seems to have "given up" in life because of a past failure? If so, share this article with him or her and offer your encouragement. Change someone's life today.

"Finish each day and be done with it. You have done what you could. Some blunders and absurdities no doubt crept in, forget them as soon as you can. Tomorrow is a new day, you shall begin it well and serenely..."

- Ralph Waldo Emerson (1803–1882)

Day 72: Baby Steps

In the beginning of the movie, _What About Bob?_, the highly neurotic and troubled Bob (played by Bill Murray) visits Dr. Leo Marvin (Richard Dryfuss) for help with his troubles. Dr. Marvin prescribes his own best seller book, _Baby Steps_ which is about breaking down the apparently insurmountable problems into small, achievable goals. While this movie is fictional, the concept behind _Baby Steps_, is very real and a great way to approach your goals and life's challenges.

A perfect example of baby steps in action is our on-line course with hundreds articles to read, about 1000 action steps to complete, over 1000 quiz questions to answer and an average of about 180 hours of study. If you were to print out each day of the course and put it into a book, it would be thicker than the average yellow-pages book with over 1000 pages of pure content. My reason for telling you all this is certainly not to turn you off from the course (or the book), but to show you how less than 30 minutes a day is much more surmountable than 180 hours of study. By breaking down the very large goal of taking a 366 day course in personal achievement into single days, our membership increases because members believe they can accomplish the small daily goals.

What about becoming a millionaire? Do you find it hard to believe that you can ever become a millionaire? After all, the most you ever had was a few thousand dollars saved up. Well what about creating product that you can sell for a net profit of $10? Can you sell about 100 of these products per day for the next three years? How about just 50 products a day for the next six years? Either way, you will be a millionaire.

The easiest way to overcome the mental limits we impose on ourselves is to take "baby steps". Break the goal down into manageable targets that you believe 100% in your mind you can reach. If you do not truly believe you can reach these targets, then break the goal up into smaller steps or increase the timeline for completion.

The next time you are faced with a problem that seems too large for you to handle, or a goal too bold to believe you can accomplish, think of Bill Murray literally taking baby steps to the elevator saying, "Baby step to the elevator". Who knows, in addition to tackling your problem or achieving your goal, you may just smile as well. :)

ACTION STEP(S):

---

1) Try this baby step approach with one of your goals or current problems. Break it down into as many smaller steps as it takes for the goal or problem until you believe you can achieve or solve it.

"The reason most people never reach their goals is that they don't define them, or ever seriously consider them as believable or achievable. Winners can tell you where they are going, what they plan to do along the way, and who will be sharing the adventure with them."

- Denis Waitley

Day 73: Inspiration from Thomas Edison

Thomas Edison (1847-1931) was one of the greatest inventors of all time.

Success is desiring knowledge. From the age of 4, Thomas Edison was known for his thirst for knowledge. This desire led his parents to introduce him to the public library at age 11, where he developed the preference of learning by self-instruction.

Success is acting on opportunity. At age 14, Edison used the information he got from working at a railroad station to publish his own weekly flyer, which ended up having hundreds of subscribers and making over $10 a day (big bucks back in the late 19th century).

Success is seeing the good in less than desirable situations. By age 14, Edison lost almost all of his hearing and was legally deaf. He naturally accepted his fate and quickly adapted his learning methods. In fact, when doctors offered him an operation that would almost certainly restore his hearing, he refused because he feared that the "added noise" would hamper his concentration in his now silent and peaceful world.

Success is imminent the moment true desire is established. In his late teens, Edison returned home to find his mother mentally ill and his father out of work and about to lose their home. It was at this point in his life when he made the commitment that he MUST succeed and make some serious money.

Success is learning from your failures. Edison's first "legitimate" invention was an electric vote-recording machine that, despite its brilliance, was too far ahead of its time to be marketable and did not sell. Edison learned a valuable lesson in marketing, and from this point on, he vowed he would "never waste time inventing things that people would not want to buy."

Success is a result of past actions that eventually are seen as valuable by others. Edison spent years tinkering with the telegraph, the quadruplex transmitter, the stock-ticker, etc., all in his spare time. Then one day, to his complete amazement, a corporation paid him $40,000 for all of his rights to the stock-ticker. This apparent "overnight" success that served as a major turning point in Edison's life was a result of years of earlier work.

Success is inspired by healthy competition. In 1879, extremely disappointed by the fact that Bell had beaten him in the race to patent the first authentic transmission of the human voice, Edison now "one upped" all of his competition by inventing the first commercially practical incandescent electric light bulb, which as we know, dramatically changed the way we all live today.

Success is a pattern that never quits. Edison obtained his last patent, his 1093rd, at the age of 83. This was less than a year before his death.

Success is perseverance. Edison is the role model for perseverance. While working on the nickel/iron storage battery, he performed 10,295 failed experiments before achieving success. In addition, almost every one of his failed inventions was followed by a success. Edison knew very well the key element of success— perseverance.

[Sources: http://www.thomasedison.com, http://www.incwell.com, http://www.biography.com]

"Genius is 1% inspiration and 99% perspiration."

- Thomas A. Edison

Day 74: Luck

Jack worked hard through school. He studied every night, did his assignments on time, and did extra credit assignments when possible. He applied to 14 of the top colleges and was accepted to two of them. Jack chose Yale where he worked feverishly for another four years. During that time he applied for dozens of internships and made many connections in the business world. Upon graduation, he interviewed for almost 50 jobs and out of his four job offers, he accepted a very attractive position as a high-level manager for a respectable company. When Jack's friends learned of his success, they would say, "Boy, is he lucky!".

How much of success is actually luck? Is the reason that you are not successful because you tend to have bad luck whereas others who are successful only have good luck? What is luck anyway? I am not going to say, "I don't believe in luck" or "luck is for losers". Luck is very real. However, I believe luck is something over which we all have a strong influence.

Luck is defined as, "the chance happening of fortunate or adverse events". The keyword here is "chance". This is important because to improve our luck, all we need to do is improve our chances. Luck is nothing more than application of the law of probability. The person who is most likely to be "lucky" at winning the lottery is the person who buys more tickets. Of course, there are those one-in-a-billion chances we hear about where one time ticket buyers win the jackpot, but not only is that extremely rare, it is also NOT success. By now you should realize that success cannot be achieved by one fortunate chance in life, or even several. Success is achieved within us and is a result of our own continual personal development.

Each of us has the ability to create our own good luck—or bad luck for that matter. First of all, you must BELIEVE that you control your destiny. The luck you have experienced in your life and the luck you will experience has much to do with you.

Although we cannot have good luck all the time, using the laws of averages and probability, we can certainly tip the scale of good luck and fortune on our side. You can have more doors opened for you, and experience more of the things that everybody refers to as "luck."

Here are some suggestions on how you can make your own good luck.

- **Be in the right place at the right time.** Although most people see this is as pure chance, it is vision, proper planning, and calculated risk taking that puts most successful people in the right place at the right time.
- **Create the circumstances in your life that lead you to good luck.** This can also be referred to as sowing and reaping. In our opening example, Jack was "lucky" to get such a great job because of everything he did in his life up to that point. He chose to work hard and apply for so many jobs. Had he not created these circumstances, his luck would no doubt be different.
- **Increase your probabilities.** The more chances you have at good luck, the more likely you are to experience good luck. Too many people go about their normal, uneventful lives just waiting for something great to happen to them without doing anything to increase their chances. Some excellent ways to increase your probability for fortunate chances are by working on your personal development, making more contacts or networking, and becoming involved in new opportunities, just to name a few.
- **Take more calculated risks.** Those who avoid risk are almost always doomed to a life of failure and bad luck. The more you can limit your chance of loss and increase your chance of gain, the better off you will be.
- **Apply the principles of success and personal achievement.** There are thousands of these, most of which are revealed in this course. Being successful, you will not be able to stop good luck and good fortune from coming your way even if you wanted to!

Then there is the law of attraction. As you start to create good luck in your life, you will experience even more good luck as a result of your existing good luck. The door of opportunity and good fortune usually opens to several more doors.

Unfortunate events or chance will come your way from time to time and despite all your efforts they cannot be avoided. However, you CAN control your response to this "bad luck". As a positive thinker and one who looks for opportunity in problems, each instance of "bad luck" will be replaced with "minor set backs" or even "new opportunities". Luck, as we know it, is all about perception.

When you understand that you create your own luck, you no longer live with insecurity—thinking that some unfortunate chance will take away your success. It is true that some unfortunate chance may take away your money or your business, but it can only take away your success if you let it.

Good luck does exist, and it is something each of us has the power to influence. What most people refer to as bad luck is generally referred to as "minor setbacks" or "new opportunities" by successful individuals. Follow the suggestions above for creating your own good luck and you too will find yourself becoming increasingly "lucky".

ACTION STEP(S):

---

1) Write down at least 5 events in your life that you viewed as either good or bad luck. If good luck, what did you do to create the good luck? If bad luck, what could have you done to avoid it? Was it really "bad luck"? What opportunities did it lead you to?

Day 75: Why Aren't You Rich?

Why aren't you rich? I love to ask this question to others. It seems like whenever I ask this question of someone, they respond by going in to their best Bob Newhart routine—breaking a sweat and stuttering. Why aren't YOU rich? We already know that riches are just a small part of success and money is not everything, blah blah blah... so for now, with that understanding, let's just talk about being rich in a purely financial sense.

Like success, the word "rich" has a different meaning for everyone. For the purpose of this discussion, let's just assume it means having more than enough money to live your dreams. If you already are rich, then play along with us anyway; you can always use this information to help others get rich.

It is time to ask yourself, **why aren't you rich?** Write down your reasons why in your success journal. I promise you, this will be an incredible eye-opener for you and a big step forward in your attainment of wealth. To help you in your thought process, here are some of the more common reasons people have come up with.

- I really do not want to be rich
- I don't know how get rich
- I am working on it
- Money is evil
- I don't have the time
- I am not smart enough
- I am not talented enough
- I am destined to be poor
- No one in my family has ever been rich
- I have been trying to get rich but I just can't
- I have responsibilities like taking care of my family and paying the bills—it is irresponsible of me to be chasing a dream
- I am waiting for the right opportunity
- I am waiting for a rich relative to pass away

- I am waiting to marry someone rich

Now that you have written down your reasons, ask yourself, "Are these the real reasons or are they excuses?" In other words, is this what you are telling yourself and others because it "sounds reasonable"? Or behind the excuse is there a more truthful reason? I am asking you to question your reasons or beliefs as to why you think you are not rich. For example, if you wrote down, "I don't have the time", don't you think you would make the time if you knew that by making the time you would become rich? If so, then isn't the real reason that you do not believe you can become rich? Go back through your list of reasons now, and write down the real reasons.

Here are some to get you started.

- I really do not want to be rich - *If you truly feel this way, you are already rich, otherwise you have some limiting beliefs about money that are holding you back from becoming rich.*
- I don't know how get rich - *If this is the case, why haven't you learned? Bookstores are full of books on how to acquire riches.*
- I am working on it - *Most people spend their lives "working on it". I rephrase the question... why aren't you rich NOW?*
- Money is evil - *Money is paper and metal, it's not evil. Do you really believe that you would use your money for evil rather than good?*
- I am not smart enough - *Refer to the quote by Calvin Coolidge (Day 1).*
- I am not talented enough - *Refer to the quote by Calvin Coolidge (Day 1).*
- I am destined to be poor - *Says who? You create your destiny so why would you create one that is not filled with wealth?*
- No one in my family has ever been rich - *That may be a true statement, but realize that has nothing whatsoever to*

do with your financial destiny. There is no gene for being rich.

- I have been trying to get rich but I just can't - *Don't try, do. Change what is not working. Believe 100% with all your heart that you can get rich. Persist. This course will reveal much information that will help you with this one.*

- I have responsibilities like taking care of my family and paying the bills; it is irresponsible of me to be chasing a dream - *It is irresponsible of you NOT to follow your dream and NOT give your family the lifestyle they deserve. We all have responsibilities and bills to pay - even rich people. Find the time or make the time.*

- I am waiting for the right opportunity - *Why not create your own opportunities? You can spend your whole life waiting and one will never come.*

- I am waiting for a rich relative to pass away - *A little on the sick side, but who am I to judge.*

- I am waiting to marry someone rich - *Why not become rich yourself first and marry someone for pure love? There will not only be more "fish in the sea", but you will also do much better on the prenuptial agreement.*

If your reasons are not in the list above, use the same line of reasoning that I have used to refute your own statements. Have fun with this... pretend you are a lawyer putting yourself on the witness stand, drilling yourself for the real reasons. Don't go easy on yourself!

Congratulations! Assuming you have done the exercise, you are now closer to being rich than you ever have been before. Now that you know why you are not rich, it is up to you to make the necessary changes in your beliefs, behaviors, and/or lifestyle to become rich. If you are not sure how, no need to worry. You will find the information you need in this course. I am not being secretive—if I could tell you to do A,B,C to be rich, I would. Like success, there are many ideas, concepts, skills, and beliefs that will help you to acquire riches. Just remember to be patient and believe in yourself.

ACTION STEP(S):

---

1) Just do the exercise in the article.

"No matter how rich you become, how famous or powerful, when you die the size of your funeral will still pretty much depend on the weather."

- Michael Pritchard

Days 76 and 77 are for "R&R"—review and reflection. Spend these days reviewing the last five articles and reflecting on the information and how it relates to your life. Now is also a good time to make sure all the action steps for the previous days have been completed.

Day 78: Going the Extra Mile

Why do so many people do just what they need to do to "get by" in life rather than go the extra mile? Some say it is because people are generally lazy and some say it is because people are generally unwilling to give something for nothing. However, I believe it is because people are just unaware of the chain reaction of positive events that come from going the extra mile. If everyone knew the great effects this gesture has, everyone would take the time to go the extra mile.

Going the extra mile is simply doing more than you are asked or expected to do. You may have tried this approach before and became discouraged or found it a waste of your time. In order to realize the benefits that come with going the extra mile in business or your personal life, **you must not expect anything in return**. You must be satisfied enough in knowing that you have helped another in need. If not, this value will be in conflict with your other values and it will not last.

Why go the extra mile? Why go out of your way for others? Besides the great feeling you get in knowing you have helped another in need, there are many reasons that will ultimately benefit you. I use the word "ultimately" because these benefits are not obvious and not immediately recognizable, however, they do have a very positive effect on your success in life.

- Going the extra mile will help you stand out from the crowd and be recognized
- Going the extra mile will bring out positive emotions in others allowing them to both remember you and feel good about you
- Going the extra mile will help you to move ahead of your competition and succeed where others fail

How and when do you go the extra mile? Do you give your customers free products or service? Do you do your employees' jobs for them? Do you give away money to your friends? Going the extra mile is not about becoming a slave or a saint, it is about offering your help in some small way. Giving away products, service, money, or doing too much for others will hurt both your business and the independence of others you are attempting to help. Ask yourself this question, "Is this something I would charge a friend for?" If not, then do it for free and do it with enthusiasm.

Here are some ways you can go the extra mile for others.

- run errands for a parent
- take a friend out to dinner
- call existing customers just to make sure they are happy with their purchase
- help a co-worker with their heavy workload
- do a personal favor for an employee

Waiters who go the extra mile get bigger tips. Employees who go the extra mile get more promotions. Businesses that go the extra mile get more customers. Go the extra mile for others in your life and expect nothing in return. Then just sit back and enjoy the by-product of success that will eventually come your way.

ACTION STEP(S):

1) Go the extra mile or offer to go the extra mile for someone else right now (or very soon). Experience how good it makes you feel knowing that you have helped another without expecting anything in return.

"There are no traffic jams when you go the extra mile."

- Anonymous

Day 79: Thank God It's Any Day

In America, we have some pretty disempowering sayings that, unfortunately, some have adopted as credos, and even worse, ways of life. Sayings like, "A bad day of fishing is better than a good day of work", "Don't work too hard", and the classic, "Thank God it's Friday". We use these snazzy sayings during "happy" hour, in conversations with friends and co-workers, and even stick them on the bumpers of our cars. It seems as if too many people universally share misery and hatred for one's work. Why not live by the words, "Thank God it's any day!"

Our week consists of seven days, five of which are traditionally reserved for "work" and two for "play". Again I say traditionally because I do not know who came up with this idea, but it wasn't someone with success in mind nor was it someone who valued family life. Nevertheless, for most working adults, this is just "the way it is". If you are not one the fortunate few who can spend all seven days with the ideal balance of work and play, there are still ways you can enjoy your "work week".

Let me ask you this question: how much would the quality of your life improve if every day of the week was as enjoyable as your best day of the week? The average working adult, and student for that matter, enjoys 2 out of 7 days of the week or about 29% of the week. Add in some vacations and personal days and we're looking at about 35%—which leaves 65% of our days spent doing things that we don't enjoy. And that's assuming we spend all of our non-work days on things we enjoy!

To be successful, you must enjoy what you do. The more passionate you are about what you do for a living, the easier success will come. I have said before that I believe perseverance is the most important part of success; well, right after persevereance comes enjoying what you do. There are two basic ways you can start enjoying every day:

1) Change what you do for a living. If you truly dislike your current job and you do not realistically see any chance of improvement in the near future, find a new job. Changing jobs or careers is one of the more stressful moves you can make in their lifetime because it usually requires taking risks and giving up security. However, it can also fill your life with new excitement and enthusiasm that you have been without for so many years. Changing what you do for a living is a serious step and should be well thought out.

2) Change your attitude. Life is perception and perception is about attitude. For every one person who "hates" their job, there are at least a dozen people who would love to have it. I would never suggest giving up on your dreams and adopt a "learn to like" attitude toward your current work, but I am suggesting a conscious change in the way you approach your work that will make it enjoyable while you work toward your dreams.

Here are some things you can do to build a more positive attitude toward your current work.

- **Do your job better.** Consider this "practice" for your success. Success is about being your best and going the extra mile. Start now by doing your job better.
- **Learn more about your job.** One of the reasons people do not enjoy their work is that they do not fully understand it. Learn all you can about what you do and you will discover a new flame that did not exist before.
- **Learn why things are done the way they are.** In the workplace, there are rules and policies, many of which are debated amongst the workers who argue that they "are not fair". Speak to someone who knows why these polices are in place. Once you understand, you will no longer have the resentment.
- **See the big picture.** If your job is in data-entry, realize that you are doing an important part of a much larger job. An organization is like a chain with many links. Each link is vital to the strength of the chain. You are not just

entering data, you are partly responsible for keeping the organization running.

- **Build amenable relationships with co-workers.** If you do not get along with your co-workers, it is easy to dread going to work. Make amends in existing relationships if needed and go the extra mile for your co-workers.
- **Solve or manage your problems.** What don't you like about work? Make a list. Consider each item on your list a problem and solve or manage the problem.
- **See your current job as a necessary rung on your ladder of success.** I strongly believe one can get ultimate enjoyment from any job if they believe they are working toward their success. What skills is your current job helping you achieve? How is your current job helping you achieve success? Even if it is as basic as giving you the money you need to move on, you are working toward your success.

A major key to success is happiness. Without happiness, success is not possible. Don't settle for two days of happiness or enjoyment a week. Change your job or change your attitude and wake up each day with excitement and passion. Adopt the credo, "Thank God it's any day".

ACTION STEP(S):

1) Do you often make disempowering statements such as "Thank God it's Friday"? If you do say this, it is telling others how you feel about your work and it is also telling your subconscious how you feel about work, even if you really enjoy your work. Think about replacing your disempowering, common, small talk one-liners with more empowering ones that will motivate others and help them to think more positively.

Day 80: Inspiration from Abraham Lincoln

Abraham Lincoln (1809-1865) was the sixteenth president of the United States.

Success is having character. "We should be too big to take offense and too noble to give it." • "Character is like a tree and reputation like it's shadow. The shadow is what we think of it; the tree is the real thing."

Success is knowing how to accept criticism and knowing enough not to criticize. "If I care to listen to every criticism, let alone act on them, then this shop may as well be closed for all other businesses. I have learned to do my best, and if the end result is good then I do not care for any criticism, but if the end result is not good, then even the praise of ten angels would not make the difference." • "I am rather inclined to silence, and whether that be wise or not, it is at least more unusual nowadays to find a man who can hold his tongue than to find one who cannot."

Success is consistently doing one's best every day. "I never had a policy; I have just tried to do my very best each and every day."

Success is realizing the true significance of failure. "My great concern is not whether you have failed, but whether you are content with your failure."

Success is understanding the secret to happiness. "Most folks are about as happy as they make up their minds to be."

Success is understanding the power of listening. "When I am getting ready to reason with a man, I spend one-third of my time thinking about myself and what I am going to say and two-thirds about him and what he is going to say."

Success is knowing how to influence others. "When the conduct of men is designed to be influenced, persuasion, kind unassuming persuasion, should ever be adopted. It is an old and true maxim that 'a drop of honey catches more flies than a gallon of gall.' So with men. If you would win a man to your cause, first convince him that you are his sincere friend. Therein is a drop of honey that catches his heart, which, say what he will, is the great highroad to his reason, and which, once gained, you will find but little trouble in convincing him of the justice of your cause, if indeed that cause is really a good one."

Success is knowing the futility of procrastination. "You cannot escape the responsibility of tomorrow by evading it today."

Success is not showing envy toward another's wealth. "Property is the fruit of labor...property is desirable...is a positive good in the world. That some should be rich shows that others may become rich, and hence is just encouragement to industry and enterprise. Let not him who is houseless pull down the house of another; but let him labor diligently and build one for himself, thus by example assuring that his own shall be safe from violence when built."

[Sources: http://www.biography.com, http://www.whitehouse.gov]

"Always bear in mind that your own resolution to succeed is more important than any other one thing."

- Abraham Lincoln

Day 81: The Law of Diminishing Returns

The law of diminishing returns simply states that at some point the same effort returns less favorable results. This law can be adapted to many areas of life. Understanding and recognition of this law play an important part in success.

If you have a gallon of your favorite ice cream and start to eat it, the first bite may bring you to your knees while groaning "ummmmm". The next few bites will be good as well, but may not have the same effect. By the time you are halfway through the gallon, you may be feeling like dropping to your knees, but for a completely different reason. Perhaps this law is the reason for the popularity of the banana split—lots of ice cream, but one scoop of vanilla, one of chocolate and one of strawberry. With each change your stomach may be just as full, but your mind has a new experience and the point of diminishing return shifts. This is the law of diminishing returns in action and it applies to all foods as well.

In business, recognition of this law and its presence is vital. In the business world, this law is often referred to as "spinning your wheels", that is, putting forth much effort with little return. However, it is harder to recognize when your actions produce great results at the onset and then diminish. Very often people become stubborn and proceed with the same action without change. Learn to recognize the point where it is time to move on to something else.

At Archieboy, we build web hosting companies. With our first web host, we reached a point where no matter how much additional effort we put into marketing and promotion of the company, we would see the same general results. This is the point of diminishing return. We then proceeded to create new hosting companies where our efforts would produce much greater returns. This strategy is commonly used in business and referred to at times as *line extension*.

The inventor of the banana split knew how to sell more ice cream and counter the law of diminishing returns by subjecting the customer to change. This is a very powerful technique used by those in marketing. For example, I have much information to get across in this book. Instead of grouping the days by general topics, i.e. motivation, time management, communication, etc., I mix up the topics almost daily. Each time the reader comes to a new topic, the interest is restored and the point of diminishing returns is pushed back. Eventually, however, the point will be reached despite the number of changes.

Recognize this law in your personal life as well. For example, in study you may find that when you read for 30 minutes at a time you retain most of the information and maintain interest, but if you push that 30 minutes to one hour, the second 30 minutes you find yourself drifting and retain almost nothing. At the 30-minute mark, the law of diminishing returns has kicked into effect.

Understanding this law will have a significant effect on your productivity and time management. As we have seen, it can also be applied to other areas of our lives as well. Learn to recognize when you are "spinning your wheels", and change your actions or behaviors to become more productive in all areas of your life.

ACTION STEP(S):

---

1) If you are interested in losing weight, try simply eating smaller portions. According to the law of diminishing returns, you can eat about 50% of the portion and still get about 90% of the enjoyment.

2) Write down all the areas in your life right now where you feel as if you are spinning your wheels. What can you change about what you are doing to see greater results?

Day 82: Getting Better Every Day

How can you NOT remain positive and optimistic knowing that in some way, every day, the quality of your life is getting better and better? This is not a hard task, even for those who consider themselves "over the hill". We are all endowed with the ability to make positive changes in our lives every day and literally become better people if we choose to.

Some people let time get the better of them. As time passes, they lose their health and vitality, and give up on their dreams while slipping into an ongoing state of depression. Others embrace the power of personal growth and personal achievement and begin to replace youth with wisdom, innocence with understanding, and lack of purpose with self-actualization. Although it may not always seem like it, time **is** on our side.

Here are some suggestions on how you can make small, daily changes in your life and become a better person tomorrow than you are today, and continue this pattern for the rest of your life.

Health and Fitness

- Begin an exercise/fitness program. Know that with each workout you are strengthening your muscles, including the most important muscle—your heart.
- Over time, start giving up unhealthy foods in your diet and replacing them with more healthy alternatives.
- Cut down and eventually give up the consumption of drugs used to change your physical state. Your body will heal itself over time but only if you give it a chance to.
- Do some research into wellness programs. Keep an open mind and explore the possible heath benefits of chiropractic care, yoga, massage therapy, meditation, etc. In most cases, you have very little to lose and much to gain.

Mind and Spirit

- Learn something new every day. There are no known limits to the amount of information the human mind can store. Keep your mind sharp by consistently challenging it.
- Continually pursue your goals and dreams. Knowing you are closer to your goals and dreams today than you were yesterday is incredibly motivating and empowering.
- Work on your personal growth. You are on the right track with this one by taking this course! If our 15 minutes or so a day is not enough for you, buy some books or audio programs on personal achievement.

Our lives can get better every day in some way. It can be as simple as learning a new word every day, or as involved as following all of the suggestions above. You are in control of the quality of life you live today and the quality of life you live in the future. Just as you would plan for your financial future, plan for your physical and spiritual future as well.

If you are the type that gets motivation from self-talk and mantras, then when you wake up, why not say to yourself, "My life is better today than it was yesterday" or if you think about it, "Today is the best day of my life". What a way to start the day!

ACTION STEP(S):

1) List at least 10 specific ways in which you can make small, daily positive changes in your life. Example, "replace my morning coffee with fresh juice".

2) From your list just created, choose at least three changes and commit to them. Once you start feeling the great benefits of self-improvement, revisit this list and commit to some more.

"Every day, in every way, I am getting better and better."

- Emile Coue

Days 83 and 84 are for "R&R"—review and reflection. Spend these days reviewing the last five articles and reflecting on the information and how it relates to your life. Now is also a good time to make sure all the action steps for the previous days have been completed.

Day 85: Read or Listen to Motivational/Educational Material

In the past 50 years or so, incredible progress has been made in the fields of personal achievement and personal development. People such as Dale Carnegie, Napoleon Hill, and Earl Nightingale, just to name a few, have devoted their entire lives to the study of success. Their lives' work has been summarized in the books and audio programs they have released. Many of these books and programs sit like hidden gems on shelves of bookstores and in warehouses, waiting for readers to discover the life-changing information contained within.

If these books and programs are really that powerful, why don't more people read and listen to them? Here are the most common reasons.

- **They do not believe the information will help them.** This is the most challenging obstacle for success authors to overcome. It takes belief, or faith, for an individual to start reading a book, start listening to an audio program, or begin a program such as this one. Ironically, many of these programs contain information that will help build the faith needed; however, those without at least a little faith, or a willingness to keep an open mind, will never take that step.
- **Self-help material has gotten a bad "rap".** In some cases, this is well deserved. There some are authors, especially on the subject of making money, that are, well... let's just say less than qualified to be giving advice. If you are buying a book on how to make a million dollars, is the author a millionaire? Did he become a millionaire by selling his "how to be a millionaire" books? Learn about the author(s) before you buy a book or audio program. Read reviews and see what others have said.
- **They did not feel they got anything out of previous programs they have tried.** At the very least, their minds were subjected to hours of positive mental conditioning. It

is actually very difficult to pick up a book or listen to an audio program and not get at least one good idea or even life-changing concept. Look for that one idea and most of the time you will find many.

Now here are just some of the benefits of reading and listening to positive, motivational, and educational material.

- **Never feel as if you are wasting time again.** How much time do you spend a week driving in your car, riding public transportation, working out, or doing any other activity in which you are, or could be, listening to content of your choice? How much time do you spend waiting; in lines, for appointments, or for others? This could be turned into some of your most valuable time spent.
- **It's motivational.** We are already aware of the power of motivation. Read or listen to the words of other optimists that inspire you and give you mental power to do just about anything you set your mind to.
- **It's educational.** Education should not stop after high school or college. To grow as an individual we should spend our lives feeding our brains with useful information. Just like many careers that require ongoing education via seminars and conferences, you should require ongoing education for your own personal achievement. Your success in life depends on it.
- **We all need proper mental conditioning.** From the time we were brought into this earth until the present day, our minds have been programmed with negativity and limiting beliefs. Some of this comes from our upbringing, friends, co-workers, the news we read and the commercials we watch. By focusing on positive material, we can literally recondition our minds and replace the negative, limiting beliefs we have about success with positive, empowering ones.

Here is my five-step process for getting the most out of non-fictional, self-help material.

1. **Read for Understanding.** Personal development programs are crammed with information and ideas that work best when they are retained in your conscious memory. Read or listen to the book or tape more than once. Each time you do, your retention rate of the information increases. Do not take in too much information at once. The average mind starts to drift and wander somewhere between 20 and 30 minutes. When this happens, take a break.

2. **Evaluate.** You certainly do not have to believe everything you read or hear. Evaluate what the author has to say with an open mind. Does it make sense to you? If you adopted the belief, would it improve your life? If so, why not give it a try? Don't be turned off by the author even if you do not agree with most of what is said. Take what you can from the program and leave the rest.

3. **Apply.** It is said that knowledge without application is not power; it is only potential power. Use and apply what you learn to your everyday life. Only then will the information be of true value to you.

4. **Review.** Go back to your books, tapes, notes, and programs often and think about the times you have applied the information. When you see the benefits, it will create a passion for learning greater than you have ever had before.

5. **Share.** Make these books, tapes, and programs easily available to those you care about. Most people will not spend just a few dollars buying their own book or tape, but they may just read or listen to it if it is there.

To me, listening to motivational material is empowering and energizing yet comforting and relaxing at the same time. Take advantage of the wealth of information on personal achievement that is available today and you, too, will soon be hooked on success.

ACTION STEP(S):

---

1) Buy (or borrow) at least one motivational self-help book or audio program within the next seven days and commit to completing the book or program within 30 days.

"Education's purpose is to replace an empty mind with an open one."

- Malcolm Forbes (1919–1990)

Day 86: Cure for Depression?

Depression is defined as "a psychiatric disorder characterized by an inability to concentrate, insomnia, loss of appetite, anhedonia, feelings of extreme sadness, guilt, helplessness and hopelessness, and thoughts of death".

I am neither a medical doctor nor a psychiatrist, so I cannot speak intelligently on the workings of chemical activity in the brain and the effects of drugs to counter these effects. I can, however, tell you my belief. I believe that just as we can cause and cure our own stress, anxiety, and headaches, our thoughts can cause and cure the "chemical imbalances" in our brains that we know as depression.

If depression is brought on by our thoughts, and we can control our thoughts, then isn't it true that we can control depression with our own thoughts? If you have a positive mental attitude, it is extremely difficult to get depressed. People with positive attitudes do not experience helplessness and hopelessness. They understand that they are in control of their own destiny as well as their thoughts and feelings. It would be fair to say, however, that this level of positive mental attitude does not come easily, and takes time to build. Thinking positively is a habit just like depression can be a habit. However, depression is a habit most people would like to do without, so it makes the habit easier to "kick".

Besides building and applying a good positive mental attitude to your daily life, here are some "miracle" cures for depression that can instantly take you out of a depressed state into one of motivation, gratitude, and energy.

- **Have goals and focus on them; do something each day that brings you closer to their attainment.** Be sure your goals, and life purpose, are empowering enough to both excite you and motivate you.

- **Ask yourself, "What am I thankful for? What is good in my life?"** Write these things down, close your eyes and experience the feelings these things bring to you.
- **Help someone else.** This one reminds me again of the movie *It's a Wonderful Life*, when the angel saved George by allowing George to save him.
- **Change your physiology.** Stand or sit up straight, take deep breaths, keep your chin up, chest out and smile.
- **Keep active.** Boredom follows lack of activity and depression often follows prolonged boredom. Do something productive—build, create, write, read, learn, play—anything that will keep your mind and/or body active.
- **Exercise.** I cannot stress enough the seemingly limitless benefits of regular exercise. Preventing and curing depression is just one of them.

We can actually sum up all of these "cures" into one: **change what you focus on**. When you feel like you may be depressed, or even just a little down, you may be that way because you are focusing on the negative in your life, not because you are suffering from the disease known as clinical depression. Try focusing on all the good things in your life, what has been, what is, and more important, **what can be**. If you cannot think of any good things in your life, then think harder. We can all at least be thankful for being alive and having the gift of free will. As an American or a citizen of another free country with opportunity, we have even more positive things to focus on. Focus on the positive and build your positive mental attitude, and depression may become an emotion you will no longer have to experience.

ACTION STEP(S):

---

1) Bookmark this article and refer to it next time you are feeling depressed or even just a little down.

Day 87: Inspiration from Sam Walton

Sam Walton (1918-1992) founded the Wal-Mart discount retail store chain in 1962 and revolutionized the retail industry. Here we have adapted Sam Walton's 10 Rules For Success—from Sam Walton: Made in America, My Story, co-authored by J. Huey, Doubleday.

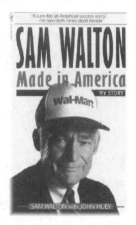

Success is committing yourself to your business. Believe in it more than anything else. If you love your work, you'll be out there every day trying to do the best you can, and pretty soon everybody around will catch the passion from you—like a fever.

Success is sharing your profits with all your associates, and treating them as partners. In turn, they will treat you as a partner, and together you will all perform beyond your wildest expectations.

Success is motivating your partners. Money and ownership aren't enough. Set high goals, encourage competition and then keep score. Make bets with outrageous payoffs.

Success is communicating everything you possibly can to your partners. The more they know, the more they'll understand. The more they understand, the more they'll care. Once they care, there's no stopping them. The gain you get from empowering your associates more than offsets the risk of informing your competitors.

Success is appreciating everything your associates do for the business. Nothing else can quite substitute for a few well-chosen, well-timed, sincere words of praise. They're absolutely free and worth a fortune.

Success is celebrating your success and finding humor in your failures. Don't take yourself so seriously. Loosen up and everyone around you will loosen up. Have fun and always show enthusiasm. When all else fails put on a costume and sing a silly song.

Success is listening to everyone in your company, and figuring out ways to get them talking. The folks on the front line—the ones who actually talk to customers—are the only ones who really know what's going on out there. You'd better find out what they know.

Success is exceeding your customer's expectations. If you do they'll come back over and over. Give them what they want—and a little more. Let them know you appreciate them. Make good on all your mistakes, and don't make excuses—apologize. Stand behind everything you do. 'Satisfaction guaranteed' will make all the difference.

Success is controlling your expenses better than your competition. This is where you can always find the competitive advantage. You can make a lot of mistakes and still recover if you run an efficient operation. Or you can be brilliant and still go out of business if you're too inefficient.

Success is swimming upstream. Go the other way. Ignore the conventional wisdom. If everybody is doing it one way, there's a good chance you can find your niche by going in exactly the opposite direction.

"There is only one boss, the customer. And he can fire everybody in the company, from the chairman on down, simply by spending his money somewhere else."

- Sam Walton (1918-1992)

Day 88: Carrot or the Stick?

There is an old analogy for positive vs. negative reinforcement that refers to how people "motivate" donkeys. A carrot is used to positively reinforce the donkey's behavior, whereas a quick and hard whack with a stick is used as a negative form of motivation. There have been numerous studies done with other animals, as well as humans, on the effectiveness of the two kinds of reinforcement. Conclusion: positive reinforcement produces greater and longer lasting results—most of the time.

Have you ever had someone, like a good friend or a family member, flat out tell you, "Wow... you got fat!"? I did, and I can tell you that despite the lack of tact and political incorrectness of this statement, it did cause me to take action to change my behaviors that caused me to gain so much weight in the first place. Success stories are filled with similar situations where parents told their kids they are "worthless" or that they "will never amount to anything". This negative reinforcement, which borders on mental abuse, caused these now successful individuals to take action to prove their parents wrong.

If you have ever had the good fortune to be a parent, you most likely had a time when you caught your 6-month-old putting small objects in his or her mouth. Well, you could praise them every time they don't have a small object in their mouth, but that is just not practical. Times like these you must use the stick (figuratively, I hope!)

We have also said that the need to avoid pain is often a greater motivator then the desire to gain pleasure. Charles Dickens understood this concept well when he used the ghost of Christmas future in motivating Scrooge to change his behavior. You don't hear stories of the CIA using chocolate cake and ice cream to get information out of prisoners.

I know... just when you thought positive reinforcement was the key to human behavior you read this and now are confused once more. So when do we use that carrot and when do we use the stick? Here are a few of my general rules that I have found apply to most situations.

1. When you want the new behavior to last, use the carrot. In the case of a military interrogation, the interrogators do not care if the one withholding the information is full of resentment after giving the information. However, the opposite may be true in the case of regular informants of police or investigators, where building a relationship and the need for both parties to benefit is important.

2. If you are motivating yourself, use the reinforcement that will have the greatest effect on you. Only you know what really motivates you. If the thought of dying a painful death as a result of lung cancer is a greater motivator than being free from a socially unacceptable habit, then quit smoking for the former reason.

3. If motivating others to do what they are already being paid to do, or are otherwise obligated to do, use a balance of negative and positive reinforcement. For example, in the case of motivating employees to do their assignments on time, you may penalize late assignments by bringing it to the employee's attention in the form of a written warning, but at the same time, praise on-time assignments by perhaps offering a small reward or recognition for a certain number of assignments all done on time.

4. For most all other situations, use only positive reinforcement.

As for telling people they are fat or worthless, don't do it. The only real motivators in these cases are not the people who make the obnoxious comments, but the people who see the comment as a wake up call and motivate themselves to make changes. In no case should one use such negative statements, because most of the time, these comments will sink in the subconscious mind of those to whom these comments are directed, and become a belief. Use tact and get your message across in a positive and empowering way.

At times you will find the stick will bring about better results. However, use the carrot whenever possible for creating lasting changes, especially when it comes to changing the behavior of others.

ACTION STEP(S):

---

1) Take some time to think about how many times you use negative reinforcement.   Should you be using positive reinforcement in these situations?

"Motivation is the art of getting people to do what you want them to do because they want to do it."

- Dwight D. Eisenhower

Day 89: Introduction to Goals

I can begin this article writing about getting in a car without having a destination, shooting a bow and arrow but not having a target, or any of the other hundreds of goal setting analogies, but I am not going to. If you passed the fourth grade, you have probably heard most of these analogies anyway so I won't insult your intelligence. I will get right to the point: proper goal setting is an important part of success. Over the next three lessons you will read about why we need goals, how to set goals, and most important, how to achieve goals. By the end of this three-part article, you will have taken a major step toward your success.

What is a goal? By definition a goal is "the purpose toward which an endeavor is directed". In this sense, everybody has goals. Unfortunately for most people, their goals are as simple as making it through the day or making it home for dinner before six o'clock. In terms of success, I like to define a goal as "an outcome that one strives to achieve by proper planning". There are two main differences between my definition and the dictionary's definition—the words "strive" and "proper planning". For a purpose to be goal, you must exert much effort or energy toward its achievement. In addition, a goal must be consciously planned beforehand in such a way that makes its achievement more possible in your mind, and therefore more probable.

To illustrate the importance of having goals, let's examine why most people do not have goals.

1) Unsure of need for goals. At the very, very least, goals allow you to put conscious effort into taking regular "baby steps" to achieve an outcome. For example, one really does not need to set a goal to go to the store and pick up some bread. This is something than can be easily and immediately done at a subconscious level. However, setting a goal for learning how to make bread would be appropriate because one can't simply just start making bread. There are several steps that must be taken before one can get to the point of actually making the bread like 1) buying a book on bread making, 2) reading it, 3) buying ingredients, etc. It is goal setting that allows one to take these small steps that will eventually lead to the achievement of the goal.

- Creating goals provides your life with purpose and direction
- Having goals allows to you focus on the future when the present seems bleak
- Reviewing your goals can fill you with excitement and motivation

2) Unsure of wants and lack of decision. Too many people wander through life waiting for opportunity to find them. They know they want things like a good job, a nice car, a nice home, love and friendship, but they have never really taken the time to be specific about what they want. They despise being broke, yet they fear success; they love the single life, yet want the security of marriage; they want to do something meaningful, yet cannot seem to get the motivation to do it. This is where the power of focus and decision comes in. If you have trouble deciding on the things you want, remember that most decisions you make today can be changed tomorrow if needed. Flexibility is an extremely important part of goal setting. Without decision, you cannot move forward.

3) Lack of belief in the power of goals. This reason is one of the easiest for me to understand. There are so many goal setting books, tapes, workshops, seminars, and gurus out there who preach goal setting as "the key to success" or the magic bullet to instant financial, spiritual, and emotional success. While I do believe having goals is an important part of success, it won't do much good without applying the many other principles of success described within this course. With authors exaggerating the benefits of goals, it is easy to see how so many become discouraged and lose faith in the power of goals.

A great example of this exaggeration is a story told by many goal setting gurus about a 1953 study done at Yale, where the 3% of the students that had goals did better 20 years later than the other 97%

combined. This story is untrue as reported by several independent investigators including the editorial staff at *FastCompany*. The fact is, goal setting is a powerful step toward the achievement of success; however, like anything else, it is the continual persistence and effort that makes goal setting as powerful as it is.

4) Belief that goals are too rigid. Assuming that you never change your goals this is true, but an important part of goal setting is being flexible and allowing new opportunity to change your goals. Columbus did have a goal... to sail to India. However, a new opportunity arose when he found America. Without his initial goal, he may never have made the discovery he did.

5) Unsure how to set goals. This will be covered in detail in the next article "How To Set Goals".

6) The fear of both failure and success in achieving goals. If this applies to you, review the articles on "The Fear of Failure" and "The Fear of Success". Along the same lines, a common objection to goal setting is, "Focusing on goals you don't have leads to disappointment." The excitement and anticipation of the achievement of a goal is a much more positive thought than focusing on the fact that you have not yet achieved it. True disappointment comes from not having any goals at all.

7) Poor self-image. Believe it or not, many people just do not believe they are worth the effort. If this applies to you, it is best to refer to the article on "Self-Esteem".

A goal is an outcome one strives to achieve by proper planning. It is something one puts conscious effort into taking regular steps to achieve. This systematic process, or formula, makes the impractical practical, the unreachable reachable, and the improbable probable. With clearly defined goals, your chances for success increase significantly.

ACTION STEP(S):

---

1) What has prevented you from setting goals? Write down the reasons why you currently do not have a clear set of written goals. Then, next to each reason, write down why that is not a good reason for not having goals.

"Many are stubborn in pursuit of the path they have chosen, few in pursuit of the goal."

- Friedrich Nietzsche

Days 90 and 91 are for "R&R"—review and reflection. Spend these days reviewing the last five articles and reflecting on the information and how it relates to your life. Now is also a good time to make sure all the action steps for the previous days have been completed.

Day 92: How To Set Goals

There are many goal setting strategies available and, just as expected, some strategies work well for some people, and other strategies work better for other people. I cannot stress enough the importance of using a goal setting strategy that works best for you. This usually requires adapting a general strategy and removing the steps you see little value in and/or adding steps of your own.

I will list all of the goal setting steps that are used to make up the strategy I have found works best. You can either adopt mine as is, or create your own strategy by using some or all of the steps listed below. Have fun with this!

Brainstorm. Before you choose a single goal to set and focus on, use a blank sheet of paper to write down as quickly as possible all the things you want in the following categories: Artistic, Career, Educational, Ethical, Family, Financial, Mental, Physical, Pleasure, Social, Spiritual, and any other. There is no need to include detail here. Once you have created this list, prioritize each of the items on your list. This will allow you to begin immediately focusing on the potential goals that are most important to you.

Goal Setting Steps

1. **Identify your goal.** Pick the goal you will be setting and write the goal in positive terms as if you have already reached the goal. For example, "I weigh a lean, mean 170 pounds". Make sure your goal is quantifiable, that is, do not simply say "I want to be lean". Write your goal with as much detail as possible at this time while remaining flexible. For example, on your way to purchase a red Ferrari, if you find that you like the silver Ferrari much better, then buy that one.
2. **Put your goal through the test by asking questions.** Is this really your goal or someone else's goal? Is this goal bold enough? Do you honestly believe you can

achieve this goal? If not, why? List the limiting beliefs you have and change your beliefs. Does this goal conflict with any of your other goals? How would you feel 5, 10, 20 and 50 years from now if you never achieved this goal? Would it really matter? Having asked and answered all of these questions about your goal, do you still want this goal?

3. **Set a "maturity date" for your goal's achievement.** It is important to have both long and short-term goals. Set the exact day that this goal will be achieved.

4. **Identify the obstacles you must overcome in order to achieve your goal.** Who or what will be an obstacle for you in the process of pursuing this goal? How can you overcome these obstacles?

5. **Identify the people, groups and organizations you need to work with in order to achieve your goal.** Must you rely on others to meet this goal? Or perhaps with help from others this goal can more easily be met?

6. **Identify the skills and knowledge needed to help you achieve your goal.** What can you learn that will help you achieve this goal?

7. **Ask yourself if you are willing to pay the price in order to enjoy the benefits.** A goal is a goal because of the effort it takes to achieve. Is that effort worth it to you? Are you willing to overcome the obstacles, work with the people, and acquire the skills needed to see this goal through? Are you 100% committed to this goal?

8. **List benefits of achieving and reasons why you are committed to your goal, and visualize yourself having already achieved the goal.** What pain will you experience in your life if you do not achieve this goal? Here you create enough leverage to convince yourself that you must absolutely reach your goal. It is this step where you turn the want into desire.

Repeat the steps above for each of your goals. Once you do this, you will have created a clear strategy to the achievement of your goals. Tomorrow, we will conclude this three-day section on goals with the most important aspect of goals, which is the achievement of them.

ACTION STEP(S):

1) Follow the steps above and put your goals on paper. At the very least, identify and complete the process for three goals.

2) Customize the strategy above if needed. Write down your own strategy on the inside cover of your success journal or print out, cut, and paste the one used in this article. You should refer to this often.

"You must take action now that will move you toward your goals. Develop a sense of urgency in your life."

- H. Jackson Brown, Jr.

Day 93: Achieving Your Goals

By now, you should be absolutely convinced of the importance of having goals and its direct relationship to success. You should have also defined and set at least three goals using some or all of the steps in the goal setting strategy in the previous article. Now it is time to create your plan of action and see your goals through.

Create your plan of action. A plan of action in this sense is essentially a "to do" list. However, the plan of action includes a list of monthly, weekly and most important, **daily actions** that will bring you closer to your goal. The concept of taking small, daily actions toward the achievement of your goals is, to me, the most important factor in achieving goals. Do your best to find some action that you can do on a daily basis that will bring you closer to your goal. Add, "review goal" or "reevaluate actions based on progress" to your daily, weekly, or monthly action here.

The second part of the plan of action, or to do list, is the list of non-recurring actions. Here you list the action, the date it needs to be done on or by, and the approximate time it will take. You can even implement your plan of action in your existing to do list if you already have one.

Here is an example of our plan of action for weighing a lean, mean 170 pounds:

DAILY: cardio exercise for one hour, eat a light lunch
WEEKLY: weigh myself and take measurements
MONTHLY: reevaluate actions based on progress

Action: lift weights at gym with trainer
Date: Sept 1,3,5,8,10,12,15,17,19,22,24,26
Time: about 1 hour per session

Follow your action plan like you would follow a written prescription from your doctor (assuming you listen to your doctor). An action plan is worthless unless you honestly plan to follow it.

Without question, you will meet adversity. For some reason, at some time, you will find yourself not as committed to reaching your goals as you were when you first wrote them down. Do not despair, for this is all part of the process. Here are some suggestions to help you stay committed to your goals and follow them through.

- **Change what isn't working.** Be flexible. If you are not making progress on your goal, or you are not satisfied with the level of progress you are making, change the action steps you are taking to reach your goal. Don't confuse activity with accomplishment. Be sure to reflect on the progress you have made, not on the time or effort you have put into the goal.
- **Know when to share your goals with others.** Here is a simple rule for when to share your goals with others: share your goal only with those who you feel will be supportive of your goals; otherwise, keep your goals to yourself.
- **Don't procrastinate.** Your goals have maturity dates and dates associated with action steps for a reason. Practice self-discipline. If you don't have any self-discipline, make getting some your #1 goal.
- **Keep motivated.** If you are taking this course and have made it this far, this should not be an issue for you. Motivation comes from within so whip some up when you need it.
- **Believe in yourself.** Millions of people reach their goals every day. Why can't you be one of them?
- **Reward yourself.** Whenever you reach a goal, celebrate. Treat yourself to something special, give yourself a pat on the back, post it on our forum and let other members know about it, eat a Scooby snack—whatever it takes. Show appreciation for yourself and your commitment.

Goal setting is not easy and achieving your goals is even more challenging. It has been said that you must pay the price for achieving your goals, but the truth is, you enjoy the benefits. You pay the price for not setting goals at all. Set goals in your personal and professional life that will provide your life with purpose and direction. The discipline you learn and character you build from setting and achieving goals is more valuable than the achievement of the goal itself, so enjoy the process and have fun!

ACTION STEP(S):

1) Create your plan of action for each of the goals you set yesterday.

2) Right now, take at least one action to the attainment of these three (or more) goals.

"What you get by achieving your goals is as important as what you become by achieving your goals."

- Henry David Thoreau

Day 94: Inspiration from Eleanor Roosevelt

Eleanor Roosevelt (1884–1962) was a humanitarian, United Nations diplomat, and First Lady; the wife of President Franklin D. Roosevelt.

Success is knowing how to deal with criticism. "No one can make you feel inferior without your consent." • "Do what you feel in your heart to be right—for you'll be criticized anyway. You'll be damned if you do, and damned if you don't." • "Long ago, I made up my mind that when things were said involving only me, I would pay no attention to them, except when valid criticism was carried by which I could profit."

Success is understanding the basis of self-esteem. "Friendship with oneself is all-important, because without it one cannot be friends with anyone else in the world."

Success is learning. "You gain strength, courage and confidence by every experience in which you really stop to look fear in the face. You are able to say to yourself, 'I have lived through this horror. I can take the next thing that comes along.' You must do the thing you think you cannot do."

Success is having character. "People grow through experience if they meet life honestly and courageously. This is how character is built." • "Only a man's character is the real criterion of worth."

Success is knowing how to bring balance to one's life. "I wish for those I love this New Year an opportunity to earn sufficient, to have that which they need for their own and to give that which they desire to others, to bring into the lives of those about them some measure of joy, to know the satisfaction of work well done, of recreation earned and therefore savored, to end the year a little wiser, a little kinder and therefore a little happier."

Success is embracing inevitable change. "My life can be so arranged that I can live on whatever I have. If I cannot live as I have lived in the past, I shall live differently, and living differently does not mean living with less attention to the things that make life gracious and pleasant or with less enjoyment of things of the mind."

Success is knowing what success means to you. "We have all made such a fetish of financial success and forgotten frequently that success of any kind, when it does not include success in one's personal relationships, is bound in the end to leave both the man and the woman with very little real satisfaction."

Success is knowing what happiness means to you. "I would not be happy unless I had some regular work to do every day and I imagine that I will always feel that way no matter how old I am..." • "Happiness may exist under all conditions, given the right kind of people and sufficient economic security for adequate food and shelter."

Success is believing in the Internet—even back in 1943. "One of the best ways of enslaving a people is to keep them from education... The second way of enslaving a people is to suppress the sources of information, not only by burning books but by controlling all the other ways in which ideas are transmitted."

[Sources: http://www.biography.com, http://www.whitehouse.gov, http://www.wic.org]

"Absence makes the heart grow fonder."

- Eleanor Roosevelt

Day 95: Advertising, Marketing, and Sales

Every day, we as the public are "sold". The average American is bombarded with hundreds of advertisements each day telling us what we need to be happy and what we need to avoid pain. Like it or not, this shapes our beliefs and values. It is very important in business and in our personal lives to understand basic marketing, know when you are being "sold", and distinguish fact from fiction. In addition to understanding them, actually applying advertising and marketing techniques in your professional and personal life is a key element of success.

Before we go any further, let us define a few terms. These terms are often confused, interchanged, and misunderstood.

Sales. As a verb, sales refers to the act of selling a product or service, usually where one or more people are involved. Sales can include direct one-on-one selling or selling to more than one person, like in the case of a presentation.

Advertising. The activity of attracting public attention to a product, service, or business, as by paid announcements in the print, broadcast, or electronic media.

Marketing. The process or technique of promoting, selling, and distributing a product or service.

To illustrate these three terms, we will use the example of XYZ Corporation. The marketing department has taken time to put together a *marketing* campaign in which they have carefully planned the methods and techniques they will use to sell their product. This campaign includes several forms of *advertising*, including print and banner advertising, as well as direct selling via their in-house *sales* force, which will sell the product mostly by telephone.

Advertising, marketing, and sales are a very important part of our economy and, I believe, one of the main reasons we live in such an abundant society. In fact, if it weren't for marketing, you would never have found this site. It is these activities that allow both organizations and individuals to get their message across to hundreds and even billions of people while giving the people more choices.

Unfortunately, not all salespeople, marketing campaigns, and advertisements are looking out for your best interests. In fact, most advertisers never really understand this basic concept: when you truly help others, you help yourself. Every day we are conditioned, misled, deceived, and even at times outright lied to by advertisers. They sacrifice long-term success for short-term gain, and effectively create lose/lose situations. We as "the public" must be aware of the techniques used by advertisers so we can avoid being taken advantage of and make our decisions based on facts. As business people, we must avoid misleading others in our marketing and know how to effectively communicate our message.

Throughout this course we will be discussing different advertising, marketing and sales techniques. Remember, even if you are not in business, understanding these techniques will play an important part in your success. At the very least, it will improve your decision making process when it comes to purchasing products or services, and perhaps, save you thousands or even millions of dollars in the long run.

ACTION STEP(S):

---

1) Commit to consciously questioning ads you come across. Learn to spot the advertiser's attempt to condition your brain to respond positively to their product. If you drink beer will you automatically find yourself surrounded by beautiful people? If you smoke Virginia Slims will you become a successful, independent businesswoman?

Day 96: Is It Right To Make So Much Money?

There are millions of people in this world who go without food every day. In the United States, one of the most abundant countries in the world, entire families live in rooms no bigger than the average walk-in closet, children wear rags as clothing, people living on the streets call cardboard boxes "home". Closer to home, your friends and neighbors work just as hard as you do and are barely getting by. They drive cars that are held together by bondo and duct tape. They have mortgages and bills that prevent them from spending the money they do make on leisure or material possessions that will bring them enjoyment. With so many people in this world less fortunate than you, is it right for you to make so much money?

Before we answer this question, let's look at what money actually is. It is a symbol of wealth. Money is given to you in exchange for something else of equal value, or it is a measure of the value of the services you provide. There are two caveats here. One, your value is not always realized the moment you provide the service. Vincent Van Gogh spent his life with little money, although he created beautiful works of art worth fortunes today, which millions of people in future generations would continue to enjoy. Two, some value is "paid back" with other forms of compensation like fame, appreciation and admiration. Mother Teresa was certainly not rich, yet spent her life doing something of tremendous value and was admired and recognized by millions. Keep in mind that these caveats are the rare exceptions, and for the most part, money is a measure of the value of the services one provides. Avoiding money either on a conscious or subconscious level will ultimately lead you to failure to become all you are capable of becoming.

Is it right to have more knowledge than others? Is it right to be more motivated and enthusiastic than others? Is it right to have more persistence than others? Is it right to have more faith than others? Is it right to be more loving, caring, and sharing than others? If you answered, "Of course it is!" to these questions, then understand that money is simply a by-product or result of these feelings and beliefs.

Having more money does not mean that someone else, somewhere, has to have less. This is why it is called "creating wealth" and not "taking wealth". In a capitalist society, it is true that competing businesses do have an effect on the wealth of other competitors, which is generally referred to as *market share*. However, even businesses have the right and opportunity to expand to new markets where they can create products or services that will benefit more people. Most certainly, you having more money does not have anything to do with your neighbor or friend, the guy living in a box on the street, or the starving children in other countries.

One of the main reasons people never achieve financial success is because they associate guilt and feelings of resentment with having money. While none of us can control the negative feelings of resentment in others, we can realize that there are no reasons to feel guilty about our own financial success. It is our birthright to be the best we can be, and we all have an opportunity to make a difference in the world. Pursue financial success just like you would any other type of success in your life. It not only is right to strive for financial success, but it is OUR right. Go for it!

ACTION STEP(S):

---

1) Are you still being held back from financial success by guilt? If so, write down your beliefs that are holding you back. Do your best to refute these beliefs. If you can't, dog ear the page in your success journal and revisit this exercise when the answer comes to you.

"All I ever wanted was an honest week's pay for an honest day's work."

- **Master Sergeant Ernie Bilko (played by Steve Martin)**

Days 97 and 98 are for "R&R"—review and reflection. Spend these days reviewing the last five articles and reflecting on the information and how it relates to your life. Now is also a good time to make sure all the action steps for the previous days have been completed.

Day 99: The Power of Belief

Many think that the benefits and the seemingly miraculous results of belief are based on speculative or abstract reasoning, or the *metaphysical*. However, this is not the case. The power of belief is proven almost daily in the medical and scientific community and is known as the placebo effect. When researchers test the effects of new drugs on humans, they give the drug to some of the volunteers and they give a *placebo*, or an inactive substance or preparation, to the rest of the volunteers. In almost all cases, some of the volunteers that were given the placebo report the same effects as those who were given the actual drug.

Irving Kirsch, a psychologist at the University of Connecticut, believes that the effectiveness of Prozac and similar drugs may be attributed almost entirely to the placebo effect. He and Guy Sapirstein analyzed 19 clinical trials of antidepressants and concluded that the expectation of improvement, not adjustments in brain chemistry, accounted for 75 percent of the drugs' effectiveness (Kirsch 1998). "The critical factor," says Kirsch, "is our *beliefs* about what's going to happen to us. You don't have to rely on drugs to see profound transformation."*

Dr. Deepak Chopra, best-selling author and one of the leaders in the field of mind, body and spirit healing, is a big advocate of the power of belief and its seemingly miraculous effects on the body. He cites several studies of patients with multiple personality disorder who display different physical traits with each personality, like visible allergic reactions on the skin, high blood pressure, and even different color eyes for each personality. He also discusses cases where several of his patients have used the power of belief to get rid of cancer in their bodies.

Success is having belief and not going though life as a cynical skeptic. Remember, thought and imagination are about the only things in this world that are limitless. The body and human spirit often are limited by what one believes is possible. Prior to Roger

Bannister breaking the 4-minute barrier to running one mile in 1954, no one else was able to achieve this goal and many thought it was not humanly possible. Shortly after Bannister's new record, many other runners broke the self-imposed mental barrier and broke the 4-minute mile as well.

There is a metaphysical part to belief. This theory states that when you truly believe in something, the forces of the universe work toward making that belief a *manifestation*, or giving physical form to the belief. A great example of this is money. Before you can acquire a significant amount, you must believe that you can. This belief over time, with persistence and practical application, will manifest itself into money.

Believe you will succeed and you will. Believe in your own abilities and have faith in yourself. As Napoleon Hill, one of the early 20th century experts in success wrote, "Whatever the human mind can conceive and believe, it can achieve."

* *Source: Kirsch, Irving , Ph.D. and Guy Sapirstein, Ph.D. "Listening to Prozac but Hearing Placebo: A Meta-Analysis of Antidepressant Medication" Prevention & Treatment, Volume 1, June 1998.*

ACTION STEP(S):

1) Do what it takes to convince yourself, without doubt, that you can succeed.

"Whatever the human mind can conceive and believe, it can achieve."

- Napoleon Hill

Day 100: The Money Machine

There are many "well to do" individuals in this country who have substantial salaries by most standards. This group of individuals usually includes doctors, lawyers, college professors, executives and others in high-paid careers. Statistically however, despite their level of income, most in this group still have financial difficulties. Once they stop working, their income stream ceases, or at least is drastically reduced. They spend their lives stressed about money and working 60-hour weeks because they feel they "have to" not because they enjoy it. This group of individuals spends their lives working for money.

If the rich do have a "secret", it is this: **don't work for money, let money work for you**. This essentially means your money should be making you more money and your income should not be dependent on your labor. This is actually not a secret, but a concept preached by investment firms, banks, and other financial institutions. They use this concept to sell people on IRAs, CDs, stocks, bonds, and other traditional investment vehicles. There is, however, a flaw with this traditional approach in making people rich: for most people, it doesn't work. In order to become wealthy using traditional investment vehicles, you need either a) a lot of money to invest, b) the willingness and the discipline to wait a long time to see your investment significantly grow, or c) good fortune, as in the case of a stock that significantly appreciates in value. Even then, you probably would not consider yourself "rich", just better off. This is a difficult concept for most people to accept because they were conditioned all their lives by parents, teachers, commercials, bankers, accountants, and financial advisors that this is where money should be invested. Traditional investment vehicles do have their place, but for the rich, they are used more as "temporary storage facilities" rather than life-long "homes".

Imagine creating and building a machine that turned coal in to diamonds. You plug it in, feed it with coal, and just sit back and let the diamonds come out. You can use the cash you get from selling the diamonds to build more of these machines and produce even more diamonds. While there is no known machine that can turn coal into diamonds, the world is full of similar "money machines" referred to as businesses.

All business owners do not take advantage of this concept and those who do are not all rich. Self-employed consultants or other laborers, skilled or non-skilled, physical or mental, are still limited by their own time. By owning a business where you market products or **other people's** services, you are establishing the foundation for wealth. This is the key to having money work for you.

Another method of having money work for you is creation. For example, when you write a book, you may spend 1000 hours creating the book. Once the book is published, you don't need to exert any more labor. You are paid royalties on each book sold and you have created a money machine. The same holds true for movie actors, inventors, songwriters, and other creators.

If have chosen a career, do it because you love doing it, not because of the money. If you are torn between a passion for a low-paying career and the desire for wealth, choose both! There are many people who have made fortunes creating businesses, marketing products or services, or writing songs or books, all while working a full-time job. Be creative and create your money machine today.

ACTION STEP(S):

---

1) What can you do that can become a potential money machine for you? Brainstorm. Take at least 5 minutes to write down as many ideas as you can (no matter how ridiculous they may seem).

2) Pick one of these ideas and take action on it today.

Day 101: Inspiration from John F. Kennedy

John F. Kennedy (1917-1963) was the 35th President of the United States.

Success is determination and perseverance. Growing up, John was in constant competition with his older brother Joe who had the advantage of being physically stronger and earning better grades in school. John never gave in or gave up and pushed himself to make many great accomplishments.

Success is having an attractive personality. Many respected President Kennedy's coolness when faced with difficult decisions—like what to do about the missiles in Cuba. Others admired his ability to inspire people with his eloquent speeches. Still others thought his compassion and his willingness to fight for new government programs to help the poor, the elderly and the ill were most important.

Success is making waves. In addition to being the youngest President ever elected at age 43, President Kennedy was also the first Roman Catholic President.

Success is making the best use of your time. In 1955, while recuperating from a back operation, John wrote *Profiles in Courage*, which won the Pulitzer Prize in history.

Success is understanding the power of goals. From the moment President Kennedy took office, he implemented and executed both short-term and long-term goals. In his short term in office, he had accomplished more than most Presidents had in their complete terms(s).

Success is sharing and caring. President Kennedy established the Peace Corps in March 1961. Through this program many young Americans were encouraged to contribute their skills to "sharing in the great common task of bringing to man that decent way of life which is the foundation of freedom and a condition of peace."

Success is understanding the importance of family. When President Kennedy was in office, the White House was reported to have seemed like a "fun place", because of the Kennedy's two young children, Caroline and John-John. There was a pre-school, a swimming pool, and a tree house outside on the White House lawn. President Kennedy was probably the busiest man in the country, but he still found time to laugh and play with his children.

Success is making informed decisions based on adequate information. President Kennedy read several newspapers while eating breakfast, had meetings with important people throughout the day, and read several reports from his advisers. He understood that better information led to better decisions.

Success is earning the admiration of others. John F. Kennedy was most admired for his winning personality, his lively family, his intelligence and his tireless energy, and people respected his courage in time of decision.

[Sources: http://www.biography.com, http://www.whitehouse.gov, http://www.jfklibrary.org]

"Ask not what your country can do for you—ask what you can do for your country."

- John F. Kennedy (1917-1963)

Day 102: Taking Risks

In the movie _Parenthood_, Gil (played by Steve Martin), with an obvious feeling of stress and frustration, comments on how chaotic his life is. His grandmother of advancing years begins to tell a story of how when she was younger, she loved the roller coaster because it goes up and down and was both frightening and exciting at the same time, whereas most other girls liked the merry-go-round that just goes round and round. Her point was clear: living the safe life without risk leads to a dull life without reward. It is the risk-takers that live their dreams and achieve success.

We have already seen that safety and security are right below physiological needs on Abraham Maslow's hierarchy of needs. According to this need theory, the need for safety and security is greater than just about all of our other needs, including the desire for greatness or self-actualization. This means we generally avoid risk to protect our level of security. This avoidance of risk is a major limiting factor in one's achievement of success.

Risk itself has many levels. For example, risking your money on a game of blackjack is not as wise as, say, risking your money on a carefully thought out business plan. The key is not avoiding risk, but limiting risk through careful thought and preparation. This is also known as taking calculated risks. Risk also comes in many forms. The world is full of brave and honorable public servants like police men and women, fire fighters, and those in the military who will risk their lives for others in a heartbeat but would not even consider investing a few hundred dollars in a start-up business. If you consider yourself a risk-taker, ask yourself, are these risks you take bringing you any closer to your idea of success?

Here are some suggestions for taking more calculated, limited risks:

- **Have confidence.** Taking risks has to do with having confidence—knowing that no matter what the outcome, you will be fine.
- **Desire greatness.** You may live a fine life full of security, but is that all you really want?
- **Do your homework.** Get all the facts to minimize the risk. The more you know, the less risky a situation becomes. Information allows you to walk away from situations that are too risky and gives you the confidence to take more calculated risks.
- **Ask yourself, what's the worst that can happen?** Put things in perspective. Asking someone out on a date can lead to temporary embarrassment at worst, but can result in a lifetime of love and happiness. If that is not a risk worth taking, I do not know what is.
- **Start small.** Risk does not have to be an all or nothing situation. For example, one does not have to quit one's current job to start a side business. This can be done on a small scale, say one hour a day.
- **Have a backup plan.** What if the chance you take does not turn out in your favor? Minimize the risk by having a backup plan.
- **Use "other people's money".** When taking financial risks, the money you risk certainly does not have to be your own. By using other people's money, you are exchanging financial risk with other types of risk, like reputation.

Do you want to spend your life going around in circles, or do you want the excitement and thrill of the roller coaster? Each of us is capable of so much more than we actually do. It is those who take the risks in life that realize their full potential.

ACTION STEP(S):

---

1) What are some of the latest risks you have taken in your life? Are you "playing it safe"? What opportunities have you missed by not taking risks? Spend a few minutes and jot down the answers to these questions in your journal.

"There are risks and costs to a program of action. But they are far less than the long-range risks and costs of comforatable inaction."

- John F. Kennedy

Day 103: Everyone has 24 Hours in a Day

How many times have you been guilty of saying "I don't have time for that" or "There is not enough time in my schedule..." or a similar phrase stating that by some freak time-space continuum disruption you have been given fewer minutes in your hour, fewer hours in your day, or fewer days in your year than every other being on earth? Isn't it true that what you really mean to say is, "I have chosen to spend my time on something else"? What a difference. The truth is, each of us chooses how to spend our time. You might be saying to yourself, "I HAVE to work or my family doesn't eat!" The fact is, you CHOOSE to work so your family can eat. It is without doubt that some choices do have some less than desirable options, but for the most part, it is a choice which you have control over. Avoiding the phrase "I don't have time...", will soon help you to realize that you do have the time needed for just about anything you choose to accomplish in life.

Not using the "I don't have time..." statement will also disable those automated responses you give yourself and others, and force you to think of the real reason why you do not want to do something. For example, when the day passes by and I am still in front of the computer, my wife says, "Aren't you working out today?" Rather than the "I don't have time today—too busy" response, my thought process goes as follows:

"There is not enough ti.... wait a minute, fact is I am too busy. Too busy doing what? Do I really have to get this done now? Is what I am doing worth giving in on my exercise program? Wouldn't I have more energy to do this later if I took a break?"

And what ends up coming out of my mouth is, "Yes... thanks for reminding me!" So not only are the words different, but this will produce different results at times as well.

If someone tells you they don't have time, ask them to elaborate or turn their answer in to a question. Be sure you have a good rapport with the person or you may come across as obnoxious. Helping others to question their sometimes automated responses will often reveal the truth.

ACTION STEP(S):

---

1) Replace "I don't have time for..." with something like "At this time, I prefer to spend my time..." The latter is a more honest statement that others will appreciate hearing.

"Don't say you don't have enough time. You have exactly the same number of hours per day that were given to Helen Keller, Pasteur, Michelangelo, Mother Teresa, Leonardo da Vinci, Thomas Jefferson, and Albert Einstein."

- H. Jackson Brown, Jr.

Days 104 and 105 are for "R&R"—review and reflection. Spend these days reviewing the last five articles and reflecting on the information and how it relates to your life. Now is also a good time to make sure all the action steps for the previous days have been completed.

Day 106: The "Good Ol' Days"

Remember the good ol' days? It was a time when bread cost a nickel, people were kind to one another, and life seemed so simple. "Ah the good ol' days... if only life were like this today, then I would be happy and successful".

The concept of the "good ol' days" must be one of our society's biggest delusions, top reasons for depression, as well as most often used excuse for lack of success. It is the gloomy belief that the world is headed downhill and life was "better" at some time in the past. Believers of this theory of gloom and doom make excuses for their lack of success by proclaiming, "if only...".

Here is a little known fact: people tend to focus on past successes and current problems. To rephrase, our minds tend to remember our own past successes as well as past global successes made by society without acknowledging the failures. Our minds also tend to focus on our current problems, no matter how insignificant. When thinking about inflation, people tend to remember when bread cost a nickel but forget that they made only ten cents an hour. Or they think about how clean the air was before automobiles, but forget about not being able to walk on a city street without stepping in horse poop. As you can see, this creates a skewed or unfair perception of reality by seeing only the successes of the past and the problems of today.

When were the good ol' days? Back in the days of colonial America where our "kinder" ancestors treated people as property? How about the early 20th century when polio was killing tens of thousands of children? The 1930s where Nazism was growing rapidly? The '40s with WWII, the '60s with the spread of drugs, the '80s with cell phones the size of toasters? The truth is that the "good ol' days" are today. It has been said, that which does not kill us, makes us stronger. As a global society, the same concept holds true: that which does not destroy us, makes us wiser and better. It is because of slavery we now have civil rights, it is because of the holocaust we have a deeper compassion for differences in the human race, and it is because of the Internet bust we have a more stable economy today.

Realize that the good ol' days are today. The world is full of opportunities today that did not exist yesterday. Every day both science and technology improve allowing people to live longer, healthier lives. Information is readily available at the speed of light allowing us to expand our minds like never before in history. Embrace today as the best time in history, for there is no better time to pursue your dreams.

ACTION STEP(S):

1) Think about the time in your life you refer to as the "good ol' days". Were they really that good or are you just remembering the good and blocking the bad? Would you really go back to that time if you could and lose all of your wisdom you have gained from that point?

"Magic Johnson, former basketball player, may run for mayor of LA in the next election. Remember the good 'ol days when only qualified people ran for office like actors and professional wrestlers?"

- **Jay Leno**

Day 107: Financial Freedom

Imagine, if you will, a life free from financial obligations and concerns. No worries about not having enough money ever again, no desire for more money because you have everything you want that money can buy. Imagine spending the 8-16 hours a day you now spend working for money on living your dream, doing whatever fills the void inside and feeling completely fulfilled each day of your life. This is financial freedom.

All of us have heard the term "financial freedom" before. However, very few people ever take the time to comprehend its significance in life. Financial freedom is NOT the same as being rich, or having a lot of money. One can have billions of dollars and still not have financial freedom. This is one of the main reasons why those who have money are not always happy or successful.

Financial freedom is about never having to work for money again and having enough money to maintain your ideal lifestyle. This means one does not have to be rich to be financially free. Theoretically, a family living off welfare checks that is completely content with their lifestyle has financial freedom, although technically broke. However, for most people, an "ideal lifestyle" includes much more than living off welfare checks.

With financial freedom comes an "enlightenment" that very few people are fortunate enough to experience. By fulfilling all your basic needs in life, your life focus can be on self-actualization, or developing your full potential. This means something different to everyone, but in all cases it is a true discovery of yourself.

In an earlier article we discussed making money work for you, rather than working for money. This is the key to financial freedom. Being free from your financial obligations means having a steady and reliable source of income that does not require your labor. The second part of financial freedom is defining your ideal lifestyle, which you should have done by now via the several life purpose and goal setting exercises. Once you understand the concept of having your money work for you, and have defined your ideal lifestyle, you have taken a huge step toward your financial freedom.

Here are some more suggestions to help you reach financial freedom.

- **Control your wants and desires.** By always wanting more you will always require more money. Make sure your wants and desires are in line with your income.
- **Have gratitude.** Enjoy what you have rather than feeling as if you must conquer and collect the material possessions on this earth. You are already wealthy.
- **Invest in assets, not liabilities.** Anything that costs you money rather than makes you money is a liability. Automobiles, boats and even houses can be, and often are, liabilities. Be careful where you put the money you do have.
- **Get rid of unnecessary liabilities.** Do you have an extra car that you rarely drive that you are paying insurance and/or property tax on? Do you have credit card debt that you are paying 19% interest on while at the same time have money in savings that you are getting only 2% interest on? Do the math and get rid of the debt.

Many rich people are not financially secure and go through life with worry and fear of losing what they have. Being free from always needing more money is something that is very attainable by anyone with the right financial attitude and aptitude.

ACTION STEP(S):

1) Calculate an approximate dollar figure it would take for you to live a life of financial freedom. How much would you need initially to purchase the things you want and how much would you

need on a monthly basis to maintain the things you have, and continue to live your ideal lifestyle?

2) Is the number you wrote down in the step above consistent with your financial goals? If not, revisit your goals and be sure your goals are set high enough to support your ideal lifestyle.

"One might think that the money value of an invention constitutes its reward to the man who loves his work. But... I continue to find my greatest pleasure, and so my reward, in the work that precedes what the world calls success."

- Thomas A. Edison

Day 108: Inspiration from Albert Einstein

Albert Einstein (1879-1955) was the Nobel Prize winner in 1921 for physics.

Success is finding opportunity in rejection. In 1901 when Einstein received his diploma, he was unable to get a teaching post, so he accepted a position as a technical assistant in the Swiss Patent Office that allowed him a generous amount of spare time. He used this spare time to produce much of his remarkable work for which he is so well known today.

Success is knowing when to keep quiet. "If A is a success in life, then A equals X plus Y plus Z. Work is X; Y is play; and Z is keeping your mouth shut."

Success is knowing how to persist. Einstein attributed much of his success not to his mathematical abilities, but his persistence. Said Einstein, "It's not that I'm so smart, it's just that I stay with problems longer." • "Insanity: doing the same thing over and over again and expecting different results."

Success is imagination. "Imagination is more important than knowledge. Knowledge is limited. Imagination encircles the world."

Success is understanding the power of questions. "The important thing is not to stop questioning. Curiosity has its own reason for existing." • "I have no particular talent. I am merely inquisitive."

Success is the appreciation of occasional solitude. Einstein's gifts inevitably resulted in his dwelling much in intellectual solitude and, for relaxation; music played an important part in his life.

Success is value. "Try not to become a man of success but rather to become a man of value."

Success is not fearing mistakes. "Anyone who has never made a mistake has never tried anything new."

Success is doing for others. In 1944 Einstein made a contribution to the war effort by hand writing his 1905 paper on special relativity and putting it up for auction. It raised six million dollars, the manuscript today being in the Library of Congress.

Success is dealing with criticism. At the time of the publication on the theory of relativity, the people who read the papers met them with skepticism and ridicule, and some even threatened him with death because of his beliefs.

[Sources: http://www.biography.com, http://www.nobel.se, http://www.einstein-website.de]

"We should take care not to make the intellect our god; it has, of course, powerful muscles, but no personality."

- Albert Einstein

Day 109: Business Systems

One day out of curiosity I decided to take a McDonald's® hamburger, remove the bun, take off the pickle, scrape off the condiments, and eat it (back in my beef eating days). Don't ask me what motivated me to do this—perhaps it was just the natural curiosity of a 13 year old. I'll never forget the mad dash I took running to the bathroom thinking I was going to lose it. I did manage to keep the hamburger down, but that experience led me to a question that I would not find the answer to until years later: if McDonald's® hamburgers taste so bad*, why are they the largest hamburger franchise in the world?

Let me ask you this, do you think you can make a better-tasting hamburger than McDonald's®? Nine out of ten people answer an emphatic "yes" to that question. If you are one of them, then why don't you own a billion-dollar hamburger franchise? McDonald's® is not the leader in mass produced processed carcasses because they have the best hamburger, but because they have the best business system.

McDonald's® is where they are today because they make a fair tasting hamburger (providing you keep the bun and don't scrape off the condiments), sell it for a good price, and really know how to run a business. It is not the product that makes the business, but the business that makes the product.

Just the other day at the mall I bought my niece her "Happy Meal™" at McDonald's®. Within seconds of ordering, our complete order was ready to go, on a tray with napkins, plasticware, and all. Before I could put my change in my pocket, the cashier was already helping the next guest. I thought to myself, "Wow... they really have an efficient system going here." As I witnessed first hand, it was this efficient system that allowed them to service about twice as many customers in the same time frame as the other businesses could in the same food court.

Success in business is not always about having the best product; it is about creating the best possible business system that will market the product. Too often when faced with slow sales, business people immediately ask themselves, "How can we make our product/service better?" rather than, "How can we better market our product/service?" Product quality is very important, but it is not the determining factor for a business' success.

This same principle holds true even if you do not own a business. Are the top people in companies always the smartest or best suited for the position? How many times have you thought, "I am sure I can do a better job than he can"? We each maintain our own "business system" which consists of the same basic components: being efficient in what we do and marketing ourselves. In the case of an individual, the individual is the "product".

Before reevaluating your product or service, and spending big money on improving a product that customers are already happy with, ask yourself the following question, "Is the problem really with our product or service?" Remember that you can please some of the people some of the time, but you cannot please all of the people all of the time. Are you basing your opinion on a large enough percentage or just a vocal few? If your goal is to increase profits, then look at factors like efficiency, negotiating better prices with suppliers, and automation. If your goal is to increase sales, then first look at your marketing and promotion.

You can have the best product in the world, but if no one knows about it, and you do not have an efficient business system in place to fill the demand for your product, then your business has a slim chance for success. Focus on the business of your product or service and success will follow.

* This is the opinion of the author and it is not a proven fact that McDonald's® hamburgers taste bad. In other words, McDonald's® people... please don't sue me.

ACTION STEP(S):

---

1) If you already have a business, can you think of any of your more successful competitors that offer a product or service of lesser quality? Why do you think they are more successful then? If you do not have a business, can you think of any of your peers in higher paid positions that are not as smart or hard working as you are? Why are they there and you aren't?

"When you're green, you're growing. When you're ripe, you rot."

- Ray Kroc

Day 110: An Extra Hour a Day

What would you do with an extra hour a day? Learn a new language? Start a business? Write a book? Learn a new skill? If you have the motivation and desire to use this extra hour, it can be yours.

Most people are under the impressions that they need "eight hours a day" of sleep because this is what they believe "the average person" requires. The fact is, each of us is different and requires different amounts of sleep. Many studies have been done on sleep and sleep disorders, only to conclude that there is no set standard number of hours of sleep per person.

Ironically, the symptoms of not getting enough sleep are very similar to those of getting too much sleep. So why not err on the side of not getting enough sleep and see what your body and mind are capable of? What if you found that with 5 hours of sleep per night, you were at your sharpest during the day with the least amount of drowsiness—and you slept better at night? What would you do with an extra three hours a day?

I have personally experienced sleeping patterns based on motivation—or my mental state. When I am motivated and highly involved in a project, I am awakened each morning around 4am with a burning desire to work on the project. During these times, my mind remains sharp, I have plenty of energy throughout the day and I sleep like a baby at night—for about 6 hours each night. During times when I am less involved in projects I sleep around 8 hours.

I have also found at times when I deprive myself of my required sleep, a mid-day, 15-30 minute "cat nap" in my desk chair does wonders for both my physical and mental state.

If there were ever a way to "buy more time", this is it. However, time is not for sale; it is yours for the taking. What you need to give in return is passion and motivation to get up the extra hour or two earlier—getting up to do household chores won't do. Give this a try by adjusting your body at a pace it can handle. Do this for the next 50 years and you will add 2-3 years to your conscious life.

ACTION STEP(S):

---

1) Start by getting up an extra 15 minutes earlier tomorrow. Spend this time on your personal development. Once you have a reason and desire for getting up earlier, you will.

"Even where sleep is concerned, too much is a bad thing."

- Homer

Days 111 and 112 are for "R&R"—review and reflection. Spend these days reviewing the last five articles and reflecting on the information and how it relates to your life. Now is also a good time to make sure all the action steps for the previous days have been completed.

Day 113: Having It All

Too many people think to be successful you must "have it all"—the latest model car, best house, newest gadgets, etc. The fact is, "all" is an infinite amount that is just not possible to be had by any one person. Our time on this earth is too limited to be spent in the pursuit of things to be had. As the very insightful comedian Steven Wright once said, "You can't have everything, where would you put it?"

An important step to true and lasting success is the realization that you don't really want it all. Success is about enjoying what you have and where you are, while pursuing achievable goals. It is like growing watermelons... you have to sacrifice some watermelons by cutting them off when small to give other watermelons a better chance to grow to full size. The same holds true for what you want in life. By focusing on a smaller number of goals and being passionate in your pursuit of those goals, you will find the achievement of the goals to be easier and more frequent.

It is the concept of wanting more that prevents many people from achieving success. Although they may be successful in the eyes of others, they do not see themselves as successful. Substitute gratitude for "it all". Instead of having the newest model automobile, have gratitude and be appreciative for the car you do have.

Let's examine a few of the more popular philosophies on "having it all".

- **"You can't have everything."** This is true; "everything" is just too much for any one person to have. However, some interpret this statement to really mean, "You can't have everything *you want*". I say why not? If your wants are reasonable enough, why can't you?
- **"You can have anything and everything you want in life."** If your desires are strong enough and you believe

you can achieve your limited wants, then anything is possible.

- **"You can have anything you want, but you can't have everything you want."** I only believe this is true if you want everything. Again, limiting your wants is the key to living a fulfilled life, and it is certainly something that can be achieved.

Where do we draw the line? On the one hand, to be successful we must set bold goals and strive to be the best we can be, while enjoying the material possessions that motivate us. On the other hand, we must exchange many of our wants and desires for gratitude. I believe that if the wants and desires are truly ours, then they are worth pursuing. When we start creating wants and desires by other people's standards of success, we set ourselves up for disappointment. I also believe that there is nothing wrong with wanting more as long as we can appreciate what we currently have. If we do not appreciate what we currently have, then "more" will not make us happier or bring us closer to success.

Start right now by adopting an "attitude of gratitude", and realize your current successes and wealth. Continue to work for and be motivated by your wants and desires, realizing that you can have anything **you** want that you pursue with passion. By controlling your wants and desires, and having gratitude for what you do have, you are taking a big step upward on your ladder of success.

ACTION STEP(S):

1) Eliminate at least one of your "thing" goals, wants or desires. It is best to eliminate a want of a better version of something that you already have. Start with something small. Once you do this, it will be easier to do with larger items.

2) Take a few moments to reflect on all you do have; family, friends, career, material possessions, physical health, mental health, and anything else that comes to mind.

Day 114: Accepting Criticism

Gautama Buddha's preaching was interrupted one day by a man unleashing a flurry of abusive invective. Calmly waiting for his critic to finish, Buddha asked, "If a man offered a gift to another but the gift was declined, to whom would the gift belong?" "To the one who offered it," the man replied.

"Then," Buddha declared, "I decline to accept your abuse and request that you keep it for yourself."

Or as Mary Katherine Gallagher (Molly Shannon), in the movie _Superstar_, so eloquently put it, "I am rubber, you are glue. What you say bounces off me and sticks to you".

Buddha and Mary knew one of the main rules to accepting criticism: one does not have to accept it!

Criticism is essentially feedback, in which there are two parts: giving and accepting. In this article we will discuss accepting criticism and how it can work toward our success.

The first rule of accepting criticism is understanding the motivation behind the criticism. Understanding this motivation helps you decide how valid the criticism is, and whether to accept it or not. Here are some of the more common reasons why people criticize.

- **Out of jealousy.** When others are jealous of your work, they will criticize with the intent of damaging your self-esteem. It is usually easy to spot this motivation because the critic will usually have something to gain by your failure.
- **Out of anger or frustration.** Often when someone gets frustrated they misdirect their frustration and start playing the blame game. This blame is dished out in the form of undue criticism. Most of the time, this criticism is

outrageous and even laughable to those with a clear head. This kind of criticism can easily be identified by the tone and the words used to criticize.

- **Concerned for one's own interest.** People have different tastes and preferences. Some critics will criticize based on their own personal preferences. Now this can be a perfectly legitimate form of criticism, as in the case where the work criticized is especially for the critic. Take for example someone who hires an artist to paint a portrait. The one who is being painted is justified in criticizing the work based on his own personal preferences, since the work was specifically done for him.
- **Concerned for mutual interest.** This is the most common form of criticism given by customers and employees. They criticize with the hopes that changes will be made that will better their situation and the company/individual in general.
- **Concerned for your best interest.** Criticism made by parents, loved ones, or good friends is usually done with your best interest in mind. This is important to realize because it is this group of "critics" that are usually the most resented for their criticism.

The second rule of accepting criticism is choosing to accept it or not. Based on the motivation of the critic, do you think this criticism has merit? If so, how much merit does it have? Accepting criticism is using the criticism to better your work or performance. Rejecting the criticism is not letting the criticism affect your work, performance, or especially your attitude.

The third rule is responding to the criticism. This is where most people damage their reputations and good will by *reacting* to the criticism negatively. A response is reaction with thought. In this case, we have already thought about the motivation of the critic and chosen to accept it or not. No matter what our response is, it should be stated positively.

Why is accepting criticism so difficult? Here are some of the top reasons:

- **Other people do not know how to criticize properly.** Most people criticize in such a way that makes us very emotional. However, we know that we cannot control how other people express themselves, but we can control how we internally respond to their criticism. Practice self-control.
- **We often take it too personally.** We must remember that it is our actions or performance that is really being criticized and not us.
- **We fail to put criticism in perspective.** If you have created a work of art that thousands of people admire, and a few express dislike, realize that you cannot please all of the people all of the time. It is true that for every one person who criticizes, there are probably ten more that feel the same way, but even with these numbers your work or performance is being enjoyed by the majority.
- **We fear failure.** Trump does not make great deals all the time, Benjamin Franklin did not always have good inventions, and Schwarzenegger certainly does not always make great movies. Our fear of failure, rather than acceptance of it, causes us to often deny the truth or at least be blinded by our own ego. When criticism is just, we must accept it graciously, learn from it, and move on.

Critics often expect harsh reactions to their criticism, probably because that is the way most people respond. Not successful people. Shock your critics by thanking them for their feedback and if you choose to accept the criticism, share with them what way you plan on using their criticism. If your critics say things such as, "You suck!" or "Your work sucks!", don't ignore it. Ask them to elaborate as to what about you or your work they dislike.

Criticism is an extremely valuable element to success. Since most success is based on providing something of value for others, it is important to value the opinions of others and change your actions based on good feedback. It is this feedback that helps us to achieve success.

Sources: Will and Ariel Durant, The History of Civilization; Harpers, Oct. 2002

ACTION STEP(S):

---

1) Ask at least two people for feedback on your work or performance. When you get the feedback, go through the three rules in the article.

"Criticism may not be agreeable, but it is necessary. It fulfils the same function as pain in the human body. It calls attention to an unhealthy state of things."

- Sir Winston Churchill

Day 115: Inspiration from Sir Winston Churchill

Sir Winston Leonard Spencer Churchill (1874-1965) was one of the twentieth century's most important figures, best known as Britain's Prime Minister from 1940–1945 and 1951–1955.

Success is knowing that your past does not equal your future. Winston was known to be a willful and somewhat rebellious little boy. His teachers wrote in letters how difficult he was, one teacher even writing, "Very bad... is a constant trouble to everybody..."

Success is progress. "Every day you may make progress. Every step may be fruitful. Yet there will stretch out before you an ever-lengthening, ever-ascending, ever-improving path. You know you will never get to the end of the journey. But this, so far from discouraging, only adds to the joy and glory of the climb."

Success is keeping your family life in order as well as your work. In 1908, Churchill married Clementine Hozier, which proved to be a long and happy marriage.

Success is knowing that effective communication is better than proper grammar. When corrected for using a preposition at the end of a sentence, Churchill gave the oft-quoted response, "This is the sort of English up with which I will not put."

Success is viewing failure as temporary. Being human, in 1914, Churchill made an error in judgment that lead to the disastrous Gallipolli landings. This error cost Churchill his job as First Lord of the Admiralty and much of his good reputation. • "Success is the ability to go from one failure to another with no loss of enthusiasm."

Success is having courage. "One ought never to turn one's back on a threatened danger and try to run away from it. If you do that, you will double the danger. But if you meet it promptly and without flinching, you will reduce the danger by half." • "Success is never final. Failure is never fatal. It is courage that counts."

Success is being able to inspire others. Churchill's role in World War II was mostly that of an inspiration. He is known today as one of the greatest speakers of the century.

Success is persistence. "We shall not fail or falter; we shall not weaken or tire... Give us the tools and we will finish the job."

Success is being optimistic. "A pessimist sees the difficulty in every opportunity; an optimist sees the opportunity in every difficulty."

[Sources: http://www.biography.com, http://www.nobel.se]

"The price of greatness is responsibility."

- Sir Winston Churchill

Day 116: Dealing with Peer Pressure

In kindergarten, it was the kids that threw clay out the window. In the fifth grade, it was the kids that skipped class. In high school, it was the kids that smoked, got drunk, and did drugs. Even in our adult lives, there are, and will always be, those people who unjustly influence the lives of others. This influence is known as *peer pressure*.

Peer pressure is the psychological force exerted by another, or others, in equal standing, which often influences one into acting or behaving in a manner that is generally inconsistent with one's normal behavior. It is this influence that one can choose to accept or not accept. It is important to understand that no one, besides you, can control the direction of your life. We are endowed with the gift of choice and decision, and we must take full responsibility for the decisions we make in life.

All peer pressure is not always bad. It is certainly possible there can be pressure to "follow the crowd" to do homework and to get good grades. Or if you hang out with millionaires, there can be pressure to make millions of dollars. The key factor is thinking for yourself and doing what is consistent with your goals and life purpose.

Peer pressure is not something that only kids face. Throughout our entire lives we deal with peer pressure. Some of the most destructive forms of peer pressure are those that cause us to "fall in line" by living a life of accomplishment far below what we are capable of, just because it is what our peers do. Giving into peer pressure as a child begins the life-long habit that keeps most people far away from success. As we know, it is never too late to change and break destructive habits.

Why do people give into peer pressure? The main reason, and the reason preached to most kids these days, is the need for belonging. This is part of Abraham Maslow's "love needs" which is right after safety needs, in the middle of the hierarchy. We all have a desire to fit in and to be accepted. However, one often looks for acceptance in groups that work against one's achievement of success. It takes a leader to delay this need for belonging and reject the pressure. Soon, others will follow and the need for belonging will be met. One must have faith.

Here are some other reasons why people give in to peer pressure, that are less known but equally as responsible.

- **The lack of self-confidence to go one's own way.** It is easier to follow the footsteps of another than to make your own. There is also a certain level of safety that comes with following another. Taking the road less traveled by making your own choices takes self-confidence and self-assurance.
- **The desire to avoid embarrassment.** Many people fear embarrassment more than death. Knowing this, it is easy to see how important effective communication can be in responding to peer pressure. For example, if a bunch of peers surround a teenager and asked him if he wants to smoke a cigarette like the rest of them have, and all the teenager can think of is, "but... my mom said I should just say no." then he is in trouble. It is best to prepare yourself and your children with witty, yet clear responses to known peer pressures. For example, in the above situation the teenager could say, "Hmmm, spend my life wasting money, offending people, having bad breath, and killing myself.... no thanks." A good response cannot only save one from embarrassment, but give others the confidence to not give in to the peer pressure as well. Those who lead are often well respected by those who follow.
- **The lack of using one's own mind.** Again it is reacting, rather than responding that causes one to get in trouble. Think about the consequences of your actions, both present and future. Don't give in and sacrifice your long-term goals for short-term gratification.
- **The lack of unbiased information.** When someone feels pressure from peers, they are often presented with biased information. Again it is preparation that can help one to

avoid peer pressure by knowing all the facts. Anticipate peer pressure in life and get the facts from a reliable source. Educate yourself and your children—don't count on the school system to do it. Some of the more common peer pressures experienced in youth that can be prepared for today are smoking, alcohol, drugs, sex, cutting class and committing crimes. The biggest peer pressure in adulthood is being expected to behave, act, and perform like your peers rather than becoming the person you are capable of becoming. Know the reasons for and against these pressures.

People are often categorized as either leaders or followers. Be a leader. Think before you act and act on what you believe. Never allow others to influence your actions or behaviors without using your own mind and be consistent with your goals in life. Success often follows those who refuse to follow others.

ACTION STEP(S):

---

1) Take a few moments to write down all your behaviors or habits that began as a result of peer pressure. Is it time to change these behaviors?

2) Take a mental journey back to a time when you did give in to peer pressure. Knowing what you now know, how could you have better handled that situation?

Day 117: Ideas for Wealth

When was the last time you said something like, "I wish they would invent something to..." or "Somebody really should..." or "Why don't they make something that...'"? If you are like most people, you probably say these words on a regular basis. Who are "they"? Who is "somebody"? Why can't the "they" and "somebody" be you?

One of the most common reasons people do not act on ideas is that they think somebody must have already thought of it. The chances are, somebody, even many others, has thought about it, but nobody has *acted on it*. Every fortune, large or small, started with an idea. Some of these ideas at one time were thought to be far fetched, silly, stupid, crazy, and even impossible. It was the inventor who had enough belief and determination to see the idea through into its physical equivalent.

Here are some more reasons people generally don't act on ideas.

- **They don't think they are inventors.** Just because you are not a plumber, doesn't mean you can't unclog your own toilet with a plunger. It does not take an electrician to change a light bulb, nor does it take an inventor to come up with and act on a good idea.
- **They don't believe in their ideas enough.** Many people make the mistake of asking other people what they think of an idea and choosing to act or not based on others' opinions. I believe it was Edison who was known for asking for others' opinions on his ideas, and if they all unanimously thought it was a BAD idea, he would act on it. Ask yourself, what is your "gut" feeling on this idea?
- **They don't know how to follow through.** Many people simply don't know what to do next after having an idea. The key is to educate yourself and align yourself with the right people who can help you see your idea through. With

the advent of the Internet, this is easier than ever before in history.

- **They fear criticism and ridicule.** What do you think Gary Dahl's family and friends thought of him when he enthusiastically explained to them that he was going to market a "pet rock" for $3.95? I can just imagine how his parents felt when trying to explain what their son was up to these days, "Oh, our Gary is working on selling rocks as pets". And of course there is the more common example of Columbus' idea of the world being round. This was the classic case of public criticism and ridicule. Those who ridicule new ideas are closed minded, and criticism from them should not be accepted.

Here is my five-step idea process that I like to follow. Feel free to adopt mine or create your own. The goal of this process is to make sure we act on our ideas worthy of action.

1. **Record it.** The moment an idea pops in your head, write it down or record it.
2. **Add it to your list.** Have a page in your success journal or a list somewhere where you transfer, write down and collect all of your ideas and review this list often. Your idea may not be strong enough to act on now, but it may be later.
3. **Carefully think through the idea and the possibilities.** Do not let "reasoning" talk you out of taking action on an idea. Most ideas probably are not worth pursuing, but do not get in the habit of letting all ideas go.
4. **Always be acting on at least one idea.** Pick your best idea at the time and act on it. Do the research. Make acting on the idea one of your goals and follow the proper goal setting steps.
5. **Know when to move on.** There is a fine line between giving up and moving on. Never give up on good ideas but know when to move on to better ideas.

It only takes one good idea to lead you to wealth. If you have 100 ideas a year and act on 10 of them and one results in wealth, you will have made it. It is not lack of knowledge or talent that keeps most people from wealth, it is lack of persistence. You are just as capable of bringing a great idea to this world as Edison, Ford, and Gates. Act on your ideas, and wealth will eventually find its way to you.

ACTION STEP(S):

1) Right now, write down at least 10 ideas you have or have had in the past that has not been acted upon already. These can be ideas for wealth, ideas that change the world, or ideas that will stop your door from squeaking.

2) Go through steps 3,4, and 5 in the five-step idea process above. Be sure you choose at least one idea to start acting on today. If you cannot, then add more ideas to your list. DO NOT STOP until you have chosen at least one idea to act upon.

"The ability to convert ideas to things is the secret of outward success."

- Henry Ward Beecher

Days 118 and 119 are for "R&R"—review and reflection. Spend these days reviewing the last five articles and reflecting on the information and how it relates to your life. Now is also a good time to make sure all the action steps for the previous days have been completed.

Day 120: Using Questions Effectively

There is a tool we have in communication that is so important, yet most people fail to make full use of this tool. It is called the question. Most people use questions for one purpose, to get information. This is a fine use of the question but certainly not the only use. Questions can be used in several ways in the art of communication. Those who use questions effectively will be more successful and influential communicators.

Did you know that most people mentally drift off during conversations, only half-listening to what the other person is saying? Did you know that I asked that question not to get information, but to get attention? Questions have an incredible effect on bringing someone back from "la-la land". People are conditioned to respond to questions so when they hear the tone of a question, their minds are once again focused on the communicator. These types of attention-getting questions are best used in speeches and lectures, especially as an opening statement.

Did you realize that in my last question, I shared some information with you? All questions get attention, but they can also serve other purposes at the same time. In this case, questions like "did you know..." or "could you believe that..." share information with the reader/listener. These questions are used as a more powerful way to get information across since it causes the reader/listener to ask themselves the question and mentally answer it. This form of information sharing works very well, but should not be abused. Information sharing questions are great for occasionally communicating important points.

How would you feel if you mastered the power of questions and were able to effectively communicate any message to anyone? How would this help you in your achievement of success? (dramatic pause...) These questions were asked to start you thinking, visualizing, and feeling emotion. The ability to communicate emotions rather than just words is a skill that very few people have. It is one of the most powerful skills of a successful communicator and the question is one of the best ways to use this skill.

Let me ask you this: Once you're rich and successful, will you still use questions for more than getting information? And thus we have the presumptive question. Notice the question is not will you become rich and successful, I have already assumed that as stated in the question. The question is about your plans on how you will use questions after you are rich and successful. The presumptive question is one of the favorite tricks of the lawyers. It gives information that is to be accepted as fact while at the same time, soliciting information. The presumptive question is also a favorite used by people in sales. This is done by assuming that you are going to buy and asking a question like, "Would you like that in green or blue?" In sales, presumptive questions make it more difficult for the prospect to say no since "no" is really not a proper answer to the question being asked (tip: a good response to the sales person using this technique on you is to ask back, "I see you like to ask presumptive questions. Why is that?").

Now that you have been introduced to several powerful uses for questions, why not start using them today?

I could have ended the article there, but I would not get a chance to explain the use of the last question: to bring to a conclusion. Leaving readers/listeners with a question that sums up your points is a great way to end a speech or writing. Once again, it gets the attention of the listeners/readers, and causes them to think. Ending this way can leave your audience with a powerful impression.

Summary of the effective uses of questions:

1. get information
2. cause attention
3. give information
4. start the other person thinking or visualizing
5. accept information as fact
6. bring to conclusion

ACTION STEP(S):

---

1) In the next few days, make use of each type of question in your verbal or written communication. This can be done in casual conversation or in casual e-mails to friends or business associates. Get used to asking these types of questions.

"The art and science of asking questions is the source of all knowledge."

- Thomas Berger

Day 121: Avoid Criticizing and Complaining

You have just found out that one of your subordinates at work made a costly mistake that may cost you your job. When you confront your subordinate about the mistake, he is obviously remorseful but you proceed to vent your frustration and say everything that is on your mind anyway. As a result, he quits, and several of his co-workers are now full of resentment toward you, and have lost respect for you. Productivity in your department is way down, and ironically, you are now at an even greater risk of losing your job, all due to your inability to effectively criticize.

In both our personal and professional lives, the ability to effectively deal with people is vital to building good character and to our success. The words criticize and complain are by definition very negative, and thus bring out negative emotions in both the giver and receiver. From this point forward, vow never to criticize or complain again. Instead, give feedback.

We have already discussed why people criticize. These are the same general reasons why people complain as well. To review, the top reasons are:

- Out of jealousy
- Out of anger or frustration
- Concerned for one's own interest
- Concerned for mutual interest
- Concerned for your best interest

We can break these reasons down into two even more general categories. 1) We criticize and complain so we can feel better and 2) we criticize and complain to bring about change in others. Now let's examine both of these reasons more carefully.

Dale Carnegie once wrote, "We are creatures of emotion, not logic". In this sense, we act and react based our emotions first, then logic second. This causes us to do and say things that "feel good" at the time but we often regret shortly after. How many times have you written a nasty e-mail only to rewrite it several times over, taking out all the harsh parts before actually sending it? Control your emotions and do not let your emotions control your actions without first filtering your emotions through your mind.

Do not allow yourself to become jealous, angered or frustrated by another's action. Practice understanding and empathy. Would you have done the same thing if you were in the other person's exact same situation? What are the reasons why the other person did what they have done? Taking a few moments to gather the facts will help you to understand, and with that understanding comes compassion.

There are times when we want to bring about a change in another's behavior. As parents we must discipline our children, as teachers we must correct our students, as managers we must direct our subordinates, and as customers we must do our best to get value from the service or product for which we are paying. It is neither harsh criticism nor complaints that bring about lasting changes; it is *eloquent feedback* that causes one to want to make lasting changes. For example, telling an employee that their performance is less than acceptable and they'd better change or they will be out of a job, will most likely persuade the employee to change, but not for a positive reason. This change will most likely be done with resentment and ill feelings, and will last only a short time.

There are two main reasons why one should neither criticize nor complain. First, criticism causes the person being criticized to feel resentment. When you criticize another's actions or behaviors, especially in a negative way, it arouses feelings of anger and resentment in most people. This resentment is one of the most powerful relationship-killers there is. Second, criticism causes the person being criticized to justify his or her actions. It is a natural response for one to become defensive when being criticized. The most common form of defense is justification. When one justifies one's actions, they are convincing themselves even more that they are right. This brings the parties further from resolution.

There will be times when you feel that criticisms and complaints are necessary. Ask yourself first, what do I plan on accomplishing by criticizing? Very often the real answer will be "so I can feel better", in which case, the criticism or complaint is not necessary. If you wish to bring about a change in another's behavior, then you must practice the art of changing people without giving offense or arousing resentment (discussed in detail later in this course). Or if you just wish to give feedback, do so in a way that leaves an overall positive impression.

Criticisms and complaints lead to resentment and ill feelings that rarely bring about positive, lasting changes. Learn to control your emotions by practicing understanding and having empathy. By avoiding criticizing and complaining, you will be better respected in both your personal and professional relationships.

ACTION STEP(S):

1) Every time you feel yourself about to criticize or complain, ask yourself what you are trying to accomplish. If it is only to vent your frustration, practice the art of redirecting your frustration into creative feedback.

"The squeaky wheel may get the grease, but it is also often the first one to get replaced."

- Unknown

Day 122: Inspiration from Jerry Seinfeld

Jerry Seinfeld (1954–) is a comedian and television actor in his long running series "Seinfeld".

Success begins with an interest. Seinfeld became fascinated by comedians as a child while watching them on television and realizing their entire job was to make people laugh. He developed a keen interest in performing while in college. He graduated with a bachelor's degree in communications and theater.

Success is often about rough beginnings. Jerry began his career working in New York comedy clubs, often without pay, while holding a number of odd jobs.

Success is knowing that persistence pays off. After much time in the comedy circuit, Jerry got his first big break when comedic legend Rodney Dangerfield saw his act and invited him to feature on his HBO special.

Success is having others believe in you. In the early days of Jerry's career, another comedic legend, Jackie Mason, caught his act and told Jerry, "It makes me sick. You're going to be such a big hit." These inspiring words stayed with Jerry for years.

Success is the result of an earlier failure or unfortunate event. Jerry appeared on several episodes of TV's "Benson". The producers of the show did not agree on his character development so they "let him go". This was so devastating to Jerry that he vowed never to do a sitcom again unless he had more control. That vow led him to partner with his friend Larry David to create one of the most successful sitcoms of all time.

Success is not accepting failure. The pilot for "Seinfeld" did not test well, in fact NBC "hated" it. However, with persistence, it began with a very slow season, followed by a much better one.

Success is doing what you love, despite the money. After almost a decade, Seinfeld called it quits at the pinnacle of his sitcom. Despite the many lucrative TV and movie offers, Jerry went back to stand up, once again, touring the local New York clubs and often performing for free.

[Sources: http://www.biography.com, http://www.jerryseinfeld.us]

"The Four Levels of Comedy: Make your friends laugh, Make strangers laugh, Get paid to make strangers laugh, and Make people talk like you because it's so much fun."

- Jerry Seinfeld

Day 123: Get a Job?

In my four years of high school and four years of college (ok, four and a quarter), the idea that I had the choice of starting my own business, or working for myself in some other way, was mentioned but a few times. As a student, the traditional approach of "study hard, get good grades, find a good job" was hammered into our brains over and over. What appears to be good, solid advice is the same advice that is creating a society of dependent and financially insecure adults.

What if.... what if we ALL followed this "sound" advice? Who would create the jobs that we are all seeking? There are only so many government jobs, and even those have to be created by someone. We would rely on the jobs that are currently available, which by attrition, would eventually decrease. The jobs that are available would be more and more competitive which would result in higher unemployment. Does this sound familiar?

Why is getting a job sold as a "better" option than creating a job for oneself?

- **Social status.** To many people, a title is more important than a raise. It does wonders for one's self-esteem and feeling of importance. Jobs come with impressive titles these days. Landing a good job gives one instant social status and bragging rights (Vice President of Pencil Sharpening?).
- **Credibility.** Somewhere, sometime, someone linked a paid job with credibility. It seems that if an employer is willing to pay someone in advance for services rendered, both the job and the employee's abilities are credible. However, those who choose the riskier path of self-employment or an opportunity heavily based on performance pay, somehow could not get a "real job".

- **Security.** For the most part, security in the workforce is a myth. One is only truly secure with confidence in one's own abilities.

- **Instant gratification.** Getting a job usually means instant gratification via a weekly, bi-weekly, or monthly paycheck. The need for immediate cash flow prohibits most people from investing in themselves and being independent from an employer. In today's business world, there are so many opportunities that can be done part-time and with little or no money down. Creating your own job is rewarding in so many ways and brings with it long-term gratification.

- **It's easier.** Depending on the job, one's abilities, skills and education, it is generally much easier to get a job than create one. Most people choose the easier path in life to their own detriment. Success is not easy, but it sure is worth it.

- **Lack of faith.** Although filled with good intentions, most parents and teachers do not encourage children and students to go for the "dare to be great" situation. With their best interest at heart, adults condition students to "study hard, get good grades, find a good job". Statistically speaking, this is the most sound advice considering an estimated 90% of all businesses fail in the first five years. However, what if students were conditioned for success? Would this failure rate be so high? What's wrong with failure anyway? Perhaps students would be better off studying persistence rather than making birdhouses.

There is more to creating a job than just securing your own financial future. Bill Gates chose to create a job for himself rather than join the existing workforce. As a result, his company, Microsoft, now employs more than 50,000 people in 72 countries, not to mention the number of jobs and opportunities it has created indirectly. This comes back to one of my favorite "keys to success" by Zig Ziglar who says, "You can get what you want by helping enough other people get what they want".

There are numerous benefits to employment as well. Without employees, companies could not operate. There will always be those who prefer the path of employment and employers are grateful for that. However, let's have a little more faith in our youth and at least introduce them to the option of creating jobs rather than taking them. It is the entrepreneurs that create opportunity, and is our duty to do our best to create a better world for the next generation.

ACTION STEP(S):

---

1) If you have children in middle school through college, talk to them about the option of creating their own job. If you are a student or already have a job, do some brainstorming. How can you create a job for yourself using the money and time available to you?

"All paid jobs absorb and degrade the mind."

- Aristotle

Day 124: Learning to Fish

On the streets, for every economically disadvantaged person begging for money there are several kind souls who help out by giving change. At home, for every dependent adolescent there is a loving parent catering to the child's every need. In business, for every needy employee there is a caring manager just trying to help. There is an old saying by Lao Tzu, the father of Taoism, which says "Give a man a fish and you feed him for a day. Teach him how to fish and you feed him for a lifetime". Too often in life we ask for fish, and too often others give fish away. Within Mr. Tzu's statement lie two keys to success.

Key number one: we must seek instruction over temporary assistance. An ambitious young gentleman knocked on the door to my home recently. He was selling magazines through a company that "teaches economically disadvantaged young adults communication and business skills to help achieve success". Needless to say, I had a great talk with the gentleman. Before we parted ways, and after I confirmed he had access to the Internet, I told him I would not be buying any subscriptions, but I would be doing much more for him. I reached in my pocket and gave him one of my YearToSuccess.com cards, which has no other information besides, "YearToSuccess.com - Are You Ready for It?". By the look on his face, I could see that he was disappointed, yet a bit curious. He may have thrown the card away or he may have actually joined Y2S, I may never know. It is not always easy to accept instruction over more temporary, yet immediately gratifying forms of assistance, but in our quest for success, we must seek the instruction and graciously accept it.

Key number two: we must offer instruction rather than temporary assistance. I am personally guilty of "giving away fish". When I sold my last company, my wife and I gave away a significant amount of money to family and employees in the company. Just over two years later, many of those we gave the money to are no better off financially than they were before the gift, and several are actually in a worse financial situation. Why? How could giving somebody a significant amount of money hurt his of her financial situation? There are actually many reasons like poor spending habits, living beyond one's means, and having a false sense of security. However, I believe the main reason is that giving someone money, or other material goods, hampers their desire to seek a permanent solution to improving their financial situation. The same holds true for doing anything for anyone where, with a little knowledge and persistence, they can do for themselves.

"Give a man a fish and you feed him for a day. Teach him how to fish and you feed him for a lifetime". Spend your life learning to fish and teaching others how to fish and you will sow and reap the seeds of success.

ACTION STEP(S):

---

1) How can you help others help themselves? (hint: refer others to this course!) What else can you do to help others help themselves?

2) Where in your life have you, or do you currently, accept temporary assistance? How can you replace that with instruction so that you are no longer dependent on the assistance?

Days 125 and 126 are for "R&R"—review and reflection. Spend these days reviewing the last five articles and reflecting on the information and how it relates to your life. Now is also a good time to make sure all the action steps for the previous days have been completed.

Day 127: Dependability

John Donne, English metaphysical poet from the late 16th century, once said, "No man is an island, entire of itself; every man is a piece of the continent, a part of the main..." As an employer, husband, and father, I can truly appreciate the concept behind this truth. No man (or woman, as it is PC to say in the 21st century) is alone in this world. We have others on whom we can depend to help us achieve success. However, before we can depend upon others, we should set an example by first understanding and practicing one of the principles of success: do what you say you are going to do, and do it when you say you are going to do it.

Dependability is a characteristic more often used to describe cars than people. Having others depend on us gives us a healthy dosage of importance that is good for our self-esteem. Doing what we say we are going to do, when we say we are going to do it, builds character that is admired by parents, teachers, spouses, peers, employers, and especially customers. It is the dependable children that get more independence, it is the dependable student that gets the better grades, it is the dependable employee that gets the promotions, and it is the dependable business that gets the customers.

Dependability, just like any other quality, is a learned behavior that can be improved with practice. Here are some tips on how to become more dependable.

- **Keep a schedule, calendar, or to-do list.** Organization and knowledge of your own workload and commitments is the key to dependability.
- **Write down everything! Don't depend on memory.** The moment you commit to action, write it down. Then, when convenient, transfer the action to your schedule, calendar or to-do list.
- **Never say "I'll try".** I am not one of those people who will tell you to completely remove the word "try" from

your vocabulary. "Try" is a valid word with many valid meanings. However, it should never be used when committing to action. This is a very weak and ambiguous response to a request. "I'll try", essentially means, "Don't count on it". If you are honestly unsure whether you can commit to the action or not, but plan to make your best attempt, instead say, "I will do my best". Otherwise, respectfully decline the commitment and maintain your integrity.

- **Request responsibility.** Ask your employer, customer, teacher, or parent if you can do anything for them. Taking this proactive approach goes a long way in bringing you closer to success.

What happens when you just can't deliver? Despite your best efforts, you find yourself not being able to do what you said, or do it by the promised time. Here are some suggestions:

- **Don't make promises you can't keep.** Prevent this situation from happening in the first place. Before making a commitment, think carefully about what it will mean if you break the commitment. Don't let others coerce you into committing to something to which you are not ready to commit. Respectfully decline commitment when needed and you will be respected for it.
- **Be up front and honest ASAP.** The moment you realize that you cannot deliver, let the other party know about it. Do not make excuses, and take responsibility for your actions, or lack thereof.
- **Apologize.** Offer a sincere apology for not being able to deliver on your commitment. Again, do not offer excuses, just a sincere apology.
- **Reschedule with an additional benefit.** I once saw this comedy skit where a guy borrowed a videotape from his friend. Each day the friend would ask if he brought the video back and each day the guy who borrowed the tape would appease his friend by saying, "No. But I'll tell you what I'm going to do..." and promising to bring it the next day plus bringing more videos, taking him out to dinner,

and other added benefits. Each day he would "sweeten the deal", but never deliver on his promises. I guess you had to see it to find it funny. Anyway, this is an illustration of how rescheduling the action with an additional benefit can appease the one the commitment was made to. Of course, this technique can only be used on occasion when needed, and should never be misused like in the extreme example above.

Do what you say you are going to do, and do it when you say you are going to do it. As leaders, we must set good examples for those who follow us. Imagine if everybody followed this rule of success, what a world it would be!

ACTION STEP(S):

1) Rate yourself on a dependability scale from 1-10 (10 being the most dependable). How often do you do what you say you are going to do? How often do you do it when you say you are going to have it done by?

2) Make a verbal commitment to another for doing something—anything—and actually do it. Follow the suggestions in the article if needed to ensure you get it done.

"No man is an island, entire of itself; every man is a piece of the continent, a part of the main..."

- John Donne (1572-1631)

Day 128: The Subject of Money

I remember sitting around with my friends, back in elementary school, talking about money. We would all talk about how great it would be to have lots of money and even discuss ideas on how to start making money. We talked about making wooden novelties in my Dad's workshop and selling them door-to-door, trading and selling baseball cards, starting a leaf-raking business, and more. The subject of money got us excited and started our pre-teen creative juices flowing. As the years went by, we spoke less and less of money until our adult lives when it became a taboo subject. What happened?

By most adults' standards of etiquette, money is a subject that should not be discussed openly among friends or other peers. Why? For most people, in their adult lives, money is an unpleasant subject. This is because they don't have enough of it. In fact, one of the top reasons married couples argue is because of financial difficulties and other strains that lack of money both directly and indirectly cause. Since it is generally not considered good etiquette to discuss any subject that makes others feel uncomfortable or even depressed, the subject of money has become taboo.

If you are one of the people who is uncomfortable talking about money, then change your associations. Talking about money openly, especially with those who have more than you do, will allow you to grow in your financial thinking. We can learn more from our friends and peers than we could by reading books from the top financial advisors. When you think about money, think about all the good you can do with it, for yourself, your family and those you've never even met. Think about how exciting it would be to have more of it, allowing you more time to do what you are passionate about. This is how you associate money with empowering feelings.

Find a group of your peers that you can discuss the subject of money with that are comfortable talking about it with you. Realize that by avoiding the subject, you are doing nothing to improve your financial education. Don't be afraid to share your financial successes and failures with others. As we help others learn, we grow ourselves.

ACTION STEP(S):

---

1) Do you like to discuss money with your friends and/or peers? If not, why not? List the reasons why. If they wanted to discuss the subject with you, would you be happy to? Or would you do so reluctantly? Why?

"Money, which represents the prose of life, and which is hardly spoken of in parlors without an apology, is, in its effects and laws, as beautiful as roses."

- Ralph Waldo Emerson

Day 129: Inspiration from Warren Buffet

Warren Buffet (1930–) is known as perhaps the greatest investor to ever live. He became the world's richest person by sticking to common sense principles in stock market investing.

Success has much to do with aptitude. Warren displayed an amazing aptitude for money and business at a very early age. At age 6, Warren bought six-packs of soda for 25 cents and resold the cans individually for 5 cents each, making a respectable 20 percent profit.

Success is learning patience. At eleven years old, Warren purchased three shares of Cities Service Preferred at $38 per share, which quickly dropped to $27 per share. Although he was an emotional wreck, he held on to the stock until it rebounded to $40 per share, at which time he quickly sold. The stock then shot up to $200 per share and Warren learned early the importance of patience.

Success is realizing the insignificance of rejection. When Warren was persuaded to apply to Harvard Business School, he was rejected because he was "too young". Warren then applied to Columbia where famed investors Ben Graham and David Dodd taught—an experience that would forever change his life.

Success is overcoming your fears. Warren knew the importance of public speaking, however, he admitted to having an "intense fear" of it. Instead of fearing it, Warren decided to do something about it. He enrolled in Dale Carnegie's public speaking course and conquered his fear.

Success is learning from your work. One of Warren's mentors, a respected investor, offered Warren a job, which he accepted.

During this time of employment, Warren learned what he needed to know about investing to become a stock market billionaire.

Success is having goals. Since 1957, Mr. Buffet has far exceeded his initial goal of beating the Dow Jones Industrial Average by 10%.

Success is creatively negotiating. When making Ken Close President of one of his companies, he felt that it would be unfair to the stockholders to award Mr. Close a stock option, on which Mr. Close insisted. Instead, Buffet proposed to co-sign an $18,000 loan that Mr. Close then used to buy his own stocks. Mr. Buffet created a win-win situation.

Success is sticking with what works. When asked by a friend why he doesn't invest in real estate, Warren replied, "Why should I buy real estate when the stock market is so easy?"

Success is believing in yourself even when the facts are against you. Warren Buffet's philosophy is and always has been to allocate capital into great businesses that are selling below intrinsic value. However, with the Internet boom, his firm was making very nominal gains while other investment firms were making their clients millionaires. Buffet's clients, and the media, began to believe Buffet had lost his touch. As Buffet expected, the market did eventually correct itself and while millions of "on paper" millionaires lost everything virtually overnight, Buffet's clients remained wealthy.

[Sources: http://www.surferess.com, http://www.askmen.com]

Day 130: A Better Way To Save

There is an age-old piece of wisdom passed from generation to generation that essentially says if you want something, save your money and buy it. We hear it all the time today. Phrases like, "I am saving up for..." or "saving for a rainy day". To save is wise, however, the way most people save is not. Most people see their income, and income potential, as limited. Thus the only way to start saving money is to cut back on spending. There is a better way—make more money.

When you save money by "cutting back", you are working with very limited resources. For example, if you make $50K per year and have $10K per year as "disposable income", this is essentially all you can possibly save. Also when you save by cutting back, you are, in practical terms, reducing your quality of lifestyle. Giving up the little luxuries in life can be damaging to your self-esteem and positive mental attitude. By making more money, you are increasing your net worth, forcing yourself to think creatively and discover new opportunities, and continuing to spend your extra money on those luxuries in life that we all enjoy so much. Most of all, you are proving to yourself that your income potential is not limited, and was not maxed out.

There are many ways you can use an extra source of income as savings versus cutting back. Here are a few ways:

- **Get a part time job.** If you have the time, look for a part-time job. Choose one where you can learn a skill, trade, or other information that will be helpful in your life's specific purpose. Don't only work for money, work for knowledge.
- **Start a side business.** This is easier now than ever before in history. You do not need a business degree, just a good idea, persistence, and perhaps a little start up cash.
- **Become an affiliate.** The Internet is loaded with opportunities for people to market products from their homes without investing any money, stocking inventory, or

even dealing with finances. Affiliate programs are a great way to boost your income. You can find affiliate programs all over the Internet (hint: look at our sponsor).

- **Ask for a raise.** When was the last time you've asked for a raise? Do you deserve a raise? Ask with confidence and you may be surprised how often you get it.
- **Find a way to increase your existing business.** If you already have a business, how can you attract more customers? How can you sell your customers more product? How can you keep more of your revenues as profit? With a business, there are many ways to tap into extra income.

Realize that your income potential is unlimited, even if your boss tells you otherwise. You are in business for yourself no matter who signs your paycheck. Use your labor, skills, and/or creativity to increase your income to save for the things you desire in life that cost money.

ACTION STEP(S):

1) Is there anything you would like to save up for? What can you do to increase your income and start saving today? Write down some ideas and act on at least one.

"A penny saved is a penny earned."

- Benjamin Franklin

Day 131: How To Get a Raise

One of the easiest ways to immediately increase your income is by asking for a raise. Many people underestimate their value and accept the standard pay schedule set the by organization they work for. Rule number one in asking for a raise is to make sure you are doing more than what is written in your job description and/or do it better than most others in the same position. If you are only doing what you are getting paid for, and doing it no better than the average employee, then your pay is most likely right where it should be.

Here are some questions to ask yourself before asking for a raise. The answers to these questions can help you determine your approximate worth to the organization where you work.

- **How long have you been at the job?** The more time you have invested in the job, the better your chances of getting a raise.
- **Did you sign an employment contract, or otherwise make an agreement to a set pay for a set time?** As a person of honor, it is right to keep our word whether it is verbal or written. You may be able to get a raise now, but you could damage your reputation and any chance for long-term success at the position.
- **Can the organization you work for afford to give you a raise?** You can be the number one employee and be crucial to the organization, but there may just not be enough money to give you a raise.
- **How unique are your skills?** Do you have a job that virtually anyone can do with little training, or does your job require very specialized skills or knowledge that you are one of the few who possess? If the latter, you have a much better chance at getting a raise.
- **How unique is the way you do your job?** I heard of this traffic cop in Provincetown, Massachusetts who does his job with a style of all his own. While he directs traffic, he

dances, spins, and hops around, putting on a good show for spectators. In fact, he is one of the reasons tourists visit the town. The city has even declared a day "Dancing Cop Donald J. Thomas Day". You can be sure that this 42-year veteran of the force can pretty much name his price and get it.

- **Do the person(s) responsible for giving raises know who you are?** Do something to stand out in a positive way. bring donuts for your co-workers, share ideas with your bosses, keep yourself in the spotlight and make an impression.

Once you are convinced that you deserve a raise, it is time to ask for it. Follow these guidelines carefully and at the very least, you will be more appreciated and respected for what you do.

- **Never fear asking, as long as you do it right.** Do not be demanding and never give an ultimatum. Just as you would ask a friend out to dinner, be friendly in your request. Have the attitude that what you are proposing will benefit both parties.
- **Ask with confidence.** Stand or sit up tall, maintain good eye contact, speak in an audible tone of voice, and eliminate the small talk. Confidence tells your boss that you are not just asking for a raise for more money, but that you feel you deserve the raise as well.
- **Ask in person.** If possible, ask for a raise in person. Over 80% of our communication is non-verbal. Allow your confidence and your ability to read people to work to your advantage. Asking via telephone is the next best way to ask for raise because you can still immediately answer any objections or concerns that arise. Finally, at times it may be required to submit a formal request via letter. If this is the case, be sure your letter is checked by at least one other person before sending it out.
- **State your request correctly.** As an employer, here are two of the ways that I most appreciate a request for a raise: 1) ask, "What would I have to do to earn a salary of ___?" or 2) "Here is what I will do for ___". Using the former as

the request, the option of not getting a raise is not even mentioned. This question causes the employer to think of ways to grant your request rather than reacting with a defensive "no". By telling your employer what you will do for the raise shows that you have carefully thought this through, and you are not looking for something for nothing. Choose the method that you are most comfortable using.

Asking for a raise is not that difficult if you feel you truly deserve it. Make sure you are doing more than is expected of you and doing it better than the average employee. Be confident and courteous in your request, state your request correctly, and you will greatly improve your chances of getting the raise you deserve.

ACTION STEP(S):

1) Are you are doing more than what is written in your job description and/or do it better than most others in the same position? If not, start doing it today.

"The only risk of failure is promotion."

- Scott Adams

Days 132 and 133 are for "R&R"—review and reflection. Spend these days reviewing the last five articles and reflecting on the information and how it relates to your life. Now is also a good time to make sure all the action steps for the previous days have been completed.

Day 134: Integrity

The word "integrity" is probably the most overused and most misunderstood word on resumes. So many people use it, but very few actually know what it means. By definition, integrity means "a steadfast adherence to a strict moral or ethical code". Whose moral or ethical code? Your parents'? The Catholic church's? Your friend's? Having integrity is doing what is consistent with **your** beliefs, and living by the moral or ethical code **you** have chosen to adopt. All too often individuals will say things they believe others want to hear, rather than saying what they believe. An example is the single guy who will say anything and everything to get that first date. Having integrity is about being and acting as the real you.

I believe one cannot be truly successful without integrity. Without integrity, one can have the appearance of success, or even short-term success. However, acting without integrity will lead to guilt, which will eventually lead to a self-destruction of one's temporary successes. Acting without integrity has even been linked to physical illnesses such as nausea, headaches and ulcers. It is the desire for short-term gain or immediate gratification that usually causes one to act without integrity, however, the damage it does to one's self-esteem, cancels out any short-term gain.

Integrity is one of the easiest qualities to detect, or detect the lack of, in people you know well. When you know someone well, you are familiar with the actions they have taken in the past and are able to detect inconsistencies. It is these inconsistencies that are usually the result of acting without integrity. When you do act with integrity, others feel as if they can trust you because your actions are more predictable. If they know your beliefs, they can anticipate your behavior and count on you. Integrity is one of the most sought after qualities by parents, employers and customers.

Do you have integrity? Let's take the classic wallet test. Answer this question to yourself and be completely honest. You find a wallet on the street filled with about $500 cash, credit cards, drivers license and other cards. What do you do? Do you

A) keep the cash, ditch the wallet
B) keep the cash, return the wallet
C) keep the cash, try to use the cards to charge as much as possible online where you won't get caught
D) return the wallet with all cash to the owner, based on the information on their driver's license.

Now, how would you answer this question if asked by a reporter on national TV? If your answer was the same for both questions, you have integrity. Yes, even if your answer was C. Integrity is about doing what is consistent with your beliefs, no matter what they are. If, by the way, your answer was anything but D, you may want to take some time to review your beliefs.

Here are some integrity-building suggestions:

- **Don't lie.** Lying is almost always associated with lack of integrity, even if the lying is "justified". Once one is labeled a liar, it is very difficult for that person to be seen as having integrity. As Baltasar Gracian once said, "A single lie destroys a whole reputation of integrity".
- **Don't exaggerate.** Exaggeration is just another form of lying, although less malicious
- **Respond, don't react.** Think before you speak or do. When we act on emotion, we do not always act in accordance with our beliefs.
- **Know your beliefs.** Before you can act consistently with your beliefs, you must know what they are.
- **Strive for long-term success.** Do not be tempted by immediate gratification at the expense of long-term success. Always keep the big picture in your mind.

If you are one who will do "whatever it takes" to succeed, you have the right attitude and certainly the spirit. Just realize that to succeed you must act with integrity at all times and your beliefs must not only be empowering, but they must be ones that do not cause harm to others. Dwight D. Eisenhower said it best when he said, "The supreme quality for leadership is unquestionably integrity. Without it, no real success is possible, no matter whether it is on a section gang, a football field, in an army, or in an office."

ACTION STEP(S):

1) When was the last time you acted without integrity? Why did you act this way? What benefit did you get? How did acting against your beliefs make you feel? What did it do to your self-esteem? What could you have done differently?

"America Online customers are upset because the company has decided to allow advertising in its chat rooms. I can see why: you got computer sex, you can download pornography, people are making dates with 10 year-olds. Hey, what's this? A Pepsi ad? They're ruining the integrity of the Internet!"

- Jay Leno

Day 135: Knowledge Is Only Potential Power

Welcome to day 135. You are over four months into this course and have no doubt been exposed to some valuable information on the achievement of success. Through the use of education, inspiration, and action, it is my goal to see to it that you turn this information into knowledge. However, knowledge itself won't get you much more than a new microwave on a game show perhaps. Knowledge is only potential power. It is knowledge, followed by action and persistence that is true power. It is up to you, and no one else, to use the knowledge you have to produce lasting results.

Think about all of the facts, dates, names, formulas, games, and more you learned going through school. How much of it do you actually remember? If you are like the rest of us, you remember very little. What you do remember is mostly the "important" information like how to read, write, do basic math, communicate and get along with others. In all the years of schooling that followed your first few years, you built upon this knowledge by putting it to use on regular basis, making it second nature. In fact, any knowledge followed by action and persistence, stores that knowledge in your subconscious mind, allowing you to use that information without consciously thinking about it. As an example, when you ride a bike, you do not think about turning, pedaling, balancing, or braking, this is all automatic; it is knowledge that you have previously followed with action and persistence, and committed to your subconscious memory. Once it is there, you will never have to "re-learn" the information again.

Use the information in this course. Put it to use in your daily life. The first few times you use a new piece of knowledge, you will need to put some effort and conscious thought into the process. However, you will soon find that conscious thought is no longer necessary. Just as the law of atrophy applies to the physical body, it applies to the mind and the information within it as well. Keep using it, and you won't ever lose it.

ACTION STEP(S):

1) Take time to once again review all the days so far in this program, or at least select days that contain information you can put to use in your life.

"Information is not knowledge."

- Albert Einstein

Day 136: Inspiration from George Foreman

George Foreman (1949–) is a business man, entertainer, preacher, writer, and professional boxer—the oldest boxer to ever win the world championship (at age 45).

Success is understanding that lack of education does not have to mean lack of success. Foreman dropped out of junior high school and reverted to a life of petty theft, before joining the U.S. Job Corps in 1965.

Success often sprouts from unfortunate events. While in the Job Corps, Foreman was on the verge of expulsion due to his belligerent attitude. Foreman's supervisor saw promise in George's physical strength and began training George to become a boxer. Foreman eventually would make boxing history.

Success is knowing your own weaknesses. "I want to keep fighting because it is the only thing that keeps me out of the hamburger joints. If I don't fight, I'll eat this planet."

Success often stems from turning points. In 1977, Foreman experienced a self-proclaimed religious awakening, immediately retired from boxing, and was ordained a minister by the Church of the Lord Jesus Christ. Foreman then established his own church, counseled prisoners, and some years later, started the George Foreman Youth and Community Center.

Success is not always about winning. In 1991, the 40-year-old Foreman lost a bout for the championship title by decision against Evander Holyfield, but gained a wealth of respect from the boxing industry for his remarkable comeback.

Success is doing the "impossible". At age 45, George Foreman regained the heavyweight title in a dramatic victory over the 26-year-old Michael Moorer. Today, Foreman is known for being the oldest heavyweight boxing champion in history.

Success is found in a strong family life. George and his wife, Mary, have 10 children, 5 boys and 5 girls. Of which, by the way, all the boys are also named "George". This odd naming convention has nothing to do with success, but I felt it was worth mentioning. :)

Success is knowing the destructive power of negativity. "That's my gift. I let that negativity roll off me like water off a duck's back. If it's not positive, I didn't hear it. If you can overcome that, fights are easy."

Success does not have to change who you are. "It embarrasses me to think of all those years I was buying silk suits and alligator shoes that were hurting my feet; cars that I just parked, and the dust would just build up on them."

[Sources: http://www.biography.com, http://www.healthy-grill.com]

"I don't even think about a retirement program because I'm working for the Lord, for the Almighty. And even though the Lord's pay isn't very high, his retirement program is, you might say, out of this world."

- George Foreman

Day 137: Power of Networking

Nowadays, when most people hear the word "networking" they think of interconnected computers or getting their PC connected to the Internet. Long before the advent of the Internet, and even before computers, there was another type of networking; the type where one interacts or engages in informal communication with others for mutual assistance or support. This form of networking is responsible for the success of many individuals and businesses today.

Throughout history, fortunes have been made by people who got their first big break by "a friend of a friend" or other similar contact. These contacts were generally made by networking. By networking with others, you are benefiting in two ways: 1) you are introducing your product or service to another and 2) you are being introduced to others who offer products and services that you may someday require. Additionally, many people use networking to form partnerships or alliances in business. It is a great way to meet like-minded people with the same goals. Networking is a true win-win situation.

Prior to the Internet, networking was almost all done face to face. However, with today's technology networking can be done virtually without having to leave the comfort of your own home. The Internet is full of discussion groups, chat rooms and organizations whose members join for the sole purpose of networking with others. Virtual networking is a great complement to traditional networking but should not be the only source of networking. There is something about face-to-face contact that cannot be achieved by virtual networking.

Here are some tips for effective networking:

- **Let everyone know what you do.** Be proud of what you do and don't hesitate to tell others about it. Give out business cards to people you meet.

- **Keep a personal contacts file.** Keep a file on everyone you meet. The more information you can collect, the better. Most important, keep a record of what they do because someday they may be of service to you.
- **Expose yourself!** Join meetings, groups, functions, chat rooms, forums—any avenue that allows you to network with others. The more exposure you have, the more contacts you can make. Check out the Y2S Workshops— these are excellent places to network with other success-minded individuals!
- **Become an expert in your field.** Once you are known as an expert in your field, your reputation will precede you. You will be able to benefit from the power of networking without even having to network!
- **Give a little.** Offer free advice, suggestions, and help. Look for opportunities to write articles or speak in public. Believe that the more you give, the more you will get in return.
- **Express interest in those with whom you network.** The best question to ask is, "So, what keeps you busy during the day?" This is an open-ended question that encourages those you meet to talk about themselves and what interests them. This is a great way to find out how others may be able to help you, as well as getting other people to like you.
- **Use the 75/25 rule.** When networking with others, allow them to talk about themselves and what they do 75% of the time and only spend 25% of the time talking about yourself and what you do. In their minds, it will seem more like 50/50. Remember, you learn nothing by listening to yourself talk.

It is that one contact that often begins one's unstoppable series of successes. We, of course, cannot always know who that contact will be, but we can play the numbers game and network with as many people as possible. It is through networking one finds opportunity and through opportunity one finds success.

ACTION STEP(S):

---

1) How can you expand your networking today? Write down 10 ways. Out of these 10 ways, act on at least one right away.

"Call it a clan, call it a network, call it a tribe, call it a family. Whatever you call it, whoever you are, you need one."

- Jane Howard

Day 138: Welcome Frustration

Back in 1995, when I had a graphic design business, I wanted to use the Internet to share designs with customers. At the time however, there were only a few "companies" offering web hosting. The first company I went with took my money and ran; the second company's server was only up for about 3 hours a day; and the third company's server was so complex, it took me hours just to upload a photo and make some basic edits to a web page. Out of total frustration, I committed the next 6 months of my life to learn all I could about Internet programming and hosting so I could do it myself, the right way. This was the beginning of Adgrafix, the company I eventually sold for 20 million dollars.

Frustration is such a powerful feeling that we automatically determine it to be negative. We call it negative because it generally does not make us feel very good. Frustration is the feeling that accompanies the experience of being thwarted in attaining your goals. This feeling, although quite painful at times, is a very positive and essential part of success. Frustration is energy that can be positive or negative, depending on what you do with it. Misdirected frustration wasted on cursing, taking it out on others, or kicking the computer is like running the air conditioner with all the windows open—a complete waste of energy.

Why should we welcome frustration, a feeling that is almost always painful? Here are a few main reasons:

- **Pain, especially emotional, can be a major self-motivator.** When motivating ourselves, the need to avoid pain often gets more results than the desire to gain pleasure. We can use this frustration to change what is not working in our lives. It is this constant change, with the desire to reach an end goal, which is known as persistence.
- **Frustration gives us emotion and energy to take action.** There are usually many things to do on the average "to do"

list. However, it is usually those items on the list that cause frustration that get done first.

- **Frustration makes our mind search for alternative action.** There is a thought process of which you may not even be aware; it is the process of searching for alternative actions when you feel frustrated. Frustration usually occurs because, at the time, no suitable alternatives can be found. However, remember that despite your conscious mind's inability to present to you a suitable alternative (I don't consider cursing or kicking the computer suitable), your subconscious mind is still busy searching. Trust your own subconscious mind to find the solution for which you are looking.

There are two primary ways to harness the power of frustration and use it as positive energy. The first way is to release the frustration physically. Frustration is a powerful motivator for exercise. Running, lifting weights, and especially hitting a heavy bag are ways to release the frustration while burning calories and getting in shape! In June 2003, a Brazilian artist opened an exhibition of punching bags in the Santa Cecilia subway station so that commuters could better relieve their frustrations.* The second primary way to harness the power of frustration is to release it mentally. This is the sometimes agonizing process of changing actions and behaviors, searching for alternatives, and just pure perseverance. However, it is this process that led to many of the greatest achievements in history.

Frustration is not bad. It may not feel too good at the time, but once you understand the power of frustration and the incredibly positive effects it can have, you will begin to use frustration to your advantage by bringing yourself closer to success. So next time you are about to kick the computer, kick a heavy bag instead or better yet, kick-start your mind and turn frustration into success.

Source: Jornal da Tarde newspaper, June 12, 2003

ACTION STEP(S):

1) Make a list of all the things that you are currently frustrated with right now in your life. Look at each item on the list and think about what you can do to turn the frustration into opportunity. If you cannot think of anything right away, remember that your subconscious mind will work on the solution for you.

"I've come to believe that all my past failure and frustration were actually laying the foundation for the understandings that have created the new level of living I now enjoy."

- Anthony Robbins

Days 139 and 140 are for "R&R"—review and reflection. Spend these days reviewing the last five articles and reflecting on the information and how it relates to your life. Now is also a good time to make sure all the action steps for the previous days have been completed.

Day 141: Express Sincere Interest in Others

Do you know that person at the party who is constantly rambling on about him or herself, not giving any one else a chance to speak? We all know that person, and the chances are many of us ARE that person. We may not realize it, but others sure do. It was Dale Carnegie who said, over 80 years ago, "You can make more friends in two months by becoming interested in other people than you can in two years by trying to get other people interested in you."

Expressing sincere interest in others is one of the key elements of human relations. By expressing sincere interest in one's appearance, qualities, history, stories, hobbies, work, family, or anything else closely related to that person, you are giving that person a sense of importance and well being.

It seems almost natural that when you express interest in others they will express interest in you. People who are interested in you, become more interesting to you. It is one of those laws of psychology that has been known for centuries. This law applies relationships of any kind.

For most of us, most of the time, expressing interest in others is not difficult. Casual conversation usually leads to questions that one can ask about another, leading them to talk more about their interests or about themselves. However, at times it can be challenging to "force" yourself to express sincere interest in others. Expressing interest without sincerity is the same as patronizing. Here are some suggestions on how to express sincere interest in others.

- **Ask questions about a person's appearance.** Do you like the person's outfit? Haircut? Are they wearing any jewelry that you admire? Do they look like they are in good shape? You can ask questions about someone's appearance without knowing them and without any previous dialog. This is a great way to begin a conversation.

- **Ask a person, "So what keeps you busy during the day?"** This is a very open question that can lead the person to talk about their work, family, hobbies, or just about anything. While they are speaking, listen for any common interests that you may share, and then ask more questions about those interests. This will keep the conversation interesting for the both of you while still allowing the other person to do the majority of the talking.
- **Compliment.** Offer the person a sincere compliment. This often leads to dialog initiated by the person receiving the compliment. A dialog that begins with a compliment is almost always a positive and memorable one.

Remember that everyone is your superior in some way and you can learn something from everyone if you just ask the right questions and do more listening than talking. As one who appreciates the value of learning, it should be easy to be able to express your sincere interest in others. When you do this, you will find yourself closer to success due to your improved relationships.

ACTION STEP(S):

---

1) Start putting this principle to work right now. Start expressing interest in others almost to the point where they say, "What are you writing, a book?" Try this with complete strangers as well and see first hand how your interest in them brightens up their day.

"I've been going on and on... enough about me, let's talk about you. What do you think of me?"

- Unknown

Day 142: Always Look for Opportunity

How many green cars did you see the last time you were on the road? Chances are, green cars were all around you but you did not "see", or at least did not notice, any. Why? Because you were not looking for green cars. Opportunity is the same way. It is all around us, every day of our lives. Since most people are not looking for opportunity, they just don't "see" it. The key is to find opportunity and do not wait for opportunity to find you.

Opportunity is defined as a favorable or advantageous circumstance or combination of circumstances. As expected, the definition is subjective. What is "favorable"? What is "advantageous"? Optimists see most situations as favorable or advantageous where pessimists rarely see themselves in favorable or advantageous situations. So who do you think will have more opportunity, the optimist or the pessimist?

Fortune and success are found in opportunity. One can go back through history and trace the beginning of any fortune or success and find that it was a result of acting on opportunity. The greater the opportunity, the greater the chance for success. One who seeks opportunity asks about every setback, "What good can come out of this?" The opportunity seeker capitalizes and excels where others remain stagnant.

To act on opportunity, you must be flexible, open-minded, motivated, and willing to take risks. You must choose which opportunities you will take action on while passing on less promising opportunities. As an active opportunity seeker, this will be your most difficult task since letting go of a good opportunity is not easy. You need to balance out your opportunities and be decisive on which ones you will pursue, which ones you will delegate, and which ones you will bypass.

Think creatively. The creative thinker sees opportunity where others do not. In 1904, an ice cream vendor named Charles

Menches ran out of dishes while selling ice cream at a state fair. None of the other vendors would sell him any plates out of jealousy and greed, figuring they would get more business. Nearby was a stand where his friend was selling a Middle Eastern, crisp, wafer-like pastry treat called *Zalabia*. "Give me Zalabia!" cried Menches. He rolled up the Zalabia, scooped his ice cream on top, and the ice cream cone was born. This creative thinking allowed Charles Menches to see opportunity where most others would only see disaster—it also made him quite wealthy!

Here are a few suggestions on where you can find opportunity:

- **Crises, problems, setbacks, and challenges.** Very often a step back is followed by two steps forward. It is these setbacks that allow us to grow by exposing us to opportunities that we just did not see before.
- **Everywhere someone's needs are not completely being met.** Think about that. How many of us are actually having all of our needs met? I do not have exact numbers on this one, but I would guess a very small percentage. This means opportunity is everywhere. Be attentive to the needs of others. What do people want? How can you fill that need and act on that opportunity?
- **Something new.** When there is a new business in town, chances are there is opportunity for those seeking employment and those selling business-to-business products or services. When a company releases a new product or service there are opportunities to market the product or service. Virtually anywhere something new is introduced, there is opportunity.
- **The local newspaper.** Local newspapers are filled with opportunities, and I am not just referring to the help wanted section. You can find many opportunities where others are selling businesses, real estate, and other assets.

Opportunity is all around us. It is constantly knocking but most people just can't hear it. Finding opportunity is a learned skill that can be developed with practice. The key is to always be looking for it.

ACTION STEP(S):

---

1) Spend one full day consciously looking for opportunity. Go about your average day, but always be thinking about possible opportunities in everything you do. This will take conscious effort at first, but with a little practice, it will become habit.

"Opportunity dances with those already on the dance floor."

- H. Jackson Brown, Jr.

Day 143: Inspiration from Ray Kroc

Raymond Albert Kroc (1902-1984) was the founder of the McDonald's Corporation; the company that changed the eating habits of the world (for better or worse).

Success is often a result of a decision made in the past. Approximately 17 years prior to founding McDonald's Corporation, Ray Kroc mortgaged his home and invested his life savings into a product called the "Multimixer" in which he strongly believed. It was because of this product he came across the McDonald brothers' hamburger chain and became a partner.

Success is knowing that your best years are still ahead of you, despite your age or current problems. Said Ray Kroc about the time he started McDonald's Corporation, "I was 52 years old. I had diabetes and incipient arthritis. I had lost my gall bladder and most of my thyroid gland in earlier campaigns, but I was convinced that the best was ahead of me."

Success is changing your goals when needed and acting on opportunity. Ray Kroc's initial intention was to open up additional stores for Dick and Mac McDonald so he could send eight of his Multimixers to each store. That goal quickly was abandoned when Ray realized the opportunity he had with franchising these hamburger restaurants.

Success is taking calculated risks. In 1961, Ray bought out the McDonald brothers for $2.7 million cash, using borrowed money, which with the interest, eventually cost him $14 million. As time proved, this was still one of the century's greatest bargains.

Success is having dedication to strict standards. Ray was committed to providing customers with consistent quality, service, cleanliness, and value.

Success is not about the money. "If you work just for money, you'll never make it," Ray Kroc said, "but if you love what you're doing and you always put the customer first, success will be yours."

Success is leadership. Under Ray Kroc's leadership, McDonald's® set standards against which other chains were measured.

Success is spotting trends. Perhaps Ray Kroc's greatest asset was the ability to spot trends. He knew almost instinctively that the fast food, eat-and-run craze would only continue to grow as Americans and other people in the world adapted to a more hectic lifestyle.

Success is being a expert salesperson. Ray Kroc was best known as a master salesperson. It was with his sales skills that he transformed a small chain of eight restaurants into perhaps the largest, most well-known franchise in the world.

[Sources: http://www.media.mcdonalds.com,
http://www.biography.com]

"You're only as good as the people you hire."

- Ray Kroc (1902-1984)

Day 144: The Use and Misuse of Pronouns in the Workplace

I do not have many pet peeves; in fact, peeves do not make very good pets. One I do have is people who work with me isolating themselves from rest of the team or organization by using words like "I", "me", or "mine", and assuming credit or ownership of that which belongs to the team or organization. For example, we once had a system administrator who would constantly refer to our servers as "his" servers. This annoyed me a bit, considering I was the one who paid in excess of $5000 per server, but it also isolated the rest of the members of our team who all had a piece of ownership in our company.

One of the biggest business faux pas one can make is taking credit for a team effort. Taking credit does not have to be telling others that you did all the work; it can be as simple as making an assumptive statement using the word "I" instead of "we". Even when you are working on behalf of a company, it is admirable to share the glory of your work and successes with the other members of the organization by using words like "we", "us" and "ours". This says much for your character.

By simply using plural pronouns, you can make others feel more of a part of what the organization is doing. This gives the others in the organization a feeling of importance that leads to motivation, increased productivity, and greater self-confidence. It encourages participation and feedback and creates an environment of learning and growth.

Here are a few suggestions in the art of using pronouns to empower:

- **Change your vocabulary.** When discussing anything that belongs to the organization, or work done that others had a part in, no matter how insignificant, use words like "we", "us" and "ours".

- **Share the good and take responsibility for the bad.** To a child, this would seem very unfair. But we are not children nor are we expected to act like children in our professional lives. Sharing your successes with others, even if they really had little to do with it, is an admirable act, so is taking full responsibility for mistakes or failures in which others may have had a part. It is during these times that using the words "I", "me" or "mine" become admirable.
- **Give up credit.** If you are really out to make someone feel important, take yourself out of the pronoun and give the other person full credit for the victory. For example, the employees in the design department who won an award may credit it to the team leader by referring to it as "her" award. The team leader would most likely correct the group by calling it "their" award, but the gesture has been made and appreciated.

Use caution when using pronouns in the workplace. A childhood habit of selfishness can develop into a bad habit that keeps success at a distance when you are an adult. Pronouns can also be used as tools to empower and motivate. Choose your words wisely.

ACTION STEP(S):

1) Next time you are about to take full credit for something, think about who you can share the credit with and do it.

"The more credit you give away, the more will come back to you. The more you help others, the more they will want to help you."

- Brian Tracy

Day 145: Success is Health

It was not until recently that I realized firsthand what a crucial part health played in success. I started having debilitating head pains almost daily. When this pain started, I would just have to isolate myself and put up with the pain for anywhere from 15 minutes to several hours. This excruciatingly painful phenomenon that lasted a long six weeks was diagnosed by neurologists to be cluster headaches. To my own surprise, I was not depressed or even down during this time. My eyes were opened by a new appreciation of life and health. During those six weeks, when I was not experiencing the pain, I started to experience appreciation and gratitude like never before.

Health is not just the absence of disease or illness, it is the presence of vitality. It is the lifelong process of prevention and commitment to wellness. If you really thought about it, you could think of something that is physically bothering you right now. Very often minor discomforts are blocked by our *reticular activating system* in our brain, which filters out all that is not important to us at any given moment. This ability of our minds to block discomfort is the same ability that prevents us from appreciating all the times we do not feel discomfort. This causes us to take our health for granted.

At the time of the headaches, I came to a realization: there are times when we cannot control what happens to us health-wise—it just happens. There are also so many ways we can take control of our health and live a healthy lifestyle. So why not do whatever is in our power to live the healthiest lifestyle possible? Then, when fate (God, destiny, chance—call it what you will, just do not call it bad luck!) comes knocking on our door, our bodies, minds and spirits will be better equipped to manage or solve any health problem that comes our way. Several years ago my cousin, who was seriously involved in bodybuilding at the time, was in a fatal car crash that instantly killed the three other passengers in the car. My cousin, who was sitting in the passenger's seat, walked away with a minor concussion and some scratches. The doctors told us that because he was in such great physical shape, he is alive today.

Health does play a crucial part in success. The absence of our health allows us to experience appreciation and gratitude on a whole new level. The presence of health allows us to live a more productive, pain-free life enabling us to get more enjoyment out of life. Being healthy is feeling good about yourself, knowing that you are taking care of your most valuable asset—yourself.

Unless you are living in a bubble somewhere, there will be times when you have to deal with illness. Here are some suggestions to keep you on the road to success at times of illness.

- **Just because your body is ill, it does not mean your mind or spirit have to be ill as well.** It is all about maintaining your positive mental attitude.
- **If your illness is temporary, see it as temporary.** Setbacks in life are common and expected. Keep your sight on your life's goals and never let temporary illness take you off course.
- **Focus your attention on anything but your illness.** Be active if possible, practice mind control and focus on empowering and positive feelings.
- **Do something about your illness and work on future prevention.** Is this something you could have prevented? If so, how? Make changes in your life if necessary to avoid illness and learn from each experience.

Remember that health is not just the absence of illness, it is the presence of vitality. Here are some suggestions to help you reach and maintain your ideal health while enjoying life to the fullest.

- **Eat well.** "Let your food be your medicine," said Hippocrates, the Father of Medicine. Many believe that the foods we eat have a significant effect on both our short-term and long-term health. We literally are what we eat. If we put garbage in, we get garbage out. Eating well does not mean eating diet foods; in fact, I wouldn't touch a frozen "diet food" dinner if you paid me. Eating well begins with learning about foods that have positive effects on your body and mind. Bookstores are loaded with books on this topic.

- **Exercise more.** Both your body and mind need activity to grow stronger. Maintain physical and mental fitness programs that keep you in your best shape.
- **Lose excess weight.** If you are like most Americans, you probably can lose a few pounds. As you lose fat, your body becomes a more efficient "fat burning" machine. Conversely, as you pack on the pounds, it becomes increasingly more difficult to lose the weight.
- **Make healthier choices.** Eating well does not have to happen overnight. In fact, I began the process almost 10 years ago when I chose to no longer eat red meat. Since then, I have made dozens of healthier choices like drinking water rather than diet soda, using olive oil in place of butter, snacking on nuts rather than candy, and other relatively painless dietary changes.
- **Don't neglect checkups.** See your doctor(s) on a regular basis. Many health problems are insignificant when taken care of early enough. Do not let your fear of doctors, or the sharp needles they stick into you, keep you from health.

Most people's definition of success includes some level of health. It is very difficult to enjoy anything, including success, if your mind is continuously focused on your illnesses, pain, heartburn, lethargy, and/or the extra 20 pounds of fat you are carrying around with you. You have full control over many aspects of your health, so take control of what you can today and live with vitality.

ACTION STEP(S):

1) If you are overweight, commit to losing just 2 pounds. This two pounds of loss fat will allow your body to burn more calories than before and start a chain reaction that just may bring you down to your ideal weight.

2) Make a healthy choice today. Choose grilled chicken or fish over a hamburger or steak. Have a glass of fresh juice instead of a cup of coffee. Snack on fruit or veggies instead of candy and pastries. A healthy lifestyle begins with small and frequent healthy choices.

3) Make an appointment for a checkup. If your last visit to the doctor took place sometime last century, it is time to make another appointment.

"What is called genius is the abundance of life and health."

- Henry David Thoreau

Days 146 and 147 are for "R&R"—review and reflection. Spend these days reviewing the last five articles and reflecting on the information and how it relates to your life. Now is also a good time to make sure all the action steps for the previous days have been completed.

Day 148: Let it Go

One of my favorite all-time recurring characters on *Saturday Night Live* is the "grumpy old man" played by Dana Carvey. Dana does his impression of an 80-year-old man who is angry at the world. This character represents a man who never let go of a lifetime of grudges, resentment and hate. While Dana's portrayal of this character is very funny, it is a sad truth that the world is full people just like this, both male and female, of all ages.

Let it go. Three little words that mean so much in the pursuit of happiness. These words apply to grudges, resentment, hate, fear, and any other negative, self-destructive feeling or emotion. One of my favorite movie lines is from *Get Shorty*, where John Travolta plays a tough, but very likeable "wiseguy" named Chili Palmer. Just after the scene where he escapes death after fighting on a roof, Karen asks Chili if he is scared. He replies, "I was." "You're not anymore?" asks Karen. Chili responds, "How long do you want me to be scared for?"

We already know that it is only possible for our brains to focus on one thing at a time. While we are focusing on fear, worry, or hate, it is not possible for us to be experiencing happiness, enthusiasm or love. As time passes, we seem to hold on to more and more of these negative feelings and emotions. When we do this, our lives become consumed with negativity and the innocence of youth is gone.

Let it go. You certainly do not need to sabotage your own happiness and success by holding on to negative emotions. You can choose to move on, forgive and forget, and once again focus on the more positive and empowering emotions. Here are some suggestions on how you can "let it go".

- **Don't let other people control your emotions.** Easier said than done, but certainly possible with practice. When another person angers or upsets you, it is only because you have allowed that person to. This is what is meant by "don't let him get to you".

- **Don't carry grudges.** A grudge is one of the most wasteful forms of mental energy there is, with some grudges lasting lifetimes. End arguments when they start. Come to a resolution as soon as possible and communicate. Don't let another's actions or behaviors cause you negative feelings. Talk it out.
- **Ask yourself, "Is feeling this way doing me any good?"** Chances are it is not. It is only human to feel negative emotions and we all feel them. However, those who understand happiness and success know that prolonged negative feelings are pointless and a complete waste of energy. Know when to say when.
- **Remain focused on your life purpose and goals.** When your mind is preoccupied with more important thoughts, such as your life purpose, it is much easier to let go of minor grievances that get in your way.
- **Put things in perspective.** Instead of spending all day angry at your significant other for not taking out the garbage, think for a moment how fortunate you are to have that person in your life.
- **Remember that we all operate on different sets of beliefs.** Everyone was not raised the same way with the same experiences in the same situations. Our belief systems are all different. We must be open minded to those who act and behave differently than we do rather than resenting or even hating them for it.
- **Make amends.** Are there any relationships right now in your life that can use fixing? Are you still living with guilt for something you did to someone years ago? It is never too late to do the right thing. Make amends and start living with a clean slate today.

Let it go. We only come around this way once and our time on this earth is precious. We can choose to live with happiness or misery. Focus your mental energy on your life purpose and goals rather than the negative emotions that suck the enjoyment from life. Enjoy your life to the fullest—you deserve it.

ACTION STEP(S):

---

1) Make amends. Are there any relationships right now in your life that can use fixing? Are you still living with guilt for something you did to someone years ago? It is never too late to do the right thing. Make amends and start living with a clean slate today.

"In my day we didn't have movies with all these special effects and action sequences. Somebody would shine a lamp on a wall in a dark room and make shadows with his hands. And we liked it!"

- Dana Carvey as "Grumpy Old Man"

Day 149: Never Be Wrong Again

High self-confidence and success are often directly related. As you become more and more successful, your self-confidence increases, sometimes to the point where you believe you are right in just about everything you do and say. Very often, you may be right, but when you are wrong, and you project a cocky attitude, others will be all over you for it.

What if through careful use of words, you could always be right and never be wrong again? How would that help you in your personal life? How about professional life? This technique is not a magic one that will make you smarter, but it is simply a communication technique that can help you to better articulate your beliefs and opinions and make it impossible for others to disagree with you. See if you can disagree with these statements:

I believe the sky is green.
In my opinion, people from Boston smell like donuts.

You may know, or at least you may think you know, that the sky is blue. You may have never smelled donuts on people from Boston, but you cannot say that those statements are wrong. Why? Because the statements use words that express opinion or belief, which, assuming one is not lying, cannot be wrong. For example, the person making the first statement is not saying the sky is green, they are saying *they believe* the sky is green. You can certainly question their belief and even present them with facts in order to change their belief, but you cannot say that they are wrong for their belief.

Stating beliefs, opinions, or facts you are unsure of (thus they are beliefs) in a way that makes it obvious it is your belief or opinion, versus stating a belief or opinion as a fact, is a habit of successful communicators. Here are some reasons why this is such an important technique:

- **Avoid arguments.** One cannot argue with your beliefs or opinions when clearly stated as such. Often people disagree with an opinion when stated as a fact just by reaction.
- **Avoid animosity.** If you state an opinion as a fact, whether you are right or wrong, if the person you are making the statement to has a different opinion, you have created friction and possible animosity.
- **Project self-confidence and not cockiness.** People are labeled "cocky" when they state opinions and beliefs as facts.
- **Prevent disagreement.** Win more debates, have greater influence over others, and just be seen as someone who is not known to be wrong.

The key to this technique is 1) knowing the difference between a fact and your opinion or belief and 2) knowing how to state your opinion or belief as an opinion or belief. Begin by asking yourself, "Can this statement be reasonably argued?" For example, if you are holding a pen you can, with certainty, say "I am holding a pen". However, if the lighting is poor, can you say with certainty that the pen is dark blue? Is it possible it is black? Or even maroon? When unsure of a fact or expressing a belief or opinion use phrases like:

I believe
I feel
I think
It is my understanding that
In my opinion
I could be wrong, but

Using words and phrases such as "can", "may", "it's possible that", "it's one of", "at times", etc., has similar benefits, but can also be argued with. For example:

It is possible that men have never walked on the moon, and the whole thing was a just a staged event to put the U.S. ahead in the space race.

The words "it is possible that" makes it difficult to disagree with this statement, unless said to a member one of the Apollo missions that actually walked on the moon. There are even some people who are not as open-minded as you or I, who would disagree with statements like this just based on what they believe are facts. So choose your words wisely.

In my opinion, this is one of the best communication techniques there is. It gives listeners or readers the opportunity to have a different opinion, but does not give them a chance to disagree with the statement made. Be careful not to abuse this technique by "watering down" known facts, but use this technique when there is even the slightest chance the fact is an opinion. As a writer or speaker, this can give you credibility with your audience while helping you to become a more successful communicator.

ACTION STEP(S):

1) Write down your top beliefs and opinions that you most often share with others. How do you state these when sharing? Write down how you will state them from now on.

"I believe that a simple and unassuming manner of life is best for everyone, best both for the body and the mind."

- Albert Einstein

Day 150: Inspiration from Walt Disney

Walt Disney (1901-1966) was the creator of Mickey Mouse and founder of the Disneyland® and Walt Disney World® Theme Parks.

Success begins with imagination. Disney is known as a pioneer, an innovator and the possessor of one of the most fertile imaginations the world has ever known.

Success begins with a dream. In 1923, Walt Disney left Kansas City for Hollywood with nothing but a few drawing materials, $40 in his pocket, and a completed animated and live-action film.

Success is solving problems. Later in his career, Disney turned his attention toward the problem of improving the quality of urban life in America. He personally directed the design of an Experimental Prototype Community of Tomorrow, or EPCOT®.

Success begins with passion. "Disneyland is a work of love. We didn't go into Disneyland just with the idea of making money."

Success is having vision. In 1965, Disney directed the purchase of 43 square miles of virgin land—twice the size of Manhattan—in the center of the state of Florida. Here he master-planned a whole Disney world of entertainment to include a new amusement theme park, a motel-hotel resort vacation center, and his Experimental Prototype Community of Tomorrow. After more than seven years of master planning and preparation, including 52 months of actual construction, Walt Disney World opened to the public as scheduled on October 1, 1971.

Success is overcoming adversity. "All the adversity I've had in my life, all my troubles and obstacles, have strengthened me...

You may not realize it when it happens, but a kick in the teeth may be the best thing in the world for you."

Success is being optimistic. Disney is one of history's best known optimists. His visions and dreams for a brighter future took shape in Epcot Center, which opened on October 1, 1982. • "The era we are living in today is a dream coming true." • "I always like to look on the optimistic side of life, but I am realistic enough to know that life is a complex matter."

Success is thinking huge. "Here in Florida, we have something special we never enjoyed at Disneyland...the blessing of size. There's enough land here to hold all the ideas and plans we can possibly imagine."

Success is welcoming competition. "I have been up against tough competition all my life. I wouldn't know how to get along without it."

[Source: http://disney.go.com, http://www.biography.com]

"The way to get started is to quit talking and begin doing."

- Walt Disney

Day 151: Let's Make $1,000,000.00

Whenever I come across a book, article, or website on making a million dollars, I notice the method used is either A) a long-term secure investment strategy that begins at age 20 and matures at age 65 or B) an attempt to get readers to sell the author's product. Well, the strategy I am about to propose is one that will take 7 years, not 45, and it does not have anything to do with selling our services. It is the same formula I used to build Adgrafix, which in 7 years I sold for 20 times the one million dollar goal. If acquiring more money is part of your definition of success, then read on.

Why one million dollars? Why not? It is a nice round number that many people use as a basis for wealth. Sure, one million dollars is not the same today as it was 25 years ago, but it is certainly an amount that most people on this earth would be happy to have.

This formula is a general formula not an exact "how to". It is up to you, using the knowledge you have already acquired in this course, to fill in the details and make this formula work for you. The formula itself is quite simple, but as powerful and real as they come. I call this the "RAM" formula, and I will explain why in a moment. This is a formula that will take seven years to make one million dollars. Your results may vary by taking longer, shorter, having less, or as in my case, having much more in the seventh year.

You begin by setting a goal to make an extra $8000 in one year. In today's economy, $8000 in one year is not that difficult to make. It is a mere $22 per day. This can be achieved with a part-time job or side business. This $8000 you make should be spent 100 percent on this goal of making a million dollars. Do not hoard this money or spend it on anything but that which will help you to double your money in the next year. This means in year two, your goal is to make $16,000, but this time, you have $8000 to work with as "investment capital". Repeat this process for seven straight years and you will have made over one million dollars.

Continue this process for one more year you can keep the one million dollars you have made in the previous year and call it quits if you wanted to.

Year 1: $8000
Year 2: $16,000
Year 3: $32,000
Year 4: $64,000
Year 5: $128,000
Year 6: $256,000
Year 7: $512,000

The numbers in this formula are the same incremental numbers used for a computer's random access memory, or RAM, thus the name the "RAM" formula.

There is a big bonus by following this formula; to make these numbers on the high end, you will almost certainly need to create something of value that can be marketed. This "something of value" which you are creating is called an asset, which, unless it is you or your time, can generally be sold when you are done with it. The sale of this asset can make you more than double all of the money you have ever earned from the asset, allow you great tax advantages, and allow you to keep more of what you make.

As I said, this is a general formula to follow. It is very reasonable, since doubling a non-fixed income in one year is a goal that is very achievable. In fact, people do it every single day. It is up to you to fill in the details by adapting this formula to your life. At the end of seven years, with patience, determination, and persistence, you will have made one million dollars.

ACTION STEP(S):

1) Devise a plan to make $8000 within the next year.

Day 152: Introduction to Affiliate Marketing

I am often asked why I think our web hosting companies do so well considering the intense competition in this market. To keep from sounding like one of our ads, I will keep the answer to this question brief. I believe our success in the industry has to do with many factors such as support, automation, software, in-depth knowledge of the industry and market, and most of all, our people. Since 1995 we have capitalized on perhaps our greatest strength— our people—and built one of the first Internet-based reseller models, known today as affiliate marketing. In the past several years, affiliate marketing has made businesses millions and ordinary people millionaires.

Affiliate marketing is a powerful form of Internet marketing that began right around the commercialization of the Internet. It is a form of network marketing that capitalizes on technology and the communication network of the Internet. Affiliate marketing allows virtually any person, with little or no qualifications besides the desire to market a product or service, the opportunity to achieve financial success while helping the organization running the affiliate program do the same. It is a true win-win situation.

If you are looking for a part-time job with unlimited potential, affiliate marketing is an ideal solution, especially if you are one who is unable or unwilling to travel. The greatest part of affiliate marketing is that there is no inventory to keep, no finances to manage, and no risk to assume. You just market the product or service and collect your commission. In addition, many affiliate programs have online education available. For example, we actually use this site, YearToSuccess.com, to help educate, motivate, and inspire our affiliates at HostingScouts.com.

Over the years I have heard some great stories from our affiliates who have used the extra income to live the lifestyle they always dreamed of, while keeping their low-paying jobs that they love.

Others have completely changed their careers based on their success with affiliate marketing. Affiliate marketing can fit nicely into just about anyone's plan for success.

Here are my three steps for affiliate marketing success (as an affiliate).

1. **Identify your market.** Do you have any unique opportunities or "ins" with a certain market, either via personal contact or a website? Do you have knowledge in a specific market to which you would be more comfortable marketing? In which market do you think you would have the most success?

2. **Choose your product or service to market.** Today, as an affiliate, you can market just about any product or service imaginable and choose the product or service based on your contacts, background, or unique opportunities. For example, if you work at a flower shop and know many florists in the industry, you may choose to market a product or service geared toward that group. Or if you happen to run a website on surfing, perhaps you can market surfing books and surfing related products. Some simple searches on Google can help you find such programs. Consider the following when choosing a program:

   o **Reputation of the company.** How long have they been around? How many affiliates do they currently have? Do they have open forums where you can communicate with their other affiliates?
   o **Marketability of the product or service.** Is this a product that is easy or difficult to sell? Is there a large enough market for it?
   o **One time commission.** How much do you get for selling the product? Is it enough to justify your effort?
   o **Residual commission.** Do you continue to get paid each month or each year after the product is sold?

It is worth looking into companies that provide residual commissions. This is a great way to leverage your time and energy and have your money work for you.

o **Support from the company.** How easy is it to get sales assistance, product support or sales support? How responsive is the company?

3. **Sell!** Nobody makes any money until a sale is made. If you are marketing via person-to-person, or marketing via the Internet, you need to be actively working on building relationships that will lead to sales. Do not just put up some ads or a website and wait for sales to come to you. In this market, you need to be active.

For organizations, implementation of affiliate marketing programs has been identified as the key element to their success. Amazon.com was one of the first well-known companies to implement an affiliate marketing program. As a result, they are the largest online e-tailer having the most products, sales and affiliates. At Archieboy, our affiliates are responsible for over 80% of our sales and that number is growing. Implementation of an affiliate program is not that difficult and certainly is worth it.

Whether you are an individual looking for some extra money or a business looking to greatly increase sales through a new channel, affiliate marketing is a new way of selling for the 21st century that can help.

ACTION STEP(S):

---

1) Take a few moments to get some unbiased information on affiliate marketing at http://www.iafma.org.

"Affiliate marketing has made businesses millions and ordinary people millionaires."

- Bo Bennett

Days 153 and 154 are for "R&R"—review and reflection. Spend these days reviewing the last five articles and reflecting on the information and how it relates to your life. Now is also a good time to make sure all the action steps for the previous days have been completed.

Day 155: How To Lose a JOB in 10 Days

One of my favorite recent movies was _How To Lose a Guy In 10 Days_. I know it sounds like a bit of a "chic flick", but it's not. It is a hilarious movie about the more common things women do to turn men away in relationships. So in the spirit of fun, I chose to write this article in the same style of what NOT to do, but instead of relationships, this is about how to lose a _job_. So if you are interested in getting fired, or if you are interested in learning what NOT to do to keep your job, read on.

In today's job market, jobs are competitive and it is generally easier for employers to find good employees than for employees to find good jobs. If you are one of the persistent individuals that have made it into a position that you really enjoy, it is up to you to keep your job. If you are truly an asset to the company, the chances are that no recession, cutback, or takeover will cause you to lose your job. What will cause you to lose your job is doing one or more of the many things the average employee does every day. So here we go...

How to lose a job in 10 days (begin sarcasm)

- **Be irresponsible.** Don't do things when you say you are going to do them, make promises and don't keep them, forget things, keep your schedule in your head, don't bother writing things down, and don't bother returning messages. After all, with so many starving children in the world, does it really matter that you miss a few assignments?
- **Don't listen.** Just because your body has to be at an important meeting, it does not mean your mind has to be there. Drift off into la-la land where you are sunning on a tropical beach. Chances are someone else at the meeting was listening and you can ask them what it was about. If asked a direct question in the meeting, simply answer, "I'll have to get back to you on that one". It is a safe answer that will work about 80% of the time. The other 20% of the

time just blame your irrelevant answer on some medication that you have recently taken.

- **Treat your co-workers with envy and resentment.** Your co-workers are really all out to get you. It is a big conspiracy against you and only you. Everyone is talking about you behind your back. Those below you all want your job and those above you want to see someone else in your job.

- **Make excuses for everything.** Buy a book on excuses and keep it handy. As long as you have a good excuse, you will never have to work another day in your life. Don't only play the blame game, but win it as well. Nothing is ever your fault, but even when you think it is, blame someone or something else.

- **Do the bare minimum.** If your company really wanted you to do more than the bare minimum, they would pay you more. Do just what you think is enough not to get fired.

- **Lack self-confidence.** When asked to do something say, "Are you serious?" or "I don't think I can do that". It is also a good idea to ask your boss at least once a day if they have any plans for letting you go.

- **Take your personal frustrations to work with you.** Have problems on the homefront? Don't take it out on your family, take it out on your customers and co-workers instead. Chances are, they deserve it anyway.

- **Criticize everything.** Nobody really knows anything at your company besides you. If everyone did things the way you think they should be done, everyone would be happy and the company would be perfect. Tell everyone how they should be doing their jobs, shoot down any ideas not proposed by you. If you do not like the way something is being done, tell everyone in the most negative way possible.

- **Maintain an unattractive personality.** Be negative, never smile or laugh, don't be friendly to anyone unless there is something in it for you. Annoy people when you get the chance. Talk about your problems and all the evil in the world.

- **Despise your job.** Follow the law of nature—leisure time is for fun and work time is for pain and boredom. If you do enjoy your job, you are really not working so you really should not be paid.

(end sarcasm)

Losing a job is not difficult; it is maintaining a job that is the challenge. However, with the right attitude and strong human relationship skills, you can have a greater sense of security in any job you choose. Just DON'T follow the advice above! :)

ACTION STEP(S):

---

1) If you are the boss, or if you were the boss, write down how you would want your employees or subordinates to perform. What qualities would you want them to have? Do you possess these qualities yourself?

"That's what I'm talking about. Where's the sexy, cool, fun, smart, beautiful Andie that I knew? The one that wanted to be a serious journalist? You're up, you're down, you're here, you're there, you're like a fricken' one woman circus."

- Ben from "How to Lose a Guy in 10 Days"

Day 156: Speed Reading for Success

It has been said that knowledge is power. We have rephrased that to "knowledge is potential power". In either case, before we can convert the knowledge into power we must first obtain the knowledge through one of our five senses. For most of us, our primary source of knowledge comes from reading. Your ability to read effectively plays an important role in your attainment of knowledge and thus an important part in your success.

Effective reading consists of both speed and comprehension. Contrary to popular belief, in most cases comprehension actually increases with speed reading since speed reading helps prevent one's mind from drifting while reading. When one's mind drifts, it is necessary to reread which not only slows the rate at which one can gather information, but it effects one's confidence in his or her reading ability as well.

In just about every career, the ability to read is a must. In higher-paying careers, the ability to read *well* is a must. Imagine being able to read twice as fast as you are currently reading without losing any comprehension. Now imagine being able to read ten times faster. This is something that is certainly possible. Speed reading will increase your ability to absorb information, which can be processed into knowledge, which can then be converted into power, which ultimately leads to greater success!

Before you can become an effective speed reader, you must a) have a good understanding of basic reading skills (like in the recognition of words without sounding out the letters) and b) have a decent vocabulary. Of course, this is all relevant to the level of information you are reading. Words that you are unfamiliar with can act as obstacles and quickly slow you down.

Tips on Speed Reading

1. **Know what information you want from a document before you start reading it.** If you know what you are looking for, you will find it and retain it in your memory much easier. For the most part, the key idea is usually placed in the first sentence of each paragraph. Scanning titles and headers can be a big help to finding information as well.

2. **Focus your eyes on blocks of words.** When we first learned how to read, we started reading each letter. We eventually moved to words, which is where many adult readers are still today. Your mind is capable of so much more; you just need to push it a little.

3. **Increase the number of words read in each block.** The goal is increase the size of a block to contain as many words as your peripheral vision can handle.

4. **Reduce the length of time spent reading each block.** Speed comes in time and with practice.

5. **Reduce the number of times your eyes skip back to a previous sentence.** This is a habit that can be broken using one of several hand methods. A common method is to place your right hand on the page and slowly move it straight down the page in a slow and even motion, drawing your eyes down as you read. This hand motion will not only help you keep your place, but it will help you to read faster as well. Make it a game, try to keep up with your hand.

6. **Avoid vocalization.** When reading, make sure your mouth is kept shut. If you are trying to keep your mouth and mind in synch, you will never advance to a fast pace and your mind will get bored waiting for your mouth and wander. Also do your best not to say the words in your head. This is more difficult, but can be done with practice. If necessary, say only the key words in your mind.

7. **Remember selectively.** Depending on the style of writing, authors usually elaborate on ideas with statistics, quotes, examples, anecdotes and other forms of clarification. If you understand the main concept being presented, then

skipping over these clarifications and not trying to store them in your memory will help you to better remember the main ideas while helping you read faster.

8. **Practice!** If you are one of the fortunate people who read for enjoyment and relaxation, then you have an advantage over those of us who prefer audio and video entertainment. Practice speed reading whenever you read but don't spend all your time buried in books practicing. As Albert Einstein said, "Reading, after a certain age, diverts the mind too much from its creative pursuits. Any man who reads too much and uses his own brain too little falls into lazy habits of thinking."

Our minds are like sponges with no known limits as to how much they can absorb. One of the major limiting factors in how much we can learn is the time we have. Speed reading can allow us to absorb much more information in the same period of time, while retaining more of what we absorb. Practice speed reading and begin enjoying the benefits.

ACTION STEP(S):

1) Read this article once more by speed reading. Practice the tips in this article.

2) Commit to increasing the pace of your reading from this point on, even if just a small percentage to start. In the long run, this will save you a significant amount of time.

"I was reading the dictionary. I thought it was a poem about everything."

- Steven Wright

Day 157: Inspiration from Mary Kay Ash

Mary Kay Ash (1915–2001) was the founder of Mary Kay, Inc. Mary Kay does business in more than 30 markets on five continents and generated 2002 sales of nearly $1.6 billion in wholesale sales worldwide.

Success is focusing on the human aspect of business. Mary's idea of P&L was "people and love" rather than "profit and loss". Mary Kay, nevertheless, powered a corporate colossus. Mary personally sent birthday cards to each employee and wrote notes of encouragement on her trademark pink stationery.

Success is encouragement. "My mother's words became the theme of my childhood," Mary said. "They have stayed with me all my life: 'You can do it.'"

Success is focusing on your aptitude. Mary was studying to be a doctor while raising three children and working sales part-time. She changed direction, however, when an aptitude test showed that her sales ability outranked her science ability.

Success stems from frustration. As the national sales director for WorldGift, Mary witnessed her male colleagues being promoted ahead of her at twice her salary. She retired from corporate sales and later started her billion-dollar empire.

Success is creating an opportunity where one does not exist. Mary theorized about a dream company in several of her books she had written after "retirement", then decided to create the dream company.

Success is pressing on when faced with adversity. Just one month before the scheduled opening of Mary Kay, Inc., Mary's husband died. But thanks to the encouragement of her children, Mary Kay, Inc. did open. Mary wrote, "I knew I would never have a second chance to put my dream into action."

Success is making sacrifices. To attend college, conduct sales, and raise three kids alone, Mary Kay sacrificed a social life—and sleep. "Each goal had a price, and my spirit of competition always helped me feel that the price was worth it."

Success is optimism. "Every successful entrepreneur I've ever met has been an incurable optimist."

Success is believing in yourself. Today, Mary Kay's company and philanthropy still live by her message. "If you think you can, you can. And if you think you can't, you're right."

[Source: http://www.marykay.com]

"Aerodynamically the bumblebee shouldn't be able to fly, but the bumblebee doesn't know that so it goes on flying anyway."

- Mary Kay Ash

Day 158: What ELSE Can I Do?

When creating YearToSuccess.com, I knew that the success of this program would be based on member referrals. This led to me to the question, "What can I do to encourage member referrals?" Once I had some basic ideas and put them into effect, I could have stopped. However, for this program to be successful, I have to continually ask myself, "What else can I do?" This question, although not always an immediate answer producer, has led me to find new solutions and create new tools to help our members share this site, thus increasing membership. Too often instead of asking what else can be done, people make statements such as, "I've done all I can." My reply to that statement is, "Have you?"

There is no limit to success nor any limit to the effort you can make or actions you can take to get you there. If you ask yourself the question, "What else can I do?" you will get an answer. If by habit you insist on responding with a statement that closes the door of possibility, then ask yourself, "If there WERE something else I could do, what would it be?" Do not let yourself off the hook so easily.

Asking yourself this question is persistence in action. You know that persistence is paramount in the achievement of success, and you know you have a practical method to persist. There is always another way. When you tell yourself that you are doing all you can, you are essentially giving yourself a way out. Only when you ask yourself what more can you do, will your mind provide you with an answer.

This is also a powerful question to ask as a leader. By asking your team, "What else can we do to accomplish our objective?" you are encouraging participation by opening up your team members' minds to the possibility that more can be done. This begins the thinking process that eventually results in solutions, good ideas, and breakthroughs.

When do you stop asking this question? When you have reached your goal or objective or have made a conscious choice to no longer spend time in pursuit of the goal or objective. There is always another way, but sometimes that other way may be to back out and cut your losses.

"What else can I do?" This question has many forms and can be worded in many ways. The purpose is to keep your mind open to possibilities and persist where others do not. Next time you feel that you have reached a dead end, ask what else can be done. The answers you receive can bring you closer to success.

ACTION STEP(S):

1) List at least three areas in your life where you feel you have reached a plateau. Now ask yourself, "What else can I do?"

"The majority of men meet with failure because of their lack of persistence in creating new plans to take the place of those which fail."

- Napoleon Hill

Day 159: Good Things About a Bad Economy

It is tough at times during a recession (oops... slow economy) to be so positive and upbeat in the presence of others who are obviously affected by such times. While I do sympathize, I also believe we live in our own little worlds and we can choose to focus on the negative or the positive; the choice is ours.

Since the beginning of existence there have been times of abundance and times of deficiency. It is important to remember that this is cyclical and times of deficiency do not and will not last. It may feel like it, but as sure as the spring will follow the winter, prosperity and economic growth will follow recession. Remembering this single fact alone can completely change your outlook on life.

An economy is only "bad" if you perceive it that way. A bad economy can be, and is, good for many people. What is so good about a bad economy?

Cleansing of the market. A slow economy it is a time of metamorphosis—like the caterpillar turning into a butterfly. It is a time when stupid financial mistakes catch up to investors and they ask themselves, "What the heck was I thinking!?" It is a time of both learning and growing. But most of all, it is a time when businesses are put to the test and have to prove what they are really made of. As prospects are few and far between, the market will decide, by an almost Darwinian process, which businesses will survive and which will perish. To the business person, this means fewer competitors. To the consumer, this means a higher quality selection.

Improved service levels. Whether you are in business or not, a slow economy seems to be a positive jolt for all in a service related business. From the plumber who returns your call promptly, to the vendor that goes the extra mile to keep you satisfied, companies begin to realize how valuable your business is and therefore treat you accordingly.

Low and negotiable prices. Believe it or not, there is balance to the economy. When times are tough, merchants reduce their prices to stimulate sales, just like the Fed lowers the reserve rate. Merchants understand that there is less money being spent, so in response they lower prices. Their vendors understand this as well, so the merchants get lower prices and so on. The key is to know to ask for the discounts or the "special deals". Ask your credit card company or your bank for lower interest rates, call your phone company and ask for lower long distance rates. You will be pleasantly surprised by the results.

Good help is *easy* to find. During a time when a large number of people are without work, or even just looking for extra income, it is easier for an employer to attract qualified help.

Being your best. Some say slow economies bring out the worst in people. While certainly in some cases that may be true, I happen to believe that slow economies bring out the best in people. For many it is a time of reevaluation—a time of reflection where changes are made to become a better person. People learn new skills or brush up on existing skills. The same holds true for businesses. For businesses, this means improving products and services, creating new products or services and streamlining operations.

The benefits of a slow economy can be summed up with one word: opportunity. Think positively. Keep in mind that prosperous times are ahead. As a consumer, you have the upper hand; it is a buyer's market. And as an employer you have the upper hand; it is an employer's market. Most of all, remember the old saying, what doesn't kill you, makes you stronger.

ACTION STEP(S):

1) How do you feel about a slow economy? How can you change your thinking to prosper in a slow economy? Jot down some ideas.

"Tough times don't last but tough people do."

- Robert H. Schuller

Days 160 and 161 are for "R&R"—review and reflection. Spend these days reviewing the last five articles and reflecting on the information and how it relates to your life. Now is also a good time to make sure all the action steps for the previous days have been completed.

Day 162: Learn How to Say NO

In the world of sales, when a prospect says "no" or "not interested", what it really means is that the prospect needs more information. It is estimated that more than 50% of the time we say no, we are doing so out of reflex or habit. At the same time, many people are pressured into saying yes when they really mean no mostly out of fear of offending or fear of standing out. Every day we end up getting stuck doing things we do not want to do, buying things we really don't want, and missing opportunities because we do not know how to say no.

My friend once told me of a time he was invited to this "party". The party took place in a hotel conference room. As soon as all of the "guests" arrived, the doors were shut behind them and out came running an overly-excited guy with a microphone welcoming everyone to the party and "letting them in" on a "ground floor opportunity". Here was a group of people who were misled by someone whom they most likely trusted into coming to what they believed was a purely social event, which really turned out to be a high pressure sales situation. The tactic used by these high pressure salespeople was to get the prospects into a situation where refusing their offer would cause them embarrassment or at least discomfort. Fortunately, my friend had enough business sense to know what was going on and enough self-confidence to reject the offer. Way to go, Keith!

In today's world of high-pressure sales, learning how to say no is a must, especially in business where just one bad purchasing decision can lead to the failure of the company. However, do not react with an immediate no without understanding the offer. This hasty reaction can result in a missed opportunity. Remember, when you say no too quickly, any salesperson with even a little experience would move on to countering the rejection, thus not letting you off the hook. So how do we get off the hook?

Offer an explanation. Most people feel that no means no and they do not need to give an explanation. While this may be true, it is not good communication. People often avoid giving explanations to salespeople because they do not want to give them information that they can counter. In these cases, or in any case where you do not feel comfortable sharing the truth, say "I am sorry, but I have to say no for personal reasons" rather than "because I said" or "just because" as an explanation. It is hard to argue with that! Another favorite of mine is "I am sorry, but I have no interest whatsoever." This is both polite yet decisive enough so that any decent sales person would simply thank you for your time and move on.

Offer a substitute. This technique works great when friends or family ask you to do something you really do not want to do. Instead of saying yes to avoid embarrassment or an awkward situation, say yes, but to an alternative proposal. At times, I am asked by friends to invest in their ideas. When I feel that it would be a poor investment, rather than simply saying no, or offering some lame excuse, I offer my assistance by offering them a free website and some advice. While they did not get the money they were looking for, they are appreciative of the assistance and I feel good as well for helping them out.

Learning how to say no is an important part of effective communication. Mastering this skill will allow to you have the self-confidence it takes to reject an offer and the tact to do it in a way that will cause embarrassment to neither you nor the person whose offer you reject. Learn how to say no and make better decisions.

ACTION STEP(S):

---

1) Practice saying no with telemarketers and door-to-door salespeople. First keep an open mind to what they have to offer instead of saying no right away. Then, if you are quite certain you have no interest, say politely and with a smile and with confidence, "I am sorry, but I have no interest whatsoever."

Day 163: Smile

"Wear a smile and have friends; wear a scowl and have wrinkles."
- George Eliot

"Nobody needs a smile so much as the one who has none to give."
- Lawrence G. Lovasik

"Every time you smile at someone, it is an action of love, a gift to that person, a beautiful thing." - Mother Teresa

Hundreds of the most influential people throughout history understood the power of a simple smile. A smile is something that costs nothing, yet is priceless. It cannot be bought or sold, only given away. The more smiles you give away, the more you get in return. A smile is a key element to both our happiness and success in life.

Smiling has enormous benefits for both the giver and receiver of the smile. Here are just some of those benefits:

- **A smile makes others feel good.** When you smile at someone, it has an immediate uplifting effect on that person. People like to be with people who make them feel good. The smile is most often returned which makes the giver feel good as well.
- **A smile leads to happiness just as happiness leads to a smile.** All of our lives we associate smiling with good feelings of happiness and laughter. This association works to our advantage when we want a quick way to become happy. Put on a big fake smile then look in the mirror. Within seconds, the fake smile will turn genuine.
- **A smile is an invitation.** A smile, along with good eye contact, is a universal invitation. It tells the person receiving the smile that the giver is friendly and approachable. This is seen frequently in both personal and professional situations.

- **A smile is comforting.** A gentle smile can ease just about any tense situation. It is especially comforting when given by one in a position of power to another, like in a doctor/patient, teacher/student, boss/employee, or parent/child situation.
- **A smile leaves favorable impressions.** First impressions are said to be made within three seconds. These first impressions are mostly based on feelings and emotions. A smile, or lack thereof, is one of most influential characteristics on another's emotions. Smile, and leave others with a favorable impression of you.
- **A smile makes you look happy, confident, and self-assured.** It is the confident sales person who makes the sales. It is the confident student that gets the good grades. It is the confident single that gets the dates. Confidence is a large part of success and smiling is way of showing your confidence to others without saying a word.

Is one expected to smile all the time? Of course not. Besides not being natural, there are times when it is appropriate to have a more serious or somber expression, like at a funeral. Here are just a few times when a conscious effort to smile should be made.

- When you meet someone
- When you enter a room
- When you make a motion that attracts attention
- When you are making a sales presentation
- When you are recording your outgoing voice mail message

How does one smile? Is it as simple as using one's facial muscles to lift up the ends of one's mouth? For a fake smile, it is that simple. A genuine smile does, however, take a little more effort. A genuine smile begins in the heart with a warm feeling, proceeds to the eyes that then force the ends of the mouth upward into a smile. Smiling is habitual; the more you do it, the more you can't help doing it.

A smile is more contagious than the common cold, and as the giver, it is a whole lot more beneficial to both you and those you come "in contact" with. It is the trademark of many famous actors and said to be the "secret of success" for many individuals. Use smiles to bring yourself and those around you more joy, happiness and success.

ACTION STEP(S):

1) Commit to making a conscious effort to smile more often.

2) Put a big fake smile right now and hold it until it is replaced by a real smile. Just imagining yourself doing this will probably make your initial smile genuine.

"It is almost impossible to smile on the outside without feeling better on the inside."

- unknown

Day 164: Inspiration from Andrew Carnegie

Andrew Carnegie (1835–1919) helped build the formidable American steel industry, a process that turned a poor young man into one of the richest entrepreneurs of his age.

Success is desiring knowledge. As a boy, Andrew attended Rolland School and developed a love for learning from his teacher that he carried with him for the rest of his life.

Success is sharing. Carnegie was perhaps the first person of great wealth to state publicly that the rich have a moral obligation to give away their fortunes. In 1889 he wrote *The Gospel of Wealth*, in which he asserted that all personal wealth beyond that required to supply the needs of one's family should be regarded as a trust fund to be administered for the benefit of the community.

Success is making the right contacts. Carnegie joined Mr. Woodruff, inventor of the sleeping car, in organizing Woodruff Sleeping Car Company. This would be the beginning of Mr. Carnegie's fortune.

Success begins in the mind. "The man who acquires the ability to take full possession of his own mind may take possession of anything else to which he is justly entitled."

Success is being a trend spotter not a trend fighter. Young Andrew was expected to follow in his father's footsteps as a weaver. But Andrew chose to play a big part in the industrial revolution instead, ironically putting most of the weavers out of business in the process with the introduction of steam-powered looms.

Success is seeking responsibility, not avoiding it. Young Andrew advanced very quickly in his career as a result of doing each job to the best of his ability and seizing every opportunity to take on new responsibilities.

Success is picking your battles. At the turn of the twentieth century, J.P. Morgan mounted a major challenge to Carnegie's steel empire. The then 64-year-old was confident he could fight Morgan off in a legal battle that would most likely last for several years; however, Carnegie chose to accept a very large sum of money and spend the rest of his days with his wife and daughter.

Success is seeking the help of others. "No man will make a great leader who wants to do it all himself, or to get all the credit for doing it."

[Sources: http://www.pbs.org, http://www.carnegie.org]

"Think of yourself as on the threshold of unparalleled success. A whole, clear glorious life lies before you. Achieve! Achieve!"

- Andrew Carnegie

Day 165: Taking Advice

It seems as if everywhere we turn others are giving us advice, or an opinion about what could or should be done about a situation or problem. A key to success is knowing the difference between good and not-so-good advice and acting on the good advice. As Wilson Mizner wrote, "To profit from good advice requires more wisdom than to give it."

Nobody can tell another person with certainty what is good advice and what is bad advice. The distinction between good and bad advice is very personal and it requires a combination of knowledge of oneself and common sense. Here are some points to consider that can help you decide which advice to take, and which to leave.

- Is the person giving the advice on the subject qualified to do so? All too often we take advice from people simply because we care about them and do not question if the advice is good or not. We assume that those who care about us would not give us bad advice. Unfortunately, the world is full of bad advice yet void of those who think they give bad advice. Question the advice itself, not the integrity or intent of the person giving the advice.
- Is this something that works for everyone, many others, or just happened to work for the person giving the advice? This is usually a tough one to answer for certain so it is best to rely on your common sense.
- Is the advice based on timely information? For the most part, advice is timeless, especially when it is about subjects that don't change much over the years, like happiness. Beware, however, of advice based on outdated information. My grandmother used to tell me I needed to eat a good breakfast every day: fried eggs, sausage and bacon. To quote Phil from *City Slickers*, when Curly suffers a coronary: "The man ate bacon at every meal—you can't do that."

- Just because it is a quote, does not make it good advice. There is a misleading, unwritten rule that states if a quote giving advice comes from someone famous, very old, or Greek, then it must be good advice. One can be just as well off taking advice from a good friend as a 14th century French poet or a child Hollywood movie star. In writing this course, I have read thousands of quotes, most of which offer some kind of advice. Quotes frequently contradict each other; for every famous person who advises something, there is another famous person advising the opposite. Many authors even seem to contradict themselves—unless kept in full context, quotes are open for interpretation.

- Is this advice based on theory or practice? While advice based on theory can be good advice, advice based on practice is usually more credible.

- Why aren't they doing it? "If stock market experts were so expert," wrote Norman Augustine, "they would be buying stock, not selling advice." There are many people who talk the talk but do not walk the walk, especially when it comes to selling advice.

- Expert or professional advice is not always the best advice. Professionals most often give advice more on the safe side and rarely take into account persistence and the human spirit. For example, a doctor may advise one to refrain from a certain sport because it would be best for the ailment the doctor is treating, but not best for the patient as a whole (holistic approach). While most professionals do have your best interest in mind, they are also concerned with lawsuits and their reputations.

Ironically, this whole course is really about advice. I say this not to make you skeptical of any advice I may have to offer, but to admit that any advice I give is advice that should be subjected to the same points above. Remember that every person you meet is your superior in some way. Be both open-minded and cautious when it comes to taking advice. A life-long habit of following good advice is a sure way to success.

ACTION STEP(S):

---

1) Commit to making a conscious effort in questioning the validity of any advice offered to you.   Remember that you are not questioning the person giving the advice, but the advice itself.

"There's very little advice in men's magazines, because men don't think there's a lot they don't know. Women do. Women want to learn. Men think, 'I know what I'm doing, just show me somebody naked.'"

- Jerry Seinfeld

Day 166: Avoiding Arguments

One of the greatest obstacles that stands in the way of success is one's own ego. It seems to be in our nature to prove our superiority, point out when others are wrong, and become very defensive when others point out when we are wrong. Constructive debating and talking out a difference of opinion are appropriate at times, but there is never an appropriate time for arguing.

An argument is characterized by the expression of disagreement in which emotions and egos often get in the way of a favorable outcome. It has been estimated that 9 out of 10 arguments end up in a lose-lose situation. Someone once said, "A man convinced against his will is of the same opinion still." Also, even if you think you won the argument by presenting stronger facts, you have lost the good will of those with whom you are arguing. In Benjamin Franklin's autobiography, he had this to say about those who argue, "...these disputing, contradicting, and confuting people are generally unfortunate in their affairs. They get victory sometimes, but they never get good will, which would be of more use to them." The best way to "win" an argument is to avoid it altogether.

The majority of people believe that the best way to win someone to your way of thinking, or get someone to see your point of view is by arguing. In fact, the opposite is true. The moment you contradict another you are putting that person on the defensive, and in an effort to protect his or her own ego, the other person will continue to disagree. Most of the time, they will just convince themselves even more that they are right and you are wrong. The ability to win someone to your way of thinking is an extremely valuable skill to have, but has nothing to do with arguing, contradicting, or proving another to be wrong.

It is without question that arguing does more damage than good. As a successful communicator, knowing when to hold your tongue and show tact is essential. Do you ever find yourself contradicting others to make yourself feel smarter or superior, to convince yourself that you are right, or contradicting just out of plain habit? If so, ask yourself what you really have to gain by doing this. How will you make the other person feel? What will others think of you for publicly delivering a strong blow to another's ego?

There will be times, of course, when others disagree with you and attempt to initiate an argument. It is most important to keep in mind the ultimate goal: to create a win-win situation. Here are some suggestions on how to do just that.

- **Welcome disagreements.** Success is about keeping an open-mind and remaining flexible. When others disagree with you, they are actually presenting you with other possibilities.
- **Do not be defensive.** Resist reacting to disagreement and control your temper and emotion. Remember that being defensive of your opinion or belief will only fuel the argument.
- **Listen.** Many times an upset or angry person just wants to be heard. Do your best not to jump in and "correct" the other person. Let them say what they need to say.
- **Look for areas of agreement.** How can one argue with you if you agree with them? You do not have to agree with all of their points, but make it known where you do agree with them. This will help build rapport.
- **Admit to areas of error.** Is anything the other person is arguing true? If you are wrong about anything, admit it quickly and emphatically.
- **Watch your language.** Use words like "I believe", "it is my understanding that", or "I could be wrong, but..." to express your opinion. It is difficult for anyone to argue with your belief.
- **Thank the other person.** Thank the other person for caring enough to express his or her disagreement. Most people who disagree really do not care enough to make it known. How can one possibly still feel belligerent toward someone who just expressed gratitude for his or her disagreement?

By avoiding arguments, you can avoid getting into potentially explosive situations or avoid saying things you will later regret. Control your emotions and use tact. Do not disagree with others for your own benefit and do your best to avoid arguments by turning them into rational "fact finding" discussions. Do this, and you will build and maintain more successful relationships in your personal and professional life.

ACTION STEP(S):

1) Implement the suggestions in this article the next time you feel an argument is about to take place.

"In Vegas, I got into a long argument with the man at the roulette wheel over what I considered to be an odd number."

- Steven Wright

Days 167 and 168 are for "R&R"—review and reflection. Spend these days reviewing the last five articles and reflecting on the information and how it relates to your life. Now is also a good time to make sure all the action steps for the previous days have been completed.

Day 169: Winning Others To Your Way of Thinking

Back in the 1930's, to the detriment of mankind, a man named Adolf Hitler was able to convince millions of people that his conduct was "in accordance with the will of the Almighty Creator". Several years earlier, a man called Mahatma Gandhi helped free the Indian people from British rule through nonviolent resistance. What did these two men on complete opposite sides of the moral spectrum have in common? They were both masters of winning others to their way of thinking.

As humans, we are endowed with the gift of free will. We can use this will to believe and think as we wish. Our beliefs can only be formed or changed by us, if we allow them and want them to be. It is through influence, persuasion, mental conditioning, manipulation, and brainwashing that we allow our beliefs to be formed or altered. Success is about winning others to your way of thinking whether it be persuading board members to move forward with your new idea, being a positive influence on the life of a child, or freeing an entire country.

There are five general methods to win others to your way of thinking: influence, persuasion, mental conditioning, manipulation and brainwashing. All are equally powerful, but the last two are negative and can have serious repercussions. It is important to our success that we learn how to effectively influence and persuade, but it is equally important to our well being that we learn how to recognize manipulation and brainwashing. Mental conditioning is considered neutral that can be positive or negative, depending on how it is used.

Influence. To influence another is to sway or affect based on prestige, wealth, ability, knowledge or position. This is a skill possessed by all leaders and successful individuals in all walks of life. There are dozens of key techniques that are used to positively influence others, many of which are contained within this course.

Positive influence is characterized by the intent to create a win-win situation. For example, "Her polite and friendly way with people made her a very positive influence on her children."

Persuasion. To persuade another is to induce to undertake a course of action or embrace a point of view by means of argument, reasoning, or entreaty. Persuasion is more assertive than influence, but may prove more effective at times. Despite persuasion's definition, argumentation should be avoided when persuading. Clear reasoning is the most effective form of persuasion for getting your points across. Open-minded individuals often will often say "convince me", in which they are basically asking to be presented with facts and reasoning so that they too can share your belief.

Mental conditioning. Mental conditioning is a technique one often uses on oneself to change a belief or create a feeling using repetition. Some common examples of this are prayer, mantras, and affirmations. Mental conditioning can also be used on others. The best-known example of this is advertising. Advertisers use mental conditioning to associate a positive feeling with their product. Through repeated exposure, our minds are conditioned to accept the association. Only through awareness can we resist this type of conditioning, but for the most part it is harmless. Do we really care if we feel excited about toilet paper? It is the positive associations with potentially destructive products that we must be careful of accepting.

Manipulation. To manipulate another is to use shrewd or devious management, especially for one's own advantage. Simply put, the main difference between influencing another and manipulating them is intent. Those who use manipulation do so only thinking about what they want, not about the wants of those they manipulate. It is not easy to detect when you are being manipulated. Once again, we must rely on our common sense to help us distinguish between influence and manipulation.

Brainwashing. The dictionary defines brainwashing as "process of systematically, forcibly and intensively, indoctrinating a person to destroy or weaken his beliefs and ideas so that he becomes willing to accept different or opposite beliefs or ideas." I do not fully agree with this definition because one cannot be "forced" to accept a belief; this contradicts the entire concept of free will. One can however, be forced to live by another's belief, against his or her own will. Remove the word "forcibly" and that is brainwashing in a nutshell. The key element to brainwashing is the creation of an environment where questioning, doubt, reason, creativity, thinking for oneself and dissent are discouraged or even punished.

There are other methods of winning others to your way of thinking that are not listed above like physical force (which only appears to work), hypnotism (which is a skill practiced by a select few), and the Jedi mind trick (which to my knowledge, has only been used a long time ago in a galaxy far, far away).

The ability to win others to your way of thinking is a key element of both leadership and success. There are just as many ways to do it wrong as there are to do it right. As a successful leader, use positive influence often and gentle persuasion when necessary. Use mental conditioning on yourself to abolish limiting beliefs or to instill empowering beliefs. Never use manipulation or brainwashing in an attempt to win others to your way of thinking and be aware when others attempt to use these techniques on you. Follow these suggestions, and you will posses the valuable skill of winning others to your way of thinking.

ACTION STEP(S):

1) Commit to never using manipulation or brainwashing in an attempt to win others to your way of thinking. Use positive influence to create a win-win situation.

Day 170: Should You Commit?

What if you were offered the position of chief ashtray licker of the XYZ Corporation? Your job, if you chose to accept it, would consist of licking dirty ashtrays clean all day long. For this job, you would be paid one million dollars for just one day's work. Would you accept it? What if you would be paid ten million dollars? Now what if there were an 80% chance that you would only be paid one dollar? What if you actually enjoyed licking ashtrays, would that change anything? Should you commit yourself to this job?

Commitment and persistence go hand in hand. If you are committed to something whether it be a goal, relationship, or a cause, you use persistence to support that commitment. Persistence does not guarantee anyone success. In fact, misguided persistence has led to ruined lives and insanity. Generally speaking, the difference between genius and insanity is success. Think about the "crazy" inventor who works around the clock on some "crazy" idea. Perception of both the inventor and idea change completely if the idea succeeds. When you commit yourself to something, especially a life purpose, you must realize that there are sacrifices you must make. We all have 24 hours in a day and each minute we spend on our goals, is one less minute we have to spend on other areas of our lives.

In our hypothetical ashtray-licking situation, there are a few variables that can affect your decision to commit to the job. These are: the possible rewards, the work itself, and the risk involved. Here is my formula for deciding whether to make a commitment or not:

Possible Rewards > Work + Risk

Unlike a mathematical formula, these variables do not have absolute or numerical values. Each variable is unique to the specific commitment. If the possible reward is greater than the work plus the risk, then it makes sense to commit. If not, then it does not make sense. Simple. What is not so simple, is giving value to each variable. This is done by using a combination of your head, heart, and gut.

Possible rewards. This is what you hope to achieve by following through with your commitment. It is called "possible" reward because no reward is really guaranteed. One's possible reward to a 9-to-5 job consists of a salary that is close to 100% certain to be paid, and a future of raises and promotions that are less than certain. Possible rewards should also include the positive aspects of the work like learning, training, and enjoyment of the work itself.

Work. This is the labor, mental or physical, that is used in the commitment. To determine this value, one should consider time needed, sacrifices to be made, and the intensity of labor. These are all the negative aspects of the labor. Any positive aspects of work should be figured into the possible rewards variable.

Risk. What are the physical, mental, or emotional risks involved in the work?

What if the only rewards that ever materialized were the positive benefits from the work itself? Would you view this as completely devastating, a bit unfortunate, or could you care less? Keep in mind all that you sacrifice for this commitment. There is a myth that one must sacrifice short-term gratification for long-term success. This does not have to be true. By enjoying and profiting from the work of your commitments, any possible reward is not as important. With this, success is in the journey and not the destination.

Choose carefully which commitments you make in life. If your existing commitments consist mostly of pain, boredom, and/or resentment, it may be time to rethink where you are committed and replace your existing commitments with new commitments in which the work itself energizes and motivates you. Keep in mind any negative consequences that may be associated with breaking a commitment. Try using the commitment formula before making your next commitment and make the best use of your limited and valuable time.

ACTION STEP(S):

---

1) Reevaluate your existing commitments using the commitment formula. Are any of your commitments centered on a large "end reward"? Are you enjoying the work portion of the commitment? Is this something you really want to be committed to?

"When work, commitment, and pleasure all become one and you reach that deep well where passion lives, nothing is impossible."

- Nancy Coey

Day 171: Inspiration from John D. Rockefeller

John D. Rockefeller (1839–1937), America's first billionaire, was the driving force behind the creation and development of the Standard Oil Company and one of the first major philanthropists in the U.S.

Success is having diligence. Rockefeller's first job was working as an assistant bookkeeper for less than four dollars a week. He showed a talent for detail and a strong work ethic from the beginning. In 1859, Rockefeller's diligence was rewarded and he was made a partner.

Success is seeing opportunity where others only see misfortune. "I always tried to turn every disaster into an opportunity."

Success is putting your own money on the line and taking risks. In 1859, with $1,000 Rockefeller had saved and another $1,000 borrowed from his father, Rockefeller formed a partnership in the commission business with Maurice B. Clark, which would be the beginning of his lucrative business career.

Success is based in part on aptitude. The commission merchant business was very competitive and Clark & Rockefeller's success was due in large part to Rockefeller's natural business abilities.

Success is encouraging leadership in others. "Good leadership consists in showing average people how to do the work of superior people."

Success is sharing. Rockefeller was 57 years old when he focused his efforts on philanthropy, giving away the bulk of his fortune in ways designed to do the most good as determined by careful study, experience, and the help of expert advisers.

Success is knowing the power of money—the good and the bad. "The impression was gaining ground with me that it was a good thing to let the money be my servant and not make myself a slave to the money..."

Success does not mean being perfect. Rockefeller appeared to many to be a man of contradictions. He eagerly crushed his competitors, "ruining" hundreds of lives in his pursuit of profit. Yet he was a deeply religious man and one of the world's greatest philanthropists.

[Sources: http://www.biography.com, http://voteview.uh.edu, http://allsands.com]

"I can think of nothing less pleasurable than a life devoted to pleasure."

- John D. Rockefeller

Day 172: It's Not Always About Trying Harder

As an amateur bodybuilder, it has taken me almost 20 years to learn first hand that success is not always about trying harder. This statement seems a bit contradictory to the principles of muscle development, since when it comes to building muscle, maximum results are produced with maximum effort. However, I have learned the hard way that trying harder at doing the wrong exercises, using poor form, and working the same muscle group too often, will not bring me closer to success. In fact, due to injury, doing the wrong things has pushed me further from my goals. In addition, genetically speaking, I can never look like a Schwarzenegger no matter how hard I try. Understanding that success is not about trying harder has helped me to do MY best, and has kept me from getting discouraged when my efforts do not pay off.

According to a study done by M. Scherneck for his Ph. D. dissertation in 1998, wasted effort is actually the leading cause of discouragement. The majority of people studied rank effort as the leading predictor of success, when in fact it is just a small part of success. People try and try, see little results, get discouraged, consider themselves a failure and give up. It is the classic case of confusing activity with accomplishment. Do you think Michael Jordan tries 1000 times harder than the average pro basketball player? Do you think Bill Gates tries 100,000,000 times harder than the average business person? If success were really about trying harder, based on their success (wealth, fame, influence) in their respective fields, this would have to be true. Common sense, however, tells us that it cannot be true.

Why is success not always about trying harder? I believe there are three main reasons why effort alone does not guarantee one success. To illustrate these reasons, we will follow Ken on his pursuit of success.

Aptitude. Ken dreamed of being a pro basketball player since he was a small boy. He would devote much of his childhood to playing basketball and practicing every chance he got. Always being small for his age, and fairly big boned, he never did too well at the sport and spent most of his time on the bench when he did actually make the team. Ken realized that despite his efforts, he did not have the *aptitude* to become a professional basketball player. He did not fit the physical profile, and perhaps he was a little less coordinated than the other players. After taking one of the many available aptitude tests in high school, Ken discovered that he had a knack for business.

Doing the wrong things. Years passed and Ken entered the business world as an entrepreneur with a start up company. Ken worked 18 hour days in an attempt to get his business off the ground, mostly at perfecting his website. He would add content, make changes daily, check every word and sentence for proper spelling and grammar, spend thousands on eye-catching animations and graphics. After about a year of this, Ken finally realized the error of his ways. The problem was never with his website, it was the fact that no one knew about his site so no one was seeing it! All this time, Ken was, as they say, "spinning his wheels".

Point of diminishing returns. Ken finally knew what he needed to do. He needed to attract people to his website. To do this, Ken ran an ad in his local newspaper. This worked great for Ken. He immediately saw return on his investment and the traffic started coming in. He ran the ad again, then again. However, the results the second and third times were not so great. Ken expanded his advertising to all the local papers, magazines, websites, TV and radio stations. As with his first ad, these ads did well for a while, and then started to produce *diminishing returns*. Ken was now spending thousands of dollars and working 18 hour days once again, "trying his best" to get the business off the ground.

Since this is a hypothetical illustration, we might as well give it a happy ending, while plugging our course... Fortunately for Ken, he discovered that success is not always about trying harder.

Success is the culmination of hundreds of principles, concepts and ideas. Ken became a member of YearToSuccess.com and started applying the principles to his business. He is now one of the most successful business people in his community, and he works no harder and no longer than the average business person.

ACTION STEP(S):

---

1) Do you feel that you are not getting very far despite your increased efforts? Are you doing the right things? What can you do differently?

"The less effort, the faster and more powerful you will be."

- Bruce Lee

Day 173: Ease of Doing Business

There are several places to shop for groceries in my town. They are all within the same approximate driving distance and they all have the same general groceries. However, one of the stores does something unique that the other stores in town do not do: the baggers push the cart out to your car, load the bags into your car, then return the carriage, while accepting nothing in return besides a "Thank you". Since my wife and I shop with two small children, you can probably guess who gets our business. Even though this store is a bit more expensive than the others in town, we feel it is well worth it. The management of this local grocery store understands and applies one of the key principles in business success: make it easy for the customer to do business with you.

Make it easy for prospects to find you. Needless to say, if the prospects do not know your business exists, they will not become a customer.

- Advertise. Reserve at least a small portion of funds to list your business in places where those looking for your product or service will be able to find it.
- Use good signage. If your physical location is hidden or tricky to find, make sure you have adequate signage that directs prospects to your place of business.

Make it easy for prospects to contact you. Most prospects will call a local number over a long distance number, hang up on voice mail or a busy signal, or visit another website if yours is down.

- Get a toll free number. If doing business outside your local area, a toll free number will greatly increase the number of sales calls.
- Get call waiting or multiple phone lines. I, like most people, will hang up on a busy signal and call the next business on my list rather than persisting to try to get through.

- Get a live answering service versus voice mail. Prospects will not hang up on real people, but they will hang up on voice mail.
- Own a website and use your web address in all of your ads. A web address is a link to unlimited information and is the most valuable piece of information you can put in an ad. Thanks to the Internet, the need for large ads has decreased since just about everyone could get all the information they need to know from your website.
- Show a contact link clearly on your home page. A website without clear contact information screams "scam". Do not make the costly mistake of hiding your contact information.
- Allow prospects to contact you via phone, e-mail, snail mail, or chat. The more options you give your prospects, the more likely they are to become customers.
- Use a reliable web host provider. Beware of "free" hosting for your business. Most top quality and reliable hosts providers charge as little as $19 per month which is well worth your business' reputation.

Make it easy for prospects to buy from you. People generally like shopping and having, but not buying. The more painless you can make this process, the more prospects you will be able to convert into customers.

- Minimize the number of forms and paperwork the customer must fill out. If this cannot easily be done, fill out the forms for the customer or at least assist them with the process. On our YearToSuccess.com member form, we increased member registration by over 60% simply by requiring only vital information at sign up, then asking, not requiring, the member to complete the information at his or her convenience.
- Use salespeople. An effective salesperson is worth his or her weight in gold providing they work with the prospect throughout the complete buying cycle, not just until the prospect has agreed to buy. Most customers are busy and do not want to be bothered with details that may be important to your business, but are not important to them.

A salesperson can act as an assistant to the customer, doing the "hard stuff" for them.

- If possible, sell your products or services on-line. E-commerce is growing at an unbelievable rate. Do not let technology scare you from this. Selling goods on the Internet can be very profitable and cost relatively little to set up.
- Accept credit cards. In just about every study done, the acceptance of credit cards has increased businesses' sales substantially. As the business climate changes, customers are carrying less and less cash. Even McDonald's accepts credit cards!
- Become a one stop shop. If you have a product that is dependent on another product, or more marketable alongside other complimentary products, then sell those other products or arrange to have your product marketed by those who market the complimentary products. For example, if you sell a toy that requires batteries, sell the batteries as well.

Listen to your customers. Customer feedback is the best way to determine how "customer friendly" your business is. Remember that it does not matter how easy YOU think it is to do business with you, it is what the prospect or customer thinks.

ACTION STEP(S):

---

1) Ask your customers for feedback regarding the ease of doing business with you. Use this feedback in making changes to the way you do business to bring in more customers.

"[The customers] had a tendency to stop shopping when the baskets became too full or too heavy."

- Sylvan N. Goldman

Days 174 and 175 are for "R&R"—review and reflection. Spend these days reviewing the last five articles and reflecting on the information and how it relates to your life. Now is also a good time to make sure all the action steps for the previous days have been completed.

Day 176: Be Flexible

When I sold my first web hosting company to a large, publicly traded corporation, I was excited about taking our already profitable and successful web hosting company to a new level. We went from 11 employees to a division of over 200 people. We now had the resources of many bright people with Harvard educations that had been in business for decades. We also had access to money to improve our current services and begin some real marketing campaigns. However, within just days, my enthusiasm began to wane with the realization that flexibility was not part of this new corporate culture. Changes that we used to implement in minutes now took months. This rigid, multi-management layered environment in an industry that demands flexibility would eventually lead to the downfall of the entire division.

In the early days of my first web hosting company, I was often criticized for "not sticking with plans". If I saw a better opportunity, I would often divert all energy to the new opportunity and let the other one go. It's like being on a busy sidewalk and seeing a dollar bill a few yards away; you start to walk toward it with the intent to pick it up, and then you see a ten-dollar bill that is even closer. How could you not change course and pick up the ten-dollar bill instead? Let someone else get the one-dollar bill, or if it is still there, get it after you pick up the ten dollar bill. It was not long before those on my team began to realize the method to my "madness".

Flexibility is an attitude that can help us succeed both personally and professionally in several ways.

- **Flexibility allows us to make better decisions.** In today's business environment, we are continually presented with new information. As we become better informed, we may realize that the decisions we made yesterday are not the best decisions today. It is never too late to make the right decision.

- **Flexibility allows us to take advantage of new opportunities.** If we go through life with blinders on, we fail to see and act on the other opportunities.
- **Flexibility can help us reach our goals faster and with less effort.** A goal properly defined allows for flexibility. Know where you want to go and have a plan for getting there, but don't pass on a better opportunity just because it is not in your original plan.
- **Flexibility can help us find our "calling" in life.** We are encouraged to have some idea of what we want to do with our life by our second year in high school (around age 15). However, for most of us it takes many more years to discover what we are passionate about. Unless you are passionate about your chosen field, remain flexible and do not fear changing careers.
- **Flexibility is part of an attractive personality.** Defensiveness and stubbornness are not qualities that others admire. Flexibility, however, shows others that you are smart enough to make decisions based on new information and not just old beliefs or ideals.

The one major drawback of goals, mission statements, business plans and other written paths for the future is that people put so much effort into the creation of these, that they are hesitant to change them. There is a stigma with "abandoning goals" or "getting off track". However, flexibility is actually a very important part of any type of goal setting.

Another reason flexibility is not embraced is because of one's ego. You will often hear one say, "I have made up my mind" or "my decision is final". The more our beliefs or ideas are challenged, the more rigid we become. This behavior is reactionary and its purpose to just protect our own ego. One must learn to let go of his or her ego if he or she is to be flexible.

Flexibility is often met with criticism because it can be confused with indecisiveness and/or quitting. True flexibility is, however, a vital part of long-term success that can keep you ahead of the curve in this ever-changing world.

ACTION STEP(S):

---

1) Make sure all of your written goals allow for flexibility. If not, rewrite your goals in such a way that will allow flexibility.

"The key word is flexibility, the ability to adapt constantly. Darwin said it clearly. People thought that he mainly talked about survival of the fittest. What he said was that the species that survive are usually not the smartest or the strongest, but the ones most responsive to change."

- Philippe Kahn

Day 177: Using Practical Knowledge To Get the Job

Gordy has been working on his own for the last 20 years as a hair stylist. He has no college education, and no experience in the "corporate world", yet yearns to enter the business world. However, his lack of self-confidence and his skewed perception of what employers are looking for keep him from getting any of the jobs for which he applies. Good news for Gordy—his best chance to get the job he desires is by acquiring the practical knowledge needed for the position. The reason this is good news is that practical knowledge does not take four years and $100,000.00 to acquire.

We can categorize knowledge into three areas. Each has its advantage and use in life.

General Knowledge. This consists of the basics like reading, writing, and arithmetic. It also includes facts and figures, dates and history, and people and places. We spend the majority of our childhood and youth learning general knowledge. It is general knowledge that allows us to function in society, build a foundation on which we can begin to acquire specific or practical knowledge, and win at Trivial Pursuit.

Specific Knowledge. Once we have chosen a field of study to pursue, we acquire specific knowledge—specific to the chosen field. This is the information we learn in trade school or the latter years of college. Many corporations list as a prerequisite specific knowledge in the form of a higher education.

Practical Knowledge. This is the knowledge that is even more specific to the work one has chosen to pursue. This includes knowledge on the organization itself, the specific duties of the job, understanding the market in which the organization operates— basically, the knowledge needed to perform the specific job.

Having practical knowledge alone certainly does not guarantee you a job. There are positions that have requirements, especially those regulated by government such as lawyers, doctors, airplane pilots, and others. In addition, public corporations may be hiring for image rather than for finding the one who can best do the job. Of course, these allegations would be denied due to discrimination laws, but in order to please stockholders, some corporations will hire the gray haired, ivy league degreed, racially and sexually balanced employees that have more letters after their names than in them. So unless you fit their public image profile, your chances of getting the job are slim.

Having practical knowledge really pays off when it comes to applying for a job with a smaller, more entrepreneurial organization. This is an organization in which the person doing the hiring is more concerned with the profitability of the organization, than being criticized for his or her hiring decision. As an employer, I can confirm that hiring employees who already know the business and the industry can save months of training, loss of productivity, and money that would otherwise have to be allocated to getting the new employee up to speed.

Here are some suggestions for acquiring the practical knowledge needed to increase your chances at getting the job you desire.

- **Visit the organization's website.** Most websites contain a wealth of information about the organization itself. Learn about the history of the organization, read any information on the principals and other members of the organization, and most of all, be familiar with what the organization markets.
- **Learn about the organization's market.** Who are the organization's customers? How does the organization get it's customers?
- **Learn about the organization's industry.** How big is the industry? How long has it been around? Who are the major players? Who are the organization's greatest competitors?

It is a good idea to demonstrate some of your practical knowledge in your cover letter, or by sending an e-mail to the person in charge of hiring. A demonstration of your practical knowledge will put you at a great advantage over the other applicants. It is true that acquiring this practical knowledge takes more time and effort than just sending a resume or filling out a standard application, but it will be well worth it.

ACTION STEP(S):

1) Begin acquiring practical knowledge on the job you are seeking. If you have a job you are satisfied with, acquire practical knowledge on that job. It is never too late to become a more valuable asset to your organization.

"Those who have knowledge, don't predict. Those who predict, don't have knowledge."

- Lao Tzu

Day 178: Inspiration from J.P. Morgan

J.P Morgan (1837-1913) was one of the world's foremost financial figures during the two pre-World War I decades.

Success is making introductions. J.P. began his career as an accountant for Duncan, Sherman & Co. in New York City, which provided a good base for J.P. Morgan's introduction into the world of banking and finance, especially because of its ties to the powerful London firm of George Peabody & Co.

Success is supporting good ideas in which you believe. J.P. funded Thomas Edison throughout the 1870s and 1880s, and laid the financial foundation for Edison Electric Company.

Success is seeking and finding opportunity. When many small companies and railroads ran into tough times after the Civil War, Morgan saw opportunities and acquired those with potential.

Success is diversification. Morgan acquired and/or financed shipping interests, coal mines, insurance and communications industries, and he provided financial backing for the U.S. government itself.

Success is using power, not abusing it. Morgan saw himself as a positive force. His banks, he believed, had helped to transform America into the world's most powerful nation, while privately he gave money to the urban poor.

Success is problem solving. "No problem can be solved until it is reduced to some simple form. The changing of a vague difficulty into a specific, concrete form is a very essential element in thinking."

Success is recognizing the power of synergy. In 1891, Morgan arranged the merger of Edison General Electric and Thompson-Houson Electric Company to form General Electric, which then became the country's main electrical-equipment manufacturing company.

Success is sharing. In 1912, J.P. Morgan gave to the Library of Congress a complete set of autographs of the signers of the Declaration of Independence, as well as giving away numerous other priceless works of art to several museums.

Success is setting goals and following them through. "The wise man bridges the gap by laying out the path by means of which he can get from where he is to where he wants to go."

[Sources: http://www.biography.com, http://www.pbs.org, http://www.netstate.com]

"You can't pick cherries with your back to the tree."

- J.P Morgan (1837-1913)

Day 179: Happiness: Part 1

In 1776, Thomas Jefferson, with the help of others, wrote in the Declaration of Independence that all men (I am sure he meant women as well) were endowed with the right to the "pursuit of happiness". Success, to many people, is simply finding and living a life of happiness. Like success, the definition of happiness cannot come from the dictionary; it must come from inside you. What is happiness to you? If you have not taken the time to define what happiness means to you, what have your spent your whole life pursuing?

Many argue that there is nothing more important in life than happiness. To some, the meaning of life is the pursuit of happiness for oneself, the happiness of loved ones, and the happiness of mankind. Sophocles wrote, "When a man has lost all happiness, he's not alive. Call him a breathing corpse."

Many people get sidetracked in the pursuit of happiness by confusing temporary pleasure with happiness. Happiness is not found in "things". Entertainment and material possessions can bring us amusement and pleasure, but not true happiness. Happiness comes from inside us—it is the way we see our world. In this sense, we create our own happiness from the way we perceive and interpret the events in our own lives. We are responsible for our own happiness. "The U.S. Constitution does not guarantee happiness," said Ben Franklin, "only the pursuit of it. You have to catch up with it yourself." Another famous American named Abraham Lincoln agreed, "Most folks are about as happy as they make up their minds to be."

Some give up the pursuit of happiness by finding contentment. The two are very different. Contentment is just living life, whereas happiness is celebrating it. John Lancaster Spalding wrote, "If we were all gentle and contented as sheep, we would be as feeble and helpless."

One can learn to be happy despite one's current situation. It begins with abandoning any self-pity and wanting to be happy. Sad but true, some people do find pleasure in self pity and sorrow, but it is pleasure they experience, not happiness, usually from the attention of others. Learning to be happy is about conditioning yourself to see the good rather than the bad, and being grateful for what you do have, not resentful for all the things you don't have.

In your pursuit of happiness, now and then it is wise to just pause and be happy. The pursuit of anything often causes us to focus on the pursuit itself rather than enjoying that which we are pursuing. Like success, happiness is a journey, not a destination.

ACTION STEP(S):

1) Write down what you are NOT happy about now in your life. How can you perceive these events differently so that they can bring you happiness? What is the "good" in those situations?

"Do you prefer that you be right, or that you be happy?"

- A Course In Miracles

Day 180: Happiness: Part 2

In order to stimulate some thought, I can tell you what happiness is to others. Use some of these ideas in creating your own definition.

Happiness is being true to ourselves. "Happiness is when what you think, what you say, and what you do are in harmony," said Mahatma Gandhi almost a century ago. Internal conflict and lack of integrity lead to guilt and ultimately misery.

Happiness is keeping busy. It is often the result of being too busy to be miserable. Boredom is one of the leading causes of depression and misery. Finding something to do, especially something you enjoy doing, whether it be a career, volunteer work or hobby, will keep the boredom away.

Happiness is accepting the inevitable. J.C.F. von Schiller said, "Happy is he who learns to bear what he cannot change!" I agree with Schiller, but I would like to change "cannot" to "cannot and will not". There are many things that we can change, if we devote enough resources to it. However, we may want something to change, but not badly enough to devote our time and energy to changing it. It is in these cases, we must accept that what is, is.

Happiness is having goals and a purpose. Helen Keller believed, "True happiness... is not attained through self-gratification, but through fidelity to a worthy purpose." Having goals and a purpose in life keep boredom away as well. Happiness is a side effect of the constant feeling of accomplishment and knowing you are headed in the right direction in life.

It is the little things in life that bring happiness. Those who base their happiness on major accomplishments are setting themselves up for a life void of happiness. "Happiness consists more in small conveniences or pleasures that occur every day, than in great pieces of good fortune that happen but seldom", wrote Benjamin Franklin. Life is full of these small pleasures: enjoying a sunset, walking on the beach, watching kids play, reading a good book, watching a good movie... the list goes on.

A Hindu proverb states that true happiness is in making others happy. This statement leads us back to one of the principles of success by Zig Ziglar who says, "You can get anything you want, if you help enough other people get what they want". By bringing another person happiness, you will find happiness as well.

Happiness is found in one's work. "The road to happiness lies in two simple principles," said John D. Rockefeller III, "find what it is that interests you and that you can do well, and when you find it put your whole soul into it—every bit of energy and ambition and natural ability you have." One's work usually occupies more than half of one's waking life. Choosing work that does not bring happiness will lead to a life that is mostly disappointing.

Happiness is found in one's family life. Both loving and being loved are sources of happiness unmatched by any other. Although we cannot control the feelings others have for us, it has been said that the best way to be loved is by loving.

Happiness and health are closely related. It is not necessary for one to be in perfect health to be happy. However, it is a well-known fact that happiness does affect health. In the Orient, it was believed that the basis of all disease was unhappiness. While we are pretty sure ALL disease is not due to unhappiness, there is truth to this. Happiness does have the power to restore health, and laughter just may be the best medicine.

Happiness is financial success and prosperity. On the tail end of happiness comes the material side of life. Acquiring is not enough to bring happiness, it is enjoying what you have acquired that can bring happiness. Writer Logan Pearsall Smith wrote, "There are two things to aim at in life: first, to get what you want; and, after that, to enjoy it. Only the wisest of mankind achieve the second."

Realize that true happiness is not the absence of feelings and emotions in the darker side of life. It has been said that there is no pleasure without pain, which may be true, but happiness and pleasure are not the same thing. I believe that one can enjoy happiness without experiencing misery. Happiness is a way of life, not a temporary feeling of enjoyment or pleasure, and temporary human emotions of anger, discouragement and pain do not have to affect one's overall happiness.

Sharing happiness is considered to be our "moral obligation" by many. George Bernard Shaw wrote, "We have no more right to consume happiness without producing it than to consume wealth without producing it." Those who have found it are encouraged to share it with those who are desperately in need of it.

It has been said that happiness consists of living each day as if it were the first day of your honeymoon and the last day of your vacation. Happiness is meant to enjoy now, not someday in the future when the economy improves, you meet the right person, you own a home, the kids grow up, you get a promotion, your business takes off, or you retire. These are the "good old days" so allow yourself to be happy today, right now.

ACTION STEP(S):

1) Write down what happiness means to you.

Days 181 and 182 are for "R&R"—review and reflection. Spend these days reviewing the last five articles and reflecting on the information and how it relates to your life. Now is also a good time to make sure all the action steps for the previous days have been completed.

Day 183: When To Live

"Live in the now", "stop and smell the roses", "don't let life pass you by"... There are dozens of quotes that all mean essentially the same thing: your mind should be focused on the present, not the future nor the past. Some tell us to be mindful of the past and take the future into consideration, but focus should be primarily on the present. To me, living in the present means being aware of your conscious choice to focus on the past, present or future—it is not necessarily having to focus on the present.

When I was in high school, I worked as a dishwasher at a local restaurant. Although this job did not pay that much, and it was considered to be "dirty" work by most of my peers' standards, I actually enjoyed it very much. For me, it was a time to mentally "zone out" and think about all the ideas that I had for making money. I would spend hours playing out just about every imaginable scenario in my head. I was motivated, excited, and most of all, I loved my job. Washing dishes is not brain surgery; after my first 10 minutes on the job it became a subconscious activity. Sure, I could have focused on the plates with regurgitated chicken bones and glasses filled with milk-soda-steak soup made by bored 12-year-olds, but during this time I chose to focus on my future, where I found more productivity, energy and enjoyment.

To this day, I spend much of my valuable time focused on the future as well as occasionally reliving positive events from my past. I do this when I am done getting all the happiness out of my present environment that I can. It is wise to stop and smell the roses, but how long are you supposed to sit there with your nose in a rose? Advocates of the "live in the now" mentality often overlook the power of daydreaming and creative visualization.

Surviving prisoners of war did not survive by living in the present and focusing on their pain, hunger, and undesirable living conditions. They survived by taking journeys in their minds, focusing on past events where they found joy, and creating a future for themselves for after they were freed. In less extreme and more everyday situations, those with monotonous jobs claim to "keep their sanity" by daydreaming about future events. Why deprive yourself of the pleasure of taking a trip down memory lane, especially when you cannot find pleasure or enjoyment in your present environment?

Before you zone out to the past or future, understand that there are very good reasons for focusing on the present. By focusing on the present, you become much more observant and notice things you may have never noticed before. You begin to appreciate things you have never appreciated before. Being focused on present activities allows you to be more productive. Focusing on the present enables you to become an active listener.

There is nothing wrong with living in the future or the past, providing you are not sacrificing your present. I am often guilty of being in an amusement park on a thrilling ride, but thinking about something else. Or going for a walk with my family but thinking about business, while missing the smiling faces of my children as they are enjoying their present environment. Time spent waiting in lines, stuck in traffic and commuting can be time well spent using your creativity and imagination. Focus on your future success and visualize yourself living a life where your goals have been met. The choice is ultimately yours.

ACTION STEP(S):

---

1) Take 5 minutes to focus on the present. Concentrate 100% on you present environment. Look at the walls, your desk, out the window, an object, or anything that is part of your present. If your mind starts to wander, don't let it. Did you notice things that you did not notice before? Did you find it hard to stay focused on the present? Focusing on the present becomes easier with practice.

Day 184: Avoid Offending Others

I will never forget a meeting that I attended when I was an employee at a very large publicly traded corporation. There were about 10 attendees, many of whom were new to the company. The head of the sales department, who was on the speaker phone, led the meeting from another location. For over 20 minutes, he released his rage on the rest of us using language unsuitable for even an "R" rated movie. At the end of the meeting, I was in a state of shock. I could not believe that a "professional" would actually behave this way. How did this guy keep his job? The other new employees and I were all extremely offended. When we raised our concern with a member of the management team, who happened to be present during the vulgarity fest, he nonchalantly replied, "Oh, he is always like that." Shortly after we discovered that just about the entire upper level management team were all "like that". From that day on, we lost respect for the management team and without a doubt, productivity suffered greatly.

Some people are more easily offended than others. The fact that some people you will be in contact with are so easily offended is not something over which you have control. You can, however, follow some basic "rules" of etiquette that will help you to avoid social blunders that can get in the way of your success.

Avoid using offensive language. Vulgar language is universally found to be offensive in professional environments. Some of the more sensitive people also are offended by poor use of the English language, over use of expressions, and even accents. Whether you choose to improve your English skills or get rid of any accent you may have is up to you, but avoiding vulgar language is a must.

Avoid making offensive comments. A comment can be a joke, an observation, a quip, or any other use of words to express an idea. Be careful that the content of the comments you make do not single out any sex, race, economic group, or social group. An example of this may be as subtle as referring to the female receptionists collectively as "the girls".

Avoid offensive actions and behaviors. Use your common sense with this one. In fact, many offensive actions and behaviors are now grounds for immediate termination (as in work, not in life) and some can even lead to criminal prosecution. I once had a meeting with a few executives of another firm. One of the VPs of this firm introduced me to the three other executives in the meeting, but skipped over the secretary who was there taking the minutes. I was personally offended that they felt this woman was not important enough for me to know her name. As a result, I began the meeting with a bad impression which eventually led me to the decision not to do business with the firm.

Please note, that I am not casting a moral judgment here. It is, however, a fact that offending others is poor human relations and will get in the way of success. If you are seeking moral guidance on these issues, consult your parents or your church. If you choose to use vulgar language, tell offensive jokes, or engage in offensive behavior of any kind outside of your professional life, beware of creating a habit that will undoubtedly find its way into your professional life.

Just by interacting with others, you risk offending someone. Those who speak more, attempt humor, and have more interaction with others are at a greater risk of offending others. The best advice I can give is live with integrity and if you do offend someone, for any reason, do not criticize the person for being too easily offended. Instead, offer a sincere apology and move on. There is a chance that the person whom you offended will respect you even more than before you offended him. Follow the suggestions above and keep your path to success free of these unnecessary obstacles.

ACTION STEP(S):

1) Take the most offensive word you currently use and remove it from your vocabulary. Never again use this word. If you find you

feel better about yourself and you see others respect you more, then repeat this action step with other offensive words presently in your vocabulary.

2) For every offensive joke you know, learn two non-offensive jokes.   Great joke sites can be found all over the Internet (ironically, most of which are considered offensive by many).

"Be thou familiar, but by no means vulgar."

- William Shakespeare

Day 185: Inspiration from Debbi Fields Rose

Debbi Fields (1956–) is the founder and former chairperson of Mrs. Fields Cookies, a $500 million company with over 650 domestic locations, and over 65 international locations in 11 different countries.

Success is going for the long shot. At age 20, and without any business experience, Debbi convinced a bank to finance an unproven business concept that appeared to have little likelihood of success. On August 16, 1977, Mrs. Fields Chocolate Chippery opened its doors to the public in Palo Alto, California.

Success is innovation. In 1989, Debbi made Mrs. Fields, Inc. the first company in the food retailing business to use technology to streamline operations and production schedules using a state-of-the-art computer system.

Success is knowing how to balance work and family life. Debbie is the proud birth mother of 5 daughters and stepmother of 5 more children. She believes in the importance of integrating family and business into one successful life.

Success is knowing that belief in yourself is more important than belief in others' criticisms. "A cookie store is a bad idea. Besides, the market research reports say America likes crispy cookies, not soft and chewy cookies like you make."—Response to Debbi Fields' idea of starting Mrs. Fields' Cookies.

Success begins with a good recipe. "First, the recipe for success requires passion—you've got to love what you do. Second, you've got to persevere. There are many challenges, and it is a scary road out there—but you have to see it through. Finally, focus on perfection. To have a product or service that will last, you have to be the best, not 'me too'."

Success is going after business, not waiting for it to come to you. The first day of business, Debbi's store had no sales by noon. Instead of waiting around, she hit the streets and gave samples out. By the end of the day, she had sold $75 worth of cookies.

Success is effective communication. Debbi joined her local Toastmasters, a public speaking organization, because she knew the importance of communication and delivering a message. Debbi commented for Toastmaster's magazine, "Getting your point across quickly and succinctly is essential".

Success is accepting risk. "People talk about success, dream about success, want to be successful. But to move to the next rung on the ladder, you've got to take risks. You've got to move out of your comfort zone."

Success is being a positive role model. "Be your child's role model. How your children feel about you is more important than anything else. I try hard to be a good role model. When I told my kids I was being honored with the Golden Gavel award, they looked over the list of past recipients and the criteria for selection. And they said, 'Mom, we're really proud of you.' Those are the best words you can ever hear."

[Sources: http://www.mrsfields.com, http://debbifields.com, Toastmasters Magazine]

"If you have a dream, you've got to reach for it. A dream won't come true by itself— you've got to make it happen."

- Debbi Fields Rose

Day 186: Using Negative Words

Being a dad, I have taught my kids many things in their cumulative six years on this earth, and they have taught me a great many things as well. As my two year old son plays with his toys, I have found myself saying proactively, and in a warning tone, "Don't throw your toys," only to realize that I just put an idea in his little head that was most likely not there seconds ago. Sure enough, seconds later, toys are flying across the room. I now say, "Play nicely with your toys please," and get much better results.

This same concept is a well-known phenomenon of human behavior that applies to people of all ages. Phrasing requests by using words like "don't", "not", "stop", "refrain from", and other negative words or phrases require that the request be processed by the conscious mind. Therefore, if we make a request using a word or phrase in the negative, and the person to whom we make the request is not actively listening, or incapable of understanding the complete request, the request is passed directly to the person's subconscious mind without the negative term. So for example, saying, "Don't stick the pencil up your nose!" to a daydreaming student enforces this action by entering his subconscious as "stick the pencil up your nose". Even if the request does pass through the conscious mind, it still enters the subconscious **without** the negative word or phrase. This is because the subconscious stores images and feelings, not words. The word "not" or "don't" cannot be visualized and therefore is omitted.

Not sure about this one? Try this... Request #1) keep your hands to your side (wait 15 seconds). Now request #2) don't itch your nose (wait 15 seconds). With the second request, did you feel an urge to scratch your nose? Even if you didn't, did you find yourself thinking an awful lot about itching your nose, like more than you have in the last year of your life? Making requests using negative words is actually an inadvertent use of the power of suggestion.

Our goals should be stated not only in the present, but in the positive for this very same reason.

I have healthy, smoke free lungs vs. I *don't smoke*
I have an abundance of money vs. I *am debt free*
I spend plenty of time with my family vs. I *am not a workaholic*

If the whole concept of the subconscious mind is still too metaphysical for you, then look at it this way: Statements made in the positive are much easier to visualize and remember than statements using negative words or phrases. How can one visualize "I am not a workaholic"? Many studies have shown that visualization increases the length of time information can be recalled. State requests in the positive so that a visualization can be made, and perhaps more important, state the request in the positive so the *right* visualization is being made.

ACTION STEP(S):

1) Verify that your written goals are using a statement in the positive and one that can be visualized.

2) Commit to making requests in the positive from now on (notice I did not say, "avoid using negative words and phrases").

"Focus on succeeding rather than not failing."

- Bo Bennett

Day 187: Building Rapport

Have you ever spoken with someone and had the feeling that you were "not on the same page" or "not speaking the same language"? How about engaged a possible romantic companion only to realize very quickly that you were "incompatible"? The chances are, you did not have good rapport (pronounced ra - poor) with the other person. The ability to build rapport is one ability to which many great communicators attribute their success.

Rapport is the feeling between two or more people that they can relate to each other. Rapport is vital in just about any communication situation. Couples who have good rapport with each other have happier relationships, sales people who can build rapport with prospects sell more, and leaders who have rapport with those whom they lead are more effective.

There are said to be three general types of people:

Visuals. A visual is one who best understands and uses sight related words to express him or herself, such as, "I see what you mean" or "Your proposal looks good".

Auditories. An auditory is one who best understands and uses sound related words to express him or herself, such as, "I hear what you are saying" or "your proposal sounds good".

Kinesthetics. A kinesthetic is one who best understands and uses feelings or touch related words to express him or herself, such as, "I feel for you" or "I feel we can use the ideas in your proposal".

It is usually not that difficult to pick up which type of person you are dealing with by listening to the words they use. Once you determine which category they fall under, use language that fits in with the type of person they are. For example, a conversation between a sales person who knows how to build rapport and a prospect may go something like this:

Prospect: *It just does not **look** good to me.*
Sales Person: *I **see**. What would make it **look** good to you?*

or

Prospect: *It just does not **sound** good to me.*
Sales Person: *I **hear** what you are saying. What would make it **sound** better?*

or

Prospect: *It just does not **feel** right to me.*
Sales Person: *I **understand**. What specifically does not **feel** right about it?*

Using words and phrases based on the visual, auditory or kinesthetic tendencies of others will help the other person relate to you better, but that alone is not the answer to building good rapport. Here are more suggestions that you can use to build the level of rapport it takes to create successful relationships.

- **Match vocabulary level.** Would you talk to a two year old the same way you talk to a college professor? Hopefully not. Most people tend to have two ways of speaking: one way to adults, and one way to those who are not yet adults. People tend to find it more important to show their superiority and mastery of language rather than communicate effectively. I remember the teachers I had in high school that spoke way over most of the students' heads. Result: bored kids with poor grades. Today, high-tech sales people who use jargon that I am not familiar with often approach me. Result: no sale. Do your best to match the vocabulary level of those with whom you speak.
- **Match speech patterns.** If you are a very fast speaker and the person you are speaking with is a slow speaker, then adjust your speed to match. Likewise, if the person you are speaking with speaks in a deep voice, then lower the pitch of your voice.

- **Find common interests quickly.** If you keep speaking about the sun and the person you are speaking with keeps bringing up the moon, talk about the moon or change subjects until a common interest is found. One can usually tell when another is interested in a subject by the enthusiasm that is shown in the other person's face.
- **Maintain good eye contact.** Good eye contact does not mean a continual glare, like a raging lunatic, but rather the avoidance of shifty eyes, especially when the other person is speaking to you.
- **Listen.** Be an active listener. Listen with your entire body, not just your ears. Lean in a bit toward the speaker and give an occasional nod. Avoid too many verbal acknowledgments such as "right", "I see...", "sure", "uh huh...", and other similar words and sounds—overuse of these are both annoying and distracting.
- **Ask questions.** Without interrupting, ask clarifying questions about something the other person had just said. This is actually just another part of good active listening.

Whether communicating with your children, parents, students, teachers, friends, employees, or boss, build rapport using some or all of the suggestions above. Do this, and it will not be long before you will consider yourself a successful communicator.

ACTION STEP(S):

1) Use one or more of these techniques to consciously build rapport with another person. You can do it without them even knowing it.

"In order to sell a product or a service, a company must establish a relationship with the consumer. It must build trust and rapport. It must understand the customer's needs, and it must provide a product that delivers the promised benefits."

- Jay Levinson

Days 188 and 189 are for "R&R"—review and reflection. Spend these days reviewing the last five articles and reflecting on the information and how it relates to your life. Now is also a good time to make sure all the action steps for the previous days have been completed.

Day 190: Never, Ever Lie

Nobody likes dishonest people, whether in a personal situation or in business. Just about the worst label one can be branded with is a "liar". Lying is like a contagious disease but rather than spreading to others, it spreads to all parts of one's life. One little lie often turns into a series of lies all constructed to support the other lies. Then, each one of those lies needs more lies to support those lies, and what was once a small white lie turns into a lifetime of dishonestly and deceit. Sooner or later, those who lie will get caught in a lie, and trust, integrity, and chances at lasting success will be lost.

Lies can be told for many reasons. Some of the reasons may appear fairly honorable, but it is important to realize that once you allow yourself to lie for any reason, you begin to justify all future lies. Perhaps the first lie you told was for what most would agree to be a very good reason; however, the supporting lies needed to cover the original lie may start doing some damage. It is best to use every bit of your creativity, communication skills, and common sense to avoid lying at all costs. Here is a list of the some of the most common reasons people lie and possible alternatives to lying for those reasons.

To feel better about oneself. Many people who lack self-confidence resort to lying, or fabrication of truth to make up for their perceived shortcomings. A classic example of this is the people who subtract a few years when giving their age, or a few pounds when giving their weight. Greater self-confidence and acceptance will omit the desire for lying for this reason. Keep in mind that by using candor, you actually make others feel better about themselves and others will perceive you to be more honest and trustworthy. So next time someone asks you your weight, say with confidence and a dash of humor, "I weigh a big, fat xxx lbs".

Worried about what others will think. A lie is often told out of fear of not fitting in or the desire to protect one's image. A teenager may come home way past his curfew, and when confronted by his parents as to his whereabouts, he may blurt out a series of lies out of fear of disappointing his parents. People often underestimate the understanding and compassion of others. It is by habit that we generally assume the worst and our minds play out the worst case scenario. Tell the truth and you will be pleasantly surprised at the results. Even if others condemn your actions or behavior, they will admire and respect YOU more for your honesty.

For attention or to appear interesting. Lying or making up stories is an easy way to get some quick attention. Our everyday lives generally do not make for interesting stories. When in conversation with others who are telling their stories (many of which are most likely exaggerated or even made up, depending on how many drinks they may have had), the need arises to "one-up" the person telling their story. To do this usually requires an exaggeration or fabrication of an even more entertaining story.

To arouse negative feelings or emotions in others. Some will tell lies just to make others feel jealous, angry, regretful or other negative feelings or emotions. One should never purposely arouse negative feelings in others, especially for self-gratifying reasons. This form of lying is used more often by kids and some adults who lack maturity and common decency.

To arouse positive feelings or emotions in others. Lying in an attempt to make others feel good is also known as flattery. Flattery is the evil twin of sincere appreciation. Those who attempt flattery are usually pretty bad at it, and are labeled as "brown-nosers". A better way to arouse positive feelings or emotions in others is to use sincere appreciation. Take a moment to think about what you can truly appreciate about the other person. Are they wearing a tie or blouse that you really like? Do they handle pressure extremely well? Are they good at what they do? It is not hard to find something you can sincerely show appreciation for in another person, you may just need to look more closely.

To protect the feelings of another. Are all lies bad? What about the overweight wife that asks the husband, "Does this dress make me look fat?" Of course, the husband could use the line from the movie _Tommy Boy_ and say, "No, no, no... Your face does". However, this type of response, depending on the sense of humor of the wife, may not go over too well. It is best to give an honest response, even if not a direct answer to the question. For example, "Honey, you are beautiful no matter what you wear"... and just hope that you are not pushed for an answer to the real question!

Out of habit. Those of us who got away with lying in childhood, most likely carried the habit into adulthood. Like any other destructive habit, lying is not easy to break, but necessary if one is serious about success. The first step is to realize how destructive lying is to one's reputation and success in life. Then, one must become consciously aware of when one is lying. Finally, and perhaps the most difficult of the steps, one must stop oneself as soon the lie begins to be told.

Lying can also be in the form of simply not letting the truth be known. This can happen by leading others on to false conclusions and not correcting them. For every reason there is to lie there is a better reason not to lie. For every problem you think a lie would solve, there is a better solution consisting of an honest approach— it just takes a little more effort and practice. Never, ever lie and you'll find you have better relationships and more success in both your personal life and in business.

ACTION STEP(S):

---

1) Think about all the lies you have told recently. Write down the real reason why you told the lie. Now, knowing what you now know, write down how you could have dealt with that situation honestly.

"Lying and cheating in advertising, in the long run, are commercial suicide. Dishonesty in advertising destroys not only confidence in advertising, but also in the medium which carries the dishonest advertisement... No one can be ill in a community without endangering others; no advertiser can be dishonest without casting suspicion upon others."

- Daniel Starch

Day 191: Creative Negotiation

The movie *Phenomenon* stars John Travolta who plays George Mally, an ordinary, blue collar, working man whose intelligence level is miraculously increased by a phenomenon. After this event, he begins to solve his everyday life problems. Consider this following scene:

Roger: *George, can I have my Bronco back? I don't have any cash now but I need my car.*
George: *Well, I need some solar panels installed on my roof.*
Roger: *I don't know anything about solar p...*
George: *Charlie Shepard does and he needs a well dug on his property. You help him dig the well, he'll help me with the panels, and I'll fix your car! Deal?*
Roger: *Yeah, deal!*

Overnight, George became a master negotiator using one of the best negotiating techniques—creative negotiation.

Negotiation occurs when two or more parties want something from each other. In traditional negotiation, usually a compromise is made and one or more of the parties give in a little to make the deal. Creative negotiation is about creating solutions that take a different approach. There are many ways to meet the wants of parties involved, however, all too often only the most obvious are presented as possible solutions. It is up to the creative negotiator to search for alternative options in which both parties do not have to make compromises, and in some cases, get more out of the deal.

It is well known that right-brain thinkers tend to be more creative whereas left-brain thinkers tend to be more analytical. What if you are primarily a left-brain thinker? Can you learn to be more creative? It depends on which study you read. I happen to believe creative thinking is a learned behavior rather than a result of some gene like the one for hair color. However, if you do not believe that, or if you want to profit from creative negotiating right away, get a creative thinker on your team. If you are fortunate enough to have a creative spouse, friend or co-worker, ask them for their ideas. Most would be more than happy to help, and feel appreciated that you care enough to ask their opinion.

Creative negotiating is not about manipulating or deceiving. It is about approaching a negotiation from a different perspective. It's about suggesting a way to a win-win solution where little or no compromise needs to be made, with the best intentions of all the parties involved. There is always another way, take the time and the mental energy to find it.

ACTION STEP(S):

1) Give your right-brain some exercise: draw, paint, build, imagine, sculpt, design—do something creative that you have never done before.

"Let us never negotiate out of fear. But let us never fear to negotiate."

- John F. Kennedy

Day 192: Inspiration from Steve Jobs

Steve Jobs (1955–) is the co-founder of Apple Computer Corporation who became a multi-millionaire before the age of 30 by revolutionizing the computer industry.

Success begins with passion. Steve would begin his journey by joining the Homebrew Computer Club where he met Apple's other co-founder, Steve Wozniak.

Success is seeing what others fail to see. Jobs is best known as a visionary, who was able to see the development of the PC industry long before its actual development. In fact, his electronics teacher at Homestead High, John McCollum, recalled he was "something of a loner" and "always had a different way of looking at things."

Success is surrounding yourself with talent and skills that you lack. Jobs knew that Wozniak was a much better engineer than he. Jobs kept his focus on the marketability of the product.

Success is seeking good advice. Jobs received marketing advice from a friend, who was also a retired CEO from Intel, who helped Jobs and Wozniak with marketing strategies for selling their new product.

Success is putting it all on the line. To start their new company, Jobs and Wozniak sold their most valuable possessions. Jobs sold his Volkswagen micro-bus and Wozniak sold his Hewlett-Packard scientific calculator, which raised $1,300 to start their new company.

Success is a result of meeting the needs of others. Apple's most successful computer, the Macintosh, had an interface that allowed people to interact easier with computers, because they used a mouse to click on objects displayed on the screen to perform some function. The user friendliness of the product made it an instant success.

Success is not without setbacks. In 1985, after being ousted from a position of power in his own company, Jobs retired as chairman of Apple Computer. This was a devastating blow to the young visionary, but a necessary step in his success.

Success is not without subsequent failures. Jobs formed a company called NextStep and planned to build the next generation of personal computers that would put Apple to shame. It did not happen. After eight long years of struggle and after running through some $250 million, NextStep closed down its hardware division in 1993.

Success is in the person, not the event. Steve Jobs later founded another company called Pixar Animation Studios. Pixar was founded in 1986; The company has won many awards, including 6 Academy Awards for *Finding Nemo*, *A Bug's Life*, *Toy Story*, and *Monsters, Inc.*

Success is making amazing comebacks. Eleven years after Jobs was ousted from a position of power at Apple, they rehired the former co-founder in hopes of turning the company around. When Jobs returned, he succeeded and was responsible for one of the most astonishing turnarounds in US history.

[Sources: http://www.biography.com, http://www.askmen.com]

Day 193: Recognition

Ever since my wife created a recognition chart for our four-year-old daughter, we have seen a level of cooperation, good behavior, and achievement like never before. This chart is nothing more than a piece of paper that hangs on our bulletin board in our home. On the paper are several different categories in which, depending on performance, my wife draws a little face with a frown, half star, or full star. Whether we are 4 or 104, all of us appreciate and will strive for recognition.

Recognition is defined as attention or favorable notice. It is the act of showing appreciation, usually publicly. Recognition is most often given in the presence of one's peers in the form of either sincere words of appreciation or some kind of award. Parents can give recognition to their children, teachers to their students, managers to their subordinates, and business owners to their customers or employees. Recognition is most often given by effective and respected leaders to those whom they lead, but can be given to anyone, by anyone.

Recognition can come in many forms: a certificate of achievement, a prize of some kind (candy bar, trip to Hawaii, new car), time off from work, being excused from a test, a gold star, free product or service, and much more. However, one of the simplest, least expensive, and most effective forms of recognition is often in the form of sincere words of appreciation. The majority of studies done on this topic have concluded that people are more motivated by recognition than by money alone. Recognition for one's achievements or efforts gives that person greater self-confidence and fulfills one of the greatest human desires—the feeling of importance.

Giving recognition does more then just make the person receiving the recognition feel good, it has a significant impact on the person's peers as well. For example, publicly recognizing just one employee will motivate the other employees, knowing that their work and achievements will be appreciated too. It gives them something to strive for.

Here are some suggestions on giving recognition to others:

- **Hold award ceremonies.** These are great to hold on a regular basis such as annually or bi-annually. They can be their own events or they can be worked into existing events such as conferences, company picnics, etc.
- **Send public notices of recognition.** This can be in the form of a memo, e-mail, ad in a local or industry periodical, or any other form of print that will be read by others.
- **Give public verbal recognition.** A few, kind, spontaneous words spoken to a group can be a very effective form of recognition. This can be done in person, over a loud speaker, or over the telephone in a conference call.
- **Be fair in your recognition.** If you are going to recognize one person for doing x, y, and z, then be sure to recognize others in the same position who do x, y, and z.
- **In small groups, recognize everybody.** Giving recognition in a group where just a few members are not recognized, creates a very awkward situation. Think about how you can recognize each member for something unique and show that recognition. Result: everyone in the group will feel important and appreciated.

To the misfortune of many, recognition, like gratitude and appreciation, is often overlooked or ignored. Recognition has the power to both motivate and inspire people, and not just the receivers of the recognition. Leaders who give recognition are more respected and admired by those whom they lead. As Gerard C. Eakedale simply stated, "recognition is the greatest motivator".

ACTION STEP(S):

---

1) Give recognition to someone you feel is deserving and, if possible, views you as a leader. If you cannot think of anyone who is deserving, then think harder. Think about all the achievements or efforts one has made.

"It is up to us to give ourselves recognition. If we wait for it to come from others, we feel resentful when it doesn't, and when it does, we may well reject it."

- Spencer Tracy

Day 194: Being Popular

In the movie *Never Been Kissed*, David Arquette plays Rob, a twenty-something year old who poses as a high school student to help his sister become popular. Rob gains instant popularity when he wins a school cafeteria tub-of-coleslaw eating contest and exclaims, "I'm the coleslaw king of the world!!!" I wish I could say that this is just a movie and that is not how popularity works in high school, but I can't. I can say, however, that this type of popularity is like building a house of cards—easily collapsible. Later in the movie we see Rob turn from hero to zero just as quickly as he became popular, when his identity is discovered. True popularity may take a little longer to build, but when built with a solid foundation, it can make one's school years some of the most enjoyable and memorable years of one's life.

What is so important about being popular? For the most part, it is about acceptance. Acceptance to the average adolescent is much higher on the hierarchy of needs than it is for the average adult. This is one of main reasons parents and teachers often find it difficult to understand the actions and behaviors of adolescents. Popularity is not only about being accepted, but it's about being liked or even admired.

Before we discuss specific ways to become popular, let's dispel some of the myths that most associate with being popular.

- You don't need to be good looking. In high school, looks certainly can help, but are far from a requirement of popularity.
- You don't need to hang out with the "popular" group. Being popular means not needing to follow the crowd.
- You don't need to do things you feel are not right. Being popular is about being a leader, not a follower.
- You don't need to beat up the toughest guy. The goal is not to have others fear you, but like you. It is hard to really

like someone when you feel physically threatened by him or her.

- You don't need to be mean to others. Popularity seems to be associated with being conceited, self-centered, and just plain mean to those who are not as popular. This is only the false popularity that does not last.

True popularity can be gained using the many success principles in this course. It is the kind of popularity that leads to a lifetime of success-centered habits. Although the following suggestions were specifically written with high school students in mind, the same principles can be applied in the work environment.

- **Be friendly with everyone.** In school, students have a tendency to befriend those who are most like them and ignore everyone else. Students are categorized by other students into groups, and rarely do any students socialize outside their group. Remember that despite the label, everyone is still a person. To be popular, show others that it is OK to socialize and even choose friends outside your own little group.
- **See the good in others.** Being genuinely friendly with others requires that you learn to see the good, or positive qualities in others while choosing not to focus on their faults. Being human, we all have faults. The key to getting others to like you is by showing genuine interest in them. Looking back to my high school days, I remember deserting many friends because I did not approve of their actions and behaviors. I chose not to bother to focus on the positive qualities of others, which caused resentment in those I deserted, and me to lose the friendship of some really great people.
- **Have self-confidence.** Self-confidence, or the lack thereof, can easily be detected by others. It is one of the most admirable qualities one can possess in high school and in life. It is the self-confident individual who takes the initiative to meet new people and socialize with the opposite sex. Those who lack self-confidence usually bond with one who possesses self-confidence as a way for them

to enter the social arena. Self-confidence is a must when it comes to popularity.

- **Stand up for yourself.** Never let others walk all over you. Nine out of ten times, those who bully others and threaten with violence are just big talkers. Bullies prey mostly on the weak minded, not necessarily on those physically weaker. If you stand up for yourself, the bully will move on.
- **Be a leader.** Being a leader is about standing up for what you believe in and learning how to say no. Never give in to peer pressure. Instead, create your own positive peer pressure by being a positive role model for others to follow. Leaders make their own choices and do things for their own reasons. If you want to win the respect of others, show others that you are not afraid to go against the crowd.
- **Don't talk about others behind their backs.** Being kind to others includes being kind to them when they are not there as well. Gossip and back-stabbing (figuratively speaking) is commonplace in high school and you can choose not to participate by simply excusing yourself from any conversation where others are being talked about negatively. Be considerate of the feelings of others.

Reputations can be changed. If you were a little scrawny, geeky kid in the fifth grade, and since then, gained weight, and grew up, you first need to lose the old self-image you may still have. Then show others that you are no longer this person through your self-confidence. If you are currently one who is disliked by others because of your attitude or the way you treat others, it is never too late to change. True popularity does not happen overnight, so have patience. Treat others with respect and kindness and work on your self-confidence, and even if you are not considered "popular" by your peers, you will have built a solid foundation for your success and happiness in life, which is far more important.

ACTION STEP(S):

---

1) Share this article with an adolescent.

2) Are there any people in your life that you have not made an effort to be friendly to simply because of the "group" they may be in? Perhaps employees in a different department, students who are more focused on school work, the guy who bags your groceries? Start by being friendly to just one person with whom you would not normally be. Then, feel free to be friendly with as many people you like.

"When people laugh at Mickey Mouse, it's because he's so human; and that is the secret of his popularity."

- Walt Disney

Days 195 and 196 are for "R&R"—review and reflection. Spend these days reviewing the last five articles and reflecting on the information and how it relates to your life. Now is also a good time to make sure all the action steps for the previous days have been completed.

Day 197: Hostile E-mails

Back in the "old" days, before e-mail, people used to use ink filled tubes called "pens" and material made of cellulose pulp, derived mainly from wood, rags, and certain grasses (paper) to compose messages to send to others. They would use a delivery system called "the postal service" to send this "mail" which took days, not seconds, for the recipient to actually receive the letter. When one was acting on anger and composed a hostile message, he had plenty of time to clear his head before actually mailing the letter; there was the process of writing the letter, addressing the envelope, putting the letter in the envelope, affixing the postage, and placing it in the mailbox. Today, one can compose a nasty message, send it, and have the recipient reading it, all within less than a minute. Needless to say, this type of instant communication causes our emotions to get the better of us in our e-mail communication. Effective handling of hostile e-mails, and avoiding sending hostile e-mails yourself, will give you a significant boost in your pursuit of success.

You start your morning by going through the prior night's e-mails. The sun is shining, the birds are singing, you are happy to be alive. Then, you read a hostile and somewhat vulgar e-mail from an obviously angry customer or co-worker blaming you for one thing or another. Almost instantly, your state is transformed from one of peace and contentment to one of anger and defensiveness. What do you do next? For most of us, we click the reply button and tell the sender of the disturbing e-mail how we really feel. While that may make us feel good in the short-term, the effects of an equally belligerent response to the original e-mail will only fuel the fire. Here is why:

- The sender of the original e-mail obviously is unskilled in communication or unable to control his emotions and will not deal with a hostile and defensive response favorably. In turn, he will almost definitely respond to your response with even more hostility and perhaps threats. This will only escalate the situation.

- By escalating the situation, you will waste hours of your valuable time rather than spending that time being productive.
- You will greatly decrease your chances of changing the opinion of the person who sent the e-mail. Your response will undoubtedly make the person more defensive.

So what are you supposed to do? Let another make unjust claims about you or your service when it is obvious to you they have all their facts wrong? Not necessarily. Forget about your ego and your desire to prove yourself right and remember effective communication. Here are some suggestions for handling hostile e-mails.

- Understand that the e-mail was most likely written at the peak of the sender's frustration. If you were to call the sender, they would probably start by apologizing.
- Ask yourself, what is your goal? What are you trying to accomplish in your response? If the answer is, "tell the person a thing or two" or to vent your anger, then just hit the delete key and move on. You will have wasted no more than the time it took to read the e-mail. And maybe, you can learn something from the e-mail—perhaps something you can change to prevent others from getting so upset. If there is something you can learn from their written fury, reply with a simple, "Thank you for sharing this with me. I am sorry I have caused you so much frustration."
- Once you have a goal in mind, use your knowledge in effective communication to compose the most effective response. Some sample goals may be to:
  - save a customer from leaving
  - calm an angry customer
  - maintain a good working relationship with a customer
  - save a friendship
  - offer a sincere apology for doing something wrong
  - prevent a lawsuit

- Start your response by admitting to, or apologizing for, any fault that may have been yours to prompt such an e-mail to be sent in the first place. This alone will have an almost miraculous effect on the attitude of the sender. For example, "I checked with my supervisor and you are correct, we did overcharge you $20 for the product. This is completely my fault—I should have double-checked the price before charging your account. I am very sorry." How can any human still be furious after an apology like that!

- Correct the sender's erroneous comments or assumptions in such a way that it does not seem like you are trying to prove the sender wrong. People do not like to be corrected and they like it even less when others to tell them they are wrong. Make it sound as if it is your fault that their assumptions are incorrect and sympathize with their position. For example, "If I were overcharged $20, I would probably think the company that overcharged me were crooks as well. However, I can assure you that our firm is not in the habit of overcharging, and we are quick to correct our mistakes."

- Let the sender know what you will be doing about rectifying the situation. In some cases, there is no "situation", there is just an unreasonable person showing a complete lack of self-control. In other cases, your best course of action is to either a) explain your point of view and reasoning as to why you will not be taking any action, b) explain or apologize for what did happen and offer a solution or c) a combination of a and b.

- If appropriate, offer a phone number or ask for the sender's phone number and talk the situation out on the phone. The true message in an e-mail can easily be misunderstood. Once when a reseller of ours was having a problem with his account, being quick with my replies, I told him in an e-mail to "re sign" as in "sign up again". He though I meant "resign" as in "why don't you just quit since you are obviously inept". Fortunately, he picked up the phone to tell me off and the situation was instantly cleared up.

What about initiating the sending of a hostile e-mail yourself? You may be thinking, "I would never do that!" The fact is, when emotion gets the better of us, we often become unreasonable and get caught up in the moment. For times like these, here is some advice.

- Write your nasty message, just don't send it! Go ahead and blow off some steam. Let the person know what you really think of them. Tell them they have ugly children and their breath stinks, even if they don't have children and you've never been in physical contact with them. Write whatever makes you feel better. Then, delete the e-mail. Tip: Do NOT enter the person's e-mail address in the "To" field... you may hit "Send" by accident.
- Do your best to compose the e-mail after your feelings of anger have subsided. Keep yourself away from the keyboard at times of high negative emotions.
- Remember that sending an aggressive, hostile e-mail causes the recipient to become defensive rather than open. If your point of sending the e-mail is to get something, chances are, the only thing you will get is a nasty e-mail back from another pig-headed individual defending his ego.

It is certainly within your power to never send another hostile e-mail again, whether initiating the e-mail or replying to one. A careful and thoughtful response to a hostile e-mail can make an exiting customer a loyal customer for life or a furious employee a respectful and productive staff member. Controlling your temper and sending only e-mails that use effective communication for persuasion will produce much more favorable results than those that use harsh criticism and vulgarities. Practice self-control when dealing with e-mail and remember Lincoln's advice, "...a drop of honey catches more flies than a gallon of gall".

ACTION STEP(S):

---

1) Start making use of your e-mail client's "Outbox". Whenever you compose a message that you feel your negative emotions have played a part in creating, do not send the message right away. Save the message without sending and it will be stored in your "Drafts" folder. Come back to it 30 minutes later, or after you have had a chance to cool off and reread it. If you still feel it is appropriate to send as is, then send it; otherwise, edit the e-mail and send your new version.

"A loving person lives in a loving world. A hostile person lives in a hostile world. Everyone you meet is your mirror."

- Ken Keys

Day 198: Just Ask

After I sold Adgrafix, my wife and I started the search for our dream summer home. After looking at dozens of homes, we started to become discouraged that our dream home was not out there. However, one day while riding our bikes in our favorite summer vacation spot, we found our dream home. The only problem was, the house was not for sale. We decided not to let a little thing like that stop us. We wrote a quick note expressing our interest on a napkin we had, and then placed it in the screen door of the house. Two weeks later, we received a call from the homeowner's real estate broker and a month later the home was ours. Since the summer of 2001, my family and I have been cherishing every moment we spend together in our dream summer home. If we had never asked the former owner if he was interested in selling his home, the home would not be ours today.

A common characteristic of successful individuals is the ability, confidence, and courage to ask for what they want. Successful sales people ask for the sale rather than waiting for the prospect to ask how to buy. Successful students ask questions about what they do not understand rather than just accepting it. Successful singles ask for dates rather than stay at home and watch reruns of "Baywatch". Successful people understand a basic, but all too overlooked truth: you must ask for things you want; very rarely will they just be given to you.

Why doesn't everyone ask for things they want? The most common reason is the fear of rejection, which will be covered in detail in a future article. The second most common reason is that people assume others know what they want. The fact is, most of us are consumed with our own thoughts and desires and are not always thinking about what other people may want. This is not necessarily being egocentric, it is just being human. If you want something from someone, you can never really be sure the other person knows what you want unless you ask the other person for what you want.

When it comes to asking for what you want, don't hold back. Those who are "lucky" in life simply ask for things they want more often. Do not fear rejection; have the confidence to ask for what you want. It is a simple but powerful truth of success: those who ask more often receive more.

ACTION STEP(S):

---

1) Ask someone for something you normally would not ask for.

"For everyone who asks receives; he who seeks finds; and to him who knocks, the door will be opened."

- Matthew 7:8

Day 199: Inspiration from Charles R. Schwab

Charles R. Schwab (1947–) is the founder, chairman of the board, and co-CEO of The Charles Schwab Corporation, which is one of the nation's largest financial services firms.

Success is overcoming difficult odds. Despite his dyslexia, Schwab remained confident as a youth, never allowing his condition to get him down or stop him from succeeding at other tasks.

Success is having enthusiasm and arousing it in others. "I consider my ability to arouse enthusiasm among men the greatest asset I possess. The way to develop the best that is in a man is by appreciation and encouragement." • "A man can succeed at almost anything for which he has unlimited enthusiasm."

Success is accepting help from others when needed. Thanks to high grades in math and science, Schwab entered Stanford University in 1955. As a freshman, he failed both French and English, but made it through his undergraduate years with the aid of understanding roommates and prepared notes.

Success is discovering your aptitude and focusing on your strengths. Schwab discovered his aptitude for economics and other business courses, which led to his earning a BA in Economics, in 1959. He went on to Stanford Graduate School of Business, where he received his MBA in 1961.

Success is striving to be your best. "Everyone's got it in him, if he'll only make up his mind and stick at it. None of us is born with a stop-valve on his powers or with a set limit to his capacities, There's no limit possible to the expansion of each one of us."

Success is not being afraid to take risks. In the early 70s, Schwab borrowed $100,000 from an uncle to start up a brokerage firm in San Francisco, called First Commander Corp.

Success is having vision and seeing it through. In 1974, Schwab's company became the country's first discount brokerage firm: Charles Schwab & Co., Inc. Schwab's vision that the stock market should be accessible to everyone proved immensely popular and profitable.

Success is overcoming rejections. "I quickly learned that if I kept at it and plowed right through the rejections I would eventually get somebody to buy my wares."

Success is helping others. Mr. Schwab is also chairman of the Charles and Helen Schwab Foundation, whose work is structured within two program areas, which each has a specific focus. The Learning Differences program area directly provides resources and guidance to children with learning differences and their parents through the operating program, Schwab Learning. The Human Services program area develops initiatives in issues that severely affect communities, specifically poverty, homelessness and substance abuse.*

Text taken from http://www.schwabfoundation.org
[Sources: http://jobs.schwab.com,
http://www.schwabfoundation.org, http://www.aboutschwab.com]

Day 200: Fear of Rejection

During my later years in college, I took a sales job with my sister and mother selling ads in a free magazine that was distributed in hospitals. Majoring in, and having quite a strong aptitude for marketing, no matter how hard I tried, I could not help thinking how I was ripping off the businesses to whom I sold the ads. In my eyes, the concept was simple: approach the businesses who count on the local hospital for business, and insinuate that by taking an ad, they are doing the hospital a favor—in short, use deceptive marketing. Due to the responses from the advertisers and the renewal rates, I was quite sure that the ads did not work. Never before did I have such a strong fear of rejection. Needless to say, I did not do very well at the job, but looking back, the experience and lesson learned were priceless.

The fear of rejection, in this sense, refers to the rejection of an offer, as in asking for a date or asking for a sale. When a person fears rejection, they are not really not fearing the word "no", they are fearing imagined or out of proportion consequences of the rejection. Asking the question, "What am I really fearing?" is a good start to overcoming fear of rejection. Here are some of the more common fears associated with rejection:

The fear of feeling embarrassed. Embarrassment is a physiological phenomenon that causes feelings of anxiety and discomfort that many would rather not have to experience. The simple way to avoid having this experience is to avoid potentially embarrassing situations. However, this leads to missed opportunities and only adds to your fear of rejection. Embarrassment is a feeling that only you can generate based on your perception of external situations. Learn to say, "So what?", and put situations in perspective.

If you cannot conquer the fear of embarrassment itself, ask yourself another question, "What am I afraid of that I will be embarrassed about?" and analyze each answer. For example, selling the ads for the hospital magazine I feared becoming embarrassed if the prospect asked me a question to which I did not know the answer. Back then, I would stutter, get all red, and say, "I'm not sure" and usually blow the sale. Now in sales, I make sure I am well prepared with answers to every possible question that is likely to be asked. When an odd question is asked that I do not have the answer to, I respond with confidence, "I do not have the answer to that right now but I could find it and get back to you". Being prepared for all of the scenarios you can possibly be embarrassed about will almost certainly wipe away the fear of embarrassment.

The fear of what others will think of you. What will others think of you and your abilities if you are rejected? Will they have less confidence in you? Will they think you are a phony? Will they think you are a loser? Maybe. (I know... not the answer you wanted to hear.) First of all, who are "they"? If "they" are those close to you like your family and true friends, they will certainly know you for who you are and not let their opinion of you be altered by one or many rejections. If "they" are strangers like a prospect, an audience, or the media, do you honestly care what they think of you? If you say yes, then realize there are over 5 billion people in this world, and the opinions of a handful of strangers really do not amount to a hill of beans. Do we think any less of stock market billionaire Warren Buffet because he was rejected from Harvard School of Business, or do we think less of Harvard? :)

The fear of facing a truth that you do not want to accept. While selling the ads for the hospital magazine, my biggest fear of rejection stemmed from not believing in the product. I felt that I was selling for one purpose only: to make money. I feared that those I was selling to would see this as well. As long as this did not happen, I could rationalize that if an advertiser received just one customer from their ad, it could pay for itself for the entire year. I knew if a prospect did bring up the deceptive marketing techniques used by the company and me, I would not be able to deny it and I would be out of a job. Rather than attempt to convince myself that I was helping these businesses by selling them these ads, I chose to leave the company.

You are not the one being rejected. In most cases, it is your *offer* that is being rejected. When a single guy asks a girl out on a date, he is presenting the girl with an offer. It is the offer that the girl either accepts or rejects. If the guy feels he is being rejected too often then he needs to "sweeten the deal", perhaps by improving the quality of the conversation prior to the offer. (Note: if you are a guy and now asking, "What conversation?" you may need more help on this subject than I have to offer.)

If after questioning your true fears and doing your best to conquer them, you still feel the fear of rejection, then learn to see rejection as success. Here's how: A rejection is nothing more than a necessary step in the pursuit of success. If it takes 10 cold calls to get one sale, then realize without the 9 rejections you will not succeed at getting the sale. Now make it a game... decrease the number of rejections it takes to get a success. To do this, learn from each rejection. Ask yourself, "Why was my offer rejected?" and, "What can I learn from this?" With each rejection, you can improve your chances of success.

It is not rejection itself that people fear, it is the possible consequences of rejection. Preparing to accept those consequences and viewing rejection as a learning experience that will bring you closer to success, will not only help you to conquer the fear of rejection, but help you to appreciate rejection itself.

ACTION STEP(S):

---

1) Do you fear rejection? Make a list of all of the real fears you may have relating to rejection. How can you better prepare yourself to deal with those fears? What are the chances that what you are fearing will actually happen?

2) How can you see the rejections you deal with as successes?

Day 201: Do It Yourself?

I once read a very amusing e-mail proving that it would be a waste of Bill Gates' time to bend down to pick up a $3000 bill, if one existed. This is because his time, according to the math shown in the e-mail, is worth more than $3000 per second. In theory, this means it costs Bill Gates $90,000.00 just to pee and another $30,000.00 if he washes his hands. Of course, there are many false assumptions here but it does prove a good point: our time has monetary value and there is a cost associated with everything we do. Besides, it sure does make an amusing story. :)

A common characteristic shared by most successful people is the value of time. Many wealthy people assign a value to their time and make decisions based on the monetary value of their time, or the opportunity cost. Successful people take it a step further; they understand the difference between immediate cost and long-term cost, and also factor enjoyment into the equation. Life is full of mundane tasks and we all have the choice of doing them ourselves or seeking help. The successful individual knows how to make this choice.

What is the monetary value of your time? Here are three of the categories in which most working individuals fit.

1. **Fixed salary.** Those who are paid a fixed salary based on an average number of hours per day, and who do not get any more money from working extra hours, can use a simple formula: take total yearly income and divide it by the total number of working hours per year. Be sure to add in bonuses and other perks that can be translated into monetary form. For example, use of a company car may be equal to another $5,000 per year or stock options may be worth about $2000 per year. A $50,000.00 per year total income with about 2400 hours of work per year would equate to about $21 per hour.

2. **Variable salary.** This is where most salespeople, independent doctors, lawyers, and other performance paid workers fall. This is a group that can make more money for working more hours. Using the same formula above, the monetary value of one hour can be calculated.

3. **Business owners.** In this sense, business owners can be defined not only as sole owners of a business, but stock holders of a business in which their efforts can directly influence the value of the company. In my first two years of running Archieboy, I did not make a dime personally. This certainly does not mean my time was not worth anything. Business owners invest their time in their businesses, which has value. The value of a business is really only realized at the time in which it, or a part of it, as in the form of shares, are sold. Therefore, for a business owner to calculate his or her monetary value of time, many assumptions have to be made, specifically, the current and future value of the business they are building.

Now that we have our approximate hourly worth, it is not difficult to put a value to life's many tasks and chores. For example, a painter can give you an estimate of painting a room, and tell you how many hours it will take him. A house cleaner can tell you that she charges $20 per hour for cleaning services. A plumber, accountant, and lawyer can all give you their hourly rates as well.

Unfortunately, this is where most people stop and make their decision between doing something themselves or paying others to do it for them. The successful individual figures in these very important factors:

- **Long-term costs vs. immediate costs.** If you want a room painted, and the professional painter's estimate is $500, and your costs are $90 for the supplies, and about 6 hours of your time at $50/per hour, the immediate costs involved would lead to believe that you are better off doing the job yourself. However, what are the long-term costs? As an amateur, you may buy the wrong paint. You may not clean the wall properly or paint at a temperature that will cause the paint to come off or begin to chip years before it should. As an amateur, you can do a number of things wrong that can cause to you spend more time by having to do things twice, waste money on supplies, or do a poor job that will not last as long as a professional job.

- **Risk of getting hurt or hurting others.** What if you fell off the ladder while painting and broke your finger, your hand, you leg, or your neck? How would this affect your ability to make money in your current job? If installing a gas heater, what if you did not make a connection tight enough and your home exploded?

- **Lost time.** When a professional quotes you for his or her time, the figure they give you most often includes the time it takes for them to prepare for the job and clean up after the job. In our room-painting example, how much time does it take to get the supplies, prepare the room, and clean up after the job is done?

- **Cost of learning.** How much time is needed to research or learn about what needs to be done? Do you have manuals or instructions to read prior to doing the job? Do you have to spend time consulting experts or professionals? Is this information that you will most likely never use again?

- **Guarantees.** Most professional help, especially those who are licensed, have some kind of guarantee on their work. This means if something goes wrong, they will make it right for no charge. If you do something wrong, it is more money out of your pocket.

- **Pros can do it better.** You may be confident in your abilities and in some cases you may be able to do a better job or higher quality work than others you would have to pay. But for the most part, pros specialize in what they do and can do a better job than the average person.

- **Enjoyment.** In my line of work, much of my work is thinking. I do enjoy many mindless activities like cardiovascular exercise, doing dishes, folding laundry and others where I can be immersed in my own thoughts. I also enjoy more stimulating activities in which I learn and expand my knowledge, like programming and web design.

Enjoyment alone can be reason enough for doing something yourself.

Consider the real costs involved in "doing it yourself" versus paying someone else, especially a professional, to do it for you. Professionals are often far more efficient at doing what they do and can free you from the often mundane and sometimes difficult chores in life. When it makes sense, spend your money on peace of mind by having a professional do the job they are best suited to do, and spend your valuable time on your goals and life purpose.

ACTION STEP(S):

1) Look over your short-term and long-term "to do" list. Would you be better off having others do any of these things for you?

"Your time is much more valuable than you believe."

- Bo Bennett

Days 202 and 203 are for "R&R"—review and reflection. Spend these days reviewing the last five articles and reflecting on the information and how it relates to your life. Now is also a good time to make sure all the action steps for the previous days have been completed.

Day 204: Random Acts of Kindness

In 1928, James E. West, the "Godfather" of the Boy Scouts, said, "...the Daily Good Turn is an important factor in the development of a habit of service and attitude of mind which offset a tendency to selfishness." The Boy Scouts refer to good deeds and random acts of kindness as "good turns" and focus on the benefit of helping others by a selfless act. In fact, selflessness (not selfishness) is a common characteristic of both successful and happy people with benefits extending far beyond displaying mere selflessness itself.

A random act of kindness is something said or done to make another feel good while expecting absolutely nothing in return, not even gratitude. To be most effective, this act of kindness is done for someone just met or someone never met, thus the word "random". A random act of kindness is neither a favor done for someone who asks, nor is it ever performed with resentment or hesitation. It is an act performed strictly for the good will of others in which the only reward to be expected is the good feeling generated from helping others.

Does the idea of performing one random act of kindness each day sound too idealistic? Why should you spend your valuable time helping someone else when you need help yourself? After all, you have to look out for yourself and your own family, right? Kindness does have its critics; there is no question about it. Since random kindness is of so rare of a quality, many people suspect ulterior motives—the "What's in it for you?" attitude. Others may respond negatively to a random act of kindness. I remember a scene in the opening credits of the '70s sitcom, "The Odd Couple", where Felix (Tony Randall) offers assistance to an elderly woman crossing a busy street, only to be hit by the woman in protest. There is risk involved in random kindness, and perhaps this risk keeps most people from performing random acts of kindness. However, successful people know how to manage risk and understand when the benefits outweigh the potential negatives.

Why spend your time performing random acts of kindness? Here are just some of the reasons*:

- **Gives life purpose and meaning.** Many people believe our main purpose on this earth is to make the world a better place. Performing random acts of kindness is doing just that. Depression is rarely found in those who believe their lives have purpose and meaning.
- **Abolishes worry and self-pity.** One of the main reasons people worry so much is because they have so much time to think about worrying! Get in the habit of thinking about others and feel your worries disappear.
- **Does away with guilt.** Being human, we all do things we later regret and many times we never forgive ourselves. Restore your faith in yourself and prove to yourself that you are a good person. Build your self-confidence back by doing for others.
- **Good begets good.** As you begin to create more good in your life, there is less room and less time for the bad.
- **Improves overall health.** Helping contributes to the maintenance of good health, and it can diminish the effect of diseases and disorders—both serious and minor, psychological and physical.
- **Manages stress.** Stress-related health problems tend to improve after performing acts of kindness. A drop in stress may, for some people, decrease the constriction within the lungs that leads to asthma attacks.
- **Contributes to emotional well being.** Helping can enhance feelings of joyfulness, emotional resilience and vigor, and can reduce the unhealthy sense of isolation.
- **Improves attitude.** Chronic hostility, which negatively arouses and damages the body, can be reduced.
- **Gives a sense of increased self-worth.** An increased sense of self-worth, greater happiness and optimism, as well as a decrease in feelings of helplessness and depression, is achieved.
- **Results in greater happiness.** Regular club attendance, volunteering, entertaining, or faith group attendance is the

happiness equivalent of getting a college degree or more than doubling your income.

A random act of kindness can be as simple as a quick praise or as grand as a million dollar donation. Here are a few of the several forms that a random act of kindness can take:

- **Sincere praise.** Telling a waiter or waitress their first day on the job what a great job they are doing. Commenting on another's well-behaved children. Showing your admiration for another's shoes.
- **Gratitude.** Thanking the postal workers for delivering your mail on time each day. Showing appreciation for the employee that goes out of her way to help you. Expressing gratitude for the police officer or firefighter who puts himself at risk for the safety of others.
- **Good deed.** Picking up trash on a street, even though both the trash and street are not yours. Volunteering your time at a senior center. Coaching a children's sports team.
- **Money / material.** Donating money to a non-profit organization. Giving cash to a complete stranger in need. Giving clothes and other items to the Salvation Army.

Perform at least one random act of kindness each day. At first, it may take effort, but very quickly it will become a habit and way of life. Living in this way will have significantly positive effects on your physical body, your mental and emotional well being, and your very own success and happiness.

ACTION STEP(S):

---

1) From this day forward, commit to performing at least one random act of kindness each day.

"No act of kindness, no matter how small, is ever wasted."

- Aesop

Day 205: Be a Trend Spotter

In the movie, _You've Got Mail_, Meg Ryan plays Kathleen Kelly, the owner of a small, children's bookstore in a big city. Tom Hanks plays Joe Fox, an executive and heir to the Fox Books superstore empire, who opens one of his superstores in the same neighborhood. After months of fighting, picketing and protesting, Kathleen is forced to close the business that served the neighborhood for over 40 years. Joe was profiting from the book superstore trend while Kathleen was living in denial. Joe was a trend spotter and Kathleen was a trend fighter.

In marketing, there are trends and there are fads. A trend is the general direction in which the market tends to move. This move is characterized by a new way of doing business, the changing needs of customers and/or a new product or style that makes an older product or style obsolete or near obsolete. A fad is a specific change in the market characterized by great enthusiasm and lasting only a short period. A trend usually does not generate as much enthusiasm, and lasts significantly longer than a fad. The "Tickle Me Elmo™" doll several years back was a fad. It was almost impossible to find one in the weeks before the 1996 holiday season; then sure enough, after the holiday rush, toy store shelves were over stocked with these annoying, overpriced false icons. Barbie® on the other hand, is a trend that started about 40 years ago and is still going strong today.

Become a trend spotter, not a trend fighter. In business, you must adapt and work with trends to be successful. Knowing how to spot trends can give you an advantage over your competition, help you to save your business, or help you to become a millionaire. It is equally important to be able to spot the fads and know the difference between a fad and a trend. You can profit from fads providing you have a short-term strategy in mind, or choose to ignore fads and choose not to sweat over the temporary impact they may have on your industry or business.

How to spot a trend, how to spot a fad, and how to tell the difference.

Back in 1995, I was one of the fortunate souls that immediately saw the Internet, not for what it was, but what it was going to be. The Internet is a trend that significantly changed the way we live. Although some still call the Internet a fad, and see us moving back more toward a paper-dependent society, I believe the Internet is here to stay. I could, however, be one of the many delusional people in business who refuse to recognize trends as fads, fads as trends, or accept trends or fads altogether, simply because they do not want to believe it.

Here are some suggestions to help you spot trends and fads and be able to tell the difference.

- **Use your intuition.** What does your "gut" tell you? You may not be able to verbalize a good reason why you feel the way you do, but somehow you just know. This is intuition.
- **Be a visionary.** Look beyond today to the future. Play life out in your mind six months, six years or 60 years. How do you see this influence in the market place?
- **Use your common and business sense.** Common sense could have told most of us that the Pet Rock was not going to be an item the world could not live without. Our business sense could have told us that people would pay $3.95 for an average rock for only so long.
- **Do not fall victim to industry hype.** Trade magazines are full of articles and ads boasting the next greatest thing since perforated toilet paper. Those with the most money can usually generate the greatest buzz, but it takes a good idea to really catch on and become a fad or a trend.
- **Put yourself in the customers' shoes.** As a customer in the marketplace, how do you see this new market influence? Is this something you feel you will need? Your children will need? Your grandchildren? Is your desire for this due mostly to "market buzz"?

Spotting trends and fads in the market place, especially before others, can put your business ahead of the competition by putting you first in the minds of the consumers. By spotting trends and fads as an individual, you can act on new opportunities that can bring you success beyond your wildest dreams.

ACTION STEP(S):

1) Think of any fad and any trend. Now write down all the reasons you think the fad was only a fad, and the trend became a trend.

"Advertising generally works to reinforce consumer trends rather than to initiate them."

- Michael Schudson

Day 206: Inspiration from Ralph Lauren

Ralph Lauren (1939–) is the founder and chairman of the Polo Ralph Lauren Corporation—a leader in the design, marketing and distribution of premium lifestyle products.

Success is not something into which you are born. Born in the Bronx, New York, Ralph Lauren has come a long way from his days of sharing a bedroom with two of his brothers.

Success is knowing what's in a name. Ralph knew that people would have a problem wearing apparel with the name "Lifshitz" on them, thus he went from the Bronx's "Ralph Lifshitz" to the fashion industries "Ralph Lauren". Lauren then founded the company Polo Fashions in 1968. He chose the name "Polo" because of the power, style and intrigue with which the brand has always been associated.

Success is often the result of two or more specialties. Ralph studied business at City College in Manhattan. Although he never attended any fashion schools, his keen sense for fashion and passion for the industry gave him his advantage in fashion. With his fashion sense and knack for business, Ralph went on to become a success.

Success is working for experience, not just for money. While attending night school, Ralph would work by day at two glove companies as a salesman. He then worked for a tie manufacturer named A. Rivetz & Co., which ultimately led to the fashion empire he leads today.

Success is sticking with what you know is right, no matter what the initial cost. In the late 60s, while Lauren was trying to develop his line of wide ties, Bloomingdale's insisted Lauren remove his name from the ties' label, and make his ties narrower. Lauren refused to sell to the department store under such circumstances. Bloomingdale's eventually agreed to Lauren's terms after seeing the brand's huge success.

Success is selling ideas, not products. Polo sells a lifestyle image of sophistication, class and taste, not mere apparel.

Success is packaging and presentation. Lauren knew that an innovative mind was not enough; it would take creative packaging and persuasive presentation for his product line to take off.

Success is not perfect. Michael Gross is the author of Ralph Lauren's biography "Genuine Authentic". In this book, he describes the life of a man that is far from perfect and not quite the same as the public image Lauren projects.

Success is following your heart, not your mother's. Despite Ralph's tremendous success and contribution to the world through his fashion and philanthropic activities, it is rumored that his mother is still quite upset that he did not become a rabbi.

[Sources: http://www.askmen.com, http://about.polo.com]

"I am not looking like Armani today and somebody else tomorrow. I look like Ralph Lauren. And my goal is to constantly move in fashion and move in style without giving up what I am."

- Ralph Lauren

Day 207: Show Respect for the Opinions of Others

I have recently been reading about riots taking place in Boston and New York, due to the 2003 Red Sox/Yankees playoffs. For the most part, these are grown men causing each other physical injury all because some believe, "Sox rule!" and others believe, "Yanks rule!" Not showing respect for another's opinion is not only a faux pas, but can, and often does, lead to anxiety, tension, failed relationships, and even unlawful actions.

An opinion is a belief or conclusion held with confidence but not substantiated by positive knowledge or proof. Of course, positive knowledge and proof is debatable, and with good argument, fact can be seen as fiction. In Day 149, you read how to properly state your opinions and beliefs to avoid argument and conflict. However, many people do not show such tact and state their beliefs and opinions as fact. It is up to you to differentiate an opinion from a fact or at least question a statement if you are unsure. If someone tells you that Elvis, the king of rock and roll, is still alive you may ask, "How do you know that?" A response such as, "I read it in the *World Weekly News*" will hopefully make it clear that the person is not stating a fact.

Once you know that someone has stated an opinion, you have four basic options. You can a) accept the opinion and keep quiet, b) state your own opinion, c) express your agreement with the opinion, or d) express your disagreement with the opinion. In any case, you should always show respect for the opinion. The best way to do this is by realizing that if you had the experiences and information, and you were in the same situation as the one stating the opinion, you would most likely have the same opinion. Respect the person for taking a stance and having enough courage to share the opinion. Never tell someone stating an opinion that he or she is wrong—this is effective communication suicide.

Accepting an opinion and keeping quiet. If you accept another's opinion, you are not agreeing with it, but more important, you are not expressing your disapproval of it. An example is asking someone his or her favorite color. Unless someone's favorite color happens to be puke green, very few people would express their disapproval. If someone has an opinion different from yours, this is most often the best course of action to take, unless you have good reason for wanting to change the opinion of the other person.

Stating your own opinion. It is generally considered rude to offer your opinion unless asked. Stating your opinion which contradicts the opinion just shared causes tension and awkwardness. If you feel it necessary to state your own opinion, follow the advice below under "expressing your disagreement with the opinion".

Expressing your agreement with the opinion. Whenever possible in conversation, express your sincere agreement with another's opinion. This is a great rapport-building strategy.

Expressing your disagreement with the opinion. Disagreeing with others is a sure way to lose good rapport. Disagreement causes defensiveness: a physiological and psychological reaction, which tightens up the muscles in one's body and causes the person to be less open to influence. Do you really feel disagreeing is necessary? What will you hope to accomplish by expressing your disagreement? If you honestly feel that you must express your disagreement, start by asking questions about why the other person feels as they do. How did they form the opinion? What facts do they have, if any, to support their opinion? Ask these questions out of curiosity and with an open mind, not with resentment or disbelief. Once you have a better idea of how the opinion was formed, you can once again choose to accept it or agree with it, without ever having had to disagree with it.

The fact is, most people can have different opinions and still go on living in harmony. It is the difference of opinions that causes conflicting actions or behaviors that must be addressed by influence and persuasion. Keep an open mind and listen to the reasoning of the other person. Question your own opinions and show respect for the opinions of others.

ACTION STEP(S):

1) Write down three situations where disagreeing with another's opinion got you in trouble or at least caused you embarrassment. Did you need to express your opinion in these situations? What were the reasons you had for expressing your opinion?

"Opinion has caused more trouble on this little earth than plagues or earthquakes."

- Voltaire

Day 208: View Life from a Different Perspective

Growing up, I lived in a middle class neighborhood, in a middle class house. The area in which I lived was very economically diverse. One town south there were neighborhoods where one would be shot at just by driving through, and one town west was where some of the wealthiest people in the country called home. Exposure to these extremes taught me to be grateful for all I did have as well as showed me the possibility of living abundantly.

Why is it that the majority of those raised in economically depressed environments continue to spend their adult lives in the same environment? Why is it that the majority of children of wealthy parents grow up to be wealthy themselves or at least well off financially? Most would agree that those brought up in wealthy households have certain advantages that others do not have. Some of these advantages are superior schooling, job opportunities, good role models, and perhaps financial assistance from parents. One of the greatest advantages, however, that is most often overlooked is the desire and passion for the child to maintain the quality lifestyle that he or she is accustomed to living. Fortunately, for those of us not raised in a wealthy environment, this desire and passion can be created.

Each one of us has our own perspective of the world in which we live. Those who live, work and play in a depressed town tend to view the world in much of the same way. Our attitudes and views on life tend to be more local than global. Even if we cannot immediately change where we live, work or play; we can immediately change our perspective of the world. By doing this, we create the desire and passion needed to aggressively pursue a higher standard of living for our families and ourselves.

There are many ways of changing our perspective of our world. We do this by giving ourselves a taste of the "good life". Here are some of the ways:

- take walks or drives through wealthy neighborhoods
- visit open houses and walk through some of these multi-million dollar homes
- eat at a really nice restaurant every now and then
- visit 5 star hotels (don't need to stay in them, just visit)
- subscribe to the *Robb Report*
- pick up full color real estate books and read the listings for the high-end homes
- walk through an expensive shopping district

The more real these experiences are, the more powerful they are. For example, a walk through a really nice neighborhood with multi-million dollar homes will make a greater impression than seeing the same homes in a magazine. Although exposing yourself to the "good life" every now and then may cost money, and seem like a waste of money, consider it an investment in yourself and your future. Dare to dream and see for yourself what is possible.

ACTION STEP(S):

1) Take a drive or a walk through the nicest neighborhood in your town or a town nearby. Visualize yourself owning one of the homes, playing in the yard with your children (if you have any or want some someday), and washing your car in the driveway.

Days 209 and 210 are for "R&R"—review and reflection. Spend these days reviewing the last five articles and reflecting on the information and how it relates to your life. Now is also a good time to make sure all the action steps for the previous days have been completed.

Day 211: The Importance of a Good Vocabulary

I wish I knew in my school years what I know today about the importance of a good vocabulary. Back then, when teachers gave us scores of words to learn, all I could think about was the fact that I had never heard any of these words spoken by my peers. To me, they were just words randomly interjected into our readings so we could be tricked into thinking that they were important. I never realized this one important fact: as my peers began to learn these new words, they began to use them, which left me "below the curve". I was only thinking about my present and not my future. Many adults never bother to increase their vocabulary for the same reason.

Nobody really knows for sure how many words there are in the English language because several sources do not seem to agree on what constitutes a word. However, the estimates I have seen suggest there are between 500,000 and 1,000,000 words. David Crystal, in the *Cambridge Encyclopedia of the English Language*, suggests that the average active (used, not just recognized) vocabulary for a college graduate might be 60,000 words. This means to have a firm grasp of the English language, we just need to learn about 10% of all the available words in the English language and not worry about the other 90%.

So why is having a good vocabulary important to your success? In short, if you speak like an idiot, people will treat you like one. I am not saying this is right, since it is a form of prejudice; however, it does happen in both personal and professional situations. Here are a few more reasons directly related to your success:

- Increasing your vocabulary allows you to use more descriptive words to better communicate your thoughts.
- Understanding the meaning of more words will allow you to better understand information that you are reading or

listening to (comprehension), thus increasing your retention.

- Having a larger vocabulary to call upon will help your verbal communication flow and allow you to start eliminating noises like "umm" and "uhh".
- Being able to use more colorful words in speaking to others will allow you to project a more intelligent image.
- Knowing more words will make you a better Scrabble player

Bookstores and libraries are full of vocabulary building courses. However, these courses all lack one important ingredient: focus on the words that will be beneficial to your specific needs and goals. For example, I recently completed an audio course on communication in which over one hour was focused on learning the collective nouns of animals. I do not think I will ever in my lifetime need to say, "Hey look! There goes a *crash* of rhinoceros". Before making the effort to increase your vocabulary, make sure you have your long-term goals in mind. Learn the vocabulary, terms, and jargon that will help bring you closer to your goals. For example, if you are currently a mechanic but your ambition is to become a doctor, then learn to speak and write like a doctor. By focusing on learning words relevant to your current and future environments, you can appear more learned while not wasting your time memorizing words you are unlikely to ever use or hear.

Another tip for expanding your vocabulary is to look up unfamiliar words as you encounter them; you are much more likely to remember words this way rather than memorizing random words that have no specific meaning to you at the time.

A word of caution... perhaps the biggest vocabulary blunder one can make is not misusing or misspelling words, but abusing them by trying to impress others with his or her vocabulary rather than focusing on effective communication. It is more important to build a strong rapport with your audience by using words you are quite sure they understand. When you must use a word you feel they might not understand, define it for them. This is especially helpful when using technical terms or industry jargon. Effective communication is about sharing ideas in a way that best translates one's thoughts into a form of communication that others can understand. Effective communication will get you much further than an extensive vocabulary ever will, and overuse of complex words can make you seem pretentious.

The goal of expanding your vocabulary should be to lift you slightly above the crowd without losing the audience in words unfamiliar to them. You should be able to understand and use the words and terms encountered in your daily life, as well prepare yourself by learning the vocabulary needed to bring you closer to your goals. Expand your vocabulary and expand your opportunities.

ACTION STEP(S):

1) Learn 10 new words, five of which relate to your current environment such as your current job, hobby, spouse or friend's job or hobby, etc. Then, learn five new words you feel you will need to know when you reach your life's long-term goals. If you find this exercise helpful, make it a point to continue learning new words on a daily basis.

"Life is tons of discipline. Your first discipline is your vocabulary; then your grammar and your punctuation. Then, in your exuberance and bounding energy you say you're going to add to that. Then you add rhyme and meter. And your delight is in that power."

- Robert Frost

Day 212: The Importance of Good Grammar

Several years ago I was watching infomercials, as I often did, and came across one of a guy selling a program that teaches others how to become rich by placing ads in newspapers. This guy, although filled with enthusiasm, made some grammatical errors on his short infomercial that, for me, were more painful to listen to than fingernails scratching a chalkboard. He said things like, "Alls you have to do is..." and "Let me ax you a question...". Two months later, after seeing his new infomercial, sans grammatical errors, I knew that others had taken offense to his mistakes as well.

I know I am not alone in being offended, or at least turned off, by grammatical errors. How do I know this? Just about every day I get an e-mail from a member of Y2S that disagrees with my use of the English language. I will say that most of the e-mails I receive are corrections of careless errors made by me, in my pursuit to keep up with my strict and self-imposed schedule. However, I do get the occasional, belligerent e-mail from an expert in linguistics criticizing my style of writing. In fact, one former member took the time to rewrite one of my articles and pointed out over 30 "mistakes". When he was done with the article it read more like a sixteenth century Shakespearean poem than what it was meant to be—an article written in informal American English to capture and maintain the interest of the readers. Good grammar is subjective and quite debatable; however, bad grammar is always bad and should always be avoided.

Many of the benefits of using good grammar are the same as having a good vocabulary, the most important one being effective communication. Grammatical errors in both speaking and writing can distract from the message itself and cause negative feelings in the listener or reader. Avoiding grammatical errors can help you avoid low grades, lost employment opportunities, lost business, and embarrassment.

There is standard and nonstandard English, American and British (Queen's) English, spoken and written English, and informal and formal English. Each style follows the same general rules but has its distinct differences. The key to good grammar is knowing when to use which style and being able to defend your reasoning. When it comes to standard versus nonstandard English, use nonstandard English only when you intend to, not because you do not know the difference.

Bookstores, public libraries, and the Internet are full of information on proper use of grammar. Take some time to read the books, listen to the tapes, visit the websites, and work on your grammar skills. You will find yourself the recipient of higher grades, more job opportunities, more business, less embarrassment, and more success.

ACTION STEP(S):

1) Take a few minutes to visit one of my favorite grammar sites at http://www.wsu.edu/~brians/errors/index.html.

"If the English language made any sense, lackadaisical would have something to do with a shortage of flowers."

- Doug Larson

Day 213: Inspiration from Dale Carnegie

Dale Carnegie (1888–1955) was a pioneer in public speaking and personality development. Dale Carnegie influenced millions of people and helped define the industry now known as "self-help".

Success begins with failure. Dale failed at almost everything he did including farming, teaching, sales, acting and novel writing. His persistence in pursuing his passion led him to eventually write *"How to Win Friends and Influence People"*, which to date has sold over 30 million copies worldwide.

Success is having self-confidence. Dale's success philosophy centers on building and reinforcing self-confidence. His career began by teaching a public speaking course at a local YMCA. When the YMCA was hesitant about giving him the salary of $2 per night, he had enough confidence in himself to suggest he work on commission instead. He was soon making $30 per night.

Success is knowing how to deal with people. "When dealing with people, let us remember we are not dealing with creatures of logic. We are dealing with creatures of emotion, creatures bustling with prejudices and motivated by pride and vanity."

Success is having a positive influence on others. Over 50 million copies of his books have sold and have been translated into just about every language. His training courses, which are still thriving today, have trained over 7 million people.

Success is learning from others. Mr. Carnegie developed his success philosophy by studying people who he admired most. His books include many stories about Abe Lincoln, Ben Franklin, Andrew Carnegie (no relation), and others.

Success is taking chances. "Take a chance! All life is a chance. The man who goes furthest is generally the one who is willing to do and dare."

Success is overcoming fears. Carnegie was very shy, which is quite a handicap to a professional public speaker. However, he believed in confronting his fears and not being discouraged by initial failures. "Do the thing you fear to do and keep on doing it... that is the quickest and surest way ever yet discovered to conquer fear."

Success is acting on opportunity. Dale wrote his best seller initially because at the time, there wasn't a textbook on which he could rely.

Success is making the world a better place. "You have it easily in your power to increase the sum total of this world's happiness now. How? By giving a few words of sincere appreciation to someone who is lonely or discouraged. Perhaps you will forget tomorrow the kind words you say today, but the recipient may cherish them over a lifetime."

[Sources: http://www.biography.com, http://www.dale-carnegie.com, Investor's Business Daily, Oct 24, 2001]

"Any fool can criticize, condemn, and complain—and most fools do."

- Dale Carnegie

Day 214: Dealing with Spam: Part 1

I'll never forget the first spam I received. It was in the summer of 1995 when I had my first e-mail account with Netcom (now Earthlink). I remember being so excited and so intrigued that someone from across the country found me and wanted to sell me something. However, I was not interested in hair loss cream so I politely responded to their e-mail thanking them for their offer and explaining to the merchant that I was only 23 years old and was not in need of such a product. In 1995, since spam was fairly rare, this was actually not a bad way to deal with spam. Today, however, spam has evolved from a harmless sales pitch to a global epidemic that is responsible for increased levels of anger and billions of dollars of lost productivity.

What is spam? Ask ten different people and you will get ten different answers. At one extreme, spam can be defined as any unsolicited e-mail. This means, unless the person you are sending an e-mail to is expecting it or has asked for it, it is spam. At the other extreme, spam is mass e-mail sent to a list of e-mail addresses that have not agreed to receive solicitations, all containing the same message sent in an attempt to sell something. In our hosting companies' policies, we define spam as the sending of e-mails in bulk (same message sent to two or more addresses) to persons or organizations with which the sender had no prior dealings. Even our definition leaves some questions to be answered but we feel it is unfair to inhibit business due to a strict definition.

So what does spam have to do with your success? Much more than most people think. According to a survey of our own Y2S members, the average member spends about 15 minutes a day dealing with spam. This includes setting spam filters, downloading and reading spam, reporting and responding to spam, and removing viruses due to spam. Fifteen minutes a day equals almost 8 hours a month—that is a full workday of productivity lost. The actual time lost is even more, however. Imagine trying to get a sound sleep and being awakened dozens of times throughout the night. The effects of the interruption of spam throughout the workday are not all that different. There is also an emotional side to the effects of spam. Spam often angers, and even infuriates, those who receive it. This feeling of anger distracts from the focus of the productive work itself. Being able to effectively manage spam, and your anger associated with spam, will help you to increase your productivity, which is a large part of success.

The first step is to accept spam as part of the Internet. Consider it cyberspace's version of the annoying flyer on the windshield. Realize that you cannot completely eliminate spam (without risking losing legitimate e-mail), but you can greatly reduce it. Do not get angry over it, just accept it. Never allow a random message sent to you take away from your happiness, no matter what the content may be.

Here are some tips on both minimizing the amount of spam that finds its way to your mailbox and minimizing the amount of time spent dealing with spam:

- **Look into commercial anti-spam software.** There is plenty on the market that can reduce spam. However, understand how this kind of software works: no software can ever tell for sure what is spam or not, at least not until global laws are in place that force identifying headers, but even then we are assuming that the law will be followed. You must "teach" software what is spam and what is not. Once software detects spam, it places it in an area where you can verify that it is spam before you delete it. Very often, this whole process takes more time and effort than simply deleting the spam that finds it way to your inbox. The advantage is that you won't have as many interruptions and you can deal with spam when you choose to.
- **Do not reply to spam.** The from or reply-to addresses on spam are almost always fake. I know so many people who spend hours constructing angry replies to spam only to find

that their replies just bounce back to them. Your best bet is to spend the one second to delete the spam.

- **Don't bother looking at e-mail headers.** Very few people are actually skilled enough to read e-mail headers and know which headers are forged and which are real. Most professional spammers know how to forge headers and cover their tracks very well.

- **Set up local filters.** Most client-side e-mail software, like Outlook™, will allow this. Just like commercial software, you may find that it takes more time than it is worth.

- **Set up server-based filters.** All of our hosting companies, and I am sure many others, have web-based filters users can set up. These work like local filters but they prevent spam from ever being downloaded to your local PC. This can also help prevent viruses from ever reaching your PC.

- **Accept e-mail sent to your e-mail address only.** Many spam filters allow for this option. This alone can eliminate over 90% of spam. However, if you are subscribed to any mailing lists, or if you frequently receive messages with your address in the "Bcc" header, those will be filtered out as well.

- **Prevent your address from getting picked up on the web.** The moment you place your e-mail on any public area of the Web, it is open for "spambots" who search millions of web pages per day and collect e-mail addresses. If you are posting your e-mail address on a web page, use the "#&64;" in place of the "@" sign or include your e-mail address in an image. (Note: Your e-mail address used for this course is only seen in private, encrypted areas.)

- **Use your own domain as your e-mail address.** If you have your own domain, you can use anything @ your domain for your e-mail address. This will allow you to use a different address for everything you sign up for or order on the Web. For example, you can use Y2S@mydomain.com for this course. Now, if you start getting spam being sent to Y2S@mydomain.com, you will know where the "leak" is and you can simply stop using or block that address.

- **Change your address.** At times, especially after years of use, you may find it easiest to just change your e-mail address. It may be easier to notify the dozen or so people whose e-mail you welcome of a new address, than to spend countless hours battling spam.

Once again, your goal should be to minimize the amount of spam you receive, not eliminate it. Eliminating spam is a pipe dream that will only cause you the loss of legitimate e-mail and potential business.

ACTION STEP(S):

1) Figure out how many hours per month you spend dealing with spam. Does spam ever upset you? Do you find that your work is interrupted by having to deal with spam?

"It typically takes from 1,000 to 10,000 spams to make one sale. If you buy from a spammer, you are PERSONALLY responsible for the next 1,000 to 10,000 spams sent... including the porn spam sent to your kids."

- Paul Myers, TalkBiz News

Day 215: Dealing with Spam: Part 2

It is important to know spammer's "tricks of the trade". These are tricks used by spammers to prevent them from being shut down, get the attention of readers, build more qualified lists, and prevent spam filters from detecting their messages. Spammers rely on deceptive practices to increase the odds that their messages will be read. Much of the deception turns into outright fraud when it comes to the offer. Learn the following "tricks" and save yourself countless hours of dealing with spam.

- **Fake name.** The "From" address will often appear like it is coming from a friend like "John Smith" or perhaps something a bit less obvious. At times, the spammer will also use your name as "From", to be sure to get you to open the message.
- **Bogus subject.** It is common for spammers to use attention-getting subjects, like "Your order" or "Here is the information you requested". Don't bother replying to them with a long e-mails asking, "what order?"
- **RE:.** Spammers will include "RE:" in the subject to make you think they are replying to an e-mail that you initiated.
- **Fake "To" header.** Spammers will often send their spams using a fake "To" address, (with a fake "From" address, of course) to make it seem like your receiving the message was an accident. The curious nature of people impels them to read the message thinking they are "spying" on someone else's e-mail.
- **The old "unsubscribe" trick.** Spammers will buy millions of e-mail addresses for pennies then send out a spam with a "If this was sent to you in error, click here to unsubscribe" message. Once the unsuspecting public clicks the link, they have just confirmed for the spammer that their e-mail address is valid. Now the spammer sells the addresses as "confirmed" e-mail addresses and the amount of spam multiplies exponentially. Never click any links in

a spam. Only click unsubscribe links in e-mails to which you know you subscribed.

- **Encryption.** Spammers now encrypt e-mails so that spam filters will not pick up keywords, like "free" or "Viagra". Before spending time setting up spam filters to block a spam, "view source" of the e-mail and see if it is encoded or if words are recognizable. If it is encoded, you can often create a filter based on the URL that is linked in the e-mail, which should not be encoded.
- **Random codes.** Spammers add random codes to both the subjects and message bodies so spam filters are thrown off. Solution: set up filters that are a bit looser, i.e., that don't require an exact match of the subject.

In addition to the many deceptions you should be aware of, here are a few serious scams that frequently appear.

- **Credit card update.** These messages appear as if they are coming from a trusted vendor or bank, asking you to update your information and/or credit card. Those who fall for this are giving up all of their personal information to identity thieves who end up charging their credit cards to the max. You can ALWAYS tell if this is fake by the URL that appears in your browser when you click the link. The URL should be of the domain name you trust and never an IP address (numbers) or an unfamiliar domain name. Besides, most reputable vendors would not ask for this kind of information by e-mail.
- **"Urgent Assistance".** This is the major multi-million dollar scam that plays on people's greed and desire for quick cash with no work. It appears to be from some foreign diplomat needing an American bank to get money out of their country. The one who helps is promised millions of dollars. The scam is, they require you to wire a "good faith" deposit of tens of thousands of dollars, after which, of course, you will never see your money again or hear from the "diplomat".
- **"Microsoft Update".** This is a message that appears to be coming from Microsoft that includes an attachment. The e-

mail instructs the user to run this file to update Windows. Microsoft would NEVER do anything like this... these are viruses and/or programs that open up your PC to hackers.

Common sense should be used where rules do not exist. There are many scams sent by spam today so use your common sense to determine for yourself what is a scam.

I have been criticized by others for having too liberal of a policy in dealing with spam. This is because I choose not to be an activist on the subject. Each person only has so much time to spend and he or she must focus energies on causes that are most important to him or her. For me, it is sharing success, not fighting spam. If spam is a cause you feel is worth fighting for, then there is much more you can do than just hitting the delete key. To learn more about fighting spam, please visit http://spam.abuse.net.

Every minute you spend in your life is either spent bringing you closer to your goals or moving you away from your goals. Unless your goals include fighting spam, time spent dealing with spam is wasted time that you can never get back. Don't allow yourself to get angered by spam. Use the advice in this article to create your own method of dealing with spam and spend the time you save working on your goals.

ACTION STEP(S):

---

1) Learn the tricks used by spammers mentioned in this article and do not allow yourself to be taken advantage of.

"Ninety percent of spam is sent by fewer than 200 people, according to Mozena of CAUCE, the anti-spam coalition. That represents an astounding degree of concentration, but virtually everyone who fights spam for a living agrees it is roughly correct."

- Unknown

Days 216 and 217 are for "R&R"—review and reflection. Spend these days reviewing the last five articles and reflecting on the information and how it relates to your life. Now is also a good time to make sure all the action steps for the previous days have been completed.

Day 218: Solving Business Problems

Did you ever find yourself asking why the town does not "do something" about the busy intersection, or why your Internet service provider does not "do something" about preventing downtime, or have you found yourself identifying any problem to which you are not offering a better solution? We all have. In general, people tend to say what is wrong with the world but very few offer suggestions on how to improve it. Even fewer people will ever take action to do anything about it. In general life situations, this is acceptable. After all, the town does not rely on its citizens to plan intersections. In business, however, more should be expected from, and offered by, an organization's team members in the form of active problem solving.

Many people who work within an organization wear two hats: 1) they are a member of an organization in which there are one or more leaders and 2) they are a leader to one or more other members of the organization. Typically, this is the employee/manager relationship. As an employee, it may be common practice to bring problems to your manager's attention. As a success-oriented employee, don't just point out the problem, do your best to solve the problem. Doing this without being asked will demonstrate your creativity and willingness to go the extra mile. As a manager or business owner, you should require that all those who report to you carefully consider the problem and possible solutions before bringing the problem to your attention. The benefits of taking this approach to solving business problems are:

- **More efficiency with time.** Fewer problems will be brought to your attention and you, as the manager, can focus on more pressing issues.
- **Quicker resolution of problems.** In many cases, employees who carefully examine problems will realize that they can solve the problems themselves, right there and then.

- **Self-reliance and independence.** This kind of policy promotes employee independence, which is one of the leading indicators of job satisfaction. It also happens to be the quality most sought after by employers.
- **Prevent worry.** As a manager or business owner, you can significantly reduce the number of "problems" that you need to deal with by adopting this policy. Fewer problems generally equal fewer worries.

What does "carefully considering problems" mean? If you are to implement a policy in your business for solving problems, it is best to give clear directions on what should be done. Here is a six step process you can adopt for carefully considering problems and offering solutions.

1. **What is the problem?** Most problems are never clearly defined, which makes solutions even more difficult to find.
2. **What are all the possible causes?** At times, the cause of the problem will be unknown. Other times, there will be many possible causes. It is best to take time to think about all possible causes so the solution can focus on these causes.
3. **What are all possible solutions?** The employee may not be qualified to offer solutions to all problems, but in some cases, they are the most qualified by having the most hands-on experience. Asking the advice of employees gives them the sense of importance to the organization and expands their creative thinking.
4. **Which solution do you suggest?** Let the employee choose the solution that makes the most sense to him or her. This gives you, as the manager, an insight into the problem solving abilities and reasoning of your employees. It also exposes any hidden talents you have on your team.
5. **Do you see any possible side effects to the suggested solution?** If you have blisters on your feet, cutting off your feet would certainly solve the problem. Of course, it would lead to much bigger problems. This step encourages employees to reconsider their solution and ensure that it makes sense.

6. **What resources do you think are needed to implement the solution?** If you found that you had mice in your house, a solution could be to move into a new house. When considering the resources needed to implement this solution you will certainly find that another solution, perhaps buying $10 worth of mousetraps, would make more sense.

In implementing this policy of problem solving, you do not want to discourage problems from being brought to your attention. You may find that some employees would rather look the other way than take the time to go though this six-step process. To minimize the possibility of this happening, be sure you make it a point to reward those who do take the time to go through this process with positive public attention, gratitude, or even prizes.

Employees who take it upon themselves to solve problems are more often looked at for advancement within the organization. Managers and business owners who encourage problem solving at the employee level have more productive and more satisfied employees. Implement these six steps to solving problems in business and enjoy the success that comes to you as a result.

ACTION STEP(S):

1) Write down how you can implement this six-step problem solving technique in your business / work life today.

2) Use this technique to tackle any one of the current problems you face. It is best to write down each step along the way.

Day 219: The Word "But"

Perhaps one of the most famous disciplinarians in history was Mike Brady, from the '70s sitcom "The Brady Bunch". In just about every episode, he would lecture one or more of his kids, with his lovely hair-of-gold wife by his side. Mike may be one of the most famous disciplinarians, but his use of the contradicting "but" and "however" sure left a lot to be desired.

The word "but" has many valuable uses in both formal and informal English. Unfortunately however, many use this word when they are criticizing or giving feedback. Most people are so used to it, they can "feel" a "but" coming. It is usually detected by somber, stern or reluctant praise or good news. The "but" that follows, then takes the attention off of the positive and puts the focus on the negative, in most cases, turning the overall tone of the message, or the message deliverer, negative.

The words "but", "however", or any other contradictory word or phrase in a criticism or while giving feedback, does one of more of the following:

- Causes resentment in those to whom the message is directed
- Causes defensiveness
- Fails to offer encouragement
- Fails to offer motivation
- Gives the impression that there are "strings attached"
- Detracts from the positive tone of the message

So how does one give feedback while avoiding contradictory terms or phrases? Simply substitute the word "and" to replace the "stick" with the "carrot". It also helps to end with a positive and encouraging comment.

Here are several examples of this principle:

No: *Jan, we know you love your sister, but it is not right to be jealous of her.*

Yes: *Jan, we know you love your sister, and being supportive of her rather than jealous of her, will show her and the rest of the world what a great person your mom and I know you are.*

No: *Greg, your mom and I appreciate what you did for your sister, but it is not right to lie.*

Yes: *Greg, your mom and I appreciate what you did for your sister. Next time, use that groovy head of yours and find a better way to help others without lying.*

No: *Cindy, we appreciate you sharing things with us, however, tattling is just not right.*

Yes: *Cindy, we appreciate you sharing things with us, especially when it is information others don't mind you sharing and did not ask you to keep a secret.*

No: *Alice, we really do like your cooking, but do you think we can have anything but red meat at least once per month?*

Yes: *Alice, you certainly are a master at preparing red meat. We would love to see what you can do with some chicken and pork dishes.*

In just about every situation, you can get the same message across in a positive way, rather than leaving the person with an overall negative feeling that he or she has just been criticized simply by avoiding using the word "but". Giving feedback in this way may not seem as natural and will take some practice and thought; however, it will soon become second nature.

ACTION STEP(S):

---

1) Make a conscious effort from this point on not to use "but" or any other contradicting word or statement after a praise or statement of good news.

"Our house is more important than money. This neighborhood is more important than money. Tell me. How many times have we borrowed each other's power tools or patched up each other's kids? We know so much about each other. I know that every January, Mr. Yeager is going to have that big Super Bowl party at his house. We know that every spring, Mrs. Simmons is going to have the prettiest daffodils on the block. We know that at 10:15 every Saturday morning, Mrs. Topping likes to walk through her living room naked. Call me old-fashioned, but these things are important, and they're not for sale. This is our neighborhood, and we're staying."

- Mike Brady - from the Brady Bunch Movie

Day 220: Inspiration from Gary Larson

Gary Larson (1950–) is the creator and artist of the cartoon called "The Far Side" which was eventually picked up by 1,900 newspapers and translated into 17 languages. Larson has published 22 Far Side books including 15 collections, five anthologies and one retrospective, each of which has made it to The New York Times Best Seller List. Thirty-one million books have been sold worldwide, and have been translated into every major language.

Success is using frustration positively. One day, in 1976, fed-up with his lack of success in the music business, Larson drew six cartoons, which he submitted to a local magazine, Pacific Search. They bought them for $90. Thus he began his new career as a cartoonist.

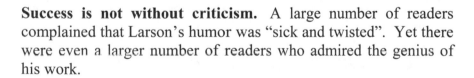

Success is using persuasion. In 1979, Larson persuaded the Seattle Times to give him a weekly panel, "Nature's Way". He knew the readers would love it—and they did—he just had to get the Seattle Times to realize it.

Success is not without criticism. A large number of readers complained that Larson's humor was "sick and twisted". Yet there were even a larger number of readers who admired the genius of his work.

Success is being different. Traditional cartoonists have always portrayed people and animals "normal-looking" or at least moderately attractive. Larson dared to be different and decided that all of his people, animals, and creatures would be goofy-looking (big noses, 1950s-glasses-wearing, foofy hair, very lumpy). This unique portrayal of his characters still makes the cartoons funny, even if you do not get the joke.

Success is taking small and frequent steps in the right direction. In 1979, Larson was determined to double his cartooning income (he was currently getting $15 per cartoon at the time) by looking for a second newspaper to pick up his panels.

Success is being persistent. Larson focused on the San Francisco Chronicle as his next "score". After submitting his portfolio, Larson called twice a day, every day, until one day, he was told that the Chronicle wanted to syndicate his cartoon and offer it to about 30 newspapers across the country in a daily panel called "The Far Side".

Success is realizing that you cannot please everyone. Before the news of the syndication was made public, the Seattle Times told Larson that it was dropping his cartoon because it was receiving too many complaints and it was just too offensive.

Success is knowing when to say when. In January 1995, to the dismay of millions of his fans, Larson stopped drawing "The Far Side". He said he felt the quality of the work was going down, and wanted to avoid what he called "the Graveyard of Mediocre Cartoons".

[Sources: http://www.biography.com, http://encarta.msn.com, http://www.salon.com]

"Great moments in science: Einstein discovers that time is actually money."

- Gary Larson

Day 221: Three Rejections = Success

I recently got a call from my brother whose website we host. He asked me how he can see statistics on an audio file that was being accessed using a URL that was bypassing his domain (for those of you who have no idea what I just said, substitute "He asked me a favor"). I told him these statistics were kept in a file he could not access—rejection #1. He then asked me how he could get access to this file. I told him there was no way to give him access to this file—rejection #2. He then asked if it is at all possible for him to see these statistics. I told him there is always a way, but it would be time consuming and costly to have a script made to do what he needs—rejection #3. Then he simply said, "Can you think of any way you can help me?" Not being one to walk away from an intellectual challenge, I immediately came up with a solution that took only seconds to implement for him. Result: he was grateful and I was happy I could help him with something that meant so much to him. My brother reminded me of one of the most important and practical principles of success: one must usually go through three rejections to get a "yes".

In this context, I am using the term "rejection" to also mean "objection". However, a rejection is most often in the form of a "no" type answer, whereas an objection is usually a statement stating why the offer cannot be accepted. An objection should normally not be seen as a rejection; it is nothing more than a request for more information. Not accepting a rejection is not being pushy; it is being persistent. It is not about being aggressive, but being assertive. Most people quit at the first rejection, but it is the small percentage who persist by not accepting the first three rejections and find success.

Think of yourself entering a room containing three large doors in front of you, while holding three golden keys. Each key unlocks one of three doors. The door is the rejection and the key is the counter to the rejection. Behind one of these three doors may be the "yes" you are looking for. Promise yourself that you will not leave the room until you have opened all three doors. If you have opened all three doors and have not found the "yes" you were looking for, then move on to the next room.

Why "give up" at rejection number four? Isn't persistence the key to success? Persistence is **a** key to success, but so is knowing when to move on. Three appears to be the magic number when it comes to rejections and the turning point in the perspective of the person to whom the offer is being made. Rejection number one is almost always reactionary; that is, the person has not really thought about the offer. Rejections number two and three are most often objections, or requests for more information. Upon rejection number four, it is best to accept the fact that the other person is not ready or willing to accept your offer. From here, you can choose to a) retreat for now, but get more information, modify your offer, or reevaluate your presentation for presenting your offer to the same person or b) move on to the next person. In either case, be sure to sincerely thank the person for their time or part ways in such a way that displays no resentment or ill feelings.

Although I am not comfortable citing any statistics on the success of this principle in action, due to all the unknown variables, I would be willing to wager that anyone adopting this principle who usually accepts the first rejection, will see at least a 50% increase in accepted offers. This applies to the salesperson selling a product, the entrepreneur selling an idea, the single guy selling himself (in a non-prostitution sense), and in any other situation where one is presenting an offer to another.

It is important to emphasize that this principle applies to an individual offer. It is not about quitting after receiving four different rejections from four different people. Not accepting a rejection may feel awkward at first, since most of us were brought up being told, "No means no!" However, remember that the "yes" is usually behind one of the three doors and to counter the first three rejections, rather than accepting them. Do not take "no" for an answer, unless it is "no" #4.

ACTION STEP(S):

1) Prove this principle to yourself—think about all times you were presented with an offer, and how many objections you made before accepting the offer.

2) Ask someone for something that is not easy to get. Do not accept the "no" until after four rejections.

"An objection is not a rejection; it is simply a request for more information."

- Bo Bennett

Day 222: Preventing Worry

The story of John D. Rockefeller, nineteenth century oil industry billionaire, is one of the most compelling stories demonstrating both the destructive effects of worry and the dramatic positive effects that managing worry can have. By age 53, Rockefeller was reported to have looked as if he were 103. He was living on liquid meals because his stomach could not take solid foods. He was well known at that time for being one of the meanest, most miserable men in business. Fortunately for Rockefeller, and for the world, he followed his doctor's advice of removing worry from his life, lived to age 98, and became one of the greatest philanthropists of all time. Preventing worry could have made Rockefeller's first half of his life as enjoyable and rewarding as his second half.

People literally worry their lives away. Besides the severe mental and emotional consequences of worry, worry has also been linked to lethargy, headaches, insomnia, ulcers, and even death. In fact, doctors often prescribe solutions to manage worry as treatment for patients who display one or more of the many physical symptoms of worry. Over the counter and prescription drugs may help with the symptoms, but it takes a change in attitude to eliminate the cause. Do not permit worry to send you to an early grave.

It has been said, "an ounce of prevention is worth a pound of cure". This is very true when it comes to worry. Worry is a habit and like all bad habits, it can be broken. The best way to break the habit of worry is by learning to prevent worry. Preventing worry can be as easy as changing your state of mind—seeing situations from a different perspective. It is making use of your positive mental attitude.

Here are some suggestions on how you can stop worry before it even starts:

- **Live one day at a time.** Worrying about the events of tomorrow and especially the events of yesterday will do you no good today. Get over yesterday's worries and move on to focusing on worthy thoughts. Prepare and take action to avoid possible troubles of tomorrow.

- **Keep your mind busy.** The mind can only focus on one thought at a time. You cannot focus on both the task at hand and your worries at the same time. You can keep switching back and forth, but that is why the activities that you choose must keep your mind busy as well as your body. Psychologists have known this for years; this is what they call "occupational therapy". Be "too busy" to worry.

- **Focus on what is right, not what is wrong.** We tend to take for granted all the things in life that are good, right, and working as they should. Our attention is drawn to that which is changing or an exception to the norm. On the news you see stories of the one fire that burned down a house, but you do not see stories of the other 2.6 million homes in the area that were NOT burned down. You hear stories about the stockbroker that lost all his money and committed suicide, but you do not hear stories about the millions of stockbrokers who live very happy lives. This skewed perception of reality causes us to worry about things that will most likely never happen to us. When you find yourself being manipulated by rare stories of misfortune, don't just think positively, think realistically and don't worry about something that will most likely never come to pass.

- **Delegate responsibilities.** The number of responsibilities one has is usually in direct proportion to the number of worries one has. As responsibilities become unmanageable, the associated worries begin to multiply. Learn to delegate responsibility and take on only as much responsibility as you can handle.

- **Laugh off sillier worries.** A silly worry is one where the chances of it coming true are incredibly slim; the results are not that devastating, and the imagined worry would make a funny story or joke. For example, after I bought this overnight suitcase with a built-in compartment for my laptop, I was worried that the compartment containing my laptop would come unzipped, the laptop would fall out, and I would never know. Then I pictured myself walking in the airport, and my laptop shooting out of the back side of the suitcase and me still walking along with a not-so-smart look on my face. I began to laugh at the image and the worry was gone for good.

- **Exercise.** Once again, the benefits of exercise far exceed just a healthy heart and a fit body. Queensland researchers have found that regular exercise alters the body's chemistry, specifically the chemical serotonin, which appears to reduce worries and make the mind less susceptible to worry and fear. Exercise also is known to burn up stress chemicals like adrenaline, which promotes a more relaxed body and mind.
- **Prevent mental fatigue.** Mental fatigue has been directly linked to physical fatigue as well as increased worry. Take regular short breaks. One of John D. Rockefeller's post-worry life secrets was to take about a 30-minute catnap each day, which he claimed revived him both physically and mentally. He did after all, live until age 98 at a time when the average expected life of a male was only about 53 years old.

If you suffer from worry, you are not alone. Nearly every individual in the world has worries despite their financial situation, age, sex, or race. Worry is not caused by external events or situations; it is caused by one's own interpretation of those events or situations. Prevent worry by maintaining a positive mental attitude and by realizing that worry will do nothing for you but send you to an early grave.

ACTION STEP(S):

1) Write down all of your worries, no matter how petty or minor. If you consider it a "worry" of yours, write it down. Now do the following: a) cross off all worries of the past, b) cross of all worries that do not related to today's events—all future worries

that you can do nothing about today and c) cross off any "silly" worries. How many are you left with?

"Worry is like a rocking chair, it gives you something to do, but gets you no where. Write that down."

- Van Wilder

Days 223 and 224 are for "R&R"—review and reflection. Spend these days reviewing the last five articles and reflecting on the information and how it relates to your life. Now is also a good time to make sure all the action steps for the previous days have been completed.

Day 225: Eliminating Worry

At age 53, John D. Rockefeller made the wisest decision of his life by choosing to manage worry rather than accepting an early death. In the many years that followed, John D. no longer let the little things in life trouble him, he let go of his greed by giving away fortunes and he learned to accepted the inevitable. He summed it up in a poem he wrote on his 86th birthday:

> *I was early taught to work as well as play,*
> *My life has been one long, happy holiday,*
> *Full of work and full of play –*
> *I dropped the worry on the way –*
> *And God was good to me every day.*

Some "experts" proclaim that worry is not all bad. They say that worry pushes us to get things done and make positive changes in our lives. Worry, they say, has been the force behind many of civilization's advancements. I believe that this force being referred to is not worry, but motivation. People can be motivated by worry just as horses can be motivated with whips. However, worry does far more emotional and physical damage than a few lashings of a whip. Bypass the worry altogether and use one of the many other emotions for self-motivation.

Even if you are one who feels worry is a powerful motivator in your life, then consider the following: it has been said that over 90% of worries are unjustified, that is, completely without benefit. These types of worries fall into one or more of these three categories:

1. **Can do nothing about.** What if the sun burns out? We will all instantly die (well technically after about 8 1/2 minutes due to the speed of light). All the worrying in the world will not prevent this event from happening, if it ever does happen. It seems silly to worry about, because we have no control over such a disaster.

2. **Choose to do nothing about.** What if the ozone layer gets destroyed? If one is really concerned with this they can devote their time and energy to one of the many causes to prevent this potential disaster. By working toward prevention, one should be contented by the feeling that he or she is doing all they can (or choose to) and worrying is pointless. If one chooses to do nothing about it, then the worry cannot really be that great, and once again, is pointless.

3. **Odds are will never happen.** What if you get struck by lightning? According to several sources, the chances are about 3000 to 1 that the average person will be struck by lightning in their entire lifetime. Then, the chances are about 300,000 to 1 that a person getting hit by lightning will actually die as a result. Would you start packing up your home and call a mover if there was even a 2 to 1 chance that you were going to be moving? How much of your mental and physical health will you waste then on worrying about events that are unlikely to happen?

If the goal was to eliminate MOST of our worries, we could stop there. But our real goal should be to eliminate all of our worries. This is not the same as never worrying again; it is about devoting the time to eliminating our worries when they first become worries. I have adapted what I believe to be the best of over a dozen techniques to create the following multi-step process for eliminating worries.

1. **Write down what you are worried about.** Do your best to carefully think of what you are really worried about. There is said to be only a few dozen or so general fears (no one seems to agree what a "general" fear is), and if you could overcome your general fears, you could eliminate worry completely. For example, one who is worried about the sun burning out is most likely really worried about death. Listing "death" as the real worry will eliminate the worry of getting eaten alive by house ants, being buried alive in tub of chunky peanut butter, and being sucked out

of an airplane window over Africa and landing in a crocodile pit.

2. **Get all the facts.** When I was suffering from severe headaches, I saw several doctors and read just about everything there is to know about the different types of headaches. With the facts, I no longer let my imagination run away with the worst case scenario. I did learn one very important lesson: the Internet is full of misinformation, exaggeration, and information from people at the extreme ends of the spectrum. Get the facts and don't allow yourself to be misled to even more worry.

3. **Analyze the facts.** Once you have enough information to help you face the worry, make some sense out of the data. What does it all mean, if anything, at this point?

4. **Ask yourself what is the worst that can happen.** At this point, you can make a more realistic assessment of what the worst-case scenario would be.

5. **Accept the worst.** Acceptance is almost always an instant cure for worry. Acceptance however, is not easy and often takes time. By accepting the worst, you are in a situation where things can only improve.

6. **Improve on the worst.** Here is where you consider the law of averages. What are the chances the worst will actually come to pass? Is it really worth worrying about?

7. **Decide what you can do about it.** Brainstorm. List everything that comes to mind that you can do about improving the situation. Spend as much time as needed on this part.

8. **Act on the decision.** If there is any point to worry, it is about taking action toward making positive changes. From your list of possible actions, decide what you ARE going to do and take action right away. Do not procrastinate. The longer you let your worries build inside, the more emotional and physical damage you are doing to yourself.

It is probable that through this process you will end up eliminating the worry before you complete all the steps. This is fine! The point of the exercise is to eliminate the worry, not to complete all the steps of the process.

A final suggestion is to keep a separate section in your success journal entitled, "Worries". Here list all of your worries on an ongoing basis. What will happen is you will review your earlier worries when entering new ones and you will being to realize that it was foolish to worry about such things. As you start to master both preventing and eliminating worry, you will no longer need to make any entries in this section.

The great American poet, Robert Frost, summed it up best when he said, "The reason why worry kills more people than work is that more people worry than work." Do not allow yourself to be a victim of worry. Break the worry habit today and face life's challenges head on.

ACTION STEP(S):

---

1) Make a list of all of your current worries. Run each worry through this process.

"Worry never robs tomorrow of its sorrow, it only saps today of its joy."

- Leo Buscaglia

Day 226: Key Contacts

Sometimes your most valuable contacts in life can be the least likely ones. In 1995, when I started our first web hosting company, we had this customer who ran a Russian dating service. His web designer eventually came to work with us, and then left to start his own web hosting business. I kept in contact and maintained a good relationship with him. Several years later, that web designer introduced me to the company that would eventually buy my company for 20 million dollars. Years earlier, I never would have suspected that an 18-year-old web designer of a Russian dating service website would ever end up being one of my most valuable contacts.

A key contact is someone who may be able to help you succeed either directly (by his or her own efforts or resources) or indirectly (by one or more of his or her own contacts). On average, each person knows about 100 other people. Having 100 key contacts is like having 10,000 contacts. Do not confuse a key contact with a prospect—they are very different. You do not solicit a key contact, a key contact solicits for you. Salespeople find prospects, millionaires find key contacts.

Besides building a valuable asset by creating a network of people who may be able to help you in your pursuit of success, you also get the benefit of meeting new people and being an interesting conversationalist. When you make a key contact, get as much information as you can about them. Since people like talking about themselves, you will be well received by people you meet.

Success comes as a result of proper building, maintaining and working your key contacts.

Building. Begin building your key contact list by listing all of the key contacts you currently have. Get out a pen and paper and think of every potential key contact you have. Next, you will want to enter the information in one of the many contact software packages available. Each record should be as detailed as possible. Most important, list the key contact's assets. I am not referring to their house, cars and stocks, but their assets that can be of possible benefit to you—like their contacts in a certain industry.

Finding new key contacts is about being as sociable as possible on a professional level and thinking of each key contact as a rung in your ladder of success. Your goal is not to sell a product or even yourself, but to learn about the other person.

The chances are, your information on most of your key contacts will be far from complete. The important information is their name, e-mail, and assets. A phone number, website, and birth date can also be helpful. Show tact when asking key contacts for this information. People generally do not like being "databased" and may react unfavorably to being asked this information. Here are some suggestions for getting this information from both existing and new key contacts:

- **Name.** This is the easy one. Just about everyone is happy to share his or her name with a new person.
- **E-mail, phone, and website.** It is best to ask someone for a business card or offer your card first. If they have a business card, their e-mail, phone number and website will most likely be on it. If they do not have a business card to share, then it is usually easiest and least awkward to get their e-mail address first. You first need to establish a reason for wanting their e-mail address. If you have a website that you would like to share with them, you can send your website URL to their e-mail address. Most people would have no problem with that.
- **Assets.** You never ask someone you have just met, "So, what can you do for me?" You must get this information out of conversation or dialog with the key contact. To do this, make sure the key contact is doing most of the talking, not you. If you are meeting the person while they are working, you can ask, "So tell me a little about what you do." If you are meeting someone in a non-business environment, ask "So what keeps you busy during the

day?" Be sure to write down the details either in a small notepad or a PDA (personal digital assistant) as soon as possible while the information is still fresh in your memory.

Maintaining. Chances are, new people you meet will quickly forget about you unless you keep regular contact with them. After making a new key contact, the first thing you should do is send that person a "nice meeting you" e-mail summarizing your conversation. Not only will this help the other person to remember you better, but it will give the other person your e-mail address.

When possible, send a personal e-mail wishing the contact a happy birthday. A quick, personal e-mail is much more meaningful than an on-line greeting card, which is usually full of ads. At the very least, send your contacts a holiday greeting via a personal e-mail every holiday season. Keep the holiday wishes general so you do not offend anyone.

Send your key contacts articles or other information that would be of interest to them, based on what you know about the key contact. YearToSuccess.com articles are perfect examples (shameless plug). Do not spam your key contacts with general information or possibly offensive e-mails that frequently circulate around the Internet. And perhaps most important, avoid mass mailing to your entire list. This can ruin your credibility and result in your key contacts asking to be "removed from your list".

Working. Eventually there will come a time when you will need to work your list of key contacts. Working your list refers to approaching one or more of the key contacts on your list with a proposition; it is not about asking favors. Always keep in mind that they are concerned about what is in it for them, not about what they can do for you. If you want something from a key contact, whether it is a sale or a recommendation, be sure you are selling that key contact on the benefits to him or her. The benefits could simply be the good feeling they get by connecting you to one of their contacts to create a win-win situation. Always be sure to show gratitude to those key contacts who help you for these reasons.

Should friends and/or family be considered key contacts? It all depends on how you feel doing business with them. If a family member or friend is not as forgiving or understanding as you may be, or is likely to feel resentment if a business dealing does not go as expected, it is best to not to consider that person a key contact.

Key contacts will prove over time to be one of your most valuable assets; they are the doorways to opportunity. Never underestimate the value of a key contact or base their value on their current situation. All people change, and some will find success of their own. Who knows, the 16-year-old cashier at your local grocery store may be the one who leads you to your fortune!

ACTION STEP(S):

1) Start building your key contact database today.

"I like to reminisce with people I don't know."

- Steven Wright

Day 227: Inspiration from John H. Johnson

John H. Johnson (1918–) is CEO and chairman of Johnson Publishing company. John H. Johnson rose from the welfare rolls of the depression to become the most successful black businessman in American history; the founder of EBONY, and JET magazines; a member of the FORBES 400.

Success is actively seeking opportunity. Like many African-American people living in the south in the 1930's, the Johnson's heard that there were more opportunities in the north and made the move.

Success is seeking knowledge and inspiration. Mr. Johnson was said to have read and been inspired by the writings of success authors since he was a teenager; including the works of Dale Carnegie.

Success is doing your best, because you never know who may be watching. Mr. Johnson proved to be an excellent student in high school. Because of his achievements, in 1936, Mr. Johnson was invited to speak at a dinner held by the Urban League. The President of the Supreme Liberty Life Insurance Company was so impressed with Mr. Johnson's speech that he offered him a job and a scholarship to attend college part-time.

Success is taking risks. Mr. Johnson ended up borrowing $500 at the Citizens Loan Corporation to start Johnson Publishing, using his mother's furniture for collateral.

Success is a direct result of helping others. Mr. Johnson's magazine, then called Negro Digest, was a magazine for giving hope to others, by documenting stories of successful African-Americans.

Success is modeling success. Modeled after *Life* and *Look*, Mr. Johnson's magazine aimed to tell the story of Black America in words and pictures.

Success is persistence. Mr. Johnson's persistence helped him to get the then first lady Eleanor Roosevelt to write an article for his magazine. The sensation this article created caused the magazine's circulation to double almost overnight.

Success is knowing how to influence people. "When I go in to see people—and I sell an occasional ad now—I never say, 'Help me because I am black' or 'Help me because I am a minority.' I always talk about what we can do for them..."

Success is loving what you do. At age 85 in 2003, Mr. Johnson is still the active chairman of Johnson Publishing. "Retirement is not in this company's vocabulary. If you are well and able to work, you can stay at the company and that's what I plan to do."

[Sources: http://www.johnsonpublishing.com,
http://www.howard.edu]

"I believe that the greater the handicap the greater the triumph."

- John H. Johnson

Day 228: Using the Web

Since 1994, the Internet, specifically the World Wide Web (or just "Web") has been constantly evolving to what it is today: a virtual global marketplace, information and education center, and communication network. The Internet has dramatically changed the way we work. No longer are we in the Industrial age where the men go off to work and the women stay behind with the children. In this new era, anyone with a PC and an Internet connection, despite sex, race, age, financial status, and physical limitations has the same opportunities to find success with the help of the Internet. However, many people are intimidated by the very thought of the Internet and limit their own success. Knowing and understanding a few basic principles can help you take full advantage of the power of the Web and help you in your journey to success.

As of this writing, there are over 3 billion public web pages on the Internet. Most of the content is garbage, but even the tiny percentage that is useful still accounts for much more information than one would find in the largest of libraries. There are more products for sale than one would find in the largest of malls, and more opportunities than one would find in all the help wanted sections from every Sunday paper in the world combined. It is not hard to see what a major role the Web can play in our success. Specifically:

- **Research.** Using your favorite search engine to find information is easy. I prefer Google (http://www.google.com) because of the lack of image-based advertising on their site.
- **Contacts.** Through browsing alone, one can make numerous targeted key contacts every day.
- **Bargains.** The Web is the ultimate marketplace where competition is fierce and prices are low. Working with reputable companies, you can save some serious money on higher ticket items.

- **Education.** There are numerous sites dedicated to providing free education and training for those who seek it. The Web, unlike books, audio, or even video is capable of interaction, which aids in the learning process.
- **Opportunities.** The Web is the ideal place for creating new and finding existing opportunities. Those who think all the good ideas have already been taken are thinking like Charles H. Duell, Commissioner of the U.S. Office of Patents who, around the start of the twentieth century, reportedly wanted to close down the U.S. patent office because he felt that everything to be invented had already been invented. The fact is, the Web is less than a decade old and as technology advances, so do opportunities. The Internet bust was not due to bad ideas, just bad investing. Today people are wiser and more cautious. This is a good thing for those with solid Internet-based business ideas or those who represent solid Internet-based businesses.

Unfortunately, the Web, like the real world, has it evils as well. These evils keep many people from embracing the power of the Web. The good news is, these evils of the Web can easily be avoided or ignored with a little education. Here are some tips, suggestions, and insights coming from a guy who has been living the majority of his conscious life in this virtual world since 1995.

Dealing with mis-information. The Web is full of information, just not all of it is based on facts. While reading biographies of the successful individuals written about in this course, I have come across web sites on just about every one of the people stating how they are/were either devil worshipers or Nazis. Verify the source of the information and do not automatically believe everything you read.

Protecting your personal information. Many years ago, there was a major security flaw in a Web browser that allowed web sites to "capture" user's e-mail addresses simply by visiting a web site that contained simple code. This security flaw has long since been fixed, but the damage still is being done today as people avoid the Web in fear that their personal information will be captured. The fact is, with the exception of extremely rare security flaws, this cannot happen unless you purposely enter your personal information on a web site or download and install a program that installs "spyware" on your PC. Before entering your personal information on a website

- Make sure the web page you are on is secure. You can tell by the URL in the address bar beginning with "https://" or by the closed lock icon on the bottom section of the browser. If the page is not secure, your information can be picked up by anyone sniffing the network (ignore the tech stuff, just know your info is not protected without a secure URL).
- Look for a privacy statement. A privacy statement is not a guarantee that the company asking for your information will do or not do everything promised in the statement, but it is certainly a good sign. Most businesses will not risk their reputation by selling their customer's information to a third party, but it is certainly possible.

Realize that very few things are free on the Web. If you do not pay for a service with money, you pay in one or more of several ways. YearToSuccess.com is "funded" by our own book sales and speaking engagements. Our members "pay" by having to see links to these products and services on our website (not a bad deal). However, most free products or services on the Web are not as kind...

- Adware. Adware is software that is bundled with other software that users download and install on their PCs. This adware "pops up" frequent ads in the form of web browser windows whether you are using the Web or not. It is very annoying to say the least. If you have this software on your PC, there are many programs you can run that will find adware and remove it.
- Spyware. Spyware is just like adware except it reads your PC for your personal information and sends it to a source that then will either sell it, or use it to market products to you.

- Ads. Ads could be in the form of banners, text ads, Flash animations, pop ups/unders, and more. These can range from discreet to very annoying. Quick tip for improving your web browsing experience: download the Google tool bar at http://www.google.com. It comes with a great pop up blocker built in.
- Spams. Many times you give your e-mail address and permission to be marketed to via e-mail in exchange for a product or service.
- Selling your information. One of the worst web "sins" a website can commit, is selling your information to a third party without your knowledge.

As a general rule of thumb, when you pay for a product or service you do not have to be concerned about any of the above. However, if you are searching for something for nothing, do your homework and search for privacy statements, FAQs, or other publicized assurances that your information will be kept private.

Keep your operating system (OS) updated. Visit the website of your OS frequently—at least once per month—and download the latest updates. This will protect you from many of the latest viruses and known security flaws.

Don't be deceived by ads. The Web is full of deceiving ads such as ads that look like windows with fake cancel buttons that launch new windows, ads that look like warning windows that tell you something must be downloaded, ads that tell you claim your "free" prize—only to later discover that the prize is free with your purchase of other products—and many more.

Only trust downloads from official sites. Download software only from sites you are familiar with and trust.

The benefits of the Web far exceed its evils. Pretty much the worst that can happen is your credit card number may be stolen, but most credit companies do not hold you responsible for that anyway. If your e-mail address gets spammed, you may have to setup some spam filters or at worst, change your e-mail address. Take advantage of this amazing tool and start working in the information age where one can find opportunity just clicks away.

ACTION STEP(S):

---

1) Look into downloading the Google tool bar. If you choose to install it, it will make searching the Web easier and faster, and it will increase your productivity by blocking pop up ads for you (you must activate this option). See http://toolbar.google.com/.

"The Internet is the most important single development in the history of human communication since the invention of call waiting."

- Dave Barry

Day 229: Spend Less Than You Earn

There is a common misconception that wealthy people have fewer money problems than the average person. Likewise, people with money problems tend to believe that more money will solve their money problems. This is rarely the case. The large majority of money problems in developed countries are not due to the lack of money, they are due to overspending, and overspending leads to debt. A 1992 Federal Reserve study showed that 43% of U.S. families spent more than they earned. Money problems, specifically, spending more than one earns, is one of the leading obstacles to finding happiness.

It is the typical trap that most people know all too well: It begins with parents trying to be helpful with the advice, "Buy the most expensive house you can afford!" The theory behind this advice is that when you use a mortgage to buy a home, you are using other people's money to grow your asset. The problem is, you are tying up all your funds in a long-term investment To the entrepreneur or investor, there is opportunity cost, or the cost of missed opportunity, associated with this money. In addition, generally speaking, the more expensive the house is to buy the more expensive it is to maintain. These maintenance costs, including time, are a liability and not an asset. If you do follow this advice, make sure you really understand what "afford" means.

At this point, the real spending begins. Credit cards are used to buy furnishings and other miscellaneous home goods. Consumers are reeled in by the "No payments 'till..." signs. Eventually, credit cards are maxed out and any disposable income is being "disposed of" by paying exorbitant interest payments. Then comes the "consolidate all your credit card debt" deal where all the debt is in one neat payment secured usually by a second mortgage on the home. Even though a vow is made never to use the credit cards again, one of life's little surprises comes along that constitutes an "emergency" and the cards, once again, start reaching their limits.

Why do so many people find it so hard to spend less money than they earn? What can be done about it? Here are some of the top reasons for overspending along with suggestions.

- **Poor planning.** Those who do take the time to prepare budgets often do not figure in life's many surprises like repairs, medical bills, or loss of income. If you do not have a budget planned, start one. Make sure you do include a reasonable amount for unknowns. Create the budget with neither an optimistic nor pessimistic view, but one as realistic as possible.
- **Desire for acceptance and/or importance.** People will overspend to meet either one of these desires. The problem is, those who will accept you only if you have money are not people with whom you want to associate yourself. Importance generally comes from what you choose to do with your time, not your money.
- **Purchases are often made more on emotion than reason.** We all are creatures of emotion and when our emotion and reason are in conflict, emotion will most often triumph. Advertisers and salespeople know this and sell based on our emotions. Think about it, how successful would a cigarette ad be if they only listed all the practical reasons why one should smoke? When we act on emotion, we tend to overlook our budget or somehow justify the purchase. It is best to purchase large ticket items or non-necessities after at least 24 hours of consideration.
- **Accustomed to a lifestyle.** A lifestyle is essentially a habit of living; a habit that is not easy to break. If one's income is reduced, the lifestyle is still usually maintained by increasing debt. Being forced to reduce the quality of one's lifestyle can have adverse effects on one's motivation, attitude, and overall happiness. It is best to live a more consistent lifestyle by saving and planning for times of reduced income.

If you are one of the many who are spending more than they earn, then break the habit now and adjust your lifestyle before you begin to earn more money or you will find yourself only deeper in debt.

Wealth begins with good financial habits. Whether you decrease your spending or increase your earning, spending less than you earn will help to you to live a life free from financial worry.

ACTION STEP(S):

---

1) Are you getting deeper in debt, or are you building wealth? If the former think about and write down the reasons why and make a plan of action for doing something about it.

"Annual income twenty pounds, annual expenditure nineteen six, result happiness. Annual income twenty pounds, annual expenditure twenty pound ought and six, result misery."

- Charles Dickens (1812–1870)

Days 230 and 231 are for "R&R"—review and reflection. Spend these days reviewing the last five articles and reflecting on the information and how it relates to your life. Now is also a good time to make sure all the action steps for the previous days have been completed.

Day 232: Self-Sabotage

I will never forget the cold day in December 1997 when I heard news that deeply shocked and saddened me. My comedic hero, Chris Farley, was dead at the young age of 33. The first reports suspected Farley died of a heart attack, since he had an obvious weight problem. However, subsequent reports would reveal that his death was the result of his own self-sabotage, like John Belushi, Elvis Presley, Marilyn Monroe, and countless other unnecessary tragedies before him. More toward the middle of spectrum, millions of people, both famous and non-famous, destroy their happiness and success by self-sabotage.

Self-sabotage is a combination of thoughts, feelings, and actions that create a roadblock to success by working against your own self-interests. It is when we consciously want something but subconsciously we make sure we don't get it. In extreme cases, self-sabotage acts as a self-fulfilling internalized death wish. Self-sabotage is ultimately due to the lack of self-esteem, self-worth, and self-confidence.

In the high profile world of fame and stardom, self-sabotage is known to result in destructive behavior, even leading to death. In the eyes of most people, these celebrities appear to have it all: money, fame, and admiration of millions of people. So where do things go wrong? Celebrities are, after all, still human, and have the same emotional issues to deal with as the rest of us. Each one of us is a manager of our own state of mind. The emotional issues of those living in the spotlight are often magnified, as are life's pressures. Those who cannot manage their state turn to drug or alcohol abuse as a quick and easy alternative, which eventually leads to their demise, or at least some time in Hollywood's second home—the Betty Ford Clinic.

Back in the real world, self-sabotage is much more common in its milder form. In this form, self-sabotage usually takes away one's success or kicks in before one can even reach any level of success. Here are some of the more common reasons for self-sabotage:

- **Fear of success.** Deep inside, there can be numerous reasons you do not want to succeed. These are referred to as limiting beliefs. You must overcome these limiting beliefs and break free from your fear of success.
- **Unworthiness.** Unworthiness is the belief or feeling that you do not deserve success. This is due to low self-esteem and or a poor self-image. Build your self-esteem and realize that you are not only worthy of success, but it is your right to live in abundance and pursue happiness.
- **Lack of belief in abilities.** Do you not believe that you have what it takes to succeed? Do you think your goals are too far-fetched or unrealistic? Rather than lower your goals, increase your self-confidence and convince yourself that you will do what it takes and you will succeed.
- **Working against true desires.** Unfortunate are those who never figure out what their true desires in life are. These are the people who think they know what they want, but never end up getting it due to self-sabotage. Well known examples are college drop-outs who choose majors based on what a parent wants them to do or employees who work for paychecks rather than the love of the work. Take the time to find out what you really want out of life and write it down.

Basically, self-sabotage is like a game of mental tug-of-war. It is the conscious mind versus the subconscious mind where the subconscious mind always eventually wins. The conscious mind can carry out actions and work toward a goal, but it will not be long before the subconscious mind reveals the true feelings and beliefs and takes control over actions. The key to eliminating self-sabotage is making sure that your conscious and subconscious mind are in harmony. You may get away with lying to others but you can never get away with lying to yourself. Believe in and have faith in yourself, and eliminate self-sabotage from your life for good.

ACTION STEP(S):

---

1) Do you find you are often playing a game of mental tug-of-war with yourself? Do you act one way but think another way? List all of the ways in which you feel "out of sync" with yourself and work on adopting the belief that will bring you closer to success.

"Self-sabotage is when we say we want something and then go about making sure it doesn't happen."

- Alyce Cornyn-Selby

Day 233: Are You Buying or Selling?

When I once again entered the web hosting industry, after the Internet bust, we assembled a salesteam of about 30 people who would call on select businesses and introduce them to one of our new hosting products. This hosting product would be part of an irresistible deal that included a free 30-day trial. To determine the success of this program, we held weekly conference calls in which our salespeople would share the results of their sales calls. The results were fairly consistent across the board: no takers. The vast majority declined the offer based on the poor economy, uncertainty of their business, lack of resources to expand their business, and many other reasons having nothing to do with our product or price. As it turned out, this salesteam was not selling anything; they were buying the excuses and hard luck stories of the prospects.

We were selling a product that could act as a substantial revenue generator for any business with an existing customer base of other businesses. Along with our free trial, it was a no-lose opportunity that could do nothing but improve the prospect's current situation. However, salespeople who accept their own hard luck stories and make excuses for their own behaviors and actions, have a tendency to sympathize with prospects who do the same. Salespeople who believe that the excuses given are legitimate reasons conclude that the prospect is better off not buying, and fail to see the benefit that the product or service being sold would bring.

Change your perspective. If you find yourself doing more buying than selling, a change of perspective may be all you need. Begin by working on yourself. Don't make excuses and don't sell yourself hard luck stories. Realize that only you are responsible for your own life and while you cannot control everything that happens to you, you can control your attitude. The same holds true for every prospect that you will ever meet.

Be an optimist. An optimistic attitude, especially in sales, can be one of your greatest assets. Being an optimist is seeing the good rather than the bad—it is seeing the brighter side of life. Seeing situations from this perspective opens the mind to creative solutions to problems. Optimists can see solutions completely overlooked by pessimistic prospects. After all, it is the salesperson's duty to demonstrate how the product or service can solve the prospect's problems.

Use tact. Tact is basically the ability to communicate without offending others. Tact separates the pushy or aggressive salesperson who annoys or offends his prospects from the assertive salesperson, who persists despite rejection or objection, having the best intentions of the prospect in mind. If a prospect tells you, "I can't buy because of this uncertain economy", contradicting their statement will only put him or her on the defense. Use tact when you respond to objections and think in terms of the prospect's point of view. An appropriate response may be, "I can certainly understand why you would hesitate in this economy. In fact, our customers appreciate our product most when the economy is slow because of the money it saves them."

In every situation where one person is attempting to sell another person a product, service or idea, a sale is made. It is either the prospect that is sold the product, service or idea, or the salesperson who is sold on a reason for the prospect not to buy. Do not let your own personality flaws interfere with your success. Cultivate an optimistic outlook on life and take responsibility for your own situation. Then, you will be more effective at helping others solve their problems by seeing the benefits your product or service can bring.

ACTION STEP(S):

1) Examine your own attitude. Are you one who makes excuses? Do you feel that life is constantly giving you lemons? If so, what can you do about it? What are you going to do about it?

Day 234: Inspiration from Fred Smith

Frederick W. Smith (1944–) is the Chairman and CEO of Federal Express Corporation; also known as the "father of the overnight delivery business".

Success is taking criticism lightly, even from those "who know best". While attending Yale University, Fred Smith wrote a paper on the need for reliable overnight delivery in a computerized information age. His professor found the premise "improbable" and, to the best of Smith's recollection, he only received a grade of C for this effort.

Success is learning all you can from your current situation. After college, Fred spent a few years in the military. While there, he observed military procurement and delivery procedures carefully. This information helped him to realize his dream of overnight commercial delivery.

Success does not always come quickly. In the first two years of business, Federal Express lost $27 million. Shortly after, the company was on the verge of bankruptcy. During this time, Smith still was confident the idea was solid.

Success is being able to negotiate. Thanks to Fred's negotiating skills, he was able to negotiate his way out of failure and managed to turn FedEx into a multi-billion dollar a year empire.

Success is continued improvement. Smith does not allow FedEx to rest on its laurels. Continuous improvement is said to be one of his fundamental management principles.

Success is fulfilling a need, even if it means creating an entire industry. "Fred Smith is the only man I have ever known who has created an entire industry," wrote Howard Baker, the U.S. ambassador to Japan and former U.S. senator from Tennessee.

Success is understanding the importance of keeping employees happy. FedEx has repeatedly been on Fortune magazine's list of the "100 Best Companies to Work For".

Success is not fearing failure. In the early 80s, Smith launched Zapmail, a program to electronically transmit documents between FedEx offices. The idea was a costly flop. "I'm not afraid to take a swing and miss," said Smith in an interview.

Success is remaining flexible. Since Smith founded Federal Express in 1971, he's kept his business nimble, always changing to meet the demands of the market and consumers.

[Sources: http://www.achievement.org, http://fedex.com, http://www.fortune.com]

"If you want to be a great leader, find a big parade and run in front of it."

- Fred Smith

Day 235: Mastermind Alliance

Henry Ford, auto industry billionaire, began his business career under the handicaps of poverty, illiteracy, and ignorance. Knowing his own weaknesses and understanding one of the key principles of success, Mr. Ford allied himself with Thomas Edison, whom he knew could help him achieve his desired goals and objectives. However, Mr. Ford's most outstanding achievements began from the time he allied himself with the great minds of Harvey Firestone, John Burroughs and Luther Burbank. Together, these men would form the mastermind alliance behind the Ford Motor Company, which was responsible for bringing affordable automobiles to the masses.

A mastermind alliance is having access to a body of knowledge and/or resources in human form that you can consult when the need arises. Many great businesses are started and run with a mastermind alliance. These masterminds consist of two or more people with varying talents, skills, and resources who work together toward a common objective. In fact, forming a mastermind could be seen as one of the key steps in the goal setting exercise—it is another way of identifying the people who can help you achieve success.

Very often, the achievement of success requires the cooperation of others. When you form a mastermind, you ideally choose members that compensate for your lack of skills or resources needed to reach your common objective.

Henry Ford was once on trial and was unable to answer a fairly simple question about history. In response to the interrogating attorney, Ford said, "Now, will you kindly tell me, why I should clutter up my mind with general knowledge, for the purpose of being able to answer questions when I have men around me who can supply any knowledge I require?" This question posed by Ford not only restored his credibility to the court, but demonstrated to many how brilliant he really was.

A mastermind, like any good team, consists of members who have different perspectives. These different perspectives are useful when it comes to problem solving. Problem solving is often like putting together a puzzle where the possible solutions are like the puzzle pieces; it takes several different pieces to complete the puzzle.

Perhaps one of the greatest benefits of a mastermind is synergy. Synergy is the interaction of two or more agents or forces so that their combined effect is greater than the sum of their individual effects. In mathematical terms, it is 1+1=3. In scientific terms, it is like mixing two or more substances to create a completely different substance. This type of synergism is the driving force behind many successes.

Before you can assemble a mastermind alliance, you must have a clear objective in mind. An objective is often synonymous with a goal, but an objective is more often a goal shared between two or more people. With a clear objective in mind, you can proceed with the following five steps for building an effective mastermind alliance.

1. **Identify and build.** Begin the creation of your mastermind alliance by identifying and seeking the types of people needed to help reach your objective. Seek members who are self-motivated, enthusiastic, success oriented, trustworthy, responsible and most of all, who possess the skills and resources needed to help reach the objective. Resources can be in the form of financial aid, contacts, time, or other forms of contribution. It is important to choose members whom you can work with and who can work with each other; however, do not choose members based solely on these criteria.

2. **Understand objective.** As the creator of your mastermind, it is your responsibility to make sure that each member clearly understands the objective. In addition, each member must believe in the group and have faith in its ability to achieve the objective. The more passionate about

reaching the objective each group member is, the better success the mastermind will have.

3. **Understand compensation.** Make sure each member of the mastermind understands what his or her rewards will be for accomplishing the objective. Remember that rewards do not always have to be all financial. Refer back to Abraham Maslow's hierarchy of needs and associate the achievement of the objective with the fulfillment of as many desires as possible. Motivate and energize the members of your mastermind alliance.

4. **Give clear direction.** It is essential that each member of the mastermind know what they need to do. Direction is meant to be general, not specific like a list of "to do" items. Leaders provide direction and managers generally provide specific action steps. Be a leader to your mastermind team members, not a manager.

5. **Set meeting times and frequency.** How will your mastermind communicate? By phone, e-mail, face-to-face meetings? How often and at what times? Make sure that the communication is frequent enough so that the members are kept focused, but not too frequent where the members are distracted from taking action toward the achievement of the objective.

A well-formed mastermind alliance can be your greatest asset for achieving any objective. You can form several masterminds, each with the purpose of accomplishing a different objective. Do your best when choosing members for your mastermind and remember that the overall success of the group is based on the contribution of each of the members. Don't waste any of your valuable time by postponing success while you work on your shortcomings. Compensate for your shortcomings by building a mastermind alliance and by beginning your journey to success right away.

ACTION STEP(S):

---

1) Create a mastermind. The objective can be as great as your life's purpose, or as little as solving an everyday problem.

Day 236: Multiple Streams of Income

Real estate millionaires do not become millionaires by investing in just one property. They do not buy just one property and rent it out, or turn over just one property for a profit. Real estate millionaires usually work several properties at one time in order to maximize their profit and make efficient use of their time. Real estate millionaires have what is called "multiple streams of income", which is essentially more than one source of cash flow. Millionaires in any industry often become millionaires by adopting this very same technique.

Multiple streams of income do not have to be within the same industry or come from the same general source. In fact, having streams of income from different industries is often more effective and provides a greater sense of security. Here are the four top general sources of income of most millionaires today.

- **Real Estate** - rental income, home appreciation, proceeds from sales
- **Financial Markets** - stocks, bonds, IRAs, CDs, money market accounts, generally any interest income
- **Business** - brick and mortar or Internet based
- **General Employment** - trading labor for a paycheck

Consider the individual who has a 9-5 job that she thoroughly enjoys, but desires financial independence. By using the mastermind principle, she can assemble a team of experts in several areas with the goal of creating streams of income. It is not necessary for her to become an expert and focus in each area, especially while working a full-time job.

Why not put all of your focus and energy on just one source of income? At times, focusing on one source of income will produce the best results, especially in the case of a startup venture where your full attention is needed. However, generally it is easier to make a little money in several areas than it is to make a lot of money in one area. Having multiple streams of income is like increasing your chances at winning the lottery by buying several tickets.

Another reason why having multiple streams of income makes so much financial sense is because at some point in anything you do, the law of diminishing returns eventually kicks in. When this happens, your maximum efforts start producing minimum results. By re-focusing your efforts on another stream of income, your chances of financial success greatly increase.

Consider for a moment that you have a problem that you need to solve: a lack of money or financial insecurity. A great way to solve any problem is by "attacking the problem from all angles". Each stream of income created is an "angle" from which you are "attacking" the problem—the lack of money. If one angle fails, you still have several more working to solve the problem. Each stream of income on its own may not be enough to solve your financial problems, but together they are. You can also substitute "problem" with "goal" and use this technique to create substantial wealth.

The majority of wealthy individuals have multiple streams of income; they do not rely on just one source. This not only helps them to achieve financial security, but often leads them to financial independence. It does not always take money to make money, but it does always take ideas and desire. Expand your thinking by asking yourself the question, "What can I do to create multiple streams of income?" The answer to this question may also be the answer to all your financial problems.

ACTION STEP(S):

---

1) What can you do today to start the ball rolling to bring in an additional stream of income? Write down all the possibilities.

"There is nothing more demoralizing than a small but adequate income."

- Edmund Wilson

Days 237 and 238 are for "R&R"—review and reflection. Spend these days reviewing the last five articles and reflecting on the information and how it relates to your life. Now is also a good time to make sure all the action steps for the previous days have been completed.

Day 239: Success is Learning

Stop learning and start doing. This is what most of us are encouraged to do at some point early in our lives, either consciously or subconsciously. The beginning of one's career is often the end of one's education as well. Sure, there may be some job training down the road and even an occasional non-fictional book or two, but nothing like the education we receive early on in life. Successful individuals embrace the habit of learning and make it a life-long process. Successful individuals are encouraged to start doing and *keep* learning.

Learning is the act, process, or experience of gaining knowledge or skill. In traditional education, topics are chosen for us and rightfully so. After all, if it were up to 10-year-olds, they would study video game cheats and the art of tormenting siblings. In traditional education, class times are fixed, as are schedules. This rigid educational system tends to turn many people off from learning early on. Learning beyond traditional education is very different; it is an unstructured process that begins with a desire within oneself to attain knowledge or a skill. This type of learning is both motivating and addictive.

So why bother learning after formal schooling is completed?

- **Law of entropy.** The law of entropy basically states that if we don't use it, we lose it. Unless we continually exercise our brain by feeding it information through learning, our ability to retain information deteriorates.
- **Perception.** Others tend to judge us based on how educated we appear to be. Although this is a form of prejudice, it happens all the time.
- **Advancement.** Continuing education can help you advance in your current career. Don't just think about degrees and titles; think about acquiring the knowledge that will help you do your job better.

- **Discovery.** We are expected to decide on a career relatively early in life. For many people, this usually leads to a life of contentment, not passion. Continue to study topics that interest you and you may discover that your true passion in life has nothing to do with your chosen career.
- **Confidence.** Continual learning builds confidence on a regular basis. Think about it, how can you not be more confident knowing that each day you become smarter and wiser?

There have been numerous successful individuals throughout history who lacked formal schooling. Yet, with the desire for knowledge, the need for personal growth, and the love of learning, they became very educated. Those who are not fortunate enough to have the opportunity of formal education are not destined for a life of ignorance. Education does not have to cost money, and it does not have to take very much time. Learning is for everyone who has the desire to embrace it.

Here are just some ways in which you can continue the learning process throughout your life.

- **Formal schooling.** If you never completed your formal schooling, it is never too late to go back. Never feel as if you are "too old" or it is "too late". Colleges are full of students of all ages. High school equivalency tests (GED) are even available on-line now.
- **Adult education.** Most communities have adult education classes on many subjects. These classes are less frequent than standard college courses and usually cost very little. Contact your town/city hall for more information and schedules.
- **On-line courses.** The Internet is the greatest source of education available today. You can find courses on just about any subject you can imagine. Some of these courses are completely free (like YearToSuccess.com) and some do cost money. However, just about all of the on-line courses can be done at home, and some even at your own pace.

- **Books, audio and video.** There are millions of non-fiction books, tapes, CDs, and videos available today on every conceivable subject. Books can be taken just about anywhere and read at one's own pace. Audio cassettes or CDs are great while driving or exercising. And videos make great teachers for visual learners. Best of all, local libraries make these incredible learning tools available for free.
- **Other classes.** Why not expand your mind while conditioning your body? Try martial arts, yoga, pilates, aerobics, swimming, tennis... the list goes on.

The key to learning is to first create the desire for knowledge. Understand that continual learning will increase your odds of success and help you reach your goals faster. Learning comes in many forms besides formal schooling and certainly does not have to stop when a career begins. Be inquisitive, ask questions, and seek answers. "Anyone who stops learning is old, whether at twenty or eighty," said Henry Ford. "Anyone who keeps learning stays young. The greatest thing in life is to keep your mind young."

ACTION STEP(S):

1) Commit to learning something new everyday: a new word, a new concept, a new idea.

2) If you have children, make it a nightly ritual to ask them, "So what did you learn today?"

Day 240: Inspire Others

In the 1970s, a young man named Rudy Ruettiger defied all odds and realized his dream of entering the University of Notre Dame and playing for the Fighting Irish football team. Rudy was a physically small young man, with little talent and a minor case of dyslexia, but had the heart of a lion. Around 20 years later, his story was made into a hit movie called _Rudy_, which inspired millions of people all over the world.

To inspire another is to fill that person with enlivening or exulting emotion. Inspiration is the spark for motivation where motivation leads to action. Leaders motivate others for a common purpose and inspire others to do something for themselves.

Inspiration is the spark needed to ignite the fire within each of us that causes us to take action. Inspiration gives us reason and desire. Leaders who can inspire others to take action for themselves have a gift that is universally sought after. Leaders in business, religion, politics, and family who can inspire those they lead rank highly among the most effective leaders.

People can be inspired by nature itself: a beautiful sunset, an ocean breeze, or a mountain stream. In fact, virtually any stimulation of one of the five senses can trigger inspiration. Some people believe inspiration is sent from a higher power in which case there is no external stimulation. Even with all of these sources, inspiration is not a frequent event. Effective leaders, however, can inspire others, or more accurately, cause others to become inspired. If you wish to inspire others, here are some techniques you can use.

- **Use positive words.** Positive words inspire positive emotions. Encourage others by reminding them of their talents, skills, and gifts. Focus on what they have done and not what they have not done. Project a positive personality.

- **Show others that you care.** People don't care about how much you know until they know how much you care. Take a genuine interest in other people.
- **Be a role model.** People are inspired by those who "walk the walk". Do not be afraid to share your own stories of accomplishment. Leaders who inspire practice what they preach and lead by example.
- **Challenge others.** Those leaders whom we love to hate are the ones who challenge us to do our best. A properly executed challenge can both motivate and inspire.
- **Share stories.** People need to believe in what is possible. Stories that people can relate to can be very inspiring. Choose stories that convey the same message you are trying get across. For example, Rudy's story is one of persistence and determination.
- **Be enthusiastic!** There is no better way to inspire others than by being filled with enthusiasm yourself. This enthusiasm is energy that easily spreads from one person to the next. To be effective, enthusiasm must be genuine; there is no faking enthusiasm.

Some of the world's greatest leaders like Lincoln, Gandhi and Churchill are best known for their ability to inspire others. Each of them used one or more of the techniques mentioned above to earn the reputation they have. Pick one of these leaders to be your inspirational role model or adopt the qualities of another inspirational leader. Being able to inspire others will no doubt make you a more effective and powerful leader.

ACTION STEP(S):

1) Learn at least one inspirational story well that you can tell to others.

Day 241: Inspiration from Jim Henson

Jim Henson (1936-1990) was more than a puppeteer and creator of the world-famous "Muppets", he was the person responsible for bringing joy to millions of people of all ages.

Success is fueled by encouragement. Jim was very close to his maternal grandmother who was an avid painter, quilter, and needleworker. She was very supportive of Jim's artistic efforts and encouraged him to use his imagination.

Success has to start somewhere. In 1954, while Jim was still in high school, he performed puppets on a local TV station. One year later, he was given his own five-minute show called, "Sam and Friends" on a local NBC affiliate station.

Success is often a result of good promotion. The success of "Sam and Friends" led to guest appearances on some of the major network talk shows of the time.

Success is seeking help when you need it. In 1961, Jim brought on puppeteer and writer Jerry Juhl, who became one of Jim's major collaborators. Later, he brought on Frank Oz, who also made significant contributions to Muppets, Inc.

Success is learning and doing. With his puppeteering well looked after by a group of talented experts, Jim was able to pursue his interests in film-making. Within a few years, he produced several experimental films that would eventually lead to his greatest success.

Success is a result of providing something of value to as many people as possible. Henson's work on Sesame Street proved to be a huge success that mostly appealed to young children. But Jim had much more grand ideas to appear to a much wider audience, thus began promotion of the idea of "The Muppet Show".

Success does not happen overnight. Jim spent years promoting the idea of "The Muppet Show" which was finally backed by a London-based television producer.

Success is a result of imagination. "The Muppet Show" was a huge success because of Jim's humor and imagination that was evident in each and every Muppet Show episode.

Success never dies. Even after Jim Henson's death in 1990, the Muppets continue to entertain and amuse both kids and adults alike.

[Source: http://www.henson.com/]

"My hope still is to leave the world a bit better than when I got here."

- Jim Henson

Day 242: Having Power

When speaking of a person, and the term "powerful" is mentioned, a common image that comes to mind is a big fat guy in a three piece suit, hair slicked back, smoking a cigar. You can probably picture this guy leaning back in his $3000 leather desk chair, barking commands at his employees. This image of power works well in Hollywood, but in the real world, true power takes a very different form.

Power is defined as the ability or official capacity to exercise control or authority. The abundance of money is often associated with power because it can give one the financial capacity to exercise such control. But money alone does not make one powerful and lack of money does not prevent one from being powerful. Gandhi is one of the greatest examples of power in recent history. Here was a man of poverty that led millions of people and freed a nation. Having power is not about being feared. As Peter Gibbons from the movie _Office Space_ says about managers who use fear as a motivator, "...but y'know, Bob, it [fear] will only make someone work hard enough not to get fired."

Power is the ability to get others to take action for their own reasons, not necessarily yours. The term "powerful" is a subjective term that usually refers to a) how much control, or influence, one has over another, b) how many people one has influence over and c) the degree of power of each of the people over whom one has influence. For example, the President of the United States is considered by many to be the most powerful person in the world. He has a) a great deal of influence over just about anyone, b) influence over almost everyone and c) influence over just about everyone who has a great degree of power.

Seeking power for the sake of being powerful is a recipe for failure. Power is a result of success; it should not be a goal in itself. People in positions of power generally earn those positions and thus earn the right to and the responsibilities of power. The moment they abuse the power, they begin to lose it. Power can be a tremendous ally on the road to success if used for the good of others. Following some basic success strategies can help you earn the right to power.

- **Make connections.** Success often comes as a result of who you know. Those who seek the right connections, or key contacts, increase their odds of success.
- **Do favors for others.** Do favors, or help others without expecting anything in return. There may come a time when you require something from someone. Those whom you have helped in the past will be much more likely to help you when the time comes. However, never expect returned favors.
- **Master the art of influence.** Influencing others is accomplished through kindness, not loathing; giving others courage, not instilling fear; and winning others to your way of thinking, not manipulation.
- **Earn respect.** You can never command respect, you must earn it. Be decisive and fair to those whom you lead. Have a positive mental attitude and offer encouragement. Stand up for yourself and project confidence.
- **Be dependable.** Do what you say you are going to do and do it when you say you are going to do it.

Money in itself is not power, just like knowledge is not power; it is only potential power. It takes action, backed by other principles of success to create power. Practice these principles and the power that comes with success can be yours.

ACTION STEP(S):

---

1) Adjust your self-image. Do you see yourself as weak, timid, or submissive? Work on projecting a more powerful image. Stand up tall (don't slouch), smile, project your voice when speaking, and most important, be confident.

Day 243: Incentive Partnership

Back in the old days of the Internet, obtaining investment money was cheap and easy. As long as you had a "dot-com" (yes, even if your business plan included a talking hand puppet with a fake microphone), you had access to the cash you needed to build your on-line empire. However, as investors began to realize the error of their ways, entrepreneurs had to use their heads more and their money less. Enter incentive partnership.

Incentive partnership is a performance-based compensation arrangement between two or more entities. Unlike the traditional employee/employer relationship, the incentive partnership rewards individuals based on efforts or results. Incentive partnerships can have rewards based on one or more of many criteria such as company-wide profits, departmental revenues, individual sales or a combination of criteria. Unlike the traditional commissioned sales professional, the reward is not solely in the form of a sales commission.

Imagine you have an amazing idea, one that you are confident can make you wealthy beyond your wildest dreams. It is an idea that has both excited you and filled you with enthusiasm. You plan out every detail of your idea, but then, reality hits and you realize that you do not have a dime to your name to hire the help needed to execute such a plan. What do you do? What if you are already in business and your problem is one of decreased productivity and low morale? The answer: form incentive partnerships. Incentive partnerships can be of great benefit to all parties involved in the following ways:

- **Makes business relationships possible.** Offering a compensation package other than a salary allows businesses to enter relationships that would otherwise not be possible, feasible, or financially sound.
- **Aids in startup.** Startup businesses or ventures often require cash for labor. That need for cash can be offset by

incentive partners who are eager to be compensated with partial ownership or some type of profit sharing.

- **Promotes unification.** In business, there is often the "us versus them" mentality between those who do the work and those who own the business or share in the rewards. When rewards are shared with those doing the work, everybody becomes the "us".
- **Promotes understanding.** When workers are compensated based on the success of the business or department, they tend to see the larger picture. Petty complaints are often eliminated as workers begin to see themselves as part of the solution to their problems.
- **Creates unified goals.** Salaried employees or commissioned salespeople usually have one main goal in mind—to look out for themselves. When workers are incentivised partners, the goals of the organization become the goals of the individual.
- **Motivates.** A fixed salary generally does not rank high on the list of motivators, especially as time passes. Incentive partnerships motivate workers in many ways: more substantial payoffs, long-term investments, and the feelings of belonging, accomplishment, and importance.

Once you are convinced that incentive partnerships can help bring you closer to your financial and business goals, it is time to take action. Here are some tips on building incentive partnerships.

- **Finding people.** Incentive partnerships certainly are not the norm and are not part of traditional industrial age thinking. Potential incentive partners will most likely have to be sold on the idea and the benefits beforehand.
- **You may need more people than you think.** If you are compensated based on partial ownership, profits, or any form of long-term and less guaranteed income, you may have trouble finding people who are financially secure enough to act on that kind of opportunity—at least on a full-time basis. If this is the case, you will most likely need several part-timers to perform the work of one full-timer.

- **Compensation.** You can compensate incentive partners by giving partial ownership of the entity, giving a portion of the revenues or profits of the company, department or division, or paying based on performance such as number of widgets assembled; the possibilities are only limited by your creativity and imagination.

Incentive partnership can be one of the fairest forms of compensation. By treating workers as owners and sharing common goals, leaders can get more productivity from those whom they lead, while creating business relationships that otherwise may not have been possible. Be open to alternative compensation plans whether launching a new venture or building an existing one, and success can be yours.

ACTION STEP(S):

1) Write down some ideas on how you may be able to use incentive partnerships now or in the future.

"Call it what you will, incentives are what get people to work harder."

- Nikita S. Khrushchev

Days 244 and 245 are for "R&R"—review and reflection. Spend these days reviewing the last five articles and reflecting on the information and how it relates to your life. Now is also a good time to make sure all the action steps for the previous days have been completed.

Day 246: Control the Conversational Climate

If you own a television set, you have most likely seen an interrogation session where one or more members of some kind of law enforcement agency attempt to extract information from a suspect or convict. Or perhaps you have seen a witness being interrogated by a lawyer in a courtroom. This is done by the interrogator attempting to rouse the witness, suspect or criminal and get him or her to act from emotion and not reason. This is an example of controlling the conversational climate. For most of us, we will not find it necessary to interrogate witnesses or criminals, but we do want to maintain control of the conversational climates in our communications with others.

When you are in control of the conversational climate, you are not necessarily controlling the topic, but you are controlling the emotions expressed and the overall tone of the conversation. This is very often more important and here's why: studies have shown that somewhere around 90% of all content of a speech, presentation, or conversation is forgotten after just one week. What is left is the impression of the emotions expressed. In personal or business situations, you want to leave others with positive emotions and good feelings.

Controlling the conversational climate is based on the premise that negative + positive = neutral or positive. To illustrate, if you have a customer who called you just to tell you how lousy your product is, by responding with positive words and comments you can make the overall tone of the call either neutral or positive. Easier said than done, right? What isn't? Controlling the conversational climate takes a positive mental attitude, self-control, understanding, sympathy, and compassion. It is the ability to counter negative emotions with the opposite emotion, and influence the other person with your positive attitude. You let the other person react from emotion, but you be sure to respond with reason.

Here are some of the more common emotions along with their positive opposite emotion.

confront **anger** *with* **forbearance**
confront **anxiety** *with* **calmness**
confront **boredom** *with* **excitement**
confront **embarrassment** *with* **confidence**
confront **fear** *with* **courage**
confront **jealousy** *with* **trust**
confront **sadness** *with* **joy**

Take positive control of the conversational climate in your speeches, presentations, formal talks, sales presentations, and even in your casual conversations and you will find that others will have a more positive impression of you as well as your ideas.

ACTION STEP(S):

1) Commit to gaining control of your conversational climates. Do not let others create an overall negative climate to your presentations, speeches, or talks of any kind.

"The happiest conversation is that of which nothing is distinctly remembered, but a general effect of pleasing impression."

- Samuel Johnson

Day 247: Having the Edge

There were once two men hiking in the Canadian Rockies. They were both fairly young, healthy, and in good shape. From a distance they noticed a mother grizzly bear walking with her cubs. As the mama bear got closer, she detected the two intruders and began to charge them at full speed. Just as one of the men was about to run for dear life, the other man calmly sat down, took off his heavy hiking boots, and began to put on his sneakers. The first man said, "Are you nuts? A full-grown female grizzly bear can run over 30 miles per hour! You will never outrun that thing!" The second man calmly replied, "I don't need to. I just need to outrun you." The second man knew what he needed to survive: an edge over his competition.

Perception-wise, there is a huge difference between first and second, even though the actual difference can be a fraction of a second, as in a race. Olympic gold medalists have gone on to fame and fortune while silver medalists have their 15 minutes of fame, then are forgotten. Businesses who bid for large contracts and win can excel, whereas those that came in second place go under. As comedian Jerry Seinfeld puts it, and I am paraphrasing here, "Think about it... if you come in second, you are really the number one loser of all the losers." Having the edge can take you from being the number one loser to being the winner.

Having the edge can be a result of physical, emotional, and/or psychological conditioning. In fact, this whole course is designed to give you the edge you need to succeed at anything you do. The long-term strategy for having the edge basically comes down to working just a little harder, and knowing just a little bit more than your competition.

There is also what is called the short-term edge. This is a quick 24-hour prep to get your mind and body in peak state for an event, such as a marathon, test, presentation or competition of any kind.

Here are some general techniques for getting the short-term edge you need to succeed.

- **Get proper sleep.** You should know by now approximately how much sleep your body needs to function at its peak. Often, the night's sleep before an important event is interrupted due to nerves and anxiety. Keep in mind that if you just lie down and close your eyes, your body will get the rest it needs. If you still feel you did not get enough sleep, try taking a 10-30 minute "cat nap" the day of the event if possible—it will do wonders.
- **Eat the right foods.** Read 10 different nutrition books and get 10 different definitions of the "right foods". I am not here to tell you what foods are right but I will tell you that you already know what foods are right for you. Think about it... which foods, and how much of those foods, leave you feeling your best? Which foods leave you feeling lethargic? Avoid the bad foods and take in the good within the 24 hours before the event.
- **Exercise.** Assuming you are not preparing for a physical event where any additional form of exercise will take away from your performance, get in at least a 20-minute cardiovascular workout. Exercise sends extra blood to your brain helping you to think more clearly. A good workout can give you the "runner's high" that lasts for several hours after the exercise. A word of caution, if you are not used to cardiovascular exercise, limit your exercise to nothing more than perhaps a brisk walk.
- **Clear your mind.** Get out a sheet of paper and a pen and write down everything that is on your mind: everything you need to do, all your current worries, anything that is consuming your thoughts. Then agree to forget about everything you wrote down until after your event. Remember that your mind can only focus on one thing at any given time.

Having the edge is being your best. You can spend a lifetime working on skills that put you ahead of your competition, but there will always be tougher competitors. Use the short-term edge to nudge your way to first place in everything you do and never again settle for being the number one loser.

ACTION STEP(S):

1) Which foods, and how much of those foods, leave you feeling your best? Which foods leave you feeling lethargic? Start jotting the answers to these questions down over the course of the next several days and determine what your "peak performance" foods are.

"Regardless of how you feel inside, always try to look like a winner. Even if you are behind, a sustained look of control and confidence can give you a mental edge that results in victory."

- Diane Arbus

Day 248: Inspiration from Michael Bloomberg

Michael R. Bloomberg (1942–) is president of Bloomberg Financial Markets, Mayor of New York City (2002–), philanthropist, and a multi-billionaire

Success stems from a good work ethic. Mr. Bloomberg financed his own education by taking out loans and working part-time by parking cars.

Success is not without its setbacks. Not too long after joining Salomon Brothers, Bloomberg was made partner in 1972. However, in 1981 when Salomon Brothers was acquired, Mr. Bloomberg was fired.

Success is having the ability to identify problems. Bloomberg became frustrated with the archaic handling of financial data. When he needed past information, he would need to find a copy of the Wall Street Journal from the date in question. The records system consisted of clerks penciling trades in oversized ledgers.

Success is having vision. Mr. Bloomberg's fascination with technology, along with his knowledge of the financial markets, allowed him to create a computer information system to oversee the management and analysis of securities data. Mr. Bloomberg had created a revolution.

Success is often about slow beginnings. In 1982, Bloomberg L.P. sold just 20 subscriptions to its service; 20 years later, Bloomberg LP had over 165,000 subscribers worldwide.

Success is overcoming obstacles. When running for mayor of New York City, Mr. Bloomberg managed to overcome a 25% deficit in opinion polls to win the mayoral election.

Success is being an optimist. "I'm able to look back, look around me, and just realize that the glass is better than half full. I never understood people who are always looking for the problems."

Success is not working for money. Mr. Bloomberg took the job as mayor of New York City for $1 per year.

Success is having the desire to make a difference. "There's no other job in government where cause and effect is so tightly coupled, where you can make a difference every day in so many different ways and in so many different people's lives."

Success is sharing. Mr. Bloomberg devotes his time, attention, and financial resources to the needs of New York City, his alma maters, as well as other causes close to his heart. His charitable donations over the years have been in the hundreds of millions.

[Sources: http://home.nyc.gov, http://news.bbc.co.uk, http://www.wnbc.com]

"I never look over my shoulder...Once finished, gone. Life continues."

- Michael Bloomberg

Day 249: Reality is Perception

In the hit science fiction movie *The Matrix*, Morpheus (Lawrence Fishburn) tries to explain the mind-baffling concept of the matrix to Neo (Keanu Reeves) who has just had his perception of reality completely changed. Neo's former perception of reality was no different than that of your ordinary late twentieth-century hacker/software programmer. When Neo made the choice to open his mind to "the real world", he realized that he was actually living a futuristic nightmare where machines were ruling the earth. Although the concept behind the movie is science fiction (or at least we think it is), it vividly illustrates how one's perception of reality is reality to that person.

If the whole concept of *The Matrix* is too "out there" for you, then consider the more common example of the disease anorexia. One who has anorexia nervosa relentlessly pursues thinness. Those with the disease report feeling fat even though they are dangerously thin. In their reality they are fat, but in other's reality, the more common reality, they actually weigh over 85% less than what is expected for their age and height. The question is, are your perceptions of reality helping you achieve success or keeping you from it?

Our reality is based on our perceptions. We base our perceptions on a number of factors like the information we take in, our experiences, our opinions, our feelings and our emotions. When we prejudge people or events, we form feelings and opinions based on limited information, which in turn becomes our reality. We can form more accurate perceptions by not jumping to conclusions or forming opinions until we have adequate information.

If we just wish to change our current perceptions, we need to seek more information. If we want to change our perceptions in a way that will help us achieve success, we still need to seek more information, but analyze that information with a positive mental attitude and with our goals in mind. For example, people with self-destructive habits and no desire to change tend to seek out only information that supports their habit and ignore other information either consciously or subconsciously. When seeking information, keep your goals in mind and you will find what you need to alter your perceptions that will bring you closer to success. Remember the proverb, "Seek and you shall find".

ACTION STEP(S):

1) Are your perceptions of reality helping you achieve success or keeping you from it? Write down any perceptions you have that may be keeping you from success. Now work on seeking more information that will alter those perceptions.

"Reality is merely an illusion, albeit a very persistent one."

- Albert Einstein

Day 250: Active Listening

Sigmund Freud, the Austrian founder of psychoanalysis, was known as one of the greatest active listeners of all time. One of his greatest contributions to the field of mental health was his discovery that in order to understand and effectively treat a patient, a doctor had to listen to his or her patients. He further explained that communication may be with direct words, with actions, or in some other disguised manner whose code is very difficult to decipher. Active listening is not just a key element of psychoanalysis, but it is the key element of successful communication.

You have most likely heard someone say something like, "I know you can hear me, but are you listening to me?" Unless one is hearing impaired, or in a completely soundproof environment, he or she is always hearing. Hearing is using our brain subconsciously to process sounds, whereas listening is focusing attention on the sounds being heard. Active listening is more effective and more interactive than just listening. It involves more physical, mental, and/or verbal interaction. Active listening should be used in place of listening in all situations: one-on-one, group presentations, personal, and professional.

So why is active listening so important? Three main reasons:

1. **Active listening is needed to get the true message.** Listening to select words or phrases, and not interpreting those words correctly can distort a message that can lead to poor decisions.
2. **Active listening can dramatically increase retention of the material.** It is said that we all have perfect memories; it is the retention with which we have difficulty.
3. **Active listening helps build rapport with the speaker.** Call it being polite, common courtesy, or showing sincere interest in the speaker, speakers appreciate active listening.

Active listeners are often viewed as great conversationalists, even though they may say very little.

In addition, active listening has other far-reaching effects that benefit both the listener and the speaker.

People tend to not listen for one of many reasons. They may be bored, distracted, or just not interested in the subject. The speaker's delivery of the message, the content, or the environment can cause boredom, distraction, or lack of interest. In any case, providing you can hear the words being spoken, you can choose to actively listen.

Here are several suggestions to help you become a more active listener. Some of these apply only to one-to-many type presentations, as in the case of a speaker addressing a large group, and some suggestions apply only to one-on-one situations, as in talking with a friend or business associate. Most of these suggestions, however, apply to any situation.

- **Clear your mind.** Anytime you have many things on your mind you should write them down and forget about them until you are ready to deal with them.
- **Make the message relevant to you.** Perhaps the main reason people do not listen is because they really just do not care about the message. If you are in a situation where not listening to the message would be disadvantageous, then convince yourself why actively listening to the message is important. Active listening begins with wanting to listen.
- **Listen more than you talk.** The common illustration is that each of us has two ears and one mouth—use them in that proportion.
- **Make good eye contact.** Look at someone when they are speaking to you. Good eye contact is not psychotic gazing, but frequently looking directly into the speaker's eyes with several breaks.

- **Take notes.** Taking notes, even jotting down key words or phrases only, can be a great way to help focus your attention on the content being presented.

- **Don't finish sentences.** When we think we know the other person is going to say, we tend to complete their sentences for them, either out loud or in our heads. This is a common way to alter the speaker's true message. When finishing a speaker's sentence for him out loud, he may find it too awkward to tell you that was not what he was going to say, and just "yeah" you instead. When finishing a speaker's sentence in your head, your version will almost always stick in your memory longer than the speaker's version.

- **Don't jump to conclusions.** The mind is capable of working many times faster than the average person can speak. This is often the main reason for "drifting" or taking the nearest mental exit. This is also why listeners tend to start forming conclusions rather than carefully listening to the words being spoken. To illustrate, on one of my favorite TV shows a riddle was presented: two coins make 30 cents and one of them is not a nickel. When others hear this riddle, they jump to the conclusion that neither coin is a nickel, even though the riddle clearly states "one of them" is not a nickel. Solving riddles is a great way to build your active listening skills.

- **Respond verbally and physically.** Your response to the speaker's message can have a great effect on the message itself. For example, if someone begins telling you a story and you begin to do the "pee-pee dance", the speaker will most likely cut their story short. Respond physically to a speaker using your body language to tell the speaker that you are interested in what he or she is saying by nodding your head or making the facial expressions that correspond with the speaker's message. Verbal responses that let the speaker know you are interested can include the occasional "right", "I see", "uh-huh", or other similar word, phrase or sound. The key here is not to overdo these physical or verbal responses or you will distract the speaker, or worse appear fake.

- **Ask questions.** Ask questions based on the content. This is a great way to show the speaker that you are interested, as well as a great way for you, the listener, to absorb more of the information. "Why" questions often make great follow-up questions.
- **Visualize.** Visualize what the speaker is saying. Create a movie in your head using colorful or outrageous characters and props.
- **Restate.** "So what you are saying is..." is a great technique to both express your interest and actively listen. When you restate what the speaker has just said, be sure not to use the same words, because then you are just repeating what was said and not restating.
- **Summarize.** If appropriate, summarize what the speaker had said when they are done speaking.

What is the speaker really saying? Active listening involves being more attentive to the words, tone and the body language the speaker is using to deliver her message. It is about focusing your complete attention on the message while involving both your mind and body. Being a good active listener is the first major step to being a great communicator.

ACTION STEP(S):

1) From this point on, consciously be aware of your own listening skills and work on the suggestions above. In addition, be aware of how others listen to you when you speak.

"Listening, not imitation, may be the sincerest form of flattery."

- Dr. Joyce Brothers

Days 251 and 252 are for "R&R"—review and reflection. Spend these days reviewing the last five articles and reflecting on the information and how it relates to your life. Now is also a good time to make sure all the action steps for the previous days have been completed.

Day 253: Sell It To Yourself First

The expression "sell it to yourself" refers to convincing yourself of the benefits of that which you are selling. Everybody is always selling something whether it is themselves, an idea, a product or a service. When you are selling something you do not believe in, you are essentially acting; and let's face it, most of us do not make very good actors.

Be sold on yourself. How confident are you in your own abilities, talents, and skills? If you were an employer, would you want to hire you? If you were a prospect, would you want to buy from you? Build your self-esteem and self-confidence by taking inventory of yourself. If you feel your inventory list is weak, then take action to improve it. If you do not see the value in yourself, nobody else will either.

Be sold on success. You must be able to answer the question, "Why should I be successful?" As you know by now, success does not come easy. It is much easier and less risky to ride the carousel of life rather than hop on the roller coaster. Do you desire a better life for you and your loved ones? Do you want to leave this world knowing that you made it a better place? You need to create a burning desire for success.

Be sold on your career. Your career is your chosen pursuit, profession, or occupation. Is this something you really want to spend the rest of your life doing? Is your career in line with your general life purpose? You must know in your head and heart that at this time in your life, you are going down the right path. When you are sold on your career, you have that deep-down feeling of knowing you are doing exactly what you should be doing. Don't confuse temporary frustration with doubt; frustration is a temporary and vital part of success; doubt is ongoing and rarely subsides.

Be sold on your organization. How do you feel about the organization for which you work? Do you believe the organization is a benefit to society? Do you have confidence in the leaders of the organization? If you have any doubts, speak to the leaders and raise your concerns. Very often the lack of information, combined with rumors, causes members of an organization to have negative perceptions of that organization. A few minutes "with the boss" can usually help.

Be sold on your product. It is especially important for anyone in the field of sales to believe in the product or service that he or she is selling. What are the benefits? Which problems will the product help the customer to solve? Do you believe the prices are fair? What about the quality? As a salesperson, you most likely know your product very well—the good and the bad. There is no such thing as a perfect product. You must believe that your product, although not without its flaws, can be of great benefit to the prospect. Know the flaws of your competitors' product as well, not so you can bad-mouth them, but so you can have more faith in your product.

To be successful, before you can sell anything to anybody, you must first be sold on what you are selling yourself. This is a universal truth that many people, in all lines of work, tend to overlook. Confidence comes from belief and it takes confidence to influence others. Believe in your product, organization, career, success and, most important, believe in yourself.

ACTION STEP(S):

---

1) Make sure you are sold on yourself, the need for success, your goals, your career, your organization, and your product. If you are not completely sold on any of these, get more information or make the changes you need to be sold.

Day 254: Self-Discipline

In the late '90s, the Internet boom made millionaires out of many investors virtually overnight. These "success stories" were in the news and magazines almost daily. People love to hear stories of overnight success, and as a result, the media loves to seek out and publish such stories. The idea of living the American dream without having to work or wait for it, is universally appealing. However, this skewed perception of what success really is promotes the "instant gratification" desire, which is one of the leading reasons people fail. True success, the kind that is achieved through personal development, is based on self-discipline.

Discipline is training expected to produce a specific character or pattern of behavior, especially training that produces moral or mental improvement. As young children, we are introduced to discipline through our parents. Later, our teachers and religious leaders contribute to our discipline. Along the way, other people like grandparents, babysitters, and/or older siblings may join in. By the time we are of age, we are all "disciplined out" and cannot wait to be on our own; free to do as we wish. What nobody ever tells us, as youths transitioning into adulthood, is the discipline cannot stop—it must be transformed into self-discipline if we are to succeed in life.

Self-discipline is the ability to adhere to actions, thoughts, and behaviors that result in personal improvement instead of instant gratification. As an adult, there is only one person who is with you 24 hours a day. This person is the only one who can choose a life of success over a life of mediocrity. This person is the only one who can write your goals and see to it that you take daily actions toward their achievement. This person is the only one who will be there for you to see that you break your destructive habits. This person is you.

One of the key elements of success, persistence, is only made possible through self-discipline. Whether your goals include becoming the next billionaire, losing weight, quitting smoking, or being the best parent you can be, self-discipline is needed to get you there.

Here are some suggestions on how you can become more self-disciplined.

- **Master your time.** Spend your time on actions that bring you closer to your goals, not further from them.
- **Focus on true desires.** Once you put your goals on the back burner, they are as good as forgotten. If your desire for instant gratification takes over, bring out your goals and review them. If you often sway from your goals, keep your written goals where you can see them on a daily basis. If you still find yourself giving in to the desire for instant gratification, change your goals and make the desire to achieve them more powerful than the desire for instant gratification.
- **Link pain and pleasure.** In your mind, associate pain with acting on your every desire and associate extreme pleasure with reaching your goals. The key is to visualize, or vividly imagine, yourself reaching your goals through self-discipline, and visualize the negative consequences of acting on your desires for immediate gratification.
- **Build your self-esteem.** Without self-esteem there is no reason you would care enough to be self-disciplined. Having the "we're all going to die anyway" attitude is not conducive to self-discipline.
- **Sacrifice short-term pleasure for long-term happiness.** Know the difference between pleasure and happiness. One can have a miserable life full of pleasures, in fact, many people do. Self-discipline keeps you working toward your goals, which to many, is the way to true happiness.
- **Beware of excuses, rationalization, and justifications.** Do not allow a miniature you dressed in a devil costume to pop up on one side of your head and sell you on instant gratification. It is amazing how desires can alter coherent thinking. Be aware of this when it is happening and allow your self-discipline to keep you from making poor choices.

- **Think about both the short and long-term consequences of actions**. If your goal is to lose 10 pounds (as in weight, not English currency), then before you eat the chocolate cake in front of you, think about the guilt that you will experience after eating the cake, your lack of self-discipline, and your long-term reasons for wanting to lose the weight in the first place.

What if you do not have the self-discipline to work on building your self-discipline? (Ahh, what irony...) If you have made it this far in the course, chances are you do. However, if you still doubt your own abilities or perhaps would just like some reinforcement, consider the martial arts. Besides self-discipline, martial arts training can help with confidence, fitness, coordination, and more.

Self-discipline is not an easy characteristic to practice. It is, however, an invaluable characteristic to have if achievement and success are important to you. True success comes as a result of self-discipline. Remember, when it comes to success, there are no shortcuts.

ACTION STEP(S):

---

1) From this point on, become consciously aware of your self-discipline or lack thereof and work on building this vital characteristic.

"Mastering others is strength. Mastering yourself is true power."

- Lao Tzu

Day 255: Inspiration from Steve Martin

Steve Martin (1945–) is an actor, writer, director, producer, film-maker, banjo player, balloon animal maker, all-around entertainer, and one wild and crazy guy.

Success is knowing how to sell—yourself. Steve worked at Disneyland after school and in the summers from age 10 until age 18. Starting off by selling guidebooks at the front gate, Steve quickly learned that "relentless cheeriness" was what he needed to far outsell the norm. This charismatic attitude is one that would help Steve succeed throughout his career.

Success does not come easy. Martin started his career as a struggling stand-up comedian by traveling from town to town sticking arrows through his head and making balloon animals. Martin reportedly told the Edmonton Sun in 1999 that these were the hardest years in his life.

Success can be a result of making good contacts. Steve's first lucky break came when his girlfriend at the time was a dancer on the very popular Smothers Brothers Comedy Hour. She passed on some of Steve's material to the head writer, Mason Williams, who loved it and hired Steve as a writer for the show.

Success is daring to be different. During his live performances, Martin took to drawing the audience together as a group and leading them out of the venue. Once, he took them all to McDonald's and ordered 274 burgers, at the last moment changing his order to "one fry to go".

Success is constantly pushing yourself. In 1987, Steve left his comfort zone by co-writing, executive-producing, and starring in *Roxanne* (1987), a modern interpretation of the story of Cyrano De

Bergerac. For his work in *Roxanne* he won a Best Actor award from the Los Angeles Film Critics Association as well as an award for Best Screenplay from the Writers Guild of America.

Success is knowing the odds. In a 1995 interview with the Toronto Sun, Steve said, "This is a sick confession, I have always been fixated on creating a body of work. I always felt that was my goal. That's why I liked doing a lot of movies. Because movies are very hard to make work, and if you do three the odds are you might have one that's any good. If you do 30, the odds are you might have six."

Success is learning to deal with failure. "You are always going to have bombs," he said. "It's always personal. I'm a little more used to it. I'm dealing with success or failure a little quicker. But it hangs in there. It's like saying goodbye to a girlfriend: It can take weeks, months or years."

Success is being creative. Martin once told reporters that he had business cards printed up for all those fans that would approach him. The business cards read something like: "This certifies that you had a real encounter with Steve Martin and found him to be kind, courteous, charming and witty."

[Sources: http://www.biography.com, http://www.movieclub.com, http://www.hollywood.com, http://www.tribute.ca, http://www.tiscali.co.uk]

"I believe that sex is the most beautiful, natural, and wholesome thing that money can buy."

- Steve Martin

Day 256: A Quick Guide to Public Speaking

"I have a dream..." Who can forget those immortal words spoken by Martin Luther King, Jr. on the steps of the Lincoln Memorial in Washington, D.C. on August 28, 1963. Dr. King managed to influence millions of people and change a nation, not because he was rich, or in a position of power, but because he was an effective public speaker. Dr. King and other highly influential people before him, like Winston Churchill, Mahatma Gandhi and Abraham Lincoln, just to name a few, mastered the art of public speaking and earned their place in history. Mastering the art of public speaking may not make you world famous, but it will most certainly help you to succeed in anything you do.

In just about every well-paid position, some form of public speaking is required whether it be presenting to the board of directors, giving a group sales presentation, speaking to a committee, or just a group of peers. The large majority of people are either terrified or just very uncomfortable with public speaking. This means the high paying jobs and the advancements are left for people like us who know that we can become effective public speakers if we put our minds to it. Better yet, we can even learn to enjoy it. So let's jump right into my quick guide to public speaking.

There are three general styles of speeches: impromptu, manuscript, and extemporaneous. In an impromptu speech, you have little to no time to prepare. For example, your boss asks you, on the spot, to bring the rest of the team up to date on what you have been working on the last week. If possible, it is best to gracefully excuse yourself for a few minutes and jot down a few key points. Then, you can be sure to cover the important points without making it sound as if you have nothing to share.

The second type of speech is a manuscript speech, which is written like a manuscript and meant to be delivered word for word. This is fine for public figures where every word uttered is vital, but when it comes to building a connection with the listeners, an extemporaneous speech is the best way to go. This kind of speech uses ideas to trigger thoughts rather than exact words. Knowing the material well will allow you to present a speech in a way that best keeps the listener's attention while allowing you to make changes based on the response of the listeners. Both the extemporaneous and manuscript styles have their own benefits so choose the style that best fits your content and your personality. Impromptu speeches should be left for impromptu situations only.

If you remember just one thing about public speaking remember this: have a point. All too often speakers stand up in front of an audience and blabber out one long stream of consciousness. Since we are masters at goal setting by now, consider your point the goal of your speech. Do you want to influence your audience? Do you want to sell them something? Do you just want to entertain them? Know your goal and build your speech around it. Here are some other suggestions that I have found to be key elements of any successful speech or presentation.

- **Have an introduction, body, and conclusion.** Follow the age-old advice, "Tell them what you are going to tell them, tell them, and then tell them what you told them." Most people find writing the body first is most helpful, then either the introduction or the conclusion.
- **Prepare.** You cannot "over prepare". The better you know the material the more confident you will be when presenting and the more flowing the speech will sound. Videotape or record yourself if possible, or at least rehearse by watching yourself in a mirror. When you are delivering your speech live, the same adrenaline that makes you nervous also helps you think better and find the right words to make your speech sound fluent.
- **Vary the pace.** Vary the pace at which you deliver the speech. Slow down, then speed up. This will keep the listener's attention. Be careful not to talk too slowly or too quickly.
- **Have good eye contact.** If you have been taught to look over the heads of those you are speaking to, forget it. Good

eye contact means making a connection with your audience by looking them straight in the eyes. If the audience is small enough, try to make it a point to make eye contact with everyone.

- **Use note cards not notepads.** Notepads are bulky, noisy, and most of all, distracting. Use note cards or notes on card stock for extemporaneous speeches. Never be afraid to use notes—even the best speakers rely on notes to ensure they communicate the points efficiently and effectively.

- **Anticipate questions.** Take the time to think about any question a listener may ask and formulate a positive answer that supports your presentation. It is OK to say you do not know the answer and tell the person you will get back to them if needed. The "I don't know" or "I can't say" answers are most effective when followed by "but I'll tell you what I do know..."

- **Try to keep your speech under 20 minutes.** Several studies have shown that 20 minutes is about the maximum amount of time listeners can stay attentive, after that, the attention levels begin to drop. Speaking is more stimulating than listening so although you may be excited to talk for longer, the chances are your listeners are ready for a break.

- **Establish credibility.** Who are you to speak about the subject on which you are speaking? Why should your audience listen to you? Establish your credibility by sharing your credentials with the listeners in a tactful way. For example, "When I was President of XYZ Corporation...", not "I was once the President of XYZ Corporation."

- **Have a strong introduction and a strong conclusion.** The introduction should be used to gain the attention of the listeners and persuade them to listen to your entire presentation. You are essentially selling them on why they should listen. Be sure you address their needs and not yours. The conclusion should consist of a powerful statement, quotation, anecdote, or other attention grabber. Never end a speech with, "that's all".

- **Have a second conclusion prepared.** After a speech or a presentation usually comes a question and answer period. Once the questions stop coming, it is best to end on a strong note. This is a great time to get your "last word" in.
- **Act on every opportunity you can to speak.** Anxiety of speaking is best subsided by experience. Also, volunteering to be the one who gives the speech will get you noticed and you will stand out as the leader. Join your local Toastmasters club (toastmasters.org) for some really great practice.

It has been said that most people fear public speaking more than death itself. While this does not mean people would rather be dead than speak in public, as some authors would like you to believe, it does illustrate why communication of ideas through public speaking is often avoided by professionals. Those who make it a point to embrace public speaking will have a major advantage over their coworkers and/or competitors. Who knows, the next time an author writes about great public speakers, your name can be on that list!

ACTION STEP(S):

1) Take the next available opportunity to speak in public.

"Using rhetorical questions in speeches is a great way to keep the audience involved. Don't you think those kinds of questions would keep your attention?"

- Bo Bennett

Day 257: Getting to YES

Am I correct in assuming that your success is very important to you? By now, you are aware of the importance of sales and how everybody sells something, aren't you? Don't you agree that sales is really about influencing others? Therefore, getting others to agree with you would be an incredibly powerful skill to master, wouldn't it?

You have just witnessed a technique used to get a "yes" response. This technique is based on the Socratic method, which is all about asking questions. This is an excellent technique for asking for referrals, closing sales, or persuading others. When you ask someone a question, assuming they are listening, they always answer it. They may not answer it out loud, and they may answer it with "I have no idea", but the question is always answered. One of the powerful uses of questions is to keep the attention of the listener or reader. The technique used above also uses questions to elicit a yes response. This "warms up" the listener by getting them in a positive frame of mind.

Let's examine how this works in detail. We begin by determining our goal. My goal was to get you to agree that getting others to agree with you is an incredibly powerful skill to master. If I had just opened with the statement, "Getting others to agree with you is an incredibly powerful skill to master" you may have agreed with me or you may not have. If you did not agree with me, you would be in "defensive mode" and even if I had proven my point later in the article you would not be as open to the idea. Now my example is a fairly easy sell, but this technique works equally as well with harder to sell ideas, products or services.

Now that we have our goal, we need to work backward and create several questions that we are confident will result in yes responses. In order for this technique to be effective, these questions must be relevant. You may be able to trick someone into saying yes by asking, "Would you like to have more money? Do you love your kids? Do you want to buy my widget?"—but their final yes will almost definitely be followed by an emphatic "NO!" Using a logical progression of questions that get yes responses make it easy for the listener to answer yes to our final question.

Here are some suggestions for formulating supporting or leading questions.

- **Use yes tags.** Yes tags are phrases like "isn't it", "don't you agree", or "wouldn't you say". These phrases can be placed anywhere in the sentence and should be mixed up for maximum effectiveness.
- **Soften your questions.** If you use hard questions as leading questions, this technique may backfire on you. A "hard" question is one that uses definite terms that leave little room for flexibility. For example, "Smoking is the most deadly habit on earth, don't you think?" is not as easy to agree with as "Smoking is one of the most deadly habits on earth, don't you think?" Remember, you want to phrase the leading questions in such a way that it is almost impossible for others to disagree.
- **Phrase in the positive.** Questions should be phrased in the positive whenever possible. My opening question, "Am I correct in assuming that your success is very important to you?" could have been written as "Am I correct in assuming that you not achieving success would be a bad thing?" The mind remembers "achieving, success, bad thing" and that is not the message to which we want our listeners to agree.

If you are thinking that this technique sounds a little manipulative, remember that the difference between manipulation and influence is intent. This technique is best used to counter other people's natural "no" defensive response, not trick them into a "yes" response. Just as a knife can be used to kill, it can also be used to heal.

Questions are a very powerful and effective form of communication that can be used in many ways. This technique, when used properly, can help you to become more influential, help you to become a better communicator, and bring you another step closer to success.

ACTION STEP(S):

___

1) Use this technique in either speaking or writing today.

"Before I refuse to take your questions, I have an opening statement."

- Ronald Reagan

___

Days 258 and 259 are for "R&R"—review and reflection. Spend these days reviewing the last five articles and reflecting on the information and how it relates to your life. Now is also a good time to make sure all the action steps for the previous days have been completed.

Day 260: Follow Through

Imagine a world where every voice mail you leave is promptly returned, where anything you ask of others is done when you want it done, and where every process you initiate gets completed without a single hitch. This world is called "Fantasyland" and it does not exist; however, many people act as if it does. To assure things get done, and get done right, you need to stay on top of them.

While working in technical support for our web hosting company, I received a phone call from an upset customer saying that he ordered a website from us three weeks prior, and despite our policy of usually setting up new accounts within one hour, his was still not setup. He continued by telling me how urgent this site was and this delay had cost his company a significant amount of money. I felt like asking "Why are you just contacting us now if this was so important?" However, I knew enough to just solve his problem and not pass the blame. It turned out that the customer had entered an invalid e-mail address and did not get his new account information. Had he contacted us three weeks earlier, the problem could have been fixed then.

We are all guilty of letting things fall through the cracks, but why? There is a certain relief associated with "putting the ball in someone else's court" or at least getting it out of your own court, especially when our "to do" list is filled with things to do. We tend to let things fall through the cracks when we are more concerned with checking tasks off our list than we are with making sure the tasks actually get done. It is not wise to depend on undependable people or people whom we do not know, nor should we blame anyone but ourselves for not following through with our tasks. The key to making sure things get done and done on time is by keeping the ball in your court. Here are some suggestions on how you can do just that.

- **Don't cross it off.** Do not cross items off of your "to do" list until the REAL task itself is complete. For example, if you have "call the doctor" on your list, what you really mean is something like "make an appointment with the doctor". Don't cross this off your list until your appointment is made and confirmed, not just when you leave a message.
- **Specify a date and time.** If you are depending on vendors, staff, or friends for something, find out specifically when you can expect action. Then, let them know you will be following up at a given date and time. For example, if you have a shipment that your vendor promises will be shipped out "this week", ask them for a specific date, then call the vendor back at least once prior to that date to make sure everything is on schedule.
- **Follow up on e-mails.** Today, many people use their e-mail client's inbox as their "to do" list. When they respond to a message or initiate an e-mail, their e-mail disappears into the sent folder and is forgotten. A great strategy is to move a copy of the message into a folder called "follow up" and review these e-mails daily.
- **Be persistent with phone calls.** Do not let your progress be slowed by busy signals and voice mail. Be persistent and keep calling until you speak with someone. Use your best judgment here and make sure you do not keep ringing a telephone line that only has voice mail.
- **Ask for confirmation.** When you depend on another for something, ask that person for confirmation that what you have asked them to do has been done. This is not only assurance on your part, but it lets the other person know that this is important to you and the task is less likely to be delayed or ignored.

Take responsibility for your tasks by following through. The object of the game is to keep the ball in your court. If something goes wrong, as it often does, you need to be there to take action to set things right. If tasks on your list do not get done because of lack of cooperation from others, you need to take action to get those tasks done some other way. Follow through on all you do, especially on your commitment to success.

ACTION STEP(S):

1) Commit to making following through a habit.

"You have to have confidence in your ability, and then be tough enough to follow through."

- Rosalynn Carter

Day 261: Under the Wing of a Millionaire

The world is full of opportunities. One opportunity specifically is overlooked every day by the large majority of those seeking wealth. This opportunity requires little or no investment, has no risk, and the benefits can be significant. The opportunity to which I am referring is meeting with a millionaire.

How can meeting with a millionaire help you to reach your financial goals? When you learned to read you were taught by someone who already knew how to read. When you learned to ride a bike you were taught by someone who knew how to ride a bike. So who do you think can best help you learn how to reach your financial goals? Unlike great books or amazing on-line courses on success (ahem), real-time, face-to-face interaction provides a level of learning and reinforcement unavailable anywhere else. Other great reasons follow:

- **Introductions.** A millionaire most likely has an impressive list of key contacts. Once you make this millionaire a contact of yours, you have what I call secondary access, or availability through referral, to all of his or her key contacts. If the millionaire likes you, he or she will most likely introduce you to others. This open door can lead to many great opportunities.
- **Opportunities.** Besides possible opportunities through key contacts, the millionaire may have some immediate opportunities for you. Even if none immediately come to mind, the millionaire mind is constantly seeking opportunity. Very often, millionaires cannot act on every opportunity themselves, but they can and do share them with those they know are looking for such opportunities.
- **Confidence.** You can read all about success and successful individuals but there is something about meeting and interacting with one who reinforces your belief that you can be financially successful. Those who are wealthy almost always interact with other wealthy individuals. As a soon-

to-be wealthy individual yourself, you too will need to be comfortable interacting with people of wealth. After all, people are people no matter how big their pockets are.

- **Advice.** For the most part, people who have succeeded where you are working to succeed are a good source of advice. However, be cautious of the advice you are given, especially when it comes to financial success, and be sure to question the advice based on your own common sense.

Why would a millionaire want to help you? What's in it for them? You will be surprised how much cooperation you will get in this area. It is a basic fact of human behavior—people love to talk about themselves, especially their own success. If given the chance to feed their ego and be made to feel important, most people will act on this opportunity. In addition, most wealthy people are sharing individuals who get a warm feeling by helping others.

Millionaires are all around us. According to the 2002 World Wealth Report published by Cap Gemini Ernst & Young and Merrill Lynch, there are 2,100,000 high net worth individuals, or millionaires, in the United States alone. Based on the 2003 World Population Data Sheet, there are just over 291 million people in the United States. This means that in the United States, about one in every 150 people you come across is a millionaire. These are mostly made up of real estate investors, business people, investors in the financial markets, and entrepreneurs. Now that we have profiled the average millionaire, and have some ideas on where to find them, it is time to contact them.

The Internet is a great tool for doing your own investigation to find out contact information of a millionaire in your local community. Whether using the telephone or e-mail, be sure to show sincere appreciation for their accomplishments, then let them know that you feel they can offer you some wisdom and advice in your pursuit of financial success. In exchange for this advice, offer to buy them lunch at the place of their choice. Spending an hour at your favorite restaurant, talking about yourself while someone else is paying is a hard offer for anyone to refuse! If by some chance your offer does get rejected, the rejection will be no worse than a friendly response expressing gratitude.

OK, so you are now set to meet this millionaire for lunch. What now? You will want to think about, or even write down, some questions that you would like to ask. When you have time to prepare, this is usually the best way to go so you can get the most out of the meeting. Make sure your questions are positive, non-personal, and non-offensive. You want the responses to make the other person feel good, not feel uncomfortable and not bring up bad memories. If you cannot think of any good questions, or have no time to prepare questions, as in the case of a spontaneous meeting, think "S-U-C-C-E-S-S":

S - How did you get *started*?
U - Do you have any *unusual* success stories?
C - How important do you feel *communication* is in success?
C - How important are the *contacts* you have made?
E - Did you always *expect* to be this successful?
S - You must have had some *setbacks*. How do you deal with failure?
S - Do you have any *suggestions* or advice for me?

Be attentive to any verbal or visual hints that may be given to end the meeting. If you start detecting shuffling in the seat, looking at the watch, or increasingly short answers, thank your guest for his or her time and pay for the lunch. Now is a good time to once again express your admiration for their accomplishments and end the meeting with a positive impression.

We use the word "millionaire" loosely here. In general, any individual that has accomplished a goal that you are striving to accomplish would do just fine. Why not make this a weekly goal? Just imagine the kind of contacts you can have after just a few weeks of making these kinds of connections. Take a millionaire to lunch this week and have a good meal with a side of success!

ACTION STEP(S):

1) Take a millionaire out to lunch.

"There's no such thing as a free lunch."
- **Milton Friedman**

Day 262: Inspiration from J. Willard Marriott

J. Willard "Bill" Marriott, Sr. (1900–1985) was the founder of what is now Marriott International, Inc., a leading worldwide hospitality company with more than 2,600 lodging properties located around the world.

Success is learning to rely on your own judgment and initiative. "My father gave me the responsibility of a man," said Marriott as an adult. "He would tell me what he wanted done, but never said much about how to do it. It was up to me to find out for myself."

Success begins with determination. Determined to get an education, Marriott worked summers selling woolen goods, eventually building up a sales force of 45 college students who sold in seven states.

Success often has modest beginnings. In 1927, Marriott successfully launched a small restaurant called "Hot Shoppes", which over the years expanded into a multi-billion dollar empire.

Success is seeing opportunity in any economy. The Depression years fueled a tremendous ingenuity in Marriott. He recognized the success of a low-cost restaurant and the failure of luxury restaurants.

Success is growth and expansion. Through the years, Marriott expanded his business from his single humble restaurant to include more locations, airlines, hotels, food chain acquisitions, theme parks and cruise ships.

Success is loving what you do. From the opening of Marriott's first business in 1927, until his death 58 years later, J. Willard

Marriott rarely rested. Whether adding locations, perfecting procedures or expanding into new enterprises, Marriott breathed, ate, lived, and dreamed about his business.

Success is paying attention to the details. "It's the little things that make the big things possible. Only close attention to the fine details of any operation makes the operation first class."

Success is living life to the fullest. "A man should keep on being constructive, and do constructive things. He should take part in the things that go on in this wonderful world. He should be someone to be reckoned with. He should live life and make every day count, to the very end. Sometimes it's tough. But that's what I'm going to do."

[Sources: http://www.horatioalger.com, http://www.marriott.com, http://www.hrm.uh.edu]

"Good timber does not grow with ease; the stronger the wind, the stronger the trees."

- J. Willard Marriott, Sr.

Day 263: Competition is Good

Back in 1996 when the commercialized Internet was still relatively new, our business was booming. There was a high demand for web hosting and we were one of the few web hosting providers at the time. We did not have to seek business, business found us. Life was grand. When we reentered the industry in 2002, we discovered that the market was a very different place. The competition had become so fierce that we were forced to change our strategy if we were to thrive, or even survive, in the industry. We ended up creating a product and a service that made us unique in the industry, as well as allowing us to operate a much smoother business model than we had in the past, setting us up for phenomenal growth. Once again, life is grand. This is all thanks to our competition.

Let's take a minute to go over Capitalism 101. In a capitalist society, competition drives prices down while increasing quality and service levels. If you have conducted business in any roller-coaster economy, like during the turn of this last century, you have witnessed this first hand. Competition obviously is beneficial for the consumer, but what about the entrepreneur or business person?

What is your attitude toward your competition? Do you feel as if your competition is responsible for taking money out of your pocket? How about taking food from your kids' mouths? Believe it or not, I have heard people in business use that analogy before. If you have an attitude like this, your business will never benefit from competition. In fact, the chances are it will eventually destroy your business. If you want your business to benefit from your competition, begin by following these three rules:

1. **Never bad-mouth your competition publicly.** Saying bad things about your competition to your customers or prospects is business suicide. Sales people are often tempted to build up their own product by putting the competition's product down. This "dirty politics"

technique may work sometimes, but almost without question does more harm than good in the long run. Try something like, "The XYZ Company makes an excellent product and offers it for a fair price. However, our customers prefer our product because of..."

2. **Never bad-mouth your competition in front of your staff.** Business owners and managers who talk trash about their competition in front of their staff are only setting a poor example for their people to follow. You cannot insist your people follow rule #1 when you break rule #2.

3. **Never blame your competition for your lack of success.** The market is what it is. You can choose how you respond to competition and the right choices can lead to you to greater success.

So how does a business benefit from competition? We have already seen that increased competition tends to increase product quality and service. However, some business people may see this as more of an added expense rather than a benefit. Here are some ways that your business can use competition to its financial benefit.

- **Create a new market.** 7up™ created a new market as a result of the extremely fierce cola industry. 7up™ created a new market by being positioned as the "un-cola". They were then the first in that market and continue today to enjoy the benefits of being first in the market.

- **Benefit from your competitor's advertising and marketing.** Have you ever seen a great commercial but had no idea who the company was behind it? Or seen a billboard with delicious food that caused you to eat at your favorite restaurant that night? I know for a fact that as a result of our competitor's marketing dollars, most of our customers are very well educated in the hosting industry and come to us because they know we can give them exactly what they require. Think about thanking your competitors rather than bashing them.

- **Use as a selling opportunity.** If your prospects are already aware of your competitor's product, then all you need to do is show them why going with your product is a better choice. Remember, if the prospect was convinced the competitor's product was so great, he would not be speaking to you in the first place.

- **Form alliances.** Competitors can make great sources of information and new business, if you create an amiable relationship with them. Most businesses in the same market are not identical, that is, their products or services may be different. Take the time to research these differences between you and your competitors and you may find opportunity for shared referrals. For example, a trendy hair salon may refer the guy looking for a bowl cut (if you are not sure what a bowl cut is, picture Moe from the Three Stooges) to "Vinny's Barber" down the street, even though they could have given the guy a stylin' $40 haircut. In exchange, Vinny sends over the teenyboppers who want to look just like Britney Spears.

Competition is good for consumers, good for the economy, and can certainly be good for business, with the right attitude and action plans. Do not adopt the belief that your competition is the enemy. Instead, use your competition as an opportunity to grow your business and succeed.

ACTION STEP(S):

---

1) Are you or anyone on your team bad-mouthing your competition? If so, it is time to correct this error.

2) List all the ways that your competition can work for your benefit.

Day 264: Sell Solutions

Paul and Fido live together in a big apartment with many carpets. Fido is a young mongrel that tends to shed more hair in a week than most other dogs do in a year. Paul has given up trying to clean the carpets with his existing vacuum, since it does not pick up a majority of the dog hair, and begins his quest to find a vacuum that will solve his problem.

Paul's first stop is "Vacuum World", where they appear to have a large selection at reasonable prices. He is approached by a salesperson who asks the type of vacuum he is looking for, and his price range. The sales person begins to go over the technical specifications of the vacuums that would "fit his needs". Paul is confused, and leaves.

Paul then stops at "Vacuum Planet", where the selection and prices appear to be comparable to "Vacuum World". Once again, he is approached by a salesperson who asks the same general questions about Paul's requirements. However, this salesperson is wise enough to know that Paul probably does not care about how many amps the vacuum is, or the fact the belt is made from a solid core of an advanced U/V resistant formulation. The salesperson sells the benefits of the vacuum: how easy it is to put away, how quiet it is, and how powerful it is. Paul is tempted to buy, but still is not comfortable. He thanks the salesperson for her time, and moves on.

Paul's next stop is at "Vacuum Earth", where he notices that the selection is not as large, but the prices are still decent. He is approached by a salesperson who asks him a strange question, "So, are you a first time vacuum buyer or did your current vacuum let you down?" Paul uses this open-ended question to explain to the inquisitive salesperson how Fido is changing the color of his carpets. The salesperson responds with a confident, "Say no more. This model here is ideal for picking up pet fur off the rugs. But the best part about this model, is the grooming brush attachment that can be used to vacuum the shedding fur from Fido before it hits your carpet!" This salesperson did something that the other two salespeople did not do: he sold the solution. Needless to say, Paul bought the vacuum from the salesperson at "Vacuum Earth".

As a salesperson, whether you are selling an idea, product or service (all of which can be referred to as "product"), it is best to think in terms of problems and solutions. Your prospect has a problem that requires a solution. How can your product solve their problem? Here are what I call the three levels of selling:

1. **Sell the product.** The salesperson is required to know as much as possible about the product itself. This includes technical specification, features, prices, options, delivery times, inventory, and other details. When a salesperson sells the product, the prospect is required to find the benefits for themselves, then determine how the benefits of the product can solve their problem. This is quite a bit of mental aerobics to ask of any prospect.
2. **Sell the benefits.** This is also referred to as "selling the sizzle". This requires the salesperson to know the product, and know the general benefits of the product. When a salesperson sells the benefits of the product, the prospect just needs to connect the benefits with the solution to his or her problem. This is a major improvement from simply selling the product but unfortunately this is the level where most trained salespeople stop.
3. **Sell the solution.** This requires the salesperson to know the specific problem that the prospect is trying to solve. This information can only be obtained by listening to the prospect and by asking the right questions. Too many salespeople jump right into the selling and neglect the information gathering. The more details the salesperson knows about the prospect's problem, the more specific the solution can be presented and the better the chances are for closing the sale. When a salesperson sells the solution, the prospect simply needs to agree. Imagine what a different

perspective the world would have on salespeople if all salespeople sold solutions.

The main difference between selling benefits and selling solutions is that the solution is specific to the prospect's problem, whereas the benefits are usually more general. The key to successful selling is to sell at all three levels. When a salesperson sells the product, the benefits, and the solution, the prospect just needs to think about how they are going to pay—cash, check, or charge.

Here are some examples of these levels of selling.

(a job interview)
Not so good: *"I am hard-working."*
Good: *"I will help your office achieve its goals by making sure the job gets done."*
Very good: *"I will see to it that the TPS reports are completed each night and I will not leave until they are."*

(persuading someone to quit smoking)
Not so good: *Showing someone a picture of a clean lung versus a smoker's lung.*
Good: *Explaining how smoke-free lungs can greatly reduce chances of fatal diseases.*
Very Good: *Explaining how smoke-free lungs will help a smoker get rid of their asthma.*

(selling a new toaster to someone who mentioned that they burn their toast too often)
Not so good: *This toaster has a dial that determines the darkness of your toast.*
Good: *This toaster can make your toast just the way you like it.*
Very Good: *This toaster has an "anti-burn" sensor so you will never burn your toast again.*

When you are focused on selling solutions, you are forced to ask questions in order to determine the exact problem. This line of questioning shows the prospects that you do care about their needs. Solution selling is more than just another selling technique; it is trend that will certainly lead you to greater success.

ACTION STEP(S):

1) Next time you sell anything to anybody, think about their problem and how your idea, product, or service will be solving it.

"There is never a good sale for Neiman-Marcus unless it's a good buy for the customer."

- Herbert Marcus

Days 265 and 266 are for "R&R"—review and reflection. Spend these days reviewing the last five articles and reflecting on the information and how it relates to your life. Now is also a good time to make sure all the action steps for the previous days have been completed.

Day 267: Three Seconds: The First Impression

It is said that people form opinions of you within the first three seconds of meeting you. I always questioned the validity of this statement until I put it to the test and realized that I do it as well. We all keep mental files on people we know or just know of. Each time one of our senses is triggered for the first time by that person, the file is opened for about three seconds and then it is closed. The first impressions that are formed are extremely important because once the file is closed, it is not easy to get reopened. We need to be sure that the first impressions we are making are the right ones.

I would like to adapt this three-second theory to include my own "sixth sense" theory. I believe we all actually have six chances to make a first impression. There are many ways we can "meet" somebody. Each way involves the use of one of our known five senses, and our more metaphysical sixth sense of intuition. For example, when we see someone for the first time we create a new file on this person based on sight only. The file is open for about three seconds, and then it is closed. However, when we are introduced to that person, the file is once again opened for another three seconds when we hear their voice for the first time and feel their handshake. Dogs form impressions based on intuition, smell and taste. We humans form our impressions mostly from sight, sound and touch. Knowing this, we need to do our best to trigger positive responses for each sense in the people we meet.

Sight. The majority of first impressions are formed by appearance. Appearance includes the clothes we wear, our expressions, our posture, eye contact and our personal grooming.

Sound. These impressions are formed when we speak. In general, it is the sound of voice.

Touch. Impressions are made the moment physical contact is made between two people for the first time. The most common form of this physical contact is a handshake.

Smell. Some people have a pleasing scent and some have a distracting odor. Detecting these smells on someone for the first time once again opens up the mental file on that person for about three seconds.

Taste. Unlike dogs, we do not go around licking other people when we meet them. As a result, we generally do not rely on our taste to make an impression on others. However, feeling differently about a romantic interest after the first kiss may very well be a result of this three-second impression formed by taste.

Intuition. Have you ever met someone and despite his or her good eye contact, great smell, warm smile and pleasing voice, something inside you keeps you from liking this person? (Dads, I am not talking about meeting your daughter's first date.) This can be your preconceived notions taking over or it may be what is called intuition. It is universally accepted that dogs have this "sixth sense", so why can't humans? Perhaps we are just not as in tune with this sense as dogs are. This is a question that we may never be able to answer.

The goal of making first impressions is to make the impressions positive. Here are several suggestions on how to make a positive first impression. Please excuse some of the overly critical and somewhat sarcastic comments, but being aware of extremes will help you to make the right impressions.

- **Dress appropriately.** This does not mean always wearing a suit, but dressing for the occasion. Be aware of the message your style of dress is sending other people. Are you wearing the same clothes you bought back in 1972? Does your shirt have a mustard stain still there from the 1994 World Series? Are you the only one dressed in jeans at your grandmother's funeral? As a rule of thumb, it is always best to dress just a little nicer than the occasion may call for.

- **Be well groomed.** Do everything your mother taught you growing up: brush your teeth, wash your face, comb your hair, etc. Adult men should keep their nails trimmed, be well shaved (or keep a trimmed beard), and beware of the unibrow (eyebrows growing together). As for adult women, keep fingernails at a reasonable length, go easy on the make-up, and unless you are going for the female grunge look, shave the armpits.
- **Smile on the inside.** When you are happy, your entire body shows it. Try to avoid meeting people when you are in a negative state or bad mood.
- **Carry yourself well.** Be attentive to your posture. Stand or sit up straight with your chin up. Portray confidence.
- **Make good eye contact.** Look at those you meet directly in the eyes and do not break eye contact while you are still shaking the person's hand. This is especially important when meeting several people at the same time.
- **Be aware of your breath.** People are rarely aware of the fact that they have bad breath. If you are one of those people, ask a good friend or someone you trust if you have bad breath. If you are a smoker or a coffee drinker, just assume that you do have bad breath and have mints ready for after your cup of coffee or smoke.
- **Air yourself out.** As a non-smoker (would you ever have guessed?), I can say that just standing near someone who smells like the Kool camel, is extremely uncomfortable and somewhat offensive. If you are smoker, you may be able to avoid these negative impressions by not smoking in closed areas or near other people.
- **Use deodorant to prevent odor, not create a new smell.** I am baffled how these strong scented deodorants stay on the market. If you want to radiate a scent, you generally do not want that scent coming from your armpits. Try unscented anti-perspirant and deodorants.
- **Use perfume or cologne sparingly.** Perfumes and colognes can be great for associating yourself with a pleasing scent. Be aware, however, that the nose gets used

to the smell over time, which generally causes people to use more and more perfume or cologne to achieve what they believe to be the same result. When this happens, negative impressions are formed. Once again, ask a good friend or someone you trust if they think you wear too much perfume or cologne.

- **Speak clearly and confidently.** When you first meet someone, never mumble or slur your words. It is best to say in a strong, confident voice, "It is a pleasure to meet you (name)", or something similar.
- **Master the handshake.** It is best to match the grip of the person with whom you are shaking hands. Avoid both the bear grip and the dead fish grip. For men, it is best to offer your hand with your palm slightly upward as a sign of openness.

Put this theory to the test yourself. Have you ever seen a picture of someone, formed impressions, then sometime later heard them speak and felt completely different about that person? Perhaps you even met them in person at a later date and found out that they are very liberal with perfume, and once again, your impression of that person changed. First impressions are based on the senses so be aware of the messages you send to others you first meet. Then, make the changes needed to ensure you are making positive first impressions. Remember, you only get six chances to make a first impression.

ACTION STEP(S):

1) Isolate yourself in a room with a mirror (full-size if possible) and practice meeting a person for the first time. Look at your posture and your expression. Does your voice sound confident or quiet and shaky? What impression would you get if you were meeting you?

2) Ask a friend if you smell.

Day 268: Rewards and Contributions

When taking my daughter to the mall a couple years ago, we came across a vending machine filled with little candies. She ran up to the machine, lifted up the metal flap to the dispenser, and poked her little fingers all around searching for the candy. I had to explain to her that she needed to first put in a quarter, then turn the knob, then get the candy from the dispenser. It took my then two-year-old daughter a couple of trips to the mall to catch on completely, yet so many people spend their entire lives "shaking the vending machine" without putting in the quarter and turning the knob. It is a universal truth that our rewards in life are directly related to the amount we contribute and those who seek something for nothing will generally get the equivalent of what they are willing to contribute—nothing.

In our vending machine analogy, think of the quarter and turning the knob as the contribution. Our contributions in life begin with some type of investment. The most common form of this investment is investment in ourselves, as in college, adult education classes, independent study, and/or personal development of any kind. Then, contribution needs action. A parent or teacher invests his time on the education or character development of a youth, whereas a salesperson may invest her time on making sales calls. Teaching and selling is also taking action, while investing. Finally, after the quarter has been put in and the knob has been turned, we get the candy. Then, and only then, will life's rewards ultimately follow.

Not all rewards are financial. Do not be discouraged if your contributions produce little or no financial reward. The chances are, your contributions are being rewarded by earning the respect and admiration of others, fame or recognition, the feeling of accomplishment, fulfillment, inner peace, or some other non-monetary reward.

Those who are willing to contribute nothing usually fall for anything. The world is full of these people with a strong desire for instant gratification. These are the people with the "get rich quick" mentality that desire all the rewards of life but are not willing to exchange patience, risk, or effort. This is the group that many deceptive advertisers and marketers secretly refer to as "suckers". It is difficult to browse the Internet and not see an obnoxious flashing ad that says, "You are an instant winner! Click here to claim your prize!" These ads are so common because they work; people actually do click on them, give up their personal information, and buy $100 worth of junk they do not need in order to get their "free" coffee mug.

If you want to get something out of life, you have to put something in. Be not only willing, but be enthusiastic to make a contribution to this world. Every one of us has something special to offer whether it be the ability to educate, motivate, create, protect, lead, solve problems, comfort, or entertain. Focus on your contributions, not your rewards, and the rewards will follow.

ACTION STEP(S):

1) Make a list of all the contributions you are currently making in your life. What rewards do you see will come as a result of these contributions? If you cannot see your desired rewards in life coming as a result of your current contributions, then you must add to this list of contributions.

"When you cease to make a contribution, you begin to die."

- Eleanor Roosevelt

Day 269: Inspiration from George Lucas

George Lucas (1944–) is a film director, writer, and producer, best known for his work with the Star Wars trilogies.

Success is realizing that life is a gift.
Just after graduating high school, George was involved in a serious car accident that changed his perspective on life. He realized that every day was a gift, and he needed to make the most of it.

Success is setting realistic goals.
George's success began by setting goals of getting good grades in school and pursuing the courses that interested him most.

Success is doing what you love despite what others may say. Lucus went to film school because he loved the idea of making films, even though very few people actually made it into the film business from film school.

Success is going with your gut. When asked about his successes in an interview, Lucas said, "Mostly I just followed my inner feelings and passions, and said 'I like this, and I like this,' and I just kept going to where it got warmer and warmer, until it finally got hot, and then that's where I was."

Success is discovering your own talents. "Everybody has talent, it's just a matter of moving around until you've discovered what it is."

Success is perseverance. Lucas believes that perseverance is one of the key qualities of a successful individual.

Success is not easy. George said that his first six years in the business were "hopeless". He borrowed money from friends and family and it did not look like he was ever going to be able to pay anyone back. It took several years for him to get his first movie off the ground.

Success is ignoring the naysayers. Before his success, people would tell George that he was in a "complete dead-end for a career". After school, Lucas moved back to San Fransisco and people told him that he could not possibly make it in the film business while living in San Fransisco. His incredible success would soon prove the naysayers wrong.

Success is learning to say no. With success comes even more opportunities. Lucas believes that if you take on too many opportunities at one time, your life becomes unfocused and you can easily sink into depression.

Success is getting others to believe in you. Lucas had a very difficult time with his first two films, *American Graffiti* and *Star Wars.* The first couple of studios Lucas took *Star Wars* to turned him down. One studio executive, however, who saw *American Graffiti* (and loved it) agreed to take on *Star Wars*, reportedly saying. "You know, I don't understand this, but I think you're a great film maker and I'm going to invest in you. I'm not going to invest in this project."

[Sources: http://www.achievement.org, http://www.cinema.com, http://www.filmmakers.com]

"If America is the pursuit of happiness, the best way to pursue happiness is to help other people. Because there's nothing else that will make you happier."

- George Lucas

Day 270: Facing Your Weaknesses

Nobody's perfect. Henry Ford was uneducated. Bill Gates was a college drop out. Arnold Schwarzenegger spoke but a few words of English coming to this country. Helen Keller was unable to see, hear or speak at all. Abraham Lincoln was belligerent. John D. Rockefeller almost killed himself with worry. John F. Kennedy was too young and George Foreman was too old. Each of these successful individuals had to face their weaknesses in order to achieve the level of success they did. To have weaknesses is to be human; to face those weaknesses is to be successful.

The key to facing your weaknesses is to first be aware of them. If you are unaware or just ignore your weaknesses, you are setting yourself up for disappointment or even failure down the road. Others may try to expose and profit from your weaknesses, or on your journey to success you may hit roadblocks or be limited by your weaknesses. Facing your weaknesses begins with awareness.

Facing your weaknesses does not necessarily mean conquering them. If your weakness is the fear of flying, then you can conquer the fear, get someone else to fly for you, eliminate the need for flying, or just take alternate transportation. Here are four effective ways of facing your weaknesses:

- **Act on your strengths to compensate for your weaknesses.** John F. Kennedy was the youngest man ever elected president of the United States. In politics, youthfulness is more associated with lack of experience and wisdom than anything else. His opponents targeted this weakness but President Kennedy continued to win the people over with his inspiration and compassion.
- **Use other people to compensate for your weaknesses.** Henry Ford knew he needed to build a mastermind that would make up for his weaknesses if he were to reach his goal of bringing affordable automobiles to the masses. Helen Keller became one of history's most inspirational

people with the help of Anne Sullivan, who acted as her eyes and ears.

- **Avoid your weaknesses.** Bill Gates was not the best scholar. His heart was just not in his studies. I am quite sure if Mr. Gates had applied himself and forgotten about tinkering with those silly computers, he could have done very well and impressed his friends and family with a Harvard degree. However, he chose to avoid studies that did not interest him and he chose impress the world instead.
- **Overcome your weaknesses.** Abraham Lincoln was known in his early days as being very belligerent. In fact, one of his harsh criticisms led him into a "duel to the death" with the man he publicly criticized. Fortunately for both of the men, their seconds stopped the duel before it began. From that point on, Lincoln committed himself to overcome his belligerent ways that eventually led him to say, "Discourage litigation. Persuade your neighbors to compromise whenever you can. As a peacemaker the lawyer has superior opportunity of being a good man. There will still be business enough."

We all have weaknesses that may be affecting our success in our personal and/or business lives. It is important to be aware of these weaknesses, then choose how to deal with them. Once this can be accomplished, your weaknesses will no longer be an obstacle on your road to success.

ACTION STEP(S):

1) Make a list of all of your weaknesses, no matter how small they may be. Now go through each weakness and choose one of the four methods above for dealing with it.

Day 271: The Art of Praise and Compliment

Every one of us has an amazing power that we seldom use. With this power, we can make another person instantly feel better, put a smile on their face and a skip in their step. In some cases, we can even give another person an emotional high that will last all day long. Of course, with any great power comes responsibility; in this case, the responsibility is using the power itself every chance we get. This power is the art of praise and compliment.

The words praise and compliment are actually synonyms for expressing approval or admiration. However, praise is more associated with accomplishment or achievement—you cannot really praise someone for his or her nice shoes. Whether you use praise or compliments, the effect is same: a warm feeling followed by a smile for both the giver and receiver.

The benefits of praising are similar to expressing gratitude. Besides good feelings all around, employees or team members who are praised are more productive and satisfied in their jobs and children who are praised are more confident and tend to focus on praise-worthy behavior. Giving sincere praise and honest compliments will help you earn the respect and trust of others.

Throughout this course I have mentioned the importance of giving praise and compliments, but not necessarily how to best do it. Here are tips on the art of praising and complimenting.

- **Follow a compliment with a question.** Did you ever notice how difficult it is for some people to accept compliments? For example, "Nice car, Bob!" may be deflected with, "It looks better than it runs." Now, instead of good feelings, there are just feelings of awkwardness and regret. Prevent this deflection by following your compliment with a question like, "Nice car, Bob! Where did you get it?" Now by answering your question Bob is "forced" to accept the compliment.

- **Compliment the person, not the object.** "Nice car, Bob!" is really complimenting the car, or perhaps the company that designed and built the car. For this compliment to have maximum effectiveness, compliment Bob on his decision to buy the car, his taste in cars, how great he looks in the car, or anything that has to do with Bob, not just the car.

- **Praise in public, carefully.** The old saying goes, "praise in public, punish or criticize in private." Generally, this is not bad advice unless your praise isolates others who feel they are deserving of praise. Public praise can cause friction so just be careful that the praising in public is appropriate for the situation.

- **Compliment often.** Compliments are free so why not give them away any chance you get? Of course, too much of anything is not a good thing (that is why it is *too much* and not just *much*), usually common sense will tell you if you are overdoing it. Do not feel that by holding back you are making the compliments and praise you do give more meaningful. While there may be some truth to this, many frequent compliments are worth much more than one big one.

- **Be sincere.** Insincere compliments or praise are called flattery and are generally detested by those who can tell the difference. If you do not truly mean it, don't say it.

- **Be appropriate.** It is probably not a good idea for a male to compliment a female employee on the firmness of her backside. Again we must call on our common sense.

Praising and complimenting others is an art that has marvelous effects on the attitude of those receiving the praise. It is something we all are capable of, but do not do it often enough. Take a few steps closer to success and practice your complimenting skills while making other people happy in the process. You can't go wrong!

ACTION STEP(S):

---

1) Compliment three people by doing the following: 1) compliment the person and not the object and 2) immediately follow the compliment with a question.

"I can live for two months on a good compliment."

- Mark Twain

Days 272 and 273 are for "R&R"—review and reflection. Spend these days reviewing the last five articles and reflecting on the information and how it relates to your life. Now is also a good time to make sure all the action steps for the previous days have been completed.

Day 274: Finding Balance

When referring to one's life, balance is a harmonious or satisfying arrangement or proportion of parts of one's life. These parts of life can be categorized many ways, the most general categories being personal and professional. These two general categories can then be broken down further. For example, a personal life can consist of love, friendship, fitness, spirituality, relaxation, and learning. The categories we choose are up to each one of us based on the importance of these categories in our lives.

Having a balanced life does not mean each day of your life must be balanced. Some work requires excessively long hours during the holiday season. Many people get more sleep and relaxation on the weekends so they have the needed physical and mental energy to forge ahead during the work week. Many spiritual people have a holy day each week, which they devote primarily to worship. Living a balanced life is seeing life as a big picture and not just a series of days.

Success ultimately depends on finding balance. Each of us has a different balance point for every part of our lives. Some believe that the moment we find that balance point we find true happiness. However, if we live an unbalanced life, we will eventually experience feelings of guilt, failure, and emptiness. When we find balance, we are essentially meeting more of our needs, and we live a more fulfilled life.

Nobody can tell us how to live a balanced life because only we can define what balance means to us. Finding balance is about using a combination of common sense, circumstance, and trial-and-error. We must determine for ourselves what is too much and what is not enough. Here is a partial list of some examples where finding balance is essential to success.

- Use humor often, but don't be a comedian (unless that is your goal).

- Be persistent, but know when to move on.
- Have definite goals, but be flexible with them.
- Build your self-esteem, but don't give yourself a big ego.
- Think huge, but be realistic.
- Exercise regularly, but don't over do it.
- Go the extra mile for people, but don't do too much for them.
- Read or listen to educational material, but make sure you spend time taking action as well.
- Reinforce positively, but use negative reinforcement when required.
- Risk some of your money, but not all of it.
- Use the power of questions, but not too often.
- Avoid criticizing and complaining, but don't let people walk all over you.
- Forgive and forget, but learn from the past.
- Smile often, but not all the time.
- Live in the present, but mentally visit the past and future every now and then.
- Avoid offending others, but don't try to please everybody.
- Avoid using negative words, but don't hesitate to tell your kids not to play with fire.
- Do some things yourself, but leave other things for others.
- Have a good vocabulary, but don't talk over people's heads.
- Use good grammar, but don't be pretentious.
- Setup spam filters, but don't let them trash good e-mail.
- Have multiple streams of income, but don't neglect focus.
- Success is learning, but success is also doing.

Balance should not be used as an excuse. It is easy to give in to instant gratification, or take the easy way out and justify one's actions as "finding balance", but that is not what finding balance is about. Finding balance is about improving the quality of your life while bringing you closer to your goals. Find balance, and you may just find success right beside it.

ACTION STEP(S):

---

1) How balanced is your life? On a sheet of paper, make three columns. In the first column, write down all the areas in your life that are important to you. In the second column, on a scale from one to ten, rate how much focus that area of your life now is getting. In the third column, rate how much focus you feel that area should be getting. Now review the chart and you can see areas where you need to start shifting focus to achieve balance.

"The best and safest thing is to keep a balance in your life, acknowledge the great powers around us and in us. If you can do that, and live that way, you are really a wise man."

- Euripides (484 BC–406 BC)

Day 275: Contentment

Contentment, or desiring no more than what one has, can be our best friend or our worst enemy. Being content with what we have is generally a good thing, especially when referring to material possessions and other "things". However, being content with our accomplishments, goals, and general position in life essentially means we have no more goals or ambitions since they have already been either reached or forgotten. Those who lack goals and direction in life also find it difficult to achieve happiness. It is this level of contentment that gets in the way of our success.

At this time, it is likely you have already experienced much success. You may have reached some of your goals or you may have achieved success in other areas where you may not have expected. It is times like these we start to get comfortable and begin to lose the burning desire that once was the driving force behind our success. When we are content, we are not frustrated, and we do nothing or very little to improve on our situation. Remember that success does not come easy; it is not about taking the path of least resistance, it is about continually challenging yourself and holding yourself to higher standards.

What is the difference between true happiness and contentment and how can you tell the difference? Although this may seem like a challenging question, you already know the answer. Ask yourself, "Am I truly happy, or am I just content?" Although you may not be able to put your feelings into words, you will be able to tell the difference.

If you feel that you have reached a point in your success where you are comfortable or contented, then it is time to review your definition of success and refocus on your goals. You may feel that you were in a more "hopeful" state of mind when wrote the goals and now your goals seem less important or maybe "too bold", but do not let your current state of contentment cloud your judgment. Review your success journal, your general and specific purpose.

Look at your dream collage. Do you really want to give up on these goals and dreams? Are you really exactly where you want to be or do you feel you have more to give?

Being content with the material things in life is said to be one of the keys to happiness and it also makes a very worthwhile goal. Contentment with your achievements in life, on the other hand, is usually more destructive than productive, and can be combated by refocusing on your goals and life purpose. In the words of John Lancaster Spalding, "If all were gentle and contented as sheep, all would be as feeble and helpless."

ACTION STEP(S):

1) Spend 15 minutes reviewing your success journal. Specifically, review your general purpose, specific purpose, goals, dreams, and ideas.

"Contentment is not happiness. An oyster may be contented. Happiness is compounded of richer elements."

- Christan Bovee

Day 276: Inspiration from Marc Andreessen

Marc Andreessen (1971–) is of the true Internet pioneers who is responsible for the World Wide Web as we know it.

Success is taking your own path. Although school sports were the main focus of the majority of Andreessen's peers, Marc had little interest in athletics. Andreessen instead pursued an interest in computers that began when he was in the fifth grade.

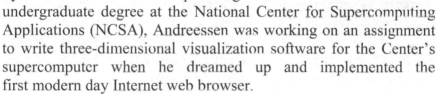

Success is a result of a dream followed by action. While pursuing his undergraduate degree at the National Center for Supercomputing Applications (NCSA), Andreessen was working on an assignment to write three-dimensional visualization software for the Center's supercomputer when he dreamed up and implemented the first modern day Internet web browser.

Success is often a result of identifying and solving problems. The user-interfaces of available browsers of the early 90s tended not to be very user-friendly. Marc decided to develop a browser that was easier to use and more graphically rich that would lead to the Web's instant popularity.

Success is seeking help when you need it. In 1992, Andreessen recruited fellow NCSA employee, Eric Bina, to help with his project. Together, the two would work many long and hard hours to create the first modern-day Web browser, called "Mosaic".

Success is often a result of a chain reaction. When making Mosaic available for more popular platforms such as Windows and MAC, its popularity skyrocketed. More users meant a bigger Web audience, which led to the creation of new content, which in turn further increased the audience on the Web and so on.

Success is often a result of making the right connections. Despite Marc's incredible work with Mosaic, because the project was developed on university time he would get neither any significant compensation nor recognition for his work. With the idea of a new start-up company (which eventually became Netscape), Marc soon met Jim Clark, founder of Silicon Graphics, Inc., a man with both the money and connections to help bring Marc's visions to the world.

Success is being able to inspire others. In developing the new web browser (Netscape), the programmers would sometimes work for 40 straight hours. As one employee recalls, they were driven by the vision of creating something better than the Mosaic.

Success is not always about cash up front. "One of the fundamental lessons is that market share now equals revenue later, and if you don't have market share now, you are not going to have revenue later. Another fundamental lesson is that whoever gets the volume does win in the end. Just plain wins."

Success is understanding the power of viral marketing. One of the "secrets" of success of the Netscape browser was the way in which it was marketed. The browser included new HTML tags that allowed Web designers greater control and creativity. Excited designers quickly began incorporating the new tags into their web pages. The new tags could only be read by Netscape, so the designers would usually include a note that their pages were best viewed with Netscape and a link to the page where it could be downloaded.

[Sources: http://www.thocp.net, http://www.ibiblio.org]

Day 277: Making Successful Decisions

Back in 1995, my wife and I had a successful graphic design business. We had a small office in a great Boston neighborhood, a few minutes walking distance from our apartment. We were not rich, but we were making enough to live comfortably in our then-current lifestyle. We then had a decision to make: we had an opportunity to sell our graphic design business, along with our steady income, and focus on Internet development. Even though our Internet revenue was only about $10 per month at the time, we made what turned out to be one of our most successful business decisions and sold the graphic design business. That one decision resulted in a chain of events that allowed us to live our dreams.

A decision is defined as the act of reaching a conclusion or making up one's mind. A successful decision is one that brings us closer to, not further from, achieving success. The decisions we make are really a result of who we are as a person; they are a reflection of our inner self. Even though the most successful individuals make poor decisions now and then, more often than not, success-minded individuals make successful decisions.

Sometimes, the least successful decision we can make is choosing not to make a decision. Being indecisive is one of the major obstacles people run into while pursuing success. If you neglect to make timely decisions...

- you can miss great opportunities
- you can be taken advantage of by others
- you let others control the direction of your life
- you often end up doing things you later regret

Fortunately, there are ways to help us make more timely and successful decisions. Let's take a look at some of the more effective ways.

- **Relate the decision to your goals.** If you consciously review your goals while making important decisions, it is not difficult to figure out which is the more successful decision for you to make. Use visualization to play out "what if" scenarios in your head. Where would you be in one, three, or five years if you decide one way? How about if you decide the other way?

- **Always think long-term success not short-term gratification.** The majority of bad decisions in life are usually a result of one's desire for immediate gratification. Successful-minded individuals think in the long-term and make decisions that way as well.

- **Don't procrastinate making a decision if you have all the facts.** Sometimes the best time to make a decision is right there and then, when you have all the information you need and the information is fresh in your mind. This is especially true for smaller, less important decisions that would otherwise compound on each other and cause unnecessary stress.

- **Get all the facts first.** Sometimes, especially for larger and more important decisions, it is best to take the time to gather as many facts as you can that will help you to make the best decision. Make sure your facts are coming from unbiased, reliable sources.

- **Never allow others to manipulate you.** Manipulation is when others persuade you to do something that is not in your best interest. Peer pressure and high-pressure sales are two common examples of manipulation. Never hesitate to tell someone you need time to "think about it" or "think it over". If you are backed into a corner with a "now or never" ultimatum, 9 out of 10 times saying "never" will be the successful decision.

- **Use your common sense.** Our common sense is the sum of all of our knowledge and experiences that tell us in our head what is the right thing to do.

- **Trust your gut.** Whether you refer to it as your gut feeling, intuition, instinct, or God, it is the unexplainable feeling inside that tells you which decision is the right one.

Some are more "in tune" with this connection than others, but if you have it, trust it.

Getting the right answer begins with asking the right question. Instead of asking yourself, "Should I do this?", ask yourself, "If I do this will it bring me closer to my goals?" Doors of opportunities are always opening, but they are not always open. You need also to be decisive and make decisions as soon as you feel you have enough information to make the right ones. Remember that just one decision can lead to chain of events that can forever change your life.

ACTION STEP(S):

1) Write down the last several decisions you made. Beside each one, write down either an "S" for successful, or a "U" for unsuccessful. Why were your successful decisions successful? Why were your unsuccessful decisions unsuccessful? How could you have made them successful?

"In a moment of decision the best thing you can do is the right thing. The worst thing you can do is nothing."

- Theodore Roosevelt

Day 278: Sacrifice

I often hear statements being made such as, "To be successful, you have to sacrifice your personal life", or "Successful people are only successful because they missed out on life's pleasures while striving for success", or even "Those with full pockets have empty souls". In fact the fear of sacrifice is one of leading causes of fear of success. It is not difficult to understand why these statements are so universally accepted: they make it easy to justify one's own lack of success. While there are those who have made poor sacrifices to get where they are, the majority of those who have achieved success have done so by making positive sacrifices that were not difficult to make. These are the sacrifices that lead to success.

Sacrifice is about giving up something of value for something else of higher perceived value. This plays an important role in success because success is about the long-term and not about giving in to instant gratification. In our pursuit of success, we often must take a step back in order to take a giant leap forward. This backward step is often known as sacrifice. The key to embracing sacrifice is taking value from that which you are sacrificing and adding value to that for which you are making the sacrifice. To illustrate, several years ago I used to drink on average two liters of diet soda a day. I knew that water was a healthier choice and I decided to sacrifice my enjoyment of drinking diet soda for my overall health. While I cannot say this sacrifice was easy, it was one of the easier sacrifices I have made because I had taken the time to research the detrimental effects of diet soda as well as the health benefits of drinking water. This research helped me to devalue the diet soda and place more value on water. It only took me about a week to learn to enjoy water more than diet soda; then, diet soda was no longer a sacrifice since it no longer had any value to me.

Here are a few positive sacrifices you can make along with some tips on how to embrace the sacrifice.

- **Sacrifice about one hour of leisure time per day for the study of personal development.** By now, you should be well aware of the importance of personal development; it is the sacrificing of the leisure time that may present the challenge. Study in a way that is enjoyable, relaxing and/or exciting to you in order to add more value to your personal development process.
- **Sacrifice buying too many luxuries and invest your money instead.** Luxuries are great to have especially as rewards for achievement. However, hold off on buying luxuries for as long as you can. There is no black and white rule for when to buy luxuries; it is about achieving balance.
- **Sacrifice higher-paying jobs for pursuing your dream.** Don't be tempted to waste your most valuable asset—your time—working for money. Make the sacrifice and do work you enjoy doing that brings you closer to your goals, even though the pay may be less.
- **Sacrifice 10% of your income for the feeling of helping others.** No matter how selfless you try to be, helping others always ends up benefiting you in some way. Welcome these benefits and accept them as you would accept gratitude.

Along with the positive sacrifices come the not-so-positive sacrifices, or poor sacrifices. These are sacrifices that we should never make because they will do more damage to our success and/or happiness than good.

- **Avoid sacrificing quality time with loved ones.** If your work requires you to spend time away from home, pick up the phone and call your loved ones. Try to avoid mentally spending time at work while physically spending time with your loved ones. One hour of quality time per day is better than a full day of neglect.
- **Never sacrifice your health.** Keep clear from frozen dinners no matter how cheap or convenient they may be. If you are on the road, spend a few extra bucks eating a good meal rather than choosing fast food. Lack of time should

never be an excuse not to take care of your body. A 10-minute workout routine that can be done in any room without weights or equipment is better than nothing.

- **Never, ever, sacrifice your integrity.** In your pursuit of success, you will frequently have opportunities to take shortcuts that will go against your ethics, morals and or values. Do not give in to this temptation. Taking these shortcuts go against everything success is about and almost always lead to guilt and regret. Remember, when it comes to success, there are no shortcuts.

No success story is complete without sacrifice. However, contrary to popular belief, the sacrifices one needs to make to achieve success do not have to be that difficult and they certainly do not have to take away from one's character. Let's remember the words of Sidney Howard who wrote, "One-half of knowing what you want is knowing what you must give up before you get it."

ACTION STEP(S):

1) Write down any sacrifices that you have made recently. Were these positive sacrifices or negative ones? What positive sacrifices can you make that will bring you closer to success?

Days 279 and 280 are for "R&R"—review and reflection. Spend these days reviewing the last five articles and reflecting on the information and how it relates to your life. Now is also a good time to make sure all the action steps for the previous days have been completed.

Day 281: Experience

What is the big deal with having experience? Why do employers require it for their higher-paid positions? Why do customers require it from contractors they hire? Why do professionals demand it from themselves? How do we get experience, and perhaps most important, how do we get around not having traditional experience? These questions are asked by students and business veterans alike. No one is ever too old or too "accomplished" to better themselves by seeking experience.

As Ebeneezer Scrooge discovered, experience, or the active participation in events or activities leading to the accumulation of knowledge or skill, is the ultimate teacher. The majority of mistakes are made early on when practicing a new skill. The common perception is, those with experience have already made the majority of their mistakes. Employers also value experience because of the costs associated with training and the productivity levels of experienced employees versus those with no experience. Experience is used as a general indicator of one's ability.

So why should adults who have "been there, done that" seek experience? Nobody is perfect. Experience is a very effective method of bringing one closer to perfection. Any one job or career can consist of several or even hundreds of skill sets. Professionals who seek to improve on these skill sets are wise to seek experience in these skill sets. For example, Toastmasters International (http://www.toastmasters.org) is an organization with local chapters all around the world that exists to help individuals build communication and speaking skills through experience. This organization has given millions of ambitious people practical experience since 1924.

There are numerous ways to get experience in the traditional sense. This is the kind of experience that most employers are looking for and/or expect.

- **Other jobs.** Take a low paying job that requires you to use the skill set on which you are working. Never think you are too good for any job nor be embarrassed by the pay. Those who think any job is beneath them are missing out on opportunities to learn from experience. Very often, experience is more valuable than money.

- **Internships.** Businesses are often willing to train people in exchange for labor. If you can afford not to get paid for your time, this can be an excellent arrangement for both parties.

- **Volunteer positions.** There are many non-profit organizations in your community that could use your help. Not only will you be gaining valuable experience, but you will be helping people as well in the process.

- **Military.** You have seen the commercials... "Be all you can be!" The armed forces can be a great organization in which to participate. Be sure you consider the commitment and the risk first, however.

- **Clubs and organizations.** Look for local clubs or organizations that will allow you to put your skills to use on a regular basis.

- **Student activities / leadership roles.** If you are currently a student in high school or college, consider taking one of the many leadership roles available.

- **Work as a temp.** Working as a temp is a unique opportunity to gain experience by working in several different firms or businesses. It is kind of like ordering the sampler platter at a restaurant: you get a taste of several things without having to commit to just one.

- **Internet opportunities.** Look for "cyber experience". There are many opportunities on the Internet especially in the technology field. For example, our company SupportFreaks.com offers a free technology consulting service called "Freebies" where techs offer free advice on computer and Internet issues on a volunteer basis.

- **Career services.** If you are a college student or have attended college at any time in your life, you most likely have access to your college's career services. This is an excellent place to seek opportunity to gain experience.

So far I have presented information on experience that you have most likely been exposed to before. This is because I feel it is important to stress the necessity of traditional experience. However, I would also like to share with you some "secrets" about experience.

When an employer posts an ad saying a certain amount of experience is necessary, what they are really saying is a) they want to be sure they get applicants that know what they are doing, b) they do not want to spend excessive money on training, or c) they want applicants who have already made their "beginners' mistakes". If you can address these concerns without having the practical experience the company may be looking for, you have a just as good, if not better, chance at competing with applicants that have the experience. In addition, never underestimate your own abilities. Ability, not experience, is what employers are really looking for. Experience just happens to be an excellent indicator of one's ability. Convince the employer of your ability, and your lack of practical experience will not be a handicap.

I have mentioned "practical" or "traditional" experience as the experiences that most employers are looking for in applicants. There are also many other non-traditional or creative ways to gain experience. Just because these are often overlooked by employers, it does not mean you should overlook them. Remember, experience is defined as the active participation in events or activities leading to the accumulation of knowledge or skill. This is quite a broad definition that allows one to be creative while gaining experience. Here are some of those creative ways.

- **Do extended research.** Research is a form of active participation that certainly does lead to increased knowledge on a given subject.
- **Interview an expert in the field.** Gain experience by "borrowing" the experiences of experts in the field. These experts often are able to share in hours their own experiences that have taken a lifetime to collect.
- **Work alongside an expert in the field.** If you can find a "mentor", even for a day, that will allow you to work

beside him or her under his or her supervision, you will get invaluable experience. Don't be afraid to ask someone for this opportunity; they will be flattered!

- **Spend time observing.** Medical students gain experience by observing their more accomplished counterparts in action. Work on your observation skills and gain experience at the same time. If your ambition is to own a deli, but you have no experience in the industry, eat your lunches at several delis. Pick up the lingo, pay attention to how they operate, ask questions, observe.

- **Start your own company.** If only for the experience, start your own company. Do you want to impress the partners at a big six accounting firm? Start your own accounting firm, even if your Aunt Bunny is your only client. Create your own experience if others will not allow you the opportunity.

Experience is one of the best teachers. Gaining experience will allow you to develop your skills and broaden your opportunities. However, never underestimate your abilities due to a lack of experience. Every great person in any field had to start somewhere without experience. The world is full of exceptionally talented and gifted people who will remain undiscovered because of their self-imposed limitations due to inexperience. Do not be one of these people. Gain either the traditional or creative experience needed to enhance your abilities and be the best you can be.

ACTION STEP(S):

---

1) What experiences would bring you closer to your goals? How can you get these experiences? Write down as many ideas as you can think of and choose at least one on which to follow up.

Day 282: Keep an Open Mind

We are presented with new ideas every day of our lives. These are the same new ideas that advance our technology, ease suffering, establish peace, and generally make the world a better place in which to live. In order for a new idea to have such a positive effect on society and the human race, it must be accepted by others. Some ideas, like the use of personal computers, have been accepted rather quickly whereas other ideas, like world peace, may just always be "too idealistic" to be universally accepted. While we cannot force our ideas or beliefs on anyone, we can learn to live with an open mind and accept new ideas that will empower us and bring us closer to success.

Throughout this course I have hinted on the importance of having an "open mind", and now I would like to explain why. Someone with an open mind is a person who is willing to accept new ideas and beliefs. In most cases, people have open minds on some subjects and closed minds on others. Unfortunately, many people have closed their minds on subjects in which they have disempowering beliefs. For example, those who were brought up with the belief "...money is the root of all evil", have a difficult time accepting the positive influences money can have. Those with open minds avoid ignorance and open themselves up to opportunity by agreeing to consider new information.

An open mind is like a good sense of humor—everyone thinks they have one; however, that is not the case. Closed-minded individuals often just consider themselves "cautious", "decisive" or justify their non-acceptance of new ideas or beliefs in some other way. Here are a few of the most common reasons why not everyone is open-minded.

- **Skepticism.** Those who have experience in life certainly have had some negative experiences. They have seen that people do or say things for their own benefit and manipulate others. Skepticism is a self-defense mechanism that protects us from being taken advantage of, but it also prevents us from accepting new ideas. Trust in your own judgment and agree to consider other ideas and beliefs

- **Stubbornness.** Some people just cannot admit they are wrong. Out of pure stubbornness, they will refuse to accept or even listen to any new ideas. If you have an issue with admitting that you are "wrong", you can, instead, admit to not having all of the information. This is a more graceful way of saying you are wrong. :)
- **In too deep.** Along the same lines as stubbornness, some people have lived their entire lives with a belief. By changing this belief, they would feel as if they have been "wrong" all this time. In fear of wasted days, months, or even years supporting an incorrect belief, these people would rather close their minds to other beliefs and ideas. Remember that it is never too late to do the right thing. Your journey down the right path begins by first getting off the wrong path.

An open mind will allow you to make better decisions in your life, while at the same time helping you to become a more understanding and sympathetic person. Lack of knowledge, or ignorance, on a subject can be avoided by having an open-minded attitude. You can choose to reject information, beliefs, or ideas after you have considered them, but not before you are even presented with them. Keep an open mind and let success find its way inside.

ACTION STEP(S):

---

1) Agree to seriously consider something that you would not have before reading this article. It may be a business proposal, a personal invitation, or a new point of view.

Day 283: Inspiration from Madam C.J. Walker

Madam C.J. Walker (1867-1919) was an entrepreneur, philanthropist, social activist, and one of America's first self-made woman millionaires.

Success is not something into which you are ever born. While some people are born into families and situations giving them advantages, Madam C.J. Walker was not one of those people. As a daughter of former slaves, orphaned at age seven, living in a time when "racial equality" was unheard of, Walker survived by working in the cotton fields.

Success is not only for the well educated. Because of her impoverished background, Walker had only a limited formal education.

Success is knowing that it is never too late to pursue greatness. For eighteen years, from 1887-1905, Walker supported herself and her daughter by working as a washerwoman.

Success begins with perceiving the world in a positive light—a perception with hope and opportunity. Friendships with other black women who were members of St. Paul A.M.E. Church and the National Association of Colored Women exposed Walker to a new way of viewing the world.

Success can be a result of acting on a crisis. At age 37, Walker found herself facing baldness due to poor diet—a common problem in those days among black women. She experimented with many homemade remedies and store-bought products none of which produced a satisfactory result. She "tinkered" with some existing solutions until she found something that worked and decided to market it.

Success is minimizing risk and maximizing gain. As a poor minority in the early 20th century, Walker was in an excellent position for success by having nothing to lose and everything to gain.

Success is knowing the importance of education. When Walker was still working as washerwoman, making about $1.50 per day, she managed to save enough money to educate her daughter. To ensure her success, Walker surrounded herself with educated people in her business and employed tutors to help her with her own education.

Success is knowing your market. Traditional marketing at the time consisted mostly of advertising. However, Walker knew that the majority of her target market, black women, were not able to read. As a result, she began a highly successful face-to-face network marketing campaign, which was very unique at the time.

Success is giving others hope. At a time when most black women were just menial laborers, Walker offered hope and opportunity by creating a professional salesforce of black women, some of whom made hundreds of dollars per day.

*[Sources: http://www.madamecjwalker.com,
http://www.princeton.edu, Investor's Business Daily - 1998]*

Day 284: Does Money Change People?

Bill was a hard-working data entry guy at ABC Processing, Inc. who was always on time and respectful to others. However, he would frequently chat with his co-workers about someday winning the lottery, telling off his boss, "not taking no crap from no one" [deliberate double negative], and sleeping in when he felt like it. One day, with a stroke of good fortune, Bill did win the lottery and did just what he promised. Shortly after, Bill's co-workers commented on how much "he changed" since he won the lottery. In actuality, the money did not change Bill; it allowed him to be his true self. Unfortunately for Bill, his expression of his true self eventually caused him to lose his job and his friends.

When I sold Adgrafix, my first company of significant value, my wife and I gave away about two million dollars. We did not become more generous when we became wealthy; we just had more to give. Contrary to popular belief, either the abundance or lack of money does not change people; it just brings out who they really are.

Do people act differently when they become wealthy? Yes, many do. Many millionaires play the part of the stereotypical millionaire even though that is not who they really are. They can act cocky, egotistical, or callous. They can also act self-assured, generous or benevolent. It does not matter how they act, good or bad, if they are not being themselves it will cause inner turmoil that will eventually lead to self-sabotage. Several years ago I thought I should "dress the part" of a millionaire so I spent quite a bit of money on dress pants, shirts and sports jackets. I was uncomfortable, felt stupid, and was tired of taking my clothes to the cleaners rather than just throwing them in the wash. I went back to my sub-$100 Eddie Bauer outfit and I am once again comfortable, confident and back to washing my own clothes.

Money itself is neither good nor evil; it is neutral. Money cannot change who you are, but the desire to "act the part" can cause you to behave in ways that are inconsistent with your personality. Don't be afraid of what you might become with money; instead, work on who you are now. When money does come your way, it will only amplify the solid character you have already built.

ACTION STEP(S):

---

1) If you reached your financial goals tomorrow, how would you act? How would you treat people? Would you act any differently than you do today? Write this down and come back to your statement after you have reached your financial goals.

"Money doesn't change men, it merely unmasks them. If a man is naturally selfish or arrogant or greedy, the money brings that out, that's all."

- Henry Ford

Day 285: Sell Yourself First

Almost daily I get the calls from monotone telemarketers who say, "Hello Mr. Benet (yes, my name is Bennett, but they rarely get it right) how are you doing today?" Then, right after that lame opening, they start with their sale pitch. My response has become as automated as their opening: "No thank you, please take me off your list." This all-too-common, fast-track sales approach has, to the detriment of the sales profession, been adopted by many sales "professionals" outside of telemarketing. Many salespeople overlook this one very important concept: before you can sell anything to anybody, you must sell yourself first.

"Selling yourself" refers to gaining the trust and confidence of those to whom you are selling a product, service, or idea. It is about establishing rapport and building credibility, and perhaps most important, it is about being likable. Building this kind of relationship prior to asking for the sale, takes down any defensive barriers that may have once existed. It allows the prospect to be more receptive and open-minded to your message. Think about it. Would you be more likely to buy a product, service, or idea from someone whom you have never met, or from a good friend? In some cases, you may buy from a good friend only because they are a good friend, not because you really need what they are selling.

Selling yourself consists of five elements. Each of these elements are essential to increasing your chances of making a successful sale.

- **Trust.** Most prospects enter sales situations with the mindset that salespeople are just looking out for their own best interests and really do not care about their needs. Building trust in a sales situation is about demonstrating to the prospect that you, as the salesperson, are indeed looking out for their best interests.
- **Confidence.** A prospect must have confidence in your ability to do what you say you are going to do, as well as

your knowledge of the product you are selling. Having confidence that you will be around after the sale is equally as important.

- **Rapport.** Building rapport is best done by finding things on which you and the prospect agree. The basic message is, "Hey, I am just like you".
- **Credibility.** Remember that when you first meet a prospect, they know nothing about you. To them, you could be a con artist, lunatic, or serial killer. The best way to establish instant credibility is by being recommended by someone the prospect knows and trusts. Another way is to tactfully share with the prospect your credentials.
- **Likeability.** You can have the greatest product at the greatest price, the trust and confidence of the prospect, great rapport with the prospect, and come highly recommended, but if the prospect does not like you, chances are she will not buy from you. Being likeable is an art in itself. In short, you must sincerely like other people if you want to be liked yourself.

As you can imagine, it is difficult to achieve all of this on the first call. This is why good salespeople never attempt to sell on the first call. Some don't attempt to sell their product until the third call and some prefer to set up appointments when more time can be devoted to selling themselves first. This is an example of consultive selling (or consultative selling) where the salesperson acts as more of a consultant by taking the time to really understand the needs and wants of the prospect. Only once the salesperson feels he has established likability, rapport, confidence, trust and credibility, does he go for the sale.

This sales process does require patience and faith. Most rookies will go right for the close in an attempt to close as many sales as possible in as little time as possible. This is playing the risky numbers game; and in a market where good prospects are hard to find, it is a game that will almost always be lost. Spend the extra time needed to build relationships and earn the respect of your prospects before trying to sell them your product, service or idea. You will find very quickly that the extra effort is well worth it.

ACTION STEP(S):

1) Whether you sell a product, service, or idea, write down some ideas on how you can first sell yourself by establishing likeability, rapport, confidence, trust, and credibility.

"The best way to sell yourself to others is first to sell the others to yourself."

- Napoleon Hill

Days 286 and 287 are for "R&R"—review and reflection. Spend these days reviewing the last five articles and reflecting on the information and how it relates to your life. Now is also a good time to make sure all the action steps for the previous days have been completed.

Day 288: Trust

It seems as if people like to dish out advice on trust just as much as new parents like to give advice on pregnancy. Ralph Waldo Emerson suggests, "Trust men and they will be true to you; treat them greatly and they will show themselves great." William Shakespeare advises, "Love all, trust a few, do wrong to none." And famed writer Stanislaw Lem cautions, "Do not trust people. They are capable of greatness." Well, when it comes to giving advice on trust, I am no different. It is not only your trust in others, but the level of trust that others have in you that play an important role in success.

Trust is defined as a firm reliance on the integrity, ability, or character of a person or thing. For this article, we will focus on trust in people (with one mention of a dog). Trust is not mere reliability. You may rely on a delivery boy to deliver confidential documents across town but you may not trust that he will not read the documents. You may trust your teenage child to make the right choices when it comes to drugs, but you may not always rely on him or her to be home exactly when they say. Trust is not global. I trust my dog, Archie, with my two young kids but I would never trust him alone near an open pizza box. Trust is not absolute. You may trust a new babysitter enough to watch your children the moment you hire her, but it can take years to build a deep level of trust to the point where you are truly comfortable.

You must trust others, as well as earn the trust of others, in order to get ahead. Trust is the foundation of all professional relationships, friendships, and love. Although you may excel in other parts of your life, without trust in your relationships, success will be just out of your reach.

Begin by learning to place your trust in others. You cannot reach success on your own; everyone depends on others for something. But trust goes beyond mere dependability. I like to think of those I trust more as extensions of myself who can help with my purpose.

A key element of success is surrounding yourself with people you can trust.

Unfortunately, people become "hardened" over time due to bad experiences of misplaced trust. These people tend to close the door on trust and adopt the "trust nobody" attitude of the overly cautious, sentencing themselves to a life of failure. Forgive the cliché, but don't let a few bad apples spoil the bunch. When others betray your trust, learn from the experience; just do not give up trust altogether.

So when can you trust someone? While there are no hard rules, I can share this advice.

- **Define the worst.** What will happen if they betray your trust? What is the worst that can happen? Can you accept that? What is the probability that the worst will happen? In my former company, I created a position for independent contractors who would provide support for our customers. These contractors basically had the "keys" to our unique business model. I was often warned that a contractor can steal our idea and enter the market as a competitor. I was willing to accept this risk and put my trust in those whom I chose for the position. Sure enough, the worst did happen and it certainly cost us business. However, we were still able to build a 20 million dollar business. Without this trust, we would have been forced into a more traditional business model that would have almost certainly failed.
- **Give those you place your trust in reason not to betray you.** The mob uses the fear of death, but you may choose something a little less Godfatherish. Review Abraham Maslow's hierarchy for some ideas.
- **Trust by association.** If someone you trust, trusts a third person, you can establish an initial trust by association. This is one of the reasons recommendations are so valuable.
- **Learn to read character.** This is not something that can be done overnight. Reading character takes time and practice. Ask yourself the question, "Do I feel that this

person will look out for my best interests?" Once you ask yourself this question, you will be in tune with the signs that will give you the answer.

- **Do they have a motive?** Do they have any reason for betraying your trust? In my example under "define the worst", the contractor who betrayed my trust was a young, bright, ambitious guy who frequently talked about not making enough money. All the signs were there; I was just too naive recognize them.

- **Do they have a history.** Once again recommendations and referrals can play an important part in trust. If others were betrayed by this person, you may be wise to make that person earn your trust first.

Once you allow yourself to trust others, others will be more likely to trust you. Here are some more suggestions on how you can be seen as more trustworthy.

- **Prove yourself.** Prove that you are looking out for their best interests as well as your own. In a sales situation, a salesperson looking to establish trust might sit down with the prospect and discuss their particular needs, and advise the prospect of what options would not work for them and why. Then, present the prospect with the option that will work for them.

- **Never lie—for any reason.** Once you tell a lie, you start a chain of supporting lies that will almost always grow out of control and you will eventually be called on one of your lies. At this point any trust that has been established is most likely destroyed.

- **Do what you say, and do it when you say you are going to do it.** Yes, reliability and dependability are not the same as trust, but trust is difficult to earn if you are not reliable or dependable.

Trust is a key element to success. Allow yourself to be more trusting, while still being cautious. Make it easier for others to put their trust in you by becoming more trustworthy. And remember that deep trust may take a lifetime to build, but only takes minutes to destroy.

ACTION STEP(S):

---

1) How trusting are you? Do you feel you are too trusting or not trusting enough? If you feel you are too trusting, write down some ways in which you can be more cautious. If you are not trusting enough, write down some ways in which you can feel more comfortable placing trust in others.

"A man who trusts nobody is apt to be the kind of man nobody trusts."

- Harold MacMillan

Day 289: Teamwork

To this day, when I think of the ultimate display of teamwork I can't help but think of the Harlem Globe Trotters. For those of you who are unfamiliar with the basketball team, they are a group of some of the most talented athletes in the world who focus on entertainment rather than competition. When they perform, they are like one person with one common mission. It appears as if each one of them knows exactly what the other is thinking at any given moment. By winning over 98% of all games played since 1927, the Globetrotters own the best winning percentage in the history of professional sports. Teamwork is the key to their success.

Teamwork is defined as cooperative effort by the members of a group or team to achieve a common goal. Effective teamwork benefits from synergy, or the combined energies being greater than the sum of the parts. Although obviously vital to team sports, teamwork and success in virtually any part of life go hand in hand. If you are one who can create, manage and/or lead teams effectively, your skills are in high demand. If you can participate in, and more importantly, excel in a team environment, you will find more opportunities for success. Organizations worldwide are beginning to realize and profit from the synergies an effective team can create. Teamwork is a trend, not a fad.

Many managers and leaders who stress teamwork are often scoffed at because they fail to sell the benefits of teamwork to the team members. Instead, teamwork is viewed by these members as just another way for management to get them to do something they really don't want to do. This attitude is detrimental to everybody, including the overall success of the team itself. Here are some suggestions on how leaders and team members alike can ensure effective teamwork.

- **Make sure each member knows their role.** Each member of the team must be clear on exactly what he or she should be doing. Each member must see themselves as a piece of the puzzle, without which, the puzzle would not be complete. Encourage all team members to step forward, in private if necessary, and ask if uncertain about exactly what they are supposed to be doing.

- **Make sure everyone is on same page.** Each member of the team must not only know what he or she should be doing, but know what the team is doing in general. This includes overall goals, mission, and purpose. More important, each member must believe in and support the purpose of the team.

- **Look out for the team's best interest.** The most effective teams are those with members that are looking out for the teams best interest, not their own. In team environments, members often find themselves in situations where they can make choices that benefit them but hurt the team. Here are a couple of examples of a member looking out for his own interests: a basketball player that hogs the ball all night in the presence of a talent scout even though the team would score fewer points and perhaps lose the game. Or a member of a business team who takes a vacation during a critical time for the team when his presence is needed.

- **Think communication.** Good communication is vital to the success of any team. Not only does the team leader have to be an effective communicator, but each team member must communicate his or her thoughts, problems, and ideas to the team as well.

- **Think of the needs and wants of each team member.** An effective team leader will recognize the team as a group of individuals, even though the goal is to perform like a single unit. The team can be most effective when each member's needs and wants are being met, and each member can connect their personal success to the success of the team.

- **Motivate.** Motivation can spread more easily than the common cold. Not everyone is a "natural" motivator, so do not rely on the team's leader to be the only source of motivation. Any member who shines with enthusiasm and can share that enthusiasm through words of encouragement, can be a great source of motivation for the team. Motivate any chance you get.

- **Learn from your team members.** Everyone is your superior in some way. Think of a team as a pool of knowledge that you can draw from at any time. Never be afraid or embarrassed to approach other team members and ask advice or for help. This is a sign of strength, not weakness.

- **Be flexible.** The team must be prepared to function effectively without all of its members. The team should be structured so the absence of any one team member would not cripple the team. This is best done by ensuring that the team consists of members with a variety of talents, skills, and abilities.

- **Be open to new ideas and suggestions.** Team members who are closed-minded do not do well in a team environment. Think of any team as a learning experience. Even if you are the star member of the team, there is always something you can learn and always room for improvement. If you do feel you are the star, then why not take what you know to the next level of learning and take the initiative to teach the other members?

- **Be able to give and take criticism.** A good team is one that is constantly evolving and changing. This requires giving feedback and acting on feedback given to you. Criticism is an art that very few people bother to study, yet the importance of giving constructive feedback versus destructive criticism can easily make or break any team.

- **Socialize.** The stronger the personal bond between team members, the stronger the team. It is important for the team and its leaders to take time to get to know each other on a personal or social level. Friendships may not always form, but a certain level of respect almost always will.

Keeping teams strong is always a challenge. There are members who seek individual glory, members who think nobody works as hard as they do, members who find it difficult to trust others, members who do not believe they are an important part of the team, and members who just have issues. Follow the above suggestions and you will find that most of these issues can be minimized or even eliminated.

Teamwork is the ultimate act of coordination and cooperation that, through synergy, can accomplish fantastic things. Building an effective team is not easy, nor is keeping one together, but it is done every day by leading sports organizations, businesses, and other groups that know the power of an effective team. So next time the Harlem Globe Trotters are in town, catch a game and see for yourself the "magic" that good teamwork can create.

ACTION STEP(S):

1) Are you a team player? Can you take suggestions from others? Do you like to work with others that are not like you? Do you consider yourself cooperative? Can you trust others? If you answered no to any of these questions think about how you can become more of a team player by following the suggestions outlined in this article.

"We must all hang together or most assuredly we shall hang separately."

- Benjamin Franklin

Day 290: Inspiration from Jackie Chan

Jackie Chan (1954–) is a director, producer, stuntman, and actor. Jackie is one of the few martial artists that have managed to make it "big" in Hollywood.

Success is not always doing what is popular, or what others want. After spending years working as a stuntman under the security of the academy where Chan studied, much to his family's dismay, Jackie went off on his own.

Success is standing out from the crowd. As a stuntman in Bruce Lee's 1972 hit film *Fist of Fury*, Jackie reportedly completed the highest fall in the history of the Chinese film industry.

Success is having a solid reputation. As the film industry grew crowded and stunt work dwindled, Jackie was still able to find work due to his reputation as a fearless stuntman.

Success does not come easy. In perfecting his craft, Jackie has broken his nose three times, his ankle, most of his fingers, both his cheekbones and his skull (patched together with a steel plate).

Success is finding your own place. Shorty after Bruce Lee's death, Jackie, like most martial artists at the time, was unsuccessful at becoming the "next Bruce Lee". It was not until Jackie invented his own unique film style by combining humor and death-defying stunts that he because famous as an actor.

Success is being inspired. Jackie got inspiration for his humorous/crazy film style from legendary film clowns such as Buster Keaton and Harold Lloyd.

Success is creating opportunity from problems. During the filming of one of Jackie's earlier movies, so many stuntmen were injured that none would agree to work with Chan again. In response, Jackie founded the Jackie Chan Stuntmen Association, whose members he personally trained and paid their medical bills.

Success does not happen overnight. Jackie's dream was always to be an international movie star. Although he has been well known in Hong Kong for decades, it was not until about 1996 when Jackie had his first American hit, *Rumble in the Bronx*. It took Jackie about 40 years to realize his ultimate dream.

Success is having a winning smile. Perhaps a large part of Jackie's success is due to his great smile that he always seems to be wearing... who knows.

[Sources: http://www.biography.com, http://www.hkfilm.net, http://www.tiscali.co.uk]

"Camera, action, jump! Boom! Ambulance! Hospital! Next stuntman!"

- Jackie Chan

Day 291: Articulation

Imagine being the human resources director for a large firm. You are reviewing applications and seeking candidates to fill a top-level position. After searching through hundreds of resumes, you come across a candidate that looks absolutely perfect on paper and you arrange an interview. Within the first 30 seconds of the interview, you realize you've made a mistake when the candidate says to you, "Thanks for invitin' me here. It's frezzin' outside—I prob'ly shoulda worn a heav'yer coat." Although the candidate looks like a professional, and has the credentials to back him up, you do not give him the job because you know his poor articulation will evoke negative perceptions in customers who speak with him.

Articulation is the process by which sounds, syllables, and words are formed when your tongue, jaw, teeth, lips, and palate alter the air stream coming from the vocal folds. Poor articulation is when the sounds of words are omitted, substituted, distorted, or just plain slurred. The two most common problem areas are adjacent words that are blended together, as in "shoulda" for "should have", and sounds in words that are omitted, as in "fishin" for "fishing". Here is a list of some of the more common problem words:

gonna = going to
woulda = would have
coulda = could have
shoulda = should have
ta = to
moun'n = mountain
foun'n = fountain
finely = finally
probly = probably
whatcha = what are you
gimmie = give me
importn = important
ya = you
and dropping the "g" from any word ending in "ing"

Poor articulation can certainly be due to physical or mental disorders beyond our immediate control. Not everyone is gifted with the ability to clearly articulate words. However, the large majority of articulation problems are due to factors within our complete control. If you are one of those people fortunate enough to have the ability to clearly articulate words, you must not take it for granted.

Here are the top three reasons most people succumb to sloppy articulation along with some suggestions for improvement.

1. **Influenced by parents, siblings, or friends that did not articulate sounds.** Most of us learn our speech patterns by listening to those around us. If our parents or other vocal influences we had while growing up did not articulate words clearly, the chances are we have adopted the same bad habits. Listen to professional speakers or radio personalities with good articulation. Take time to talk to yourself (preferably when no one is around) and work on the words that give you the most trouble.

2. **Just plain lazy.** It is easier to say "nothin'" then strain to articulate that trailing "g". It seems to be natural to look for easier ways of doing things and speaking is no different. However, we know by now that success is not about taking the easy way out. Concentrate and become aware of your articulation and work to improve it where needed.

3. **Speaking too quickly.** When we rush our speech it is difficult not to combine sounds of words together or omit certain sounds in words. Slow down. Think about the moving of your mouth, and even exaggerate the movement of your mouth at first if necessary.

Poor articulation is often a result of years of bad habit. The good news is, while it may seem challenging at first to clearly articulate all of your words, clear articulation will quickly replace poor articulation and become a new habit. You have already started to become aware of your articulation and you will now notice whenever you slur your words.

Good articulation does not mean "changing who you are" or "speaking like a snob"; think of it as just being appropriate. Good articulation is not the same as being formal; it is just not being lazy. Nobody will think less of you for using good articulation.

Articulation and the adequacy of our speech affect our social, emotional, educational, and vocational status, as well as the overall quality of our lives. Make a conscious effort to no longer slur your words. You will find that others will perceive you to be more educated. You will find yourself to be more self-confident than ever before while having more opportunities that can lead you to success.

ACTION STEP(S):

1) Create your own "slur" list of the words that you commonly fail to articulate clearly. Practice these "problem words" often until they are no longer problems.

"Speak clearly, if you speak at all; carve every word before you let it fall."

- Oliver Wendell Holmes

Day 292: Patience

Success has been summed up into three words: passion, persistence, and patience. Although many people who pursue success have the passion, and some the persistence, very few posses the virtue of patience. This course is called "Year To Success", not "24 Hours To Success" or even "30 Days To Success". Why? Marketing people tell me, in order to sell more books, I should appeal to the desires of instant gratification and create a course that infers success within a much shorter period of time. However, my goal is not to sell books, nor to deceive anyone; it is to help as many people as possible live more fulfilling lives by achieving success and reaching their full potential. This is only possible with patience. I believe the importance of patience is best summed up by the Dutch who say, "A handful of patience is worth more than a bushel of brains".

Having patience is being capable of calmly awaiting an outcome or result; not being hasty or impulsive. Impatience is just another name for instant gratification, one of the greatest afflictions of human kind. Patience is often said to be a result of having several other virtues and qualities such as tolerance, compassion, understanding, flexibility, and a good sense of humor. Or as Saint Augustine said, "Patience is the companion of wisdom".

We all know that patience is important in life and is a respectable quality and virtue to possess, so why is it so rare a virtue? The answer is lack of faith. In order to have patience, you must have faith that the result or outcome will be favorable. Without faith, or belief in a favorable outcome, feelings of uncertainty and anxiety set in, otherwise known as impatience.

When others ask you to "have patience" or to "be patient", they are essentially asking you to have faith that the outcome or result will be favorable. If you do have this faith, then it is good advice. However, if you do not have this faith, then you are not being impatient, you simply have the feeling that you are getting nowhere and you should change your course of action. Patience should never be used as an excuse for continuing to do the wrong thing.

Patience is a state of mind that can allow you to live a more enjoyable and successful life. Or as George-Louis de Buffon said, "Genius is nothing but a great aptitude for patience." Fortunately, patience can be developed. Here are some suggestions on how you can build an aptitude for patience.

- **See the big picture.** If you are waiting in line at the department of motor vehicles to get your drivers license renewed, keep in mind that it is something you need to do just once every five years. Waiting one hour for the privilege of being able to enjoy the freedom of driving for five years is not a bad deal. Put things in perspective.
- **Think long term.** Impatience is often the result of myopia, or lack of thinking in the long term. Ask yourself this question, "Will it really matter a year from now if I have to wait an extra [time frame] for [whatever]?" Again, it is about putting the situation in its proper perspective. Once you do this, the anxiety will subside and you will be practicing patience.
- **Refocus your mind on other things.** When you are impatient, you are only impatient because of what you are focusing on or thinking about. Be a positive thinker. Do not focus on the fact that you are waiting for something, rather focus on the positive result for which you are waiting. I practice this every time I am waiting in an extremely long line at Disney World. The two and a half hour wait for Space Mountain does not bother me when I am focused on the anticipation of the thrill of the roller coaster.
- **Seek encouragement.** History is full of stories of incredible successes that were a result of patience. Thomas Edison spent years trying to control the electric process that created light. Colonel Sanders spent years trying to sell his chicken recipe. Helen Keller spent many hard years learning to do things that were simple for most others.

Seek out those who have practiced patience where you require it most and learn from them.

- **Realize that wait adds value to the reward.** The old adage that says, "Good things come to those who wait" is a plug for having patience. Success itself is one of the greatest examples of this. Lasting success takes time, and therefore takes patience.

- **Avoid comparison.** Impatience is often a result of making faulty comparisons. If a peer of yours has reached a level of success that you desire, realize that your circumstances are not the same as your peers. Parents often lose patience with their children because they have heard about their friends' children who have advanced at a quicker pace. What these parents do not realize is that their own children may be far ahead in other areas—it is unfair to demand the best of everything.

Aristotle once wrote, "Patience is bitter, but its fruit is sweet." It is not easy to practice patience but those who do are rewarded in many ways. Patience can be learned like any other skill. Patience should also be practiced like any other skill as well. Learn to recognize faith as well as the absence of faith and know when to change your actions or sit back and "have patience". Overnight success dies hard whereas lasting success requires passion, persistence, and patience.

ACTION STEP(S):

---

1) Write down where, at this time in your life, you feel impatience. Are you impatient with your spouse? Your children? Your friends or co-workers? Are you impatiently awaiting a certain event or date? Apply the suggestions in the today's lesson to each area where you feel impatience.

"Adopt the pace of nature: her secret is patience."

- Ralph Waldo Emerson

Days 293 and 294 are for "R&R"—review and reflection. Spend these days reviewing the last five articles and reflecting on the information and how it relates to your life. Now is also a good time to make sure all the action steps for the previous days have been completed.

Day 295: Being Your Best

Imagine a world where everyone around you was successful. All of your peers were over-achievers, every business in your area was thriving, and everyone you met was a multi-millionaire who appeared to be happy and living fulfilling lives. Now imagine, if you will, how you would feel living in such a world with your current level of achievement. Would you feel any less successful? Do you think your level of achievement would stay the same or increase?

Being your best is about holding yourself to a higher standard and realizing your full potential. We all have the need for belonging, and this need is met by pushing ourselves to a moderate level of achievement based on the society in which we live. Should we be letting other people set the pace for our success, or lack thereof? Do you tend to base your own potential on the potential of "the crowd", and see those who succeed as exceptions? Perhaps it is time to compare our potential and ability to the only person who really matters—ourselves.

How can you learn to be your best, hold yourself to a higher standard, and live up to your full potential? Here are just a few ways.

- **Realize.** Realize that you are an individual and not a member of a herd. Realize that effort alone is not the key to success and you are not currently being the best you can be.
- **Adopt.** Adopt qualities that you admire and respect in others.
- **Believe.** Believe that you are destined for greatness and the only reason you are not there yet is because you have not realized your full potential.
- **Affirm.** If you are one who likes affirmations, then say to yourself, "I am better than this". Being your best is like

striving for perfection—you will never get there, but it certainly does not hurt to make the effort.

- **Integritize.** (Yes, this is a made up word to mean, "live with integrity"—just trying to keep consistent with my one word bullet items). Although living with integrity will not necessarily help you to be better than you currently are, it will keep you from falling back.

It seems like common sense that we would all strive to be our best, so why don't we? Some people buy the excuse, "I am what I am". This is true, we are who we are but that does not mean we cannot change. There is nothing wrong with striving to become a better person. There are also those who fear they will become one of those people who act like they are "too good" for others, or have a "holier than thou" attitude. You are not, nor ever will be, better than anyone else besides the person you are now. Remember that, and you will not only have greater respect for all others, but they will have greater respect for you as well.

Being your best is a goal that should be at the top of your list. It is a generic goal that can take a lifetime to achieve. It is, however, a goal where the pursuit alone will increase your chances of living a more fulfilled and successful life.

ACTION STEP(S):

1) Do you feel that you are living up to your full potential? If not, make a list of the things you can do to help you be your best.

"You are not, nor ever will be, better than anyone else besides the person you are now."

- Bo Bennett

Day 296: Make the Best of a Bad Situation

I remember the first time I got a flat tire. I was a teenager and only had been driving for about a year. I knew from being in the car with my parents and from watching TV that when you get a flat tire you are supposed to call the car derogatory names, look up to the sky and yell, "Why me God?", then just be angry while changing the tire. So that is exactly what I did. Later, when I shared my "tragic" story with others, I realized how exciting the experience really was and how the experience actually made me a more confident driver. All too often we react based on how we think we are supposed to react in such a situation, as opposed to taking just a moment to think about the good in the situation and how we can make the best out of the "bad" situation that we cannot change.

The ability to make the best out of a bad situation can play an important role in success. It has been said that one's true character is revealed in times of adversity. It is in times of adversity when others see us for who we really are, and not just who we are trying to become. There are many obstacles along the road to success. When we encounter these obstacles, our behavior and actions will usually determine if we proceed down the road to success, turn back, or stay where we are indefinitely. At the same time, others will judge us based on our response to adverse situations.

Making the best of a bad situation is all about attitude and action. First, realize that you may not have any control over the situation; you do have complete control over your response to the situation. Then, choose the appropriate action that will allow you to make the best out of the situation. Here are a few examples:

Waiting in a long line. I was recently in line at the post office and witnessed a lady huffin' and puffin' while complaining how long the line was to anyone who would listen. "Why can't they get more help?!" she exclaimed, along with saying, "This is ridiculous!" every 30 seconds or so. When she finally left the post office, just about everyone in the room let out a sigh of relief. When you find yourself in a long line, begin by realizing that your impatience will not make the line go any faster, then do something to keep yourself occupied: read a book, strike up a conversation with another person, or review your goals in your head.

Being stuck in traffic. The next time you are stuck in traffic, look at the people in the other cars. Although the suffering of others is generally not a source of humor, it is quite humorous watching how people respond to traffic. While in my car, I recently looked over at a gentleman waving his arms in fury screaming at the traffic. He then looked at me, looking at him, and we both started laughing. Like waiting in line, your fury will not make the traffic go away. Take advantage of this time by listening to an audio book, or learning a foreign language on audio.

Getting fired or laid off. How can one make the best of such a devastating event as getting fired? Think of getting fired or laid off as an exchange of security for the opportunity to pursue your true desire. Talk to others that have been fired, laid off, or had their businesses go under, who are now on their new career path. More times than not, these people will say that their "misfortune" turned out to be the best thing that has happened to them.

Here are some general things to remember when faced with a bad situation:

- **It is pointless and non-productive to be worried, angry, bored or upset.** Although these are usually some of the initial reactions to adversity, we must learn to take control of our emotions and move to a more productive state of mind.
- **See the big picture.** In most situations we refer to as "bad", they are really quite insignificant when looking at the big picture. If you are taking a week's vacation with your family, you miss your flight, and you are fortunate enough to get a flight that leaves 6 hours later, realize that only a small portion of your vacation is effected. Accept the situation and then make the best of it.

- **Look for good in a bad situation.** Just about every bad situation has the seed of an equivalent or even greater good; you just need to know where to look. This is where a positive mental attitude really comes in handy. At the very least, bad situations can be written off as good experience. As Dan Sanford says, "Experience is what you get when you don't get what you want."
- **Maintain a good sense of humor.** A good sense of humor can make light of just about any bad situation. Saturday Night Live's Jack Handy once said, "Dad always thought laughter was the best medicine, which I guess is why several of us died of tuberculosis." I know that quote has little to do with making the best of a bad situation, I just thought it was funny.

The next time you find yourself in a bad situation, remember attitude and action. At first, you may feel like you are fighting your true emotions, but remember that negative emotions will only make the situation worse while positive emotions can quickly spread and make the situation better for everyone involved. The ability to make the best of a bad situation is a sign of true leader.

ACTION STEP(S):

---

1) Most of us find ourselves in bad situations quite often. Commit to making a conscious effort to make the best out of the next bad situation in which you find yourself.

"It's not the situation... It's your reaction to the situation."

- Robert Conklin

Day 297: Inspiration from Michael Dell

Michael Dell (1965–) is founder and CEO of Dell, Inc., the largest personal computer company in the world, as well as a regular at the top of the Forbes richest people under 40 list.

Success is having the entrepreneurial spirit. At age 12, he formed a direct marketing company, which offered a national stamp auction through the mail. Four years later, he created a venture for selling newspaper subscriptions through target marketing, and bought a BMW with the $18,000 he earned.

Success does not take much money or an ideal environment. Michael founded the Dell Computer Corporation in 1984 with nothing more than $1,000 and an idea that started out of his dorm room.

Success is doing what you are passionate about. Dell went to college intending to become a doctor. Meanwhile, his hobby was working with computers. His hobby won out.

Success is being efficient. Dell, Inc. is now worth billions because Michael saw an opportunity for bypassing the middleman, who adds little value to the products, and sells custom-built PCs directly to end users.

Success is having vision. Dell offered the first toll-free technical support and on-site service in the PC business—services which are now standard practice throughout the industry.

Success is making your mark. With the addition of Dell Computer Corporation to the Fortune 500 in 1992, Dell is now the youngest CEO of a company ever to earn a ranking on the Fortune 500.

Success is sharing. Michael Dell has established a number of foundations within his organization committed to philanthropic and community services. These foundations work to advance educational, environmental, business, economic, and social issues.

Success is making opportunity for others. In just 18 years, Dell, Inc. has grown from a one-person operation to a company of 46,000 employees.

Success is being able to show leadership. Mr. Dell has been honored many times for his visionary leadership, including in 2003 being named one of the top-ten most powerful people in business by Fortune magazine.

[Sources: http://www.askmen.com, http://www1.us.dell.com, http://www.biography.com]

"It's through curiosity and looking at opportunities in new ways that we've always mapped our path at Dell—There's always an opportunity to make a difference."

- Michael Dell

Day 298: Little Courtesies

Both Harry and David were in line for a supervisor position at a large industrial business. They were both equally qualified, were hired on the same day, and had just about equal abilities in every way. Cindy, the VP of human resources, had a tough decision to make. After the final interview, Cindy had made up her mind and had given David the supervisor position. Why? Simply because David began the interview by thanking Cindy for the opportunity to interview. When it comes to success, little courtesies can go a long way.

Courtesies are polite behaviors, gestures, or remarks. While entire books have been written on manners, this article focuses on a few select behaviors that apply to both professional and personal situations, which are most likely to influence your level of success.

Being courteous is about showing respect for others. By showing others respect, you in turn will be shown respect. People like to be respected; therefore by showing respect, people will like you more for it. Often when in a position of power, one forgets or feels he does not have to show courtesy to those "beneath" him. He feels that by showing courtesy it would somehow lessen his power. Actually, the opposite is true. Showing courtesy is a way to get others to like you, which will help you to have more influence over them. When it comes to courtesy, we are all on the same level— no one is beneath or above anyone else.

Some of the most powerful courtesies are verbal. The two most powerful and well-known courtesies are "please" and "thank you". Some others are

can you please
would you be so kind
I would appreciate it if
excuse me
I am sorry

Other courtesies include gestures. Here are some ways to practice your courteousness.

- **The handshake.** Be the first to extend your hand. For a more meaningful handshake, try a) the two-handed handshake, b) the left hand on the other person's right shoulder handshake, c) the handshake with a one-armed hug, or d) the very powerful, handshake with a respectful nod.
- **The hello.** Be the first to say "hello". A "hello" is generally considered to be more courteous than a "hi" or a "hiyadoin".
- **The meal.** When dining in a business or even personal setting, do not sit down until the other members of the party have sat down; the same thing goes for starting to eat. Of course, use common sense: if a guest is late or using the restroom, have a seat.
- **Open doors for people.** This is not some obscure proverb—I mean literally, open doors for people. This is especially appreciated when the other person has their hands full. There is nothing wrong with going through the door first in order to keep the door open for the other person without being in his or her way.
- **Never point.** Pointing with a single "pointer" finger is almost always considered rude. Instead, use open hand palm up to do your "pointing".

If you are a woman who refuses to open a door for a man because of some 50s sexual politics, or a man who refuses to extend your hand to a woman for whatever reason, get over your sexist issues. Everyone, regardless of sex, deserves to be shown respect through common courtesy.

Being courteous is being affable, attentive, ceremonious, civil, civilized, complaisant, considerate, courtly, cultivated, debonair, elegant, gallant, genteel, gentle, gentlemanly, gracious, ladylike, polished, polite, refined, respectful, soft-spoken, suave, thoughtful, urbane, well-behaved, well-bred, well-mannered, and well-spoken. But most of all, being courteous is part of being an overall good person.

ACTION STEP(S):

---

1) Thank somebody today for something, even if it is something they have done for you long ago.

"Be courteous to all, but intimate with few, and let those few be well tried before you give them your confidence."

- George Washington

Day 299: Priorities and Procrastination

There is an old saying that goes, "Never put off until tomorrow what you can do today". This is a perfect example of bad advice. First of all, I do not agree with that statement simply because of the absolute word "never". My second issue is with the word "can". We can all spend our day staring at the wall, but just because we are capable of doing this, certainly does not mean we should. These "words of wisdom" contained in that old saying that was written to battle procrastination, ignore one of the very important principles of success: spend each day doing what you need to do, should do, and want to do, in that order. In other words, prioritize.

Once again, we see the 80/20 rule in effect. In respect to time management and the average person, 80% of one's productivity is a result of 20% of one's time. Conversely, 80% of one's time is spent on only 20% of the activities that are considered productive. The key to greater achievement, productivity, and success, is being able to shift the scale so more of your time is spent on more productive activities.

Easier said than done. The biggest challenge we face as mere mortals is having the discipline to do what needs to be done, when it should be done, rather than do what we want to do when we feel like doing it. At times, we choose to do the less important tasks of our day simply because we do not look forward to doing the tasks that really need to get done. This is actually a very common example of procrastination, or the act of needlessly postponing or delaying.

There is only one reason we procrastinate: we associate more pain with doing what needs to be done than not doing what needs to be done. Therefore, the key to avoiding procrastination and focusing more on the tasks that need and should get done, is associating more pain with procrastination of your priorities, and more pleasure with getting them out of the way. Here are some facts to consider about priorities and procrastination:

- **Procrastination is a leading cause of stress.** Dreaded, but necessary tasks are like dark clouds that follow you around wherever you go. Realize that once these tasks are out of the way, you will be able to relax more. Your days will be less stressful the sooner these tasks are completed.
- **Procrastination effects concentration.** It is more difficult to concentrate and focus when your priorities are not being taken care of.
- **Procrastination takes away from your happiness.** Realize that every thought you have of what you should be doing but are not doing takes away a bit of your happiness. There is also happiness that comes with the feeling of accomplishment, or knowing that you are doing just what needs to be done and doing it when you need to do it.
- **Anticipated pain is often worse than pain itself.** You may think dealing with your important tasks right away may be painful, but when it comes down to actually doing it, you will realize that it was not that bad. Procrastination actually causes unnecessary pain.
- **Taking care of priorities makes room for more priorities.** When you get the more important tasks out of the way, you make room for even more important, productive tasks. This is the formula for increasing productivity that leads to greater success.
- **You do not have to eliminate your wants.** Go ahead and do what you want to do, just don't spend as much time doing it. If your day consists of two hours of mindless organizing that you enjoy as "downtime", try gradually reducing that time.

Priorities take precedence over that which you "can" do today. Priorities are those tasks or activities that you need or should do today. Rather than accepting clichés such as "Never put off until tomorrow what you can do today", you are better off adopting the philosophy, "Make the best possible use of your time", which does require sacrifice and self-discipline. The overall goal is not to deprive yourself of the more pleasurable activities, but to substitute the wasteful activities with more productive ones that give you the same or even greater pleasure. At the very least, simply prioritizing the tasks and activities you are already doing by doing what needs to be done, what should be done, and then what you want to do, in that order, will make a world of difference and lead you to greater success.

ACTION STEP(S):

1) Do something right now (OK, after you finish this article) that you have been putting off.

2) Commit one day this week to doing those tasks and activities that you have been putting off.

"Procrastination is, hands down, our favorite form of self-sabotage."

- Alyce Cornyn-Selby

Days 300 and 301 are for "R&R"—review and reflection. Spend these days reviewing the last five articles and reflecting on the information and how it relates to your life. Now is also a good time to make sure all the action steps for the previous days have been completed.

Day 302: The Squeaky Wheel

Imagine yourself a member of a large team. As a member of this team you are aware of many problems with the team itself as well as the problems the team has with the authority that governs the team. What do you do about it? Do you play it safe and say nothing, or do you go to the authority figure with your list of grievances? There is an old saying, "the squeaky wheel gets the grease"; however, the squeaky wheel is also the first one to get replaced.

Unless you are in some extreme circumstances, like some military organizations or legal situations (high school can often fall into this category), it is generally NOT a good idea to hide or bury your concerns, but it is best to bring them to the attention of a superior or managerial figure within the organization or group. However, there is a difference between making your concerns known and being the "squeaky wheel".

- The squeaky wheel *complains* whereas the concerned group member *gives feedback.*
- The squeaky wheel complains about every issue on his or her mind *without carefully considering* it, whereas the concerned group member gives feedback on *only those issues of real concern* that he or she has carefully considered.
- The squeaky wheel is *concerned with only him or herself,* whereas the concerned group member *knows the only good solution is a win-win situation for all parties involved.*
- The squeaky wheel is seen by the authority figure(s) as the *squeaky wheel that needs replacing,* whereas the concerned group member is seen by the authority figure(s) as *a respected leader of the group who cares about the success of the group and the organization.*

Whether you are a customer who complains in hopes of getting coupons, discounts or deals, or an employee who complains in hopes of getting better working conditions, fewer hours, or more money, consider changing your approach. Here are some suggestions:

- **It is not what you say; it is how you say it.** Remember the immortal words of Lincoln who said, "a drop of honey catches more flies than a gallon of gall".
- **Pick your battles.** If we all look hard enough, we can all find many things to complain about in all areas of our lives. Learn to focus on the positive and work on solving the more pressing concerns with the authority figure(s) involved. You will be taken more seriously and your points will be considered more valid, rather than just being seen as a "complainer".
- **Make it one issue.** If possible, combine your issues or problems into one larger issue and break down the issue together with the authority figure(s). Approaching someone with "I just have one issue..." goes over better than the series of "and another thing...".
- **Prove that you are looking out for more than your own best interest.** To be effective at making changes that will benefit you and your group, you must demonstrate that you are looking out for the best interests of everyone involved, and do it sincerely. If you can't honestly find a way to create a win-win situation, then it may be best to keep quiet and let another team member who can, do the talking.
- **Drop the "us versus them" mentality.** Once again, if positive changes are to be made all parties have to benefit. See the big picture. See the extended team.

As the squeaky wheel, you will get attention, but it will be negative attention. You will be associated with complaints, troubles and headaches. Change your attitude to one of creating a win-win situation where you have the best interests of all parties in mind. Once you do this, you will no longer be the wheel that needs replacement; you will be the leader who deserves respect.

ACTION STEP(S):

---

1) Are you a concerned group member, squeaky wheel, or one who says nothing? Think about the role you play and how you can become more influential.

"The true leader serves. Serves people. Serves their best interests, and in doing so will not always be popular, may not always impress. But because true leaders are motivated by loving concern than a desire for personal glory, they are willing to pay the price."

- Eugene B. Habeckerin

Day 303: Create a Successful Website

For almost a decade now, people from all over the world have been finding great success on the Internet through the creation of their own websites. To this day, the concept of a website still amazes me: it is a way to instantly distribute information and communicate with people all over the world for very little, if any, cost. Never before in history has there been such a cost-effective and widely available opportunity for so many people to find success. Although not necessarily easy, by understanding the basics and some of the "secrets" of creating a website, even as a novice, you can create a successful website.

What is a "successful" website? Simply put, it is a website that achieves its purpose. Just as you must define what success means in your life, you must define what it means for your website. Your objective may be to communicate a message, sell a product, or collect information. You may want to meet this objective on a limited budget and by spending only a limited amount of your time and energy. One must consider all these factors in determining the overall success of a website.

The creation of a successful website can be broken down into four stages: 1) the planning stage, 2) the creation stage, 3) the promotion stage, and 4) the maintenance stage. Each stage is vital to the overall success of the website. If you can create one successful website, you can create several; perhaps you can create multiple streams of income and be well on your way to financial freedom.

1. **Plan.** The planning stage is mostly done in your head and perhaps on paper. Begin by creating your website in your mind.

- **The Idea.** Everything starts with an idea and a website is no different. Do some research on the Internet to see if there is a market for your idea. Even if many people are already doing what you are thinking about doing, can you do it better? If so, go for it.

- **Value.** According to recent figures, there are well over three billion web pages on the Internet. Is your website going to add value to the Internet? Think value.

- **The Domain.** Do not under or over estimate the importance of a good domain name. On the one hand, a good domain name that can be easily spoken and remembered can be of great value when promoting a website. The words used in a domain can also be of value when listing the site with search engines. On the other hand, do not be misled to believe a domain is everything. A good domain is not a miracle business-generator and most people who pay more than $15 per year for their domain pay far too much. Remember that in most cases (yahoo.com, lycos.com, aol.com) it is the website that added value to the name and not the other way around.

- **Hosting.** Where are you going to host your website? Two of the basic choices are with a "free" host, or one that charges monthly fees. I have written articles on this topic for our own web hosting division, so if you are interested visit http://www.hostselect.info/whattolookfor.php.

- **Funding.** Creating a successful website costs money. Even if you do everything yourself, you are exchanging your time which is worth money. Is this website going to be one that you finance by your own money and labor, or will it generate some level of income to pay for itself, and perhaps make you a profit? Here are three basic ways to generate revenue from a website:
  - Accept on-line donations. There are many services that make it very easy to accept on-line donations. This works well for websites that are not focused on making money. Donations are not likely to make you rich, but they can help you pay for the development and ongoing maintenance of the website.
  - Sell products or services. This is the most common form of finance for business websites. These sites are also known as "e-commerce" websites. Using

the latest technology, one can securely sell products or services on-line, or at least advertise the products and services on-line and make the actual sale off-line.

- o <u>Advertise.</u> If you plan on having a high-traffic website, you may consider selling advertising space on your website. To do this, you will need to have some tracking software in place and, more important, have potential advertisers that would be willing to pay you for advertising space.

2. **Create.** When you are ready to create your website, there is much for you to consider. With today's software and web creation tools, just about anyone can create a decent website, but it still takes the artist to create the magnificent website. However, a successful website does not have to be a magnificent one, just an effective one. Do not let the lack of funds get in your way of creating a website—you can always design it yourself and have it redesigned later when the funds become available.

- **Design.** Don't do something just because you can. Some designers use too many fonts, excessive animations, and tacky javascript tricks just because they can.
- **Colors.** Some colors go together well, and some don't... in fact most do not. Use one of the many "color schemer" tools available on the Internet to pick out colors that work well together.
- **Background.** Do not choose a background that makes text difficult to read. If you do choose to use a background image or color, consider placing text in tables with a white background.
- **Images.** Nothing says "amateur" like a poor image. Make sure the images you choose for your website are web quality (72 dpi) and not distorted. Do not let HTML tags alter the size of your image. Also, be sure your images are not too large. Try visiting your site on a dial-up connection to really put it to the test.
- **Printable.** Do you want people to print out the content on your website? If so, make sure it prints out well. If not,

perhaps create a special website just for printing, or if you are up for the challenge, convert your website into pdf (Adobe Acrobat) format.

- **Forms.** Forms are great for receiving information from users. Most forms are easy to set up providing a "script" is available on the server. These forms e-mail you the data entered by the user.
- **Links.** Avoid external links, or links linking to websites other than your own. Visitors very easily get lost and you do not want users to leave your website. If you do link to external sites, consider opening the link in a new window.
- **Content.** Your site can look amazing but if it lacks good content then people will not stay, nor will they come back. It has been said that an advertisement is a sales pitch in writing. Consider a website a form of advertisement. Write your content like you would write a sales presentation. What action are you trying to get the visitor to take? Think, "call to action".
- **Dynamic content.** A website with dynamic, or constantly changing content, is one that will keep users coming back for more. Discussion boards, chat rooms, tips of the day, anything that will make your website different tomorrow than it is today.
- **Interactivity.** Websites are capable of being so much more than on-line brochures. Take advantage of the tremendous power of the Internet and embrace some of the technology that will help you attract and maintain visitors.
- **Navigation.** Make your menus as clear and descriptive as possible. Make it easy for visitors to find what they are looking for and most of all, make it easy for visitors to take action.

3. **Promote.** Once your site is created and tested, it is time to get the word out. Promotion is not a one day event; it is usually a continual process that lasts as long as the website itself. Promotion is a key ingredient to the website success formula. When you launch a website, you are essentially competing with billions of other websites. How are people going to find your website? There are entire books written on this subject alone. My advice: think

creatively. You may find greater success promoting your website off-line than you will on-line.

One of the biggest mistakes made by website owners is wasting time and money by lowering their prices, redesigning their website, and rewriting their copy, when in fact they really need to be getting more traffic to their site. The next time you feel your problem is with your prices, design, or copy, think about the boy who setup the lemonade stand in his garage over one mile away from the street.

4. **Maintain.** Very few websites run themselves completely. In fact, I am not aware of any that do. There is always some manual intervention needed to keep a website running effectively, which requires either your time or money.

- **Automation.** Begin by automating as much as possible. If it costs some money to have a script developed to automate tasks, which will save you hours per week, then it is most likely worth it. Think long-term.
- **Support.** If you have visitors, the chances are you will have visitors with questions. For unique questions that cannot be answered by an autoresponder or on a FAQ, or to accommodate your visitors that like to work only with real people, you will need to have a support system in place. This can be as simple as an e-mail address that you respond to, or as complex as an international support department with a sophisticated intranet back-end. Take care of your visitors and they will take care of you.
- **Security.** If you have a good web host provider, security should not be a major issue. However, you should still be careful with sending passwords, credit cards, and other personal information through non-secure connections. Always change your passwords on a regular basis.

Plan, create, promote, and maintain. Each step is equally important and vital in the success of any website. A successful website is the result of a good idea from a successful thinker. To most creators, a website is a very personal thing that they take pride in maintaining and sharing with the world. Create a website and at the very least, enjoy the feeling of accomplishment that goes along with the creation.

ACTION STEP(S):

1) Time for some brainstorming... what kind of website could you create? Write down as many ideas as you can think of and consider acting on your best idea. It can prove to be a very rewarding experience.

"It may not always be profitable at first for businesses to be on-line, but it is certainly going to be unprofitable not to be on-line."

- Esther Dyson

Day 304: Inspiration from Arthur M. Blank

Arthur M. Blank (1942–) is the co-founder of The Home Depot, which is the world's largest home improvement retailer and is the second largest retailer in the United States.

Success is not something into which one is born. Arthur Blank was born in Queens, New York in 1942 and with his parents and brother shared a series of one-bedroom apartments.

Success is having entrepreneurial spirit. In his college years, Arthur launched his own landscaping company, laundry business, and even found time to baby sit on the side.

Success is moving onward and upward. In 1978, Arthur Blank and Bernard Marcus (other co-founder of The Home Depot) were fired from the Handy Dan home improvement chain where they were working at the time. This was the event that let to their creation of The Home Depot.

Success is brainstorming. The idea for the Home Depot was mapped out on a napkin by Arthur and Bernie at their favorite coffee shop.

Success often means having to take a step backward in order to take a giant leap forward. When the first three Home Depot stores were opened in Atlanta in 1979, they lost nearly one million dollars.

Success is innovation. The Home Depot has been incredibly successful due to some of the innovations it has brought to the marketplace, such as warehouse-sized stores with large inventories, very low prices, and exceptional customer service provided by skilled professionals.

Success is making a difference. Blank believes in the importance of making a difference—professionally and personally. In addition to the company's financial success, during his 23 years with The Home Depot the company donated more than $113 million to communities, and Home Depot associates provided hundreds of thousands of hours of personal volunteer time.

Success is keeping fit. Arthur is a strong believer in work-life balance; he still makes time daily for working out and remains an avid runner.

[Sources: http://www.homedepot.com, http://www.zeromillion.com, http://www.lemonadestories.com, http://www.cba.gsu.edu]

"Bleeding orange means investing in employees, being present and accounted for in your community, giving back to those less fortunate, knowing that we are not that smart and listening to those that are, and not standing on the sidelines."

- Arthur M. Blank

Day 305: Dealing with Difficult People

It all starts in preschool. You are minding your own business while building a magnificent castle out of wooden blocks. Just as you are putting the finishing touches on tallest tower, some kid named Billy Sanderson, wearing a t-shirt that reads "Born To Be Bad", pretends he's Godzilla and destroys your creation. He then turns to you, opens his big mouth with his two little pointer fingers, sticks out his tongue, then runs off. After you take a moment to digest the situation, you pick up a wooden block, and like an Australian hunting down a kangaroo with a boomerang, you forcefully whip the block at your fleeing adversary. While he cascades into a pile of tinker toys, a feeling of satisfaction overcomes you knowing that you have just dealt with your first difficult person. Unfortunately, dealing with difficult people becomes more challenging outside of preschool. What we need as adults are techniques and philosophies, not wooden blocks.

A difficult person is not the same as an angry person, although a difficult person can be, and often is, angry. A difficult person is not just one who engages in debate or stands up for what he or she believes. A difficult person is characterized by being unreasonable. To be fair and to avoid casting labels on people, all people can be difficult at times. However, it just takes one instance of unreasonable behavior for someone to earn the label "difficult".

For some people, being difficult appears to be in their "nature". Some people actually get joy and satisfaction from arguing, criticizing, condemning and complaining. Some people are conditioned to be that way due to a lifetime of negative experiences; being difficult is their defense. Others just want to be heard; they want a sympathetic ear and someone who will give them the attention they desire. No excuse, however, can justify the unyielding and irrational behavior of a difficult person.

Ideally, avoiding difficult people is better than dealing with them. However, when mere avoidance is not possible or practical, we must deal with difficult people. When you find yourself in a situation confronted by a difficult person, try this three-step process:

1. **Control your emotions.** Never allow a difficult person to get you down or angered. Not controlling an emotion such as anger can be seen as a sign of weakness, which can be further exploited. Acting in anger only leads to regret. When you remain calm, there is a good chance that the difficult person will calm down to match your demeanor.

2. **Separate yourself from the situation.** A "trick" difficult people use is making you one with the situation. For example, while standing in line to return a defective movie I purchased, I witnessed a customer yelling at the clerk, "How can you sell such junk?!" That fact is, the clerk is not at all responsible for selecting the items that particular superstore carries. Separating yourself from the situation will help you to remain calm and handle the situation more effectively.

3. **Do your best to get the difficult person to think and act rationally.** This is best accomplished by getting the other person to calm down. Now as a general rule, it is not a good idea to tell someone in a heightened emotional state to calm down or relax; this would only make the other person more defensive. Instead, use your knowledge of human behavior to help the other person see the situation from your point of view.

   o **Identify a common goal.** Show the other person that you are on the same side and that you both want a fair resolution to the problem. For example, no matter how unreasonable a person is being, never tell that person that they are being unreasonable. Instead, make sure you let him know that it is his request that you feel is unreasonable, then offer an alternative solution. "I feel your request is unreasonable, and I am quite sure my boss will as well. But here is what I suggest we do..."

- o **Agree on as many points as possible.** No matter how unreasonable the ranting of another may be, there are usually one or two points on which you can agree. Listen closely for these points and make it known that you agree with them. This will help you to establish trust.

- o **Ask questions.** One of the reasons people act unreasonable at times is they fail to ask themselves some obvious questions. This is quite common: when we don't want to know the answer we don't ask the question. To illustrate, I often deal with customers who demand refunds on months of web hosting service because they say that they "didn't use it". Instead of directing them to our service level agreement where our policy is clearly stated, I say "Even though you did not use the service, we still provided the service and incurred the associated expenses. Do you think it is fair that you should not pay for the service during this time?" Usually, that gets an "I guess not" response but if it does not I use the somewhat ironic analogy, "What do you think the cable company would say if you demanded six months credit because you told them you have not been watching TV?"

- o **Inject humor.** Since difficult people generally do not have good senses of humor—at least not while they are being difficult, this one can be a bit risky. However, reasonable people who are just having a bad day or acting out of character will generally respond well to a little humor. By the way, the best counter to the standard "What? You think this is funny?" response to humor is, "No, but I thought my joke was."

You should never expect to turn every difficult person around; you can only do your best. If at any time you feel the threat of physical harm, let the person know that they are making you feel uncomfortable and if possible call for backup (manager, supervisor, friend). Sometimes a great attitude and exceptional diplomatic skills is not enough to break through a life-long pattern of another's unreasonable behaviors. However, possessing the ability to deal with difficult people will be of tremendous value to you in many situations, and it is an ability that can help you to get ahead in just about anything you do.

ACTION STEP(S):

---

1) The next time you have the opportunity, spend about 15 minutes eavesdropping on conversations at a store's returns and exchanges counter. Pay attention to the clerks' responses.

"Reasonable people adapt themselves to the world. Unreasonable people attempt to adapt the world to themselves. All progress, therefore, depends on unreasonable people."

- George Bernard Shaw

Day 306: Reading Body Language

Recently I was at a social event where I was engaged in a casual conversation with another guest. As he was talking to me, my children were getting antsy and wanting to go. I frequently, but politely, glanced over at them, giving them the "one moment" hand signal and turned my body toward the door, while still making eye contact with the other guest who was still talking to me. After what seemed to be at least five minutes, my son had dropped his pizza on the floor allowing me to interrupt the other guest, excuse myself, and rush over to assist my son. Although I did not speak the words, my body language was screaming, "I really have to go now" for several minutes; the other guest who was doing the talking just did not see it. Result: an awkward situation that could have easily been avoided.

It is said that over 90% of communication is more than just the words we use and 60% of our communication is nonverbal, or body language. It is also believed that nonverbal signs have about five times more impact than verbal ones. To illustrate, imagine yourself meeting two new people. The first person coldly says, "Nice to meet you" while not even making eye contact with you. The second person says nothing, but looks on you with a warm smile and open arms, then proceeds to give you a compassionate hug. After you say to yourself, "OK...this is weird," you realize the spoken words or lack of spoken words actually meant very little. The ability to read or effectively interpret body language can

- help you to close more sales by allowing you to detect apprehension and excitement in prospects
- help you in your personal life by allowing you to detect when others are interested in you
- help you detect when people are being dishonest with you
- help you to become a more effective communicator
- make you a better poker player

In general, having the ability to read body language is an important part of success.

Body language can be both a natural and a learned behavior. Some body language is cultural as in the handshake or the bow. Some body language, like dramatically removing the spectacles to show intense interest, is picked up from watching movies. Some body language does appear to be natural, such as the facial expressions that represent our emotions. In reading body language, it is important to understand that it is an art and not a science; that is, just because someone folds their arms does not mean they are being defensive—they could just be cold. It is up to you to use other indicators such as your common sense to know the difference.

Here are just some of the more common nonverbal signals and their generally accepted interpretations.

- **Body not facing you while speaking:** let me go!
- **Looking at watch or clock:** bored
- **Doodling:** bored
- **Foot tapping:** anxious or bored
- **Open body (neither arms nor legs crossed):** open mind, acceptance
- **Arms or legs crossed:** defensive, not accepting what you are saying
- **Starting to walk away while talking:** do not want to spend time talking—in a hurry
- **Fidgety hands:** nervousness or lying
- **Shifty eyes:** mostly lying
- **Leaning in:** interested
- **Leaning away:** uninterested or disagreeing
- **Hands behind head while leaning back in chair:** confidence, superiority, accomplishment
- **Hand covering mouth:** nervous, lying, bad breath
- **Slouching / head down:** lack of confidence, lack of enthusiasm

Once you can read body language, you can also use body language to project the image or emotion you desire. For example, expressive individuals use their whole body when speaking. This makes them appear more interesting and enthusiastic. If you are giving a sales presentation to a prospect, you want to avoid shifty eyes and covering your mouth while speaking. Since people tend to mirror body language, if you want someone to accept what you are saying, don't cross your arms or lean away.

Just as it is important to actively listen, it is important to actively watch, or listen, with your eyes as well as your ears. People more often say what they mean with their body language than they do with their words. Be a more effective communicator by becoming a keen observer of body language.

ACTION STEP(S):

1) Next time you speak with someone, pay particular attention to their body language. What does their body language tell you? Does it match what they are saying with words?

Days 307 and 308 are for "R&R"—review and reflection. Spend these days reviewing the last five articles and reflecting on the information and how it relates to your life. Now is also a good time to make sure all the action steps for the previous days have been completed.

Day 309: Resolutions

January 1, the date when millions of people around the world make what they call "New Year's resolutions". January 3, the date that about 50% of those people "fall off the wagon". By February 1, more than 90% of those "resolution" makers decided that their "resolutions" were not that important after all. Most people make New Year's resolutions as frivolously as deciding what to watch on television. Even if you are one of the few with the best intentions of keeping to your commitment, if you can't resolve to do something right now, the chances are you won't do it in the new year.

Resolution is defined as the state or quality of being resolute—firm determination. A resolution is not a goal, or not something that you "try" to do; it is something you do. When you make a resolution, there is no turning back, and failure to stick to your resolution is not an option. Most true resolutions are made in moments of inspiration. It is like a moment of pure clarity when you just know with your heart, mind, and soul that you do not just want to do something, but must do something. To find this moment of inspiration and clarity, arm yourself with enough "whys", or reasons why you are committed to this resolution.

Resolutions can be divided into two general categories: the "give up" resolutions and the "to do" resolutions, each with their own specific ways to help ensure successful resolutions.

The "give up" resolution. When you resolve to give something up, you must have a reasonable substitute prepared. The better the substitute (the more pleasurable and less painful) the more successful the resolution will be. For example, if you resolve to give up drinking cola and other carbonated, sugared or artificially sweetened beverages, then have a drink ready to substitute—hopefully one that is better for your health.

The "to do" resolutions. Although resolutions should not be confused with goals that you may or may not reach, resolutions, like goals, must be as specific as possible. A resolution such as "get in shape" is very vague where no specific actions are given. However, a resolution to "jog on the treadmill for at least five miles a day, four days a week" is much better.

For any resolution, realize that once it becomes a habit, it becomes much easier to adhere to. How long something takes to become a habit depends on both the person and the something. As time passes, the uncomfortable feeling of change inevitably subsides. Have faith.

There is a law that can be your best friend or worst enemy when it comes to resolutions. This is the law of momentum. An automobile uses more gas to get going then it does to maintain its current speed. Like an automobile, resolutions take more energy to begin than they do to maintain. If you were to consistently step on the gas, then jam on brakes, you would not get very far before running out of gas. The same holds true for your resolutions. Once you resolve to do something, conserve energy and stick with it.

A resolution is not a goal, it is a commitment backed by firm determination. When you resolve to do or not to do something, you remove all other options. If you can't start your New Year's resolutions right now, the chances are you will not be able to keep them in the new year, and your "resolutions" are nothing more than items on your wish list that will most likely remain there year after year. You have got the will power and the ability inside you— make true resolutions right now.

ACTION STEP(S):

1) Make at least one resolution today—right now.

Day 310: The Martial Arts

I will never forget that one summer night back in 1985 in Bridgeport, Connecticut, when I was 13 years old. I was with a group of friends in a mini-mall parking lot, waiting for our ride home. All of the stores had closed and just a few of the parking lot lights had remained on—it was not the best place for a bunch of kids from the "good side of town" to be after dark. In the distance, we saw a large group of older kids approaching. When they spotted us, they stopped and only one of the group members came forward. By this kid's appearance, we could tell he was a local, and by his words and actions we could clearly tell he was looking for trouble. In that moment, I felt completely helpless and vulnerable like never before. Just minutes later, our ride arrived and we were free from danger. But it was in that moment of complete vulnerability that I made the decision to learn how to defend myself so I never had to feel that way again.

The general term "martial arts" refers to the many styles that instruct in the art of hand and foot fighting that have been developed over a period of 2,000 years. Today, martial arts are practiced by close to 20 million people in over 100 countries, recently evolving into a modern international Olympic sport. But martial arts is much more than a sport; like success, it is a lifetime process of self-improvement and self-discovery. Martial arts helps us realize our true potential both physically and mentally. Here are just some of the benefits:

- **Discipline.** Through martial arts, we learn how discipline can help us in anything we do.
- **Patience.** The fluidity and gracefulness of style and technique takes years, even a lifetime, to master. By seeing frequent improvements in our own abilities, we learn patience.
- **Balance and coordination.** We build balance and coordination by consistently taking control of our bodies and concentrating on our form. We learn that our minds

have complete control over our bodies; it just takes practice to exercise that control.

- **Self-confidence.** Once one feels confident in the ability to defend oneself, a feeling of confidence like none other is developed. I believe this level of confidence has helped me to avoid more conflicts in both my childhood and adult life than any diplomatic communication skill I possess.
- **Self-control.** Martial arts is not about learning how to fight, it is about learning how to defend. The entire philosophy of martial arts revolves around peace and self-control. Once trained in martial arts, you can use non-violent, defensive, and controlled moves when necessary instead of throwing fists, which is most people's only defense.
- **Defense.** Someday within your lifetime, you may need to defend yourself or your loved ones. Being prepared for such an unfortunate event significantly reduces the fear associated with the possible event.
- **Fitness.** Training in martial arts is a great physical activity, from the relaxing workouts of Tai Chi to the more aggressive workouts of Tae Kwon Do.
- **Concentration, focus and visualization.** Breaking boards is not just for show; it takes an extreme amount of mental energy. Through martial arts, we learn to develop these mental skills that are so valuable in life.
- **Goals.** Most martial arts are rank based systems, that is, students are rewarded frequently by promotion in rank, usually signified by a color belt. This system of rewarding achievement gives students something to look forward to; it gives them goals.
- **Influence.** Joining a martial arts class is just another way to surround yourself with positive people and meet new friends. It is, and should be, a social and enjoyable journey.

It is unfortunate that many people get turned off by martial arts because they do not ask themselves the right questions when looking for a school. So in the spirit of success, here is a quick guide to choosing the right martial arts school.

1. **Choose the right instructor.** I believe that the most important factor is finding the right instructor. The instructor sets the example for the students to follow. You want an instructor that possesses the qualities and characteristics that you seek. You may need to try out a class or two before you can get a good sense of his or her character.

2. **Consider convenience.** Look for schools that are within a reasonable commute from your place of work or home. Look for schools that have classes that fit your schedule. Do not let inconvenience be a roadblock.

3. **Choose a style.** There are many styles in the martial arts; all of which have different focuses and techniques. Choose a style that fits your goals. Here is a brief introduction to the most popular styles:

Aikido: A method of unarmed self-defense. It encourages discipline and a non-violent attitude. Its movements are made of joint twisting, grabbing, and bending.

Hapkido: An art form that uses a variety of counter-attacks and a combination of kicking and grabbing techniques. The art is at least 80% kicking, 20% grabbing and twisting techniques.

Jeet Kune Do: Founded by Bruce Lee, Jeet Kune Do is a combination of the best techniques of many styles into one concept.

Judo: Judo is a method of turning an opponent's strength against him. It uses a lot of throwing and flipping techniques.

Karate: An offensive and defensive art form that contains both hand strikes and kicking techniques. It includes a variety of blocks and powerful blows.

Kenpo/Kempo Karate: An American style of Karate. It is a combination of short hand and kicking techniques. It is also influenced by Chinese Kung Fu.

Kung Fu: Kung Fu is a flowing art that requires balance and combination techniques. It also includes a huge arsenal of weapons.

Kickboxing: Also called full-contact karate, kickboxing utilizes the techniques learned in karate or kung fu in the ring, as well as boxing techniques and training.

Tae Kwon Do: Tae Kwon Do is a native Korean art that is comprised of 90% kicking. It is extremely popular among children in America.

Tai Chi: Tai Chi is practiced in the west today and can perhaps best be thought of as a moving form of yoga and meditation combined.

Martial arts is not about fighting; it's about building character. I believe that the skills that I have learned in my martial arts training has helped me get where I am today. Consider joining a martial arts class for its physical, mental, and social benefits, or if you are raising children over the age of four, consider introducing them to martial arts. The skills, abilities, and character built will, without question, help you (or your children) to achieve success.

ACTION STEP(S):

1) Take at least one self-defense class. There are classes at local YMCAs, gyms, and of course at the many independent martial arts studios.

Day 311: Inspiration from Dave Thomas

David Thomas (1932-2002) is the founder of Wendy's, one of the world's largest restaurant chains of over 5,000 restaurants located throughout the U.S. and in 34 countries.

Success is humility. In his books and in interviews, Thomas talks of being approached by those who recognize him from television and say he must be someone famous. Dave says he replies, "I'm nobody, really. I just make hamburgers for a living."

Success is having positive influences in your life. Dave's adoptive grandmother, Minnie Sinclair, taught Dave that as long as you work hard you will never have enough time to feel bad for yourself. Miss Sinclair also taught him that he should never cut corners (thus the square hamburgers) because the minute you begin to cheat yourself, you begin to lose quality and performance.

Success is in moments of inspiration. After the death of Dave's birth mother, and his father's divorce of his stepmother, Dave and his father began to eat out more. This was when Dave got the idea of someday owning his own restaurants.

Success is in moments of conviction. In his youth, Dave was fired from several jobs, some due to the fact that he had to lie about his age. Dave's father was so upset that he told Dave that he would never be able to hold down a job as long as he lived. Dave was so affected by his words that he made a vow to himself that he would never lose another job as long as he lived.

Success is getting experience. After his employer became an early Kentucky Fried Chicken franchise in 1956, Mr. Thomas worked closely with Colonel Sanders, instituting now-famous innovations and acquiring his own hugely successful Kentucky Fried Chicken franchise in Columbus, Ohio from stores he 'turned around.' He later returned to KFC management, in charge of 300 stores.

Success is thinking huge. Dave opened the first Wendy's Old Fashioned hamburgers restaurant November 15, 1969 in Columbus, Ohio. Then, in 1973, Dave began franchising the Wendy's concept.

Success is promotion. Dave was a great promoter. One of Wendy's most successful promotions ever was with the "little old lady" Clara Piller (now an 80s icon). She was the old woman who made famous the line, "Where's the Beef?"

Success is thinking of others. Thomas established the Dave Thomas Foundation for Adoption in 1992, a not-for-profit organization focused on raising public awareness of adoption issues.

Success is for the "average guy". Dave Thomas was an adopted child who dropped out of high school and had no advantages growing up. Dave proved that success is anyone's; they just have to want it and take it.

[Sources: http://www.medaloffreedom.com, http://columbusoh.about.com, Thomas R.David. Dave's Way-A New Approach to Old Fashioned Success. New York: G.P. Putham Sons, 1991.]

"It all comes back to the basic. Serve customers the best-tasting food at a good value in a clean, comfortable restaurant, and they'll keep coming back."

- Dave Thomas

Day 312: The Referral

Imagine a referral so powerful that with it, you become an instant success in anything you do. Such a referral does exist—it comes from the daytime talkshow queen Oprah Winfrey. As an author, a referral from her on her show means your book will be an almost guaranteed best seller (yes, I did send her a copy of my book). Other powerful forms of referrals come from critics, as in art, food, film, and others. However, the most common form of referral is the personal referral, which can be just as powerful but is usually directed to a much smaller audience or even a single individual. It is the personal referral that helps the employee get the job they desire, the salesperson make sales, and the businessperson succeed.

It is understood that prospecting can be one of the most difficult parts of the sales process. Successful sales is about being efficient with your time. The average salesperson wastes much time breaking down the door of resistance to each prospect he or she approaches. A referral is like the key to the door that allows the salesperson to walk right in. A referral is based on the concept of trust by association; if someone you trust trusts a third party, then you will most likely trust that third party as well. Consider the woman who agrees to go on a blind date with her best friend's cousin, just because her best friend thought it would be a good idea. Or the office supplies salesperson who gets an instant appointment with the very busy president of a large corporation, just because they both share the same good friend who speaks highly of the salesperson. Good referrals will increase your sales success rate significantly.

The referral process can be broken down into three important parts:

1. Who and when to ask for a referral
2. How to ask for a referral
3. How to use a referral

The goal in this process is to be as smooth as possible so as to avoid resistance from those whom you ask for the referrals, and from those on whom you use the referrals.

1) Who and when to ask for a referral. The best source of referrals are current or past customers whom you believe are satisfied with your product. Some feel it is a little aggressive to ask for a referral the moment a sale was made, and would rather wait until the first follow-up call. However, in some cases it is best to ask for referrals the moment service is rendered, while the customer is "hot". Asking friends and family for referrals can be effective, but also a source of much conflict if anything goes wrong. Use your own judgment here.

2) How to ask for a referral.

- **Ask in real time.** Many studies have shown that you are much more likely to get referrals when asking in person or on the telephone. It is generally not a good idea to rely on forms that customers must fill out and return.
- **Ask for three referrals.** When you ask for a specific number, such as three, you most often will get it. By asking specific questions, you will get specific answers. If you were to ask for just "referrals" you may get the response, "Let me think about that and I will get back to you" which is generally a blow-off answer.
- **Ask about the relationship.** When you ask for the referrals, do not only ask for contact information, but ask how they are associated with the person. For example, after the customer gives you the names and numbers of three people, you may ask, "And are these business associates?" This information will come in handy later on.
- **Make sure the customer is satisfied.** Asking for referrals from an unsatisfied customer can be a very awkward experience. You can use "yes" questions

to turn a neutral customer into a satisfied customer. For example, ask "Is [the product or service] working well for you?", "Do you feel it was money well spent?" Ask questions you are confident will give you "yes" answers that will help the customer realize how satisfied they really are.

o **Show the benefit.** Remember the question that is on the mind of customers, "What's in it for me?" Before asking for the referrals, show the customer how he will be helping those he refers, not hurting. This can usually be done by saying something similar to, "Mr. Customer, since [your product or service] has helped you [benefit], can you think of three of your [business associates, friends, family, etc.] that I would be able to help as well?"

3) How to use a referral. Remember a referral is your key to the door of resistance. If you encounter a secretary, administrative assistant, or other gatekeeper, take out your key. If you are asked the question, "What is this regarding?" say, "Mr. Smith, from XYZ Corp., suggested I give Mr. Jones a call." Identify both the person who referred you and their company. When you do get to speak directly to the prospect, make the referral as indirect as possible. Mention the person who referred you and their relationship to the prospect. For example, "I have been helping your brother, Tim, with [project] and he thought I might be able to help you as well".

Never be afraid to ask a good customer for a referral or ask a friend to "put in a good word" for you in a social situation. One good referral can potentially lead to an endless supply of prospects, most of whom will give you little to no resistance. This is the secret of the efficient and successful salesperson.

ACTION STEP(S):

---

1) Make a list of those business associates, friends, and family that may be able to "put a good word" for you. Call upon members of this list when the time is right.

"In sales, a referral is the key to the door of resistance."

- Bo Bennett

Day 313: Hope

"Refusal to hope is nothing more than a decision to die." Powerful words from the best-selling author and perhaps foremost expert on understanding the gift of hope, Bernie S. Siegel, M.D. Hope is a gift, and perhaps one of the greatest gifts bestowed upon mankind. But hope, when misunderstood, can also be a curse. It is this false hope that causes more people to fail and lose control of their lives than those that just give up on life. A key element to both success and happiness is understanding the power of hope.

There are a few words in the English language that are are often interchanged with the word hope. These words are wish, faith and pray. However, each word is does have significant differences. To hope is to wish for something with expectation of its fulfillment. A wish is a desire, longing, or strong inclination for a specific thing, with no specific level of expectation. Faith is a belief that does not rest on logical proof or material evidence, whereas a prayer is a reverent petition to God, a god, or another object of worship. The confusing of these words with each other usually just results in a minor grammatical faux pas, but when any of these words, especially hope, is confused with action, the results are much more devastating.

Aristotle described hope as a waking dream. Dreams are vital to success and achievement, but dreams without action are just dreams. Hope is no different. Those who spend their lives just hoping may live a positive life, but it would be a life of dreams and not one of achievement. Your hopes are only good to one person—you. All great achievement throughout history is a result of action, not just hope.

So why is hope one of mankind's greatest gifts? The mental power of hope combined with the physical power of action is one of the greatest forces we humans possess. A lawyer may hope for the best results for her client, at the same time being sure to prepare the best case possible. The Red Sox may hope to win a World

Series, while doing their best to make sure they are up to the physical and mental challenge. Hope, by itself, also has its place. Hoping for things we have no control over is one of the ways we can alter our own perception of the world to our favor. This hope is the fuel that keeps us going in the darkest of times. It is hope that allows us to visualize a brighter future. "Hope itself is a species of happiness, and, perhaps, the chief happiness which the world affords," wrote Samuel Johnson.

The pain and suffering of millions of people could be eased if they removed just one word from their vocabulary—hopeless. One of the most influential women in modern American history, Clare Boothe Luce, said it best, "There are no hopeless situations; there are only men who have grown hopeless about them." While some situations may not be within your control, since hope comes from within, there is always hope.

Hope can be both a blessing and a curse. To avoid the curse, never rely purely on hope when action can be taken. To enjoy the blessing, use hope along with action to accomplish the seemingly impossible. And when a situation is out of your control, hang on to hope; even though it may be all you have, it may prove to be enough.

ACTION STEP(S):

---

1) Are you in a situation now that you believe to be "hopeless"? Recall the words of Clare Boothe Luce, "There are no hopeless situations; there are only men who have grown hopeless about them." Think more carefully about the situation and do not lose hope.

2) What are you hoping for now? Is there any action you can take that will make your hopes become realities? If so, take the action.

"Hope sees the invisible, feels the intangible and achieves the impossible."

- Anonymous

Days 314 and 315 are for "R&R"—review and reflection. Spend these days reviewing the last five articles and reflecting on the information and how it relates to your life. Now is also a good time to make sure all the action steps for the previous days have been completed.

Day 316: Dare To Be Different

There never was, nor ever will be, anyone exactly like you. Physically, your fingerprints, voice, eyes, teeth, and DNA can distinguish you from any other person living or dead. Mentally, your thoughts, dreams, and experiences are yours and only yours. So why does the world consist of so many "average" people? Why do so many people fight their desires for greatness and work so hard at "blending in with the crowd"? Why don't more people dare to be different?

Collectively, societies create and define what are called "norms". These societal norms tend to serve as standards to which most people adhere. Average people are only average because they choose to look, speak, and act like others who fit in this norm. Norms, for the most part, are a necessary part of any society and can help individuals avoid negative attention, like running though the city naked. Adhering to norms also, however, causes individuals to miss out on positive attention that comes as a result of actions and behaviors that are not part of the norm.

What are considered normal behaviors and actions are often based on our desire for instant gratification. As we already know, acting on this desire is one of the greatest obstacles on the road to success. Our psychological need for belonging is constantly directing us to the norm. In order to satisfy our higher need of self-actualization (where we find success), we must place a lesser importance on the need for belonging. Realize that by being different, you are not alone. Everyone is different and everyone is unique in his or her own way; however, very few people have the courage to express themselves.

It has been said that the difference between insanity and genius is success. In actuality, the difference between *apparent* insanity and genius is success. Walter P. Chrysler was a nut who bought a new car and immediately took it apart and put it back together several times until the world discovered that his eccentric behavior led to his fortune. Wilbur and Orville Wright were two nuts who were trying to fly like birds—until they actually succeeded, now they are historical heroes. Chrysler, the Wright brothers, and thousands of others who achieved great success had the courage to deviate from the norm and be different.

Being different does not necessarily have to mean being an outcast of society. In high school, I had a chemistry teacher who used to celebrate students' birthdays by writing their names with a highly flammable liquid on the classroom floor, shutting off the lights, setting liquid on fire, and leading the class in "Happy Birthday". Although this one act had very little to do with chemistry, it created a bond between the teacher and the students. To this day, I remember more from that tenth-grade class than any other class and I will never forget Mr. Norris.

Although all people are very unique and different from each other, most people tend to behave similarly in order to "fit in". If your need for belonging is strong, then fit in with people like Chrysler and the Wright brothers, not with the unhappy, work-despising, 20 pounds overweight, $20K-in-debt individual whose only joy in life comes from a bottle and the rare two-week vacation. Have the courage to do what others will not do. Stand out and get noticed. Dare to be different.

ACTION STEP(S):

1) Do something to stand out from the crowd: wear a crazy tie or a silly hat, help a stranger in need when others ignore the stranger, do anything (neutral or positive) to differentiate yourself from the masses.

Day 317: Building the Perfect You

I remember playing video games that let the players choose their character. Each available character has strengths and weaknesses, yet all the characters are equal overall. For example, in the game "Tekken", at times I would to choose the bear, who's very strong but tends to be very slow. Other times, I would choose Lee who was very fast, but not that strong. In real life, we all have our strengths and weaknesses, but unlike these video games, by no means are we all equal. In real life, we have the ability to maximize our strengths and minimize our weaknesses. All it takes is conscious effort and awareness.

For the purpose of this article, assume that your actions, behaviors, and thoughts make you who you are today, since you have a certain degree of control over these. Also understand that I use the word "perfect" loosely, knowing that perfection is, for the most part, unattainable. Building the perfect you is about consciously adopting empowering qualities and abandoning the negative qualities you have subconsciously adopted over the years. These qualities come in the form of

- mannerisms
- gestures
- words (expressions, sayings, vulgarities)
- reactions
- habits
- hobbies
- ideas
- beliefs

Who are you? Think about those people in your past and present who have been an influence to you: family, friends, teachers, spiritual leaders, actors, and even world leaders. Can't you see some of their qualities in yourself? Parents are so concerned with their children being negatively influenced by their peers, yet as adults do not realize that they are influenced in the same way.

Being influenced by others is not something one "grows out of". Once you are consciously aware of this influencing process, you can begin by "rebuilding" yourself by changing your actions, behaviors, and thoughts. Then, start adopting the positive qualities from those you admire most.

We are all, to some degree, a product of our environment. Subconsciously we have become like those who have been an influence to us in our lives. We do not have to accept this as who we are—we can choose to change who we have become and start becoming the person we really want to be. Do not let habit and adversity to personal change get in the way of your success. Take the time and make the effort to build the perfect you.

ACTION STEP(S):

---

1) (Note: This can be a very long exercise, but one that is well worth it) Make a list of all your negative qualities, or qualities that you feel may be getting in the way of your success. Be honest with yourself. Now, consider each quality and think about where you got it. Was it from a parent? An old friend? A movie? If you can make the connection that the quality was a result of negative influence, it is easier to abandon.

2) (Note: This can be a very long exercise, but one that is well worth it) Make a list of all of the people in your life, or in history, that you admire most. Write down what it is you admire about them most. What actions are these people taking? By taking the same actions, can you adopt those qualities? If not, how can you adopt those qualities?

Day 318: Inspiration from Bruce Jenner

Bruce Jenner (1949–) earned the title of "World's Greatest Athlete" by winning the gold medal in the decathlon at the 1976 Olympic Games in Montreal.

Success is overcoming adversity. Jenner grew up terrified of reading due to dyslexia, but he says his struggles with the reading disorder helped him learn to overcome adversity. "I firmly believe that deep in their soul everyone has a champion that can overcome obstacles and do great things."

Success is hard work. "You have to work hard at things to be good," Jenner says. When preparing for the Olympics, he trained six to eight hours every day for four years.

Success is loving and pursuing what you are good at. Jenner does appear to have the aptitude for athletic ability. Jenner writes in his book, "By the time I turned two, I'd already developed a big chest, wide shoulders and boundless energy, prompting my dad to nickname me Bruiser."

Success is mostly in the attitude. "I always felt that my greatest asset was not my physical ability, it was my mental ability."

Success is moving forward. Unlike many who go downhill after their 15 minutes of fame, Jenner's success in life continues to this day. Besides an Olympic gold medalist, Jenner is known to millions as a motivational speaker, TV personality, sports commentator, commercial spokesperson, entrepreneur, actor, producer, and a terrific father of ten children.

Success is being a positive role model for others. Jenner leads by example. He wants his kids to take their health seriously, so he eats healthy meals.

Success is not in what you do, but how you do it. Jenner teaches his kids how to meet goals and free their harshest critic and best cheerleader: the champion within. "I don't care what arena kids choose to play in – sports, music, school, figure skating – I encourage my kids to find something in life to get excited about when they wake up in the morning."

Success is remaining humble. When asked how he would like to be remembered, Jenner states he would like to be remembered as a good parent.

Success is found in good advice. "Start early and begin raising the bar throughout the day."

[Sources: http://brucejenner.com, http://iparenting.com, http://abilitymagazine.com]

"I learned that the only way you are going to get anywhere in life is to work hard at it. Whether you're a musician, a writer, an athlete or a businessman, there is no getting around it. If you do, you'll win—if you don't, you won't."

- Bruce Jenner

Day 319: Modesty and Self-Promotion

Since the day we were born and all throughout our youth, we have been overly praised for our accomplishments. When we first say "blah-blah" we were given a big hug and a "hurrraaayy!". When we made our first drawing of a house, which looked more like a house after a tornado had struck it, the drawing was hung on the refrigerator for all to see and admire. Then one day, we are taught that when we bring our accomplishments to the attention of others, it is called "bragging", and what used to get praise now gets scorn. For many people, without the praise, the desire for achievement is lost and others feel that boasting and bragging are necessary for all great achievements. This confusion about humility and modesty continues throughout our adult lives. Fortunately, there are some general guidelines that can keep you modest while making your achievements well known.

There is no question that humility and modesty are admirable qualities. However, these very admirable qualities also can be stumbling blocks on the road to success. There are so many talented people whose talents, achievements, and potential contributions to this world go undiscovered due to their desire to remain modest. Through the proper use of self-promotion and understanding of modesty, one can remain both humble and modest while being recognized for their achievements and talents that lead to success.

To brag or to boast is to glorify oneself in speech or talk in a self-admiring way. Self-promotion is to make one's own accomplishments, talents, and potential contributions known to others. The difference is not in what you say, but how, why, and to whom you say it.

HOW: Consider the following statement: "I was just promoted to the new VP of Marketing which comes with a 20% pay increase and a company car." Imagine a really snotty person saying this statement while bragging. The accent would be on the word "I", the chin would be up in the air with the eyelids half closed, and there would be a little nod at the end of the statement as if to say, "good for me and bad for you". Now imagine a humble person saying the same words, but with excitement and the accent on "the new VP". Modesty is not always what we say, but how we say it.

WHY and WHOM: What is the purpose of making the statement? To whom is it being said? The "why" can be sharing, self-promotion, or bragging, depending on to whom it is being said (I said these were general guidelines, I did not say they were simple).

- **To make oneself feel good.** When we are proud of our accomplishments and filled with excitement, we have this inner desire to share the news with others. Perhaps the sharing of this news makes the situation more real to us, or perhaps we are just looking for some mild praise. In either case, we must carefully choose the people with whom we share the news. Close family and good friends are there for us as much as we are there for them. They are the ideal candidates for sharing the "good news".

- **To make others feel inferior or show one's superiority.** When one speaks of his or her own accomplishments or talents simply to make others feel inferior or in an attempt to prove superiority, he or she will most certainly be seen as boasting or bragging. For example, imagine the earlier statement about the promotion being said to co-workers who were in line for the same promotion.

- **To get others to like or respect you.** This is a common form of bragging most often used by young adults especially in the area of courting. It is a form of self-promotion, but for the wrong reasons. For example, if someone is trying to get to know you better, and you happen to be the state golf champion, tell that person that you enjoy golf and play frequently. If the other person persists with a line of questioning as to your ability, then answer the questions honestly and with modesty, but never volunteer information as to your above average ability in a social situation.

- **To get others to trust you.** Some people trust others unless given a reason not to, and others trust no one unless given a reason. When dealing with people in the latter category, it may be necessary to confidently state your credentials to earn their trust. For example, if your boss is asking for a volunteer to be the team leader on a new project, it would be wise to respond confidently telling her about the similar project you have successfully completed in the past. Again, speak with confidence and not with conceit.

- **To prove yourself in a business situation.** In just about all business situations, bragging, minus the self-admiring attitude, is considered good self-promotion. Do not be the quiet, shy type in business who remains just another face in the crowd. Have faith in your future contributions and let those who can help you achieve success know what you are capable of.

Here are two "laws" relating to self-promotion that you can use to your advantage in your pursuit of success.

The law of connection. The law of connection states that the stronger the connection to you, the weaker the influence of the information. For example, everyone looks their best on a resume. Employers know this, which is why they require referrals or recommendations from previous employers. When information on your accomplishments, talents, and/or abilities are delivered by a third party, especially one with nothing to gain by your success, it makes a more powerful impact. The most powerful impact comes as a result of someone discovering your talents on their own.

The law of status. The law of status states that the higher the status of the person, organization, or institution promoting you, the more powerful the impact. The perfect example of this is testimonials. Authors, companies, and others that use testimonials, will list testimonials starting with the most well known or respected people giving the testimonial. In this case, who said it is more important than what is said.

There is no doubt that the line between modesty and good self-promotion is a fine one. It is important to be proud of your accomplishments and promote yourself but at the same time remain humble and earn, not seek, the respect of others. It is not necessarily what you say, but how, why, and to whom you say it that makes the difference. Master this concept, and you will have taken a significant step in your journey of success.

ACTION STEP(S):

1) Think about those in your life with whom you wish to share information about your accomplishments. Are they supportive? Does the information make them feel worse about themselves or do they share your excitement?

"It is important that you recognize your progress and take pride in your accomplishments. Share your achievements with others. Brag a little. The recognition and support of those around you is nurturing."

- Rosemarie Rossetti

Day 320: Six Words To Successful Communication

There are six words in the English language that anyone interested in effective marketing and communication should know how to use. These words are what, who, where, when, why, and how. In both business and personal situations, answering these single word questions can add clarity, brevity and most important, effectiveness to your written and verbal communications.

Ahhh. You have just read this concept in action. **What:** six words (what, who, where, when, why, and how). **Who:** anyone interested in effective marketing and communication. **Where/When:** In both business and personal situations. **Why:** can add clarity, brevity and most important, effectiveness to your written and verbal communications. **How:** answering these single word questions. In the opening paragraph, I gave you "the bottom line"—the very basis of the article. Now in the rest of the article, I will expand on the concept. Hopefully, the opening paragraph has stimulated your interest enough to read the entire article.

This technique can be used in more than just articles. It can be used in speeches, presentations, advertisements (print, radio, TV), websites, briefs, and even in conversation. The fact is, most people have a relatively short attention span and it is up to you, the speaker, writer, or marketer, to communicate your idea before your audience loses interest. Remember, just because what you have to communicate is interesting to you, does not necessarily mean that it is interesting to your audience.

This "six-words" technique can be adapted in many ways. For example, for most topics, you can answer more than one "how" question. "How can using this technique help me to succeed?" "How can I use this technique in my personal communication?" For some topics there may not be an answer to one or more of the six questions, or at least not an answer worth giving. At times, you may choose not to answer all of the one-word questions but leave the audience "hanging" in order to entice the audience to take action.

We have all listened to people who ramble on and on in casual conversation, who we wish would practice this technique. Perhaps we were even one of those people at one time. This technique is great in personal conversation when finding topics of mutual interest. For example, not too long ago when I was getting my haircut, the woman cutting my hair assumed that I was interested in football and starting talking for over 10 minutes about the New England Patriots. After persisting to ask me questions about the subject about which I knew almost nothing, she caught on to the fact that I was clueless about the subject. She could have summed up her 10 minute story in a 15 second headline and saved both of us 9 3/4 minutes. If I were interested, I would have asked for more information or continued talking about the topic. She still did a good job on my hair so her communication faux pas did not affect her tip.

Use this technique both in business and personal situations for more effective communication. It is not enough just to state your point, you must communicate your point. Keep your audience interested and get your message across to more people in less time.

ACTION STEP(S):

---

1) The next time you have something "interesting" to tell someone, sum it up in a few sentences answering what, who, where, when, why, and how, and wait for the other person to prompt you for more details.

"Parents are not interested in justice, they're interested in peace and quiet."

- Bill Cosby

Days 321 and 322 are for "R&R"—review and reflection. Spend these days reviewing the last five articles and reflecting on the information and how it relates to your life. Now is also a good time to make sure all the action steps for the previous days have been completed.

Day 323: Believe in Yourself

I have a great idea for a reality TV show. We begin with 10 people who are successful in their fields, but not famous or even well known. Dress them up in clothing a homeless person would wear, give them a new identity and a history of nothing more than a grade school formal education and a series of odd jobs, then drop each one of our "participants" off in a major US city. The goal is to a) stay in the game and not quit and b) to acquire as much wealth as possible by the end of the season (about 3 months). The rules are that the participants cannot reveal their true identity and they cannot accept help from anyone they know in their real lives. What an awesome show that would be. We would witness the human spirit in action as well as characteristics and qualities of truly successful individuals. How would you do as a participant on that show?

There are so many people who appear to be successful and happy, who are financially well off, yet live in a constant state of fear. This is the fear of financial loss, which is almost universal to all those who are new to wealth. What if I lose my job? What if the market crashes? What if my business fails? All of these "what ifs" conjure up unpleasant thoughts for just about everybody; but those who believe in themselves, in their abilities, talents, and determination, do not fear these potential unfortunate events. A common characteristic among successful people is their knowing that if they lost everything financially, in time they would get it all back and more.

Unless you are a lottery winner or an heir/heiress to a fortune, you have earned what you now have. You must believe that your success is not due to random luck, but is a result of the circumstances that you have created, or at least influenced in the past. Those who fall down and don't get back up are the ones who lack the self-confidence and belief that they are the reason for their success, and if needed, can do it all again.

Donald Trump is a man who proved that success is not in what you have, but in who you are. Here is a man with enough belief in himself to come back from being $900 million dollars in debt to net worth of over a billion dollars in a relatively short period of time. When disaster struck Donald, he did not resign himself to flipping burgers to "make ends meet". His strong self-image and belief in himself allowed him to get right back on top.

Fortunately, very few of us will ever be put to the test of such drastic misfortune. Your belief in yourself is like a no-cost insurance policy that will keep you from fear of financial loss and allow to you enjoy what you have earned. Your talent, abilities, determination, and your other characteristics have gotten you where you are today. Believe in yourself and enjoy success.

ACTION STEP(S):

1) Take a few minutes to visualize yourself as a participant in the fictitious reality TV show mentioned above. How would you do? What would you do? Does the idea of starting from scratch with nothing but your abilities, talents, and determination excite you or terrify you?

"The 1990's sure aren't like the 1980's."

- Donald Trump

Day 324: Help Others Discover Their Own Gifts

Every day, people settle for less than they deserve. They are only partially living or at best living a partial life. Every human being has the potential for greatness but very few people realize this potential. Their natural gifts and hidden talents remain hidden and unused. A good leader is one who can tell another how to reach his or her potential; a great leader is one who can help another discover this potential for him or herself.

I believe every human being has gifts. Some call these gifts talent, ability, aptitude, or "good genes". No matter what they are called, or how we got them, it is universally recognized that we have them. Untapped potential is the difference between where a person is now and where he or she can be. Just about everybody lives with some sort of "gap" between where they are and where they can be. To be a great leader and get the maximum performance out of your people, you need to lessen this gap by helping them discover their own gifts.

There are many "side effects" to helping others discover their own gifts besides being a great leader. Parents and teachers are well aware of the warm feeling that comes with knowing that they, in some way, were responsible for improving the life of another. Some people report a sense of fulfillment of an obligation that exists as a result of someone helping them in the same way at some time. When you help another discover his or her own gifts, this process reinforces your own success and builds your self-confidence.

There is a difference between telling someone how to reach his or her potential (the classic parent/teenager discussion) and helping that person to discover it for him or herself. Here are some suggestions on how you can help others discover their own gifts.

- **Be an inspiration to others.** Be inspired yourself and you will be inspiring to others.
- **Be a role model to others.** Practice what you preach. Learning by example is one of the most effective ways to learn.
- **Share good books.** Do you know any good books that you can share or recommend to others that will help them be their best? I am sure if you really think about, you can think of at least one. :)
- **Teach something you know well.** When you teach, you also help others to learn. When we learn, we grow. It is in this growth process where we discover our hidden abilities.
- **Ask thought-provoking questions.** To help someone realize that their voice is good enough to make a career of singing, it is more powerful and effective to ask "What is your greatest strength?... And how can you profit from that?", than simply to say, "You should sing professionally".

Whether an employee, a best friend, or a complete stranger, if the opportunity is there to improve a life by helping another person discover their talents or abilities, then act on it—even if there is no apparent direct benefit to you. Practice this to become a better leader by making the world a better place one person at a time.

ACTION STEP(S):

1) Do you know anyone who can be so much more than what they are? How can you help them to realize their potential? Do what you can to improve one life today.

"The greatest good you can do for another is to help that person discover their own riches."

- unknown

Day 325: Inspiration from Jeffrey P. Bezos

Jeffrey P. Bezos (1964–) is the founder and CEO of Amazon.com, the Internet's largest e-commerce site with annual sales over $3.9 billion (2002).

Success is following your passion. In high school, Jeffrey fell in love with computers. He entered Princeton University planning to study physics, but soon returned to his love of computers, and graduated with a degree in computer science and electrical engineering.

Success is knowing that a good education opens doors. As a 1986 summa cum laude, Phi Beta Kappa, Princeton graduate, Bezos joined FITEL, a high-tech start-up company in New York. Two years later, Bezos began working for Bankers Trust Company in New York, where he led the development of computer systems and became the company's youngest vice president in 1990.

Success is having vision and seeing opportunity. In 1994, when "e-commerce" was still unheard of, Jeffrey Bezos observed that Internet usage was increasing by 2300 percent a year. He saw an opportunity for a new sphere of commerce, and immediately began considering the possibilities.

Success is asking the right questions. In a methodical fashion, Bezos reviewed the top twenty mail order businesses, and asked himself which could be conducted more efficiently over the Internet than by traditional means. Books were the obvious solution.

Success is gathering the info needed to succeed. Bezos attended the American Booksellers' Convention to learn everything he could about the book business.

Success is talking a leap of faith. At the time Bezos had the idea for Amazon, his employers were not ready to back the idea. Jeff knew that the only way to get the business going would be to leave the security of his current job and go off on his own.

Success is adding value to a name. It is not the name that makes the business, it is the business that makes the name. Prior to 1994, "Amazon" was just another noun. Today, it represents a new industry where billions of dollars of goods are being sold each year.

Success is continual improvement. Bezos and his team continued improving the Amazon.com website, introducing such unheard-of features as one-click shopping, customer reviews, and e-mail order verification.

Success is not being afraid of the "big boys". In 1997 when Amazon.com when public, many skeptics wondered if the company could compete with already established book giants such as Barnes & Noble and Borders once they established an Internet presence. Just two years later, the market value of shares in Amazon was greater than that of its two biggest retail competitors combined, and Borders was striking a deal for Amazon to handle its Internet traffic.

[Sources: http://www.achievement.org, http://www.time.com, http://www.askmen.com]

"Work hard, have fun, make history."

- Jeffrey P. Bezos

Day 326: Words of Wisdom: Part I

Words of wisdom are pieces of advice passed on over the years, which influenced countless people around the world by shaping and defining their lives. Some of these words come from authors, poets, politicians, historical figures, and religious writings, whereas some seem to be as old as time itself and their origins remain unknown. I have read and contemplated over 10,000 of these sayings, proverbs, aphorisms, and quotes over the years and have compiled a list of just over 300 that I believe bring people closer to success. Over the next three lessons, I will share these with you. Don't just read each one, contemplate its meaning and consider these words of wisdom: *One line of wisdom can change your life more than volumes of books.*

Action

- Be afraid only of standing still
- Spend your time and energy creating not criticizing
- Action without thought is like shooting without aim
- Suppressing a moment of anger may save a day of sorrow
- Motion is not necessarily action
- Action first, prayer second
- Do more, hope less
- He who knows no laziness will know prosperity
- Do something every day that you don't want to do, but know you should do
- Every action has an opposite and equal reaction
- Every man must bear the consequences of his own actions
- Constant occupation prevents temptation
- Inactivity breeds ignorance
- If you do nothing, nothing will happen
- If you wish for a thing and do not get it, try working for it
- The smallest deed is better than the grandest intention
- It is never too late in life to make a new start
- Do things that make you smarter
- The energy we use in getting even would be better spent in getting ahead

- A journey of a thousand miles must begin with a single step
- There are those that wait for something to happen, and those that make something happen
- Oversleeping will never make your dreams come true
- There are those who have ideas and there are those who do something about them
- Imagine what you would attempt to do if you knew you couldn't fail, then do it

Adversity

- Face adversity with a smile
- You learn more from people who disagree with you than from those who agree with you
- See problems as opportunities for growth and self-mastery
- With no winter, the spring would not be so pleasant
- The crisis of yesterday is the joke of tomorrow
- Accept temporary inconvenience for a permanent improvement
- Don't let a rut become a grave
- The best way to handle any crisis is to remain calm

Anger

- Don't criticize others when you are angry with yourself
- Let anger die quickly
- One who cannot tolerate small ills will find it hard to accomplish great things
- Do not become angry with people who do not agree with your opinion
- Every minute you are angry you lose 60 seconds of happiness
- Keep your head when those around you are losing theirs
- Don't carry grudges
- No situation is so bad that losing your temper will not make it worse
- Let go of anger; it hurts you more than the person at whom you are angry
- Bury the hatchet

- Showing anger is a sign of weakness

Arguing

- The only way to get the best of an argument is to avoid it
- Never say, "You're wrong!"
- If you are wrong, admit it quickly and emphatically
- The weaker the argument, the stronger the words
- Do not argue if you know you are wrong
- Show respect for other people's opinions
- It is not who is right but what is right that's important
- It takes two to fight

Assistance

- Don't be afraid to ask for help

Attitude

- Think positively and positive things will happen
- The best is yet to be
- Focus on the big picture
- Even the longest day will come to an end
- Concentrate on your strengths instead of dwelling on your weaknesses
- The optimist sees the doughnut, the pessimist sees the hole
- Hope for the best, but prepare for the worst
- The willingness to do creates the ability to do
- Expect nothing and you will not be disappointed
- If you look hard enough, you can find the positive in any situation
- Improve your performance by improving your attitude
- No one can make you feel inferior without your consent
- Change your thoughts and you will change your mood
- Avoid negative people, places, and things
- You cannot lose what you never had
- Everything is good for something

Belief

- Faith is stronger than hope
- Believe in the goodness of others
- Everything happens for a good reason

Benevolence

- Forgive and forget
- Be kind to strangers
- Try to make someone happy each and every day
- Show respect for all living things
- Don't talk about people behind their backs
- Be kind to the unkind
- It is nice to be important, but it is more important to be nice
- Be the first to forgive
- Society succeeds when it is easy for people to do good deeds
- Compliment people every day
- Make the other person feel important—and do it sincerely
- Make others feel appreciated
- Choose being kind over being right
- Don't deny anyone the opportunity to do something nice for you
- Value all life
- Lift people up
- If you want to feel good, help others
- Always stop to think when your fun will cause another's unhappiness
- Let the other person save face
- Within each person is a treasure, but sometimes you have to dig for it
- Say hello to others

Change

- If you do what you have always done, you will get what you have always gotten
- Dump your unwanted baggage

Character

- Character is what we are; reputation is what others think we are
- Personality opens doors; character keeps them open
- Never promise more than you are willing to give
- Adversity tests whether you are what you thought you were
- Give people more than they expect—cheerfully
- Practice what you preach
- Keep an open mind
- Ability helps you get to the top, but character keeps you from falling
- Perform whatever you promise
- Remember the power of kindness
- Never subtract from your character to add to your popularity
- Share the credit
- People with tact have less to retract
- Never use profanity
- Do more than is expected
- Maturity is about experience, not age
- Keep your promises
- Be genuinely interested in other people
- If you take care of your character, your reputation will take care of itself
- A person's reputation can be ruined by one lie
- Don't keep people waiting

ACTION STEP(S):

1) Choose three (3) sayings on this page that mean the most to you and write them down in your journal, memorize them, and share them with others.

Day 327: Words of Wisdom: Part II

Almost every wise saying has an opposite. For example, "the squeaky wheel gets the grease" and its opposite "the nail that sticks up gets nailed down". Both sayings sound good and are persuasive in communication; that is why some of these sayings have survived since the beginning of recorded history. It is up to you to decide if the words you read or hear make sense to you. Never accept an idea just because it sounds good.

Choices / Decision

- Every path leads two ways
- He who follows another is always behind
- It takes just one decision to change your life forever
- Your head must take your heart into consideration when making decisions
- It is OK to change your mind
- Either lead, follow, or get out of the way

Commitment

- Don't make commitments you don't plan to keep

Courage

- It is better to be a coward for a minute than dead for the rest of your life

Communication

- Don't criticize, condemn, or complain
- You have two ears and one mouth; use them in the same proportion
- Silence is the hardest argument to refute
- Think why you are saying no before saying no
- Think why you are saying yes before saying yes

- If you can't say anything nice, don't say anything at all
- Call people by name
- Words have the power to destroy or heal
- Give honest and sincere appreciation
- Don't try to top others' stories
- Talk less and say more
- When you have nothing to say, say nothing
- Silence is sometimes the best answer
- Encourage others to talk about themselves
- The key to communication is saying something so that your audience can understand it
- Ask questions that other people will enjoy answering
- If little ears should not hear it, then big mouths should not say it
- Stack two layers of praise around every critique
- Great minds discuss ideas, average minds discuss events, small minds discuss people
- Be interested and you will be interesting
- Talk about your own mistakes before criticizing those of another person
- Criticize the behavior, not the person
- Diplomacy is thinking twice before saying nothing
- The answer depends on the question

Competition

- Do not disparage your competitor

Death

- There is only one way to enter this world, but many ways to exit it

Destiny

- Take charge of your own destiny
- Assume responsibility for the quality of your own life
- Decide who you want to become
- The past does not determine the future

- Successful people believe that they are destined for great things
- Destiny is not a matter of chance, it is matter of choice

Excellence

- Whatever is worth doing at all, is worth doing well
- If it isn't broken, improve it

Excuses

- Being human is a privilege, not an excuse

Experience

- Experience is what you get when looking for something else

Failure

- Do not be ashamed to fail
- If God wanted us to accept failure as "His will", He wouldn't have given us persistence.
- The key to failure is trying to please everybody
- Everyone gets the same 24 hours in a day—the difference is how they use it
- When something in your life breaks down, put it back together again
- You never really lose until you quit trying
- Failure isn't falling down, it's staying down

Fairness

- Life isn't fair

Giving

- Our own success should contribute to the success of others

- Helping other people with their troubles helps you to forget your own
- You always help yourself by helping others
- You get out of the world just what you put into it

Genius

- A genius is a crackpot whose crazy idea actually works

Goals

- If you aim at nothing, you usually get it

Happiness

- The world likes a happy person
- Be responsible for your own happiness
- Happiness does not consist in things, but in thoughts
- Create rituals of things you look forward to doing on a regular basis
- Be happy with what you have while working for what you want
- Get what you want, then enjoy it
- Relish small pleasures
- Some pursue happiness—others create it
- Do not rely on others for your happiness
- The happiness of your life depends on the quality of your thoughts
- Find joy in what you have
- Authentic happiness is always independent of external conditions
- Work enjoyed is as much fun as leisure
- Love and work are two of the most important ingredients of a happy life
- Happiness is hard to find in ourselves and impossible to find anywhere else
- Live beneath your means
- Nothing in excess
- It takes thirteen muscles to frown, and only two to smile

Health

- Become addicted to good and healthy ways
- Health is the greatest of human blessings
- Have enough reasons for wanting to stay healthy
- Cheerfulness is the principle ingredient in health
- Get in shape and stay there

Hope

- Never take away hope from another

Humor

- Humor is the best ice-breaker
- Lighten up

Individuality

- Think for yourself
- Leave the herd and think for yourself
- It is harder to stand up against a crowd than to go along with it
- Treat other people as individuals
- Don't expect other people to solve your problems

Management

- Ask questions instead of issuing orders

Meaning of Life

- Use your life to make something that will outlast it
- Your achievements live longer than you do
- The meaning of life is to find meaning
- Play the hand that's dealt you
- Find your own philosophy

Miscellaneous

- Even logic has its limits
- Hunger is the first course to a good dinner
- Seek and ye shall find
- Dramatize your ideas
- Never ask a barber if you need a haircut
- Age is only important if you are cheese
- The nail that sticks up gets nailed down
- Always leave them wanting more
- All the negatives of politics do not come close to outweighing the few positives

ACTION STEP(S):

1) Choose three (3) sayings in this lesson that mean the most to you and write them down in your journal, memorize them, and share them with others.

"Knowing others is wisdom, knowing yourself is Enlightenment."

- unknown

Days 328 and 329 are for "R&R"—review and reflection. Spend these days reviewing the last five articles and reflecting on the information and how it relates to your life. Now is also a good time to make sure all the action steps for the previous days have been completed.

Day 330: Words of Wisdom: Part III

The wisdom is not in the words; it is in the interpretation and the meaning behind the words. With so few words used to create such powerful statements and ideas, it is understandable why there are so many interpretations of each. As a general rule, the fewer the words, the more interpretations there are. In some cases, quotes, sayings, proverbs, and other words of wisdom have a completely different meaning when taken out of context. It is the beliefs you adopt and the actions you take as a result of the words that are most important.

Open-Mindedness

- Realize that there are other points of view

Opportunity

- Profit from your mistakes
- Be open to new ideas

Passion

- Do not work just for the money
- Doing something you love is never a waste of time
- All great things in life are achieved with passion
- Show enthusiasm in both work and leisure
- The more you love, the more you love life
- He enjoys life who makes others enjoy it
- Profit from what you love doing

Patience

- Given enough time, running water can hollow out a stone

Perception

- To the ant, a few drops of rain is a flood
- The mind can make things better or worse than they actually are
- Life is what your thoughts make it
- An imagination can make reality more enjoyable
- The difference between stumbling blocks and stepping stones is the way you use them
- The optimist sees opportunity in every difficulty
- Wherever you are right now has the potential to be paradise
- The memory of the past is usually better than the actual past
- The good old days were never really that good
- Don't let someone else's reality become yours
- The grass may be greener on the other side, but it still has to be mowed
- The only normal people are the ones you do not know very well

Persistence and Determination

- Hang on longer than your competition
- Don't expect different results from the same behavior
- When you come to the end of your rope, tie a knot and hang on
- Never give up on what you really want to do
- By improving your own life, you begin to improve the world

Personal Growth

- Hold yourself to a higher standard
- Begin a program of self-mastery
- Become a skilled learner
- Act like the person you want to be
- Spend your years ripening instead of rotting
- Bring something to the table

- We become strong only after we have acknowledged our weaknesses
- Learning is addicting
- Do not put self-imposed limitations on yourself
- Inspired people inspire people
- Raise the bar in your life
- Improve yourself every way that you can
- Small daily changes make life spectacular
- When you cease to grow, you begin to die
- It is not what you are, it is what you do not become that hurts
- Small changes add up to a big change

Problem Solving

- When you can't solve the problem, manage it
- A problem adequately stated is a problem well on its way to being solved
- Do not look where you fell, but where you slipped

Preparation and Prevention

- An ounce of prevention is worth a pound of cure

Procrastination

- Do not wait for a rainy day to fix your roof

Progress

- Look back and see how far you have come

Recovery

- The sun shines after every storm
- This too shall pass
- Make the best of a bad situation

Regret

- Put your mind in gear before you put your tongue in action
- Yesterday will never come again, but you have today
- Careless hurry may cause endless regret
- Present neglect makes future regret
- Regret nothing
- If you would not write it and sign it, do not say it
- Planning your future saves you from regretting your past

Rejection

- You cannot please all of the people all of the time

Relationships

- A marriage is made in heaven, but the details are worked out on earth
- Time spent with your children is not wasted
- Love is something you give, not something you look for
- Better alone than in bad company
- In a friendship, because you share, the good times are doubled and the bad times are cut in half
- Love your children for who they are, not for what you want them to be

Relaxation

- Get the butterflies in your stomach to fly in formation

Responsibility

- Stop blaming others for your failures
- Quit blaming everything on your parents
- Hold yourself accountable for the way you feel
- It is up to you to make your life great

Risk

- A person must risk something of significance in order to achieve something of significance

Sales

- If you can sell it to yourself, then you can sell it to anyone
- You get what you pay for
- Everyone is selling something

Skepticism

- Look at the source as well as the advice
- Examine what is said more than who said it
- Question authority
- Question everything

Security

- Don't throw away the old bucket until you are sure the new one holds water
- There is no security on this earth; there is only opportunity

Self-Control

- You will know what is more than enough before you know what is enough

Self-Discovery

- Examine what you believe in

Self-Esteem

- Stick up for yourself
- Promote yourself but do not demote another
- If you make yourself a doormat, you will be stepped on

- The biggest human temptation is to settle for too little
- Do not sell yourself short
- Feeling good about yourself is a sign of success
- The more content you are with yourself, the fewer material things you need

Success

- There is no elevator to success—only stairs
- The dictionary is the only place success comes before work
- The more you lean on somebody else, the leaner are your chances for success
- Use your own definition of success

Teamwork

- Snowflakes are some of nature's most fragile things—but look at what they can do when they stick together

Time Mastery

- You always find time to do the things you really want to
- Do not fight a battle if there is nothing to win
- Be on time
- Time should be spent solving problems, not worrying about them
- Since you cannot make more time, spend the time you have more wisely
- Never say you do not have enough time
- Make sure the prize you chase is worth the effort
- Don't major in minor things

Trust

- Trust can be destroyed faster than it can be built
- Good people can do bad things
- It takes years to build trust, but only seconds to destroy it

Wealth

- No luxury should be purchased with debt
- Have more money by having fewer wants
- Share your wealth
- Love what you do
- Life becomes less complex when you eliminate needless wants

Wisdom

- One line of wisdom can change your life more than volumes of books
- Wisdom is to the soul as what health is to the body
- Wisdom should be shared
- Wisdom is revealed through action, not talk

Worry

- Why worry?
- If you are worrying about dying, then you are not spending enough time living
- Exercise instead of worry
- Worry gives you something to do, but it does not get you anywhere
- It does not make sense to worry about things that cannot be changed

ACTION STEP(S):

1) Choose three (3) sayings from this lesson that mean the most to you and write them down in your journal, memorize them, and share them with others.

2) Choose your favorite saying from the last three lessons, print it out in large letters on a single sheet of paper and hang it on your wall where you can see it every day.

Day 331: Importance of Customer Feedback

As a father of two small children, every day I deal with "feedback". When my daughter says she wants to eat less dinner so she can have more room for dessert, or when my son wants to do nothing but watch movies all day long, I basically tell them what is best for them—and that is that. This technique is fine for small children but does not work too well with customers. Unfortunately, many business leaders today treat their customers just like pre-teen children who have no idea what is best for them. Listening to your customers, and more important, acting on the feedback they give is one of the best ways to transform a struggling business into a successful one.

Not being in tune with your customers is like living in an alternate reality; the way you think your customers feel about your product is not always the same as what your customers really think about your product. Too many business people would rather live in ignorant bliss than accept the true reality about their product or business. The fact is, even if the true reality may be harsh, in most cases it is manageable.

The reasons for accepting customer feedback are quite obvious to some, but not so obvious to others. Your customers are ultimately the ones responsible for your paycheck. By listening to your customers needs and desires, you can tailor your product and service to better meet their demands. This will ultimately lead to greater success.

Below are just a few of the more common forms of accepting feedback. Depending on your business and your customer base, some will work better than others.

Suggestion box: a physical box with a pen and paper where customers can give feedback. This is great for gyms, retail stores, and other locations where customers visit.

Feedback form: this can be mailed or delivered with the invoice at the completion of a job. The questions can be structured to prompt the customer for the right kind of information. This is great for service professionals, painters, and other contractors.

On-line: an e-mail address, on-line form, and interactive forum are all good for feedback. Ideal when the majority of customers are on-line customers.

Focus group: getting a group of customers together for a discussion about your product is most common with a new product launch but can be used for feedback on existing products or services as well. Works best when the customers do not have far to travel.

Surveys: phone, snail-mail, and e-mail surveys are all pretty annoying to most customers but they can also be the most informative. Remember that very few people who feel indifferent about the product ever fill these out without some kind of compensation; as in a product discount or coupon, it is either the very happy or very upset customers who invest the time to take these surveys.

Here are the three basic rules for customer feedback:

1. **Make it easy for customers to give feedback.** There is a bumper sticker that reads "Complaints? Call 1-900-complain. $9.95 per minute". This is a humorous example showing how difficult it can be to find an organization willing to accept your feedback. If possible, allow the customer to give feedback anonymously. In cases such as giving feedback, anonymity breeds honesty.
2. **Thank the customer for the feedback.** If a customer is giving feedback, even in the form of a non-diplomatic complaint, realize that you are benefiting from this. Although kind words should be enough, customers feel appreciated more when some form of compensation is given. If giving a gift of some sort is possible and appropriate, then do it.

3. **Analyze the feedback.** Is this feedback based on an isolated incident? Have you received similar feedback before from other customers? Is this customer being reasonable in their requests and/or suggestions? Will acting on this feedback benefit the organization as well as other customers, or just this one customer? You certainly do not have to act on all suggestions, but you certainly should consider them. Customer feedback should be used as just one of the sources of information in decision making, never the primary source. There are times when you know your product better than anyone and your vision and determination will make it work despite public opinion.

Simply making it easy for customers to give feedback can do wonders for the overall attitude of your customer base. Actively seeking feedback, as in offering some form of compensation for the feedback, shows your customers that their feedback is important to you. Acting on the feedback and implementing reasonable changes based on customer feedback is a sure way to win over your customers and increase the success of your business.

ACTION STEP(S):

1) Ask for customer feedback, even if your "customers" are your students, co-workers, or other group. Be sure to thank them even if the feedback is negative, then consider the feedback.

"Not being in tune with your customers is like living in an alternate reality; the way you think your customers feel about your product is not always the same as what your customers really think about your product."

- Bo Bennett

Day 332: Inspiration from Dr. Martin Luther King, Jr.

Dr. Martin Luther King, Jr., (1929–1968) was named Man of the Year by Time magazine in 1963; and became not only the symbolic leader of American blacks but also a world figure.

Success is having a good foundation upon which to build. Martin Luther attended segregated public schools in Georgia, graduating from high school at the age of fifteen; he received a B. A. degree in 1948 from Morehouse College. After three years of theological study at Crozer Theological Seminary in Pennsylvania where he was elected president of a predominantly white senior class, he was awarded a B.D. in 1951. He then enrolled in graduate studies at Boston  University, completing his residence for the doctorate in 1953 and receiving the degree in 1955.

Success is making a difference. As a member of the executive committee of the National Association for the Advancement of Colored People, in 1955 Dr. King accepted the leadership of the first great Negro nonviolent demonstration of contemporary times in the United States, the bus boycott that lasted 382 days. On December 21, 1956, after the Supreme Court of the United States had declared unconstitutional the laws requiring segregation on buses, Negroes and whites rode the buses as equals.

Success is standing up for what you believe in, no matter what the consequences. King was arrested many times, his home was bombed, he was subjected to personal abuse, but at the same time he emerged as a Negro leader of the first rank.

Success is knowing and using the power of words. "I refuse to accept the cynical notion that nation after nation must spiral down a militaristic stairway into the hell of a thermonuclear destruction. I believe that unarmed truth and unconditional love will have the final word in reality. This is why right temporarily defeated is stronger than evil triumphant."

Success is extreme dedication and firm commitment. In the eleven-year period between 1957 and 1968, Dr. King traveled over six million miles and spoke over twenty-five hundred times, appearing wherever there was injustice, protest, and action; and meanwhile he wrote five books as well as numerous articles.

Success is knowing the power of peace and love. "Violence as a way of achieving racial justice is both impractical and immoral. It is impractical because it is a descending spiral ending in destruction for all. It is immoral because it seeks to humiliate the opponent rather than win his understanding; it seeks to annihilate rather than to convert. Violence is immoral because it thrives on hatred rather than love."

Success is sharing. At the age of thirty-five, Martin Luther King, Jr., was the youngest man to have received the Nobel Peace Prize. When notified of his selection, he announced that he would turn over the prize money of $54,123 to the furtherance of the civil rights movement.

Success is being your best. "If a man is called to be a street sweeper, he should sweep streets even as Michelangelo painted, or Beethoven composed music, or Shakespeare wrote poetry. He should sweep streets so well that all the host of heaven and earth will pause to say, here lived a great street sweeper who did his job well."

Success is inspiring others. Dr. King's charismatic leadership continuities to inspire men and women, young and old, in this nation and around the world.

Success is having a dream. "I have a dream that my four children will one day live in a nation where they will not be judged by the color of their skin, but by the content of their character. I have a dream today. I have a dream that one day down in Alabama with its vicious racists, with its governor having his lips dripping with the words of interposition and nullification, one day right there in Alabama, little black boys and black girls will be able to join hands with the little white boys and white girls as sisters and brothers. I have a dream today."

[Sources: http://www.nobel.se, http://thekingcenter.com/]

"Injustice anywhere is a threat to justice everywhere."

- Dr. Martin Luther King, Jr.

Day 333: Don't Be a "One-Upper"

Have you ever found yourself in a conversation with one or more people sharing stories? Have you ever noticed the "one upper" in the group that always feels the need to tell a story that is more dramatic that the one just told, or make a statement that immediately takes the positive attention off another? Are you, or have you ever been, the "one-upper"?

When you finish telling a story or explaining a situation you were in, and the person you are talking to responds with "Oh yeah, well listen to this...!" Basically, what they are telling you is that your story means nothing to them because they have a better one. When someone tells you something of significance to them, all they want is a sympathetic ear and to know that they have been heard. Even if you have a more dramatic story, use tact.

Here are some examples of a person named Pat being "one-upped" in both personal and business situations. Imagine yourself being Pat. How you would you feel?

Pat: *Hey guys, I just found out that the boss chose my team to lead that big project!*
One-upper: *Yeah? Well my team just won an award for the best ad campaign!*

Pat: *The other day I bought these shoes on sale for just $30!*
One-upper: *I bought the same pair two weeks ago on-line for $20.*

Pat: *When I was a kid, I fell 20 feet from a tree and broke my leg in two places.*
One-upper: *I fell out of a tree as well, but broke both legs and an arm!*

Here are a couple of quick suggestions regarding "one-upping":

1. **Decide if your story will help the listener.** For example, if your friend just told you that she got in a car accident and dented the door, just to get it off her chest, the best response may be "I am sorry to hear that. I am glad that you are not hurt... doors can always be fixed but people always can't." However, if that same person told you this following it up with "I don't know what I am going to do", then it may be appropriate to tell her about the time you got in an accident and how you handled the situation. Bottom line—does your story benefit the listener or just you?

2. **If you are among friends and you truly have a story more fascinating than the one just told that you feel you must share, lead into it gracefully.** You can do this by first making a statement reflecting on the story just told, asking questions, or at least waiting a few moments before jumping right in. If at all possible, wait for another time to tell your story—let the person who just told the story have the glory.

The key is to be a good listener while having consideration for the other person's feelings. Don't be like a twelve-year-old at camp who begins every sentence with "Oh yeah? Well wait until you hear this..." Use tact in your personal and business communications and try not to "one-up" anyone.

ACTION STEP(S):

---

1) The next time someone shares a story with you, be sensitive to this issue. Fight the urge to tell a "more fascinating" story, especially if others are present.

"Communication works for those who work at it."

- John Powell

Day 334: Meeting People

Imagine that you work for XYZ Corporation, a large company that manufactures widgets. The company sends you and a few of your coworkers to an international widget convention where there will be thousands of your suppliers and potential customers. Once there, your coworkers are busy meeting others while you quietly keep to yourself because you do not see yourself as a "people person". When the conference is over, your boss asks you for a list of the contacts you have made. You then realize that your lack of social skills may have just cost you your job.

I am generally a quiet person who keeps to myself. I appreciate solitude more than a social event full of small talk. At times, like when I go to the gym, I purposely avoid eye contact with other members because I am there to workout, then leave, not to socialize. But I do understand that, at times, my future success and happiness depends on my ability to meet others. For example, the majority of people in the higher paid and status positions are those who have excellent social skills. When seeking a life-long companion, your selection increases significantly if you have the ability to meet other people, rather than making an eternal commitment to the first acceptable person who comes along. If you too are the quiet type, it just takes a little practice and a slight attitude adjustment to master this skill and turn it on when needed.

Let's begin with attitude.

- **Establish a desire for meeting others.** If you're being sent to a conference to make contacts and improve your relationships with existing vendors and customers, realize that your job may be on the line.
- **Overcome shyness.** Being shy is nothing more than a lack of self-confidence combined with the fear of rejection (see Day 200).
- **Learn to like people.** In the USA, we say "innocent until proven guilty". Adopt a similar attitude with people.

Assume all people are good people unless they prove otherwise. If you dislike people, it shows in facial expressions, body language, and actions—it is like wearing a "Go Away" doormat around your neck.

- **Don't appear desperate.** Desperation, like a dislike of people, shows right through. The best way not to appear desperate is not to be desperate. Have confidence that you will meet many people. The odds are, other people will want to meet you as well.

Now that we have the right attitude, or frame of mind for meeting people, we are ready to take action. Here is a five-step process that works wonders.

1. **Evaluate the situation.** Is it appropriate to say hello to a stranger or would it seem very awkward? In the movie _Crocodile Dundee_, Dundee visits New York for the first time and is seen walking down a busy city street saying "G'day" to just about everyone. At the other extreme, when two people pass each other walking, and no other people are in sight, that lack of some kind of greeting or acknowledgment can seem very awkward. Be friendly and greet people in more situations than not.
2. **Make eye contact and smile.** If you are passing another person, or at least one of you is in motion, then look the person in the eyes with a warm and natural smile. This sends a non-verbal message to the other person that you are friendly and receptive to a greeting. That person can either avoid eye-contact or return the eye-contact and smile, meaning they too are receptive to a greeting.
3. **Say hello (or other greeting).** Once the other person has made eye contact with you as well, say "Hello" or some other appropriate greeting while maintaining your eye contact and smile.

At this stage, you have established yourself as a friendly, confident person. If this is another person that you see on a *regular basis, like a person at your school, gym, or work, you may want to just stop here until a better time to start a conversation. However, if you feel the chances are slim that you will ever see that person again, then proceed with the following steps.*

4 **Determine if the other person is receptive to conversation.** Use some common sense here to avoid the appearance of desperation. Is the other person preoccupied with another activity or do you think they are open to a conversation? As the saying goes, desperate times call for desperate measures. If you feel as if this will be your only opportunity to meet a person who you really want to meet, then proceed regardless of the potential awkwardness.

5. **Begin the conversation.** The best way to begin a conversation is with a topical and relevant question or statement that can easily lead to conversation. When someone is said to be "smooth", they can ease into conversation without any awkward or uncomfortable moments. Here are some suggestions:

   o **Don't ask generic questions and stay away from clichés.** Lines like "Do you have the time?" followed by unrelated conversation is not being smooth. However, asking another "Do you have the time?" in the middle of a clock store can be pretty funny.

   o **Find something topical and relevant to talk about.** An opening line such as "So what brings you here today?" may be ideal for a prospect visiting your booth at a trade show. This can lead to conversation about their needs and how your product can fill those needs.

   o **Introduce yourself later after some talk.** In most cases, beginning a conversation with an introduction is not the best idea. Generate interest first—create this interest so the other person wants to know your name.

   o **Never start off by talking about weather.** When people have absolutely nothing to talk about, they talk about the weather. It is the "safe" topic people usually fall back on; it is not a good topic with which to start.

Congratulations! You have successfully begun mastering the art of meeting people. From here it takes practice. This process helps you initiate a conversation, then you can use what you already know about communication, specifically allowing others to talk about themselves or better yet, finding common interests to keep the conversation going strong. The more people you can successfully interact with, the better your chances of success.

ACTION STEP(S):

---

1) Using these techniques (or a variation of), meet 10 new people.

"If you think it's hard to meet new people, try picking up the wrong golf ball."

- Jack Lemmon

Days 335 and 336 are for "R&R"—review and reflection. Spend these days reviewing the last five articles and reflecting on the information and how it relates to your life. Now is also a good time to make sure all the action steps for the previous days have been completed.

Day 337: The Proposal

Imagine that you have a great idea. You anxiously set up a meeting with a person who can help you to implement this idea. While setting up the meeting, you briefly explain the basis of the idea and while this person seems interested, you are asked to submit a formal proposal at the meeting, as well as deliver a brief presentation. Now you start to sweat. A formal what?

A proposal, although very formal sounding, is nothing more than prepared persuasion. Throughout this course, we have covered many persuasive techniques that can be used to help others see your point of view. In a proposal, we can use one or many of these techniques to convince another person or group of people to take action. A well-written proposal can be even more persuasive than an extemporaneous, persuasive conversation—it solidifies and organizes ideas and thoughts into a document or presentation that can leave a powerful impression on those to whom it is delivered.

Entrepreneurs and small businesses have the luxury of acting quickly on ideas alone. To some, this is a key to the "entrepreneurial spirit" and the major part of success. To others, this kind of "hasty" action can lead to the demise of a venture or business. Many people rely on proposals to help them make more informed decisions. Some people use proposals to help justify their decisions with others. And some people may just not be convinced enough by an idea alone—"Sounds good, but I will need to see something in writing". Whatever the reason may be, writing and/or delivering an effective proposal can play a large part in your success.

Here is a guideline for an effective proposal that can be used for both written and oral proposals. The length of your proposal should be dictated by the person requesting the proposal, the complexity of the objective, and/or your personal judgment. A proposal should be long enough to contain the information needed to convince the audience to take action, yet not too long as to cause the audience to lose interest.

1. **The introduction.** The introduction should be short and sweet. It should include the overall objective of the proposal (summarized in one or two sentences), summarized course of action and benefit. For example, if this article were a proposal my intro may be

   A well-written proposal can play an important part in your success. By following a proven format for writing a proposal and using one or more persuasion techniques, you will have significantly greater success in getting others to accept your ideas.

   You may want to write the introduction last since most of the information in the introduction comes from the body.

2. **Define the audience.** Who is your audience? What is in it for them? What is the benefit to the audience? Remember that it is not important how YOU benefit, at least not to the audience. To keep their interest and be as persuasive as possible, make sure you address the needs and wants of the audience. Keep this major point in mind while writing and delivering your proposal.

3. **Establish a need.** Your proposal should solve a problem or meet a need. Explain this need. Remind the audience that the need exists with as much detail as possible.

4. **Outline course of action.** What is your recommended course of action? The level of detail may vary depending on the same factors that determine the overall length of the proposal. If possible, break the course of action into steps or bullet points.

5. **Identify the cost of taking action.** What is the cost of taking this action? There are always costs associated with action, but they are not always financial costs. It is best to list these costs and address any concerns the costs may raise in the proposal, rather than these issues being raised when you are not present to address them.

6. **Identify the cost of NOT taking action.** Fear can be a powerful motivator. In fact, the majority of those who live a healthy lifestyle do so knowing that neglecting health can lead to an early grave. When appropriate, use fear to vividly illustrate the costs associated with not taking action. Make some future predictions if it will help strengthen your case.

7. **Identify the benefit of taking action.** End the body on a powerful and positive note by illustrating the benefits to the audience by taking action. Draw upon both emotion and reason. Listing benefits in a bullet format can work very well.

The Conclusion. Finally, wrap up your proposal with a summary and clearly request that some kind of action be taken. Throw in a startling fact, statistic, or a powerful quote—anything that will leave an impression on the audience as well as further support your point.

There is no one way to write a formal proposal so do not fear "doing it wrong". Remember that the goal is to persuade. Having the opportunity to write and/or deliver a proposal is a great thing that can certainly help others to embrace your ideas. A well-written proposal, or formalized persuasion, is a powerful tool that can be used to help you succeed.

ACTION STEP(S):

1) Read a proposal—any proposal. You should be able to find one on the Internet. Look for the characteristics described in this article and see how it rates as a well-written proposal.

Day 338: The Sales Roadblock

At some point, in every salesperson's career (remember that we are all salespeople in one way or another), a "roadblock" is hit. This is when a product is just not selling or at least not selling as well is it can be. At this point, many salespeople give in and start to blame elements that they cannot change—as in the price or the product. When businesses hit this roadblock, they start blaming elements that they cannot change—as in the "market" or economy. In reality, there is usually one or more elements that the salesperson or business can change that can knock down the sales roadblock. The key is to ask the right questions.

One of the most common business mistakes that can quickly lead to a business' demise, is making the assumption that the problem is with the price. Believe it or not, lowering the price is taking the "easy road" and often just leads to a business model that does not work. It is reasonable to assume that by lowering the price of a product, more will sell. While this may be true, it does not mean that revenues or profits will increase and certainly does not guarantee more sales. Before you make a hasty decision to lower prices, take some time to ask yourself these questions: Where is the problem? Is it with the market, the attitude of those selling the product, the product itself, or the price? The goal is to address the real problem.

The Market. Begin by looking at the market. Is there a need for your product? The product would not have been developed if someone did not believe there was a need at one time. Is there still a need? Did circumstances change? Do you have enough exposure to this market? You can have the best product for the best price, but unless people know about it, it will not sell. Is the product effectively being marketed to the target audience? Does the packaging of the product deliver a powerful enough message to get the prospect to take action?

Attitude. What is the attitude of those selling your product, or if you are selling a product, what is your attitude? Do you believe in the product that you are selling? Do you feel the price is well worth product? To be successful at selling, believing in the product is essential.

The Product. Does the product live up to its promises? Does the marketing material deceive the public into buying a product that is really inferior, or is the product as good or better than the marketing suggests? Can the product be improved to be more marketable?

The Price. Finally, after all of the above concepts have been considered, look at the price. Is the price just too high for what the market is willing to pay? If your product is more of a commodity, it is easy to base your price on comparable products. Unique products can be more difficult to establish a price. Keep in mind that it is usually easier to lower a price after a product's release than to raise the price. Make sure that any price decreases you make can be part of a profitable business model.

The time will come when you too hit a sales roadblock. It is important not to make blind assumptions and do not jump to conclusions. Analyze the market, your attitude, the product, and then the price. Address the real problem and you can save yourself time, energy, and money as well as overcome any sales roadblock that may get in your way.

ACTION STEP(S):

---

1) Use this sales roadblock exercise to see how you can sell more of what you are now selling. Why wait for a roadblock?

Day 339: Inspiration from Fred Deluca

Fred DeLuca (1948–) is the founder of Subway sandwich shops; the most successful franchise ever with over 20,300 restaurants in 72 countries.

Success is often a side effect of a "problem". In the summer of 1965, the ambitious 17-year-old Fred Deluca wanted desperately to attend college but did not have enough money. Opening a sandwich shop was the solution.

Success is seeking help from others when needed. Fred sought assistance from a long-time family friend, Dr. Peter Buck, who offered him the idea of starting a sandwich shop, and the financial backing ($1000) to do it.

Success is "learning how to fish". While Dr. Buck could have easily loaned Fred the money for school, he loaned Fred a much smaller amount that would be used to help Fred create his own source of income to pay for his own school.

Success is setting goals and striving to reach them. Over the years, both Dr. Buck and Fred worked very hard at making their sandwich shops (Subway) succeed. They had a goal of opening 32 submarine sandwich shops within 10 years. By 1974, eight years after their first store, they owned and operated 16 units throughout the state of Connecticut. Although it seemed unlikely that they would double that number in two years, DeLuca focused on reaching his goal.

Success is making deals when needed that others can't refuse. DeLuca figured that the fastest way to expand the business was to go out and find a franchisee. He approached his friend Brian Dixon with the opportunity and even offered to loan Brian the money to buy their restaurant in Wallingford, Conn. DeLuca even said that if Brian didn't like the business, he could return the store to them and owe them nothing. Dixon refused at first but eventually moved forward becoming the first Subway franchisee.

Success is being flexible. "It's not necessary to be so structured in this world. With all the people who work here (Subway), whether you are real structured or not, it is not going to affect how much work they do. People have inside of them a certain work ethic, and, if you appeal to them nicely, they'll respond and give all they can give."

Success is in the business system, not necessarily the product. Subway developed a business system such that cost of starting a franchise up is relatively small compared to other franchises and business in general. Through economies of scale, the system is able to provide tremendous cost savings passed on to franchisees. The cost of the franchise was relatively low per average store. The equipment, financing, supplies, training and more is supported by the franchiser to give the franchisee the best opportunity for success.

Success is often learning along the way. "We didn't really know the franchising business, and it's [a very] different business from the store operations business," Fred Deluca says. "Just because we knew how to run stores didn't mean we knew how to run a franchising company—at that point, we were in the beginning stages of learning how to be a franchiser."

[Sources: http://www.subway.com, http://www.qsrmagazine.com, http://www.ltbn.com, http://www.entrepreneur.com]

Day 340: Initiative

As a youngster, I must admit that my taking-out-garbage initiative left a lot to be desired. No matter how full the garbage was, I would force whatever I had to dispose of in the trash container and make it fit. I had a similar policy for pretending I did not see the dog poop on the carpet. Ultimately, I had to take out the garbage and clean up the poop anyway, but I had to be told (or yelled at) to do it. In retrospect, I should have accepted my fate as the household garbageman/poop picker-upper and taken the initiative to take out the garbage when full and pick up the dog poop when present. But why deprive my parents of the joys of parenthood? :)

Initiative, a characteristic that is present in virtually every successful individual, is defined as the power or ability to begin or to follow through energetically with a plan or task: enterprise and determination. The prefix "init" means to begin. While initiative does not necessarily mean having to follow through, those with initiative either do follow through themselves or see to it that the task is properly delegated. Perhaps the most important part of this definition is the word "energetically". Taking the initiative is not about mumbling "Yeah... I guess I'll do it"; it is about accepting the plan or task with commitment.

Initiative (or personal initiative) is the characteristic that people possess that allows things to get done. Leaders must have initiative. Without it, leaders are simply workers in leadership positions. Those who demonstrate initiative also demonstrate a leadership quality—perhaps the greatest leadership quality that gets one noticed.

Personal initiative is not something you should want to possess just to get noticed however. Personal initiative is the driving force that allows you to get things done in your own life. It is the characteristic that distinguishes a "someday I'll" person from a "been there, done that" person. People with personal initiative get things done.

Now that you can see how taking initiative can benefit you both personally and professionally, here are some suggestions for how you can take the initiative more often.

- **Force it.** Initiative requires energy, not necessarily passion or desire. You can take the initiative when the need arises simply because you know it is the best course of action to take toward your success.
- **Volunteer.** Initiative is, after all, a form of volunteering. Without spreading yourself too thin, seek responsibilities— energetically.
- **Don't wait until you are asked to do something.** If you know something needs to be done, and it is something that you need to do or should do, then do it—or at least take responsibility for it and add it to your "to do" list. As an adult, I personally find it embarrassing to ask another adult to do something they should be doing, and conversely, being asked by another to do something I should be doing.

People with initiative get things done in both their personal and professional lives. Organizations that have leaders with initiative are organizations that are committed to progress. Achievements begin with action and action is a result of initiative. Commit to being the person who takes the initiative and become a better leader and a more productive person.

ACTION STEP(S):

1) When was the last time you were recognized for "taking the initiative"? Start to become more proactive in everything you do.

Day 341: Think One Step Ahead

Computer programming is a passion of mine. I think what I enjoy most about it is the logical thought processes needed to make a program function correctly. It is like a series of advanced puzzles and mind games. A good program will be written to handle any situation that it may encounter using a series of "if-then-else" statements. For example, if a user chooses option B, then display all features for option B, otherwise, display options for A. In order to create a good program, the programmer must think ahead and prepare for as many situations as possible. In order to create a good plan of action in our real lives, we must also think at least one step ahead and prepare for as many situations as possible.

Thinking ahead is a thought process that uses if-then-else statements to predetermine courses of action based on different outcomes. It is also the process of thinking things through and getting the most out of each potential outcome whether it be good or bad. This technique can be used for a specific task, as in planning a marketing campaign, or used to plan out your entire life.

Despite our confidence and persistence, there are things that we cannot control. We cannot control the economy, the markets, unforeseen disasters, and we cannot predict the outcomes of all events, but we can anticipate them. If we can anticipate an outcome, we can also prepare for the outcome and minimize its negatives and maximize its benefits. By preparing for all possible outcomes with a series of plans, we can increase our own confidence and the confidence level in those whom we lead.

Many people have the "play it by ear" attitude. This can be a great laid-back attitude to have, and not bad for a relaxing vacation, but not the best attitude to have when a successful outcome is important. Very often, thinking just one step ahead can make the difference between failure and success.

Thinking one step ahead begins with listing all of the possible outcomes for your current decision, or current course of action. For each possible outcome, you will then want to create a course of action that can bring you as close to success as possible. Depending on the likelihood of the outcome, your plan of action can range from general to extremely detailed. By thinking one step ahead, you will never be caught with your guard down. Here are some examples of thinking one step ahead:

Professional long-term: If your current business generates $x in revenue in the next five years, then proceed with your detailed plan to open up more stores. Otherwise, proceed with your detailed plan to carry a wider range of products.

Personal long-term: If you are accepted to XYZ school, then spend the next several years studying while working part-time. Otherwise, look for a full-time career.

Professional short-term: If your client accepts the proposal, then devote your energy for the next 6 weeks to this project. Otherwise, spend two weeks contacting other prospective clients.

Personal short-term: If you can get a room for a decent price, then take the kids to Walt Disney World for spring break. Otherwise, have many fun activities ready to do locally.

Remember, the key is not in making the statement itself, but having courses of actions carefully planned for any outcome (or any likely outcome) that can occur. If you make it a habit to do this, you will be able to handle surprises and unexpected outcomes much more gracefully and with much more efficiency. Think one step ahead and you will never be left behind.

ACTION STEP(S):

---

1) What possible outcomes are there for your current course of action? Make a detailed plan for each possible outcome. Be sure to make the absolute best of each situation.

"If everyone says you are wrong, you're one step ahead. If everyone laughs at you, you're two steps ahead."

- Charles Thompson

Days 342 and 343 are for "R&R"—review and reflection. Spend these days reviewing the last five articles and reflecting on the information and how it relates to your life. Now is also a good time to make sure all the action steps for the previous days have been completed.

Day 344: Be a Mentor

When I am asked what my favorite hobby is, I answer, "Helping others to succeed". I do not say this because I want people to think of me as an overly-nice guy, but for me, helping others to succeed is a source of total pleasure and enjoyment. This is certainly not a unique quality; it seems to be in our nature to want to help others. We all may not possess the wisdom needed to help others succeed, but just about everyone possesses enough wisdom in some area to help someone with something. By being a mentor, we can help others while we help ourselves.

A mentor can loosely be defined as a wise and trusted counselor or teacher. However, a mentor/mentee (or mentor/protégé) relationship is often more personal and less rigid than that of a teacher/student relationship. Where teachers are mostly looked upon for information, and counselor's guidance, mentors provide advice, encouragement, and inspiration. It is important to note that teachers, counselors, friends, and even lawyers can also be mentors.

While money is considered a valuable asset, an even more valuable asset that you can share is your wisdom in a particular area, which is made up of your knowledge and experience. When you mentor someone, besides the personal fulfillment and enjoyment of helping another, you benefit by learning even more yourself. Learning is a never-ending process that happens to be a very beneficial side effect of mentoring. Mentoring is also a form a leadership. Mentoring gives you practical leadership experience as well as practice as a leader. Leading just one person to start can turn into leading an entire organization or even a nation.

Anyone can be an mentor, but not everyone can be a good mentor in every situation. Being a good mentor requires the right set of circumstances and qualities. Below are some of these circumstances and qualities. Remember not to sell yourself short.

Although you may not think you will make an ideal mentor, the chances are you will make a fine mentor.

- **Knowledge.** To be a mentor, you have to have a certain degree of knowledge in the area in which you are mentoring. This may sound obvious, but some people love to give advice just because others are willing to listen to them. There are also those who feel that because they have not mastered the material, they do not possess enough knowledge to help others. Former con-artist Frank Abagnale Jr. once taught a class where he was supposed to be a student, simply by reading one chapter ahead of the rest of the class. Just knowing a little bit more is all it takes.
- **Experience.** Experience is a something that cannot be quantified, although many people try. Some people have 10 years experience where others have one year of experience repeated 10 times. Learning from experience and altering your actions and behaviors as a result, is what makes experience a valuable teacher. The more experience you have, the more wisdom you can share as a mentor.
- **Confidence.** A mentor must have self-confidence. It is confidence of the mentor that helps give the mentee his or her confidence.
- **Salesmanship.** When you a mentor, you are selling ideas.
- **Empathy.** Mentors should be able to identify as well as understand a mentee's situation, feelings, and motives.
- **Caring.** More than just understand, mentors should care about those whom they are mentoring.
- **Inspire.** Mentors who can inspire through their words or actions are most respected by those whom they are mentoring.
- **Time.** A Mentor must have enough time to give the mentee the attention he or she requires.
- **The right mentee.** For many reasons, some people are just not "compatible". If you do not have luck with a mentee, do not give up on being a mentor. Keep looking.

Being a mentor can be a very rewarding experience in several ways. Think about areas in which you would make a good mentor. Think about people or groups of people that you can mentor and actively seek out mentoring opportunities. While your favorite hobby may not be mentoring, the chances are that you will find another source of enjoyment in mentoring.

ACTION STEP(S):

1) Write down areas in which you would make a good mentor.

2) Write down the names of people or groups of people that you can mentor.

3) Actively seek out mentoring opportunities.

"The best mentors are the people in your life who push you just a little bit outside your comfort zone."

- Leigh Curl

Day 345: Vision

Walt Disney was a man of vision. From the time he created his world-famous cartoon mouse, to the present day, many years after his death, his vision continues to turn into reality. In 1965, Disney took a leap of faith by purchasing 43 square miles of land in central Florida where he would eventually build his empire. Although he did not have all the resources needed to turn his vision into reality, nor did he have exact details on how he was going to do it, he did have the vision, which proved to be enough.

Vision, the kind used to succeed, is "seeing" with imagination and taking action to make the vision reality. It is seeing what others lack the imagination and creativity to see. Vision is more than just imagination; it is imagination with belief. When someone is said to have vision, they are seen as having an intelligent foresight.

When one has vision, they can "see" a goal or objective and have faith in its attainment. This experience serves as a mental blueprint to success. Leaders with vision not only have more confidence in themselves and the direction they set for those whom they lead, they also have more loyal followers who have been sold on the vision as well. Many successful people rank having vision as one of the key elements to their success.

So isn't vision something you either have or don't? I believe that everyone has vision, and like virtually every other aspect of success, vision is something that can be developed with practice. Here are some suggestions on how to use your imagination and power of belief to develop your vision.

- **Ask a lot of "what if" questions.** What if I had a million dollars to make my plan work? What if I had all the help I needed? What if I could not fail and nothing were to stand in my way? These types of questions jump start the imagination and help you realize the possibilities.

- **Realize that there are no "impossible" or "ridiculous" ideas.** Allow your imagination to create any kind of vision and later start thinking about the practicality of the vision. Keep the thought processes flowing!
- **Never worry about criticism.** Many people see their vision as "too grand" or never follow up vision with action due to the fear of criticism or ridicule. Have faith in your vision and never let those who lack vision get in your way of success.
- **Take a risk.** If you are one of those detail-oriented people who will not move forward on a plan until every detail is thought out and worked out before hand, then good for you. This is an admirable quality to possess, but also one that can get in the way of great achievements. With vision, you see the goal and are confident that you can achieve it, but sometimes problems that come up in the planning stage are best left to be resolved at the time they are encountered. I know this is a hard concept for some to accept (especially loan officers), but a leader with vision, in times of desperation can accomplish amazing things. Don't give up before you even begin.

After more than seven years of master planning and preparation, Walt Disney World opened to the public as scheduled on October 1, 1971. Although Disney never lived long enough to see his vision become a reality—he did not need to. To him, Walt Disney World was already a reality.

ACTION STEP(S):

---

1) What is your vision for the future? Spend at least 10 minutes to write down your vision with as much detail as possible. Remember, you have the power to change what you don't like and make what you do like a reality.

Day 346: Inspiration from Alexander Graham Bell

Alexander Graham Bell (1847–1922) was the inventor of the telephone.

Success is following your heart. Throughout his life, Bell had been interested in the education of deaf people. Pursuing this interest ultimately led him to the invention of the telephone.

Success is having vision. Shortly after the telephone's invention, Bell had written to his father, "The day is coming when telegraph wires will be laid on to houses just like water or gas—and friends will converse with each other without leaving home."

Success is being a keen observer. Bell was a gifted pianist, who as a teenager, noticed that a chord struck on one piano would be echoed by a piano in another room. He realized that whole chords could be transmitted through the air, vibrating at the other end at exactly the same pitch. In the years to come, this simple observation would eventually lead him to the creation of the telephone.

Success is asking the right questions. Bell hoped to convey several messages simultaneously, each at a different pitch. However, he could not see a way to make-and-break the current at the precise pitch required. He would eventually find the answer to his question, "How could pitch be conveyed along a wire?"

Success is being inspired. While visiting London, Bell and his father were fascinated by a demonstration of Sir Charles Wheatstone's "speaking machine." Upon their return to Edinburgh, Melville Bell, Sr. (Alexander's father) challenged

Alexander and his older brother to come up with a model of their own.

Success is overcoming adversity. Alexander Graham Bell had his share of personal tragedies. In the late 19th century when Tuberculosis was at its peak, the disease claimed the lives of both of his brothers within the span of four months. Bell himself was battling the disease when, at age 23, he moved with his parents to Canada.

Success is generosity. In testimony to the effectiveness of his work and generosity of his spirit, Helen Keller would dedicate her autobiography to Alexander Graham Bell.

Success is promotion. Alexander Graham Bell introduced the telephone to the world at the Centennial Exhibition in Philadelphia in 1876.

Success is continuing to do what you are passionate about. After Bell became rich and famous for his invention of the telephone, he continued to make contributions to the world of science and technology though his inventions.

Success is sharing. Eager to infuse a love of science and the natural world in others, Bell lent considerable financial and editorial support to both *Science Magazine* and *National Geographic*.

[Sources: http://www.fitzgeraldstudio.com, http://www.pbs.org]

Day 347: Reading People

Ask any poker player and they will tell you the importance of reading people. People do not always say what they mean nor do they mean what they say. People's actions and behaviors do not always reflect their true intentions. Your ability to read people will not only help you to be a better poker player, but it will help you in business and in virtually all aspects of your life.

The ability to read people is both a science and an art. First there is understanding how the human body responds to stimuli. For example, you are meeting with a client in your office and the client's stomach is making more noise than the construction workers with the jackhammers outside your window. This may be a good time to offer your client a snack, or perhaps lunch. Then there is interpreting their words and actions to best understand their true intentions. This is the artistic part.

Although being able to read people can be very beneficial in just about all areas of life, I believe it to be most useful in business, or in a professional situation. Here are what I consider to be the top three major benefits:

1. **To find out a person's true needs or wants.** Many people for one reason or another do not always express what they really want. Instead, they "beat around the bush" or ask for things they think they want or need. For example, an employee may ask for a raise, when in fact what they really want is more recognition at work. Understanding this can save a employer thousands of dollars per year.

2. **To be able to predict people's actions.** In any negotiation session, having the ability to read those with whom you are negotiating can make the difference between success and failure. Negotiation is an interactive game where your next move is based on the response or action of the person with whom you are negotiating. By predicting responses and

actions, you can be better prepared for any outcome and have the edge in negotiations.

3. **To have a better rapport with people.** When you can read people, you can cater to their needs and desires more effectively. This will certainly improve your personal and business relationships.

Learning to read a person is all about being observant. In general, the more you observe people, the better at reading people you will become. However, each individual has his or her own unique characteristics and responses. The more you know a person, the better you will become at reading that person.

Here are some suggestions on how you can enhance your "people-reading" skills.

- **Ask yourself, "What's in it for them?"** By knowing what a person stands to gain or lose, you can deduce what their true needs and wants are. Be empathetic.
- **Learn to read body language.** Body language, including facial expressions, is a direct result of feelings and emotions. Everyone can read body language to an extent, but it is those who learn to read what most others don't who have the advantage.
- **Listen for nuances in voice.** If you hear the words themselves and fail to listen to how words are spoken, the odds are you are missing the real meaning behind the message. Become a keen observer of voice and you will soon be able to detect when people say something other than what they really mean.
- **Ask questions.** Lawyers, psychologists, and clever business people know that asking the right questions can help them understand a person better. If an angry customer demands a refund, the right line of questioning could help you find out that it is not a refund the customer really wants, but a product that works the way they expected. This can lead to a satisfied customer as well as an upsell.

We can all read others to a certain degree. Generally, we can read those we know better than those we don't know, and some people are more difficult to read than others. Pay attention to people—how they move, what they say, how they sound, and how they respond. By being a keen observer of people you will enhance your people-reading abilities as well as your chances of success.

ACTION STEP(S):

1) Attempt to predict the actions and thoughts of the next three people with whom you deal. Use the techniques above.

"Those who do not rush to fill silence often have a high degree of poise and self-awareness."

- unknown

Day 348: Finding Good People

If finding good people were as easy as choosing ones with the best resume, human resource managers would have the easiest job in the company. What is a resume? Basically it is a written exaggeration of only the good things a person has done in the past, as well as a wish list of the qualities a person would like to have. There are those with very impressive resumes who may be "burned out" and just looking for an organization to take them. Then there are those with less-than-impressive resumes who have not yet had the opportunity to achieve what they are capable of achieving. To find good people you need to value people for what they can do, not for what they have done.

For the past nine years, I have run some very successful companies. When it comes to the success of an organization, I believe that a key element is the organization's people. With the right people in place an organization can achieve great success. In the past nine years, I have never once asked for a resume. I personally don't care what someone has done in the past; I want to know what they can do for me now and in the future. Since I cannot see the future, I must rely on my ability to value a person professionally based on a five key factors (remember ABCDE).

- **Ability.** Does the applicant have the ability to do the job? If they are doing the job now on their own or for someone else, that is usually a good indication that they do possess the ability. Here is where we do need to look at history. Have they done the job in the past? Or have they just been trained to do this job?
- **Belief.** Does the applicant believe that they can do the job, and do the job well? What is the confidence level of the applicant? Do they say "I guess I can do it" or "Not only can I do the job, but I will be sure to do it better than anyone else!"
- **Character.** This is a big one. I do not care how qualified a person may be, or even if I do believe that a person can

make the company a lot of money, if the person has a lousy attitude, is dishonest, or otherwise does not have good character (by my standards) I will not consider making the person part of the team. It is true that one bad apple can spoil the bunch.

- **Desire.** Is the person applying for the job simply because they need the money? If money were not an issue, would they do the job for free? The person who can find pleasure in their work, no matter what the work may be, is the kind of person I want working on my team.
- **Enthusiasm.** It is amazing the difference in performance between a team that watches the clock waiting for the end of the day, and a team that is enthusiastic about accomplishing an objective. People who are or who can become enthused are not only more productive, but a great influence on other members of the team.

Together, all of these factors help me to determine the applicant's overall potential to do the job.

I understand that this hiring method will not work in all situations. I certainly would not want my local hospital to hire doctors without detailed background checks and assurance of their skills. But even in situations such as this, more weight can certainly be given to the above criteria, rather than the content of the resume and the applicant's history itself.

Realize that you pay for a person's history. A Harvard graduate will cost more than a community college graduate. Make sure that you are paying the higher price because of what the person can do for you, not what they have done for themselves. If possible, you can minimize your risk by taking the person on as a contractor, rather than an employee. Or perhaps agreeing to hiring on a trial basis.

Seeking good people with potential may be a better strategy than seeking people with good resumes; it certainly has worked for me and my businesses. This is because my businesses also have leaders who know how to help others reach their potential. Value people on a professional level based on their potential, not on their history, and build an organization of achievers rather than a team of "has beens".

ACTION STEP(S):

1) Examine your own history and potential. Do your history and past achievements do you justice or are you capable of more? Or do you feel that your resume "over sells" you?

"The will to win, the desire to succeed, the urge to reach your full potential... these are the keys that will unlock the door to personal excellence."

- Confucius

Days 349 and 350 are for "R&R"—review and reflection. Spend these days reviewing the last five articles and reflecting on the information and how it relates to your life. Now is also a good time to make sure all the action steps for the previous days have been completed.

Day 351: Three Questions to Diplomacy

One of the common characteristics shared by just about every great leader in history, is the mastery of the art of *diplomacy*, or using tact and sensitivity in dealing with others. Diplomacy is more than saying or doing the right things at the right time, it is avoiding saying or doing the wrong things at any time. Although there are times when we want to tell others exactly how we feel, there are ways to communicate our message more effectively while strengthening relationships and being sensitive to the feelings and emotions of others. This is the art of diplomacy.

A few harsh words can destroy a relationship. Those who lack diplomacy find themselves in more negative relationships than those who are diplomatic. Those who lack diplomacy tend to burn more bridges (end relationships poorly) than those who are diplomatic. But diplomacy is more than just about preserving relationships; it can help you to make better decisions and it can prove to be an invaluable asset in negotiating win-win solutions.

Although politicians have to be masters of diplomacy, since their careers can easily be ruined by a few wrong words, everyone should strive to be diplomatic. Business people who say the wrong thing, at the wrong time, to the wrong people, not only put their own careers at risk, but put the success of their company, and all those who work for it, at risk as well. In our personal lives, the cause of many problems can be traced back to the lack of diplomacy. Fortunately, being diplomatic in your personal and professional lives can be as easy as asking yourself three simple questions.

1. **How will the other person feel?** Would you want someone to say to you what you are about to say to them? Always consider the person's feelings. It may take more effort to rephrase a statement, but it is well worth it.
2. **What assumptions am I making?** The lack of diplomacy usually stems from making false assumptions. Generally,

the assumptions made are that you are right and the other person is wrong. Even if you are quite certain that you are "right", if you are going to make assumptions, it is best to assume that the other person is doing what they believe is best. Those who assume that "everyone is out to get them" are generally considered some of the worst communicators.

3. **Am I letting my emotions get in the way?** Are your comments or actions fueled by emotion rather than reason? Remember that a few seconds of uncontrolled emotion can lead to a lifetime of regret. Respond, don't react.

Great leaders are diplomatic. They understand the importance of dealing with people and preserving relationships. Good people are diplomatic because they understand the importance of being sensitive to the feelings of others, no matter who the "others" may be. Practice diplomacy in your personal and professional lives and you will enhance your reputation and relationships.

ACTION STEP(S):

---

1) Commit to practicing diplomacy in your everyday life.

"Diplomacy... the art of restraining power."

- Henry A. Kissinger

Day 352: Recognize the Dead End

Imagine yourself exactly where you are today ten years from now. You are in the same job or business and making the same pay. You know no more than you did ten years ago, since your experience has been limited to the same year of experience repeated ten times. The only things you have to show for the last ten years are perhaps a few extra pounds around the mid-section and some more gray hair. Although some people may see this as great job security, those who are focused on success and personal growth see this as ten years of wasted time. One of the best things you can do for yourself is to ensure, on a regular basis, that you are making progress in your life by recognizing the "dead end".

Before we can do something about a dead end, we must learn to recognize one. Whether you are a business owner, employee, independent contractor, or unemployed (either voluntarily or involuntarily), you run the risk of being stuck at a dead end. Although every business and job has a future, it may not be the future you had in mind for yourself. A dead end is not characterized by income potential alone; it is also about personal growth (learning, experience, etc.), happiness, and contributions to society. For example, teaching in an elementary school, although income potential is certainly limited, can bring one tremendous wealth in the form of personal fulfillment and would not be considered a dead end. Conversely, working at a job you despise, with little chance of promotion and no personal satisfaction would be seen as a dead end.

Those who fail to recognize a dead end can spend years "stuck" at the dead end, only to one day look back and ask, "What happened?" One of the worst forms of regret is a wasted life.

It is equally important not to falsely label your current situation as a dead end, as it is to recognize a dead end. Those who change vocations or directions in life solely for the pursuit of money, end up worsening their situation more times than not. Likewise, those who are impatient and determine a dead end by a "slow month" or a denial of a raise, end up making poor decisions based on their temporary situation.

So the question is, how does one recognize a dead end? Here are some suggestions.

- **Analyze the market.** Is your market expanding? Is demand increasing or decreasing? Is your organization getting an increasing or decreasing share? What do you think the future holds for the market? Where there are growing markets, there are usually increasing opportunities.
- **Analyze the competition.** Are more people entering the market? How does this affect market share? Does this appear to be a trend? "Flooded" markets are those with too much product and not enough demand, and usually a sign of a dead end.
- **Analyze technology.** Do you see technology rendering your business or your position obsolete? If so, it may be best to get out before you are forced out.
- **What is your attitude?** Are you burnt or burning out? Or do you remain motivated and positive in what you do? If you find yourself in a situation where you feel you cannot stay motivated and positive, get out.
- **Visualize your future based on your beliefs, not on your hopes or wishes.** Are you selling yourself a dream or is your prediction of your future based on your goals and actions? If you do not truly believe that you are on the right path to success, then you are at a dead end.

You can never really recognize a dead end unless you make a conscious effort. While there are millions of people who claim to be in "dead end jobs", the majority of them do nothing about their situation except complain. If you are one of these people, ask yourself, "Is this really a dead end?" and consider the non-monetary benefits. If you do find yourself at a dead end, then take a leap of faith and do something about it. Remember that dreamers only dream and successful people take action.

ACTION STEP(S):

---

1) Carefully examine your current situation. Are you growing personally or professionally? Is what you do helping others? Are you headed to where you want to be financially? Or are you at a dead end? If you are at a dead end—do something about it.

"Worry compounds the futility of being trapped on a dead-end street. Thinking opens new avenues."

- Cullen Hightower

Day 353: Inspiration from Christopher Reeve

Christopher Reeve (1952–) is an actor (Superman), director, writer, and role model for countless people around the world.

Success is being a kid at heart. Reeve credits his acting success to his ability to remain youthful in his thinking. "The ability to retain at least some of this childhood innocence is essential to fine acting."

Success is multi-tasking. After graduating high school, Reeve toured the country as Celeste Holm's leading man in *The Irregular Verb to Love*, then went on to pursue a college education, while working simultaneously as a professional actor.

Success is taking action. Acting jobs did not come to Reeve; he had to find them. This meant frequent auditions. Reeve eventually auditioned and successfully screen tested for the 1978 movie *Superman*, which launched him to "super" stardom.

Success is challenging yourself. Rather than limit himself to the heroic roles for which he seemed so well suited, Reeve frequently sought after the challenging parts that cast him against his type— playing characters that were gay, sociopathic, or villainous.

Success is progress. Reeve believes that progress in one's life comes from setting your own challenges and then doing the best you possibly can to succeed.

Success is overcoming adversity. In 1995, in a tragic horse-riding accident, Reeve was thrown from his horse and instantly paralyzed from the neck down and unable to breathe. Reeve spent six long months in painful rehabilitation before he was able to return to his home. Since that tragic day, Reeve has been living his life unable to move from the shoulders down and unable to breathe on his own.

Success is not quitting. Less than a year after his injury, Reeve began to accept invitations for speaking engagements, despite his extreme difficulty with traveling. Reeve is now a best-selling author. Reeve also continues acting by narrating, hosting and even accepting major roles in films. Reeve made his directorial debut with the critically acclaimed HBO film *In the Gloaming*.

Success is doing your part to make the world a better place. Reeve is a supporter of The Foundation for a Better Life, which creates public service campaigns to communicate the values that make a difference in our market segments—values such as honesty, caring, optimism, hard work, and helping others.

[Sources: http://www.christopherreeve.org,
http://www.chrisreevehomepage.com]

Day 354: How to Handle Mistakes

Perhaps one of the largest and most well-known mistakes of all time was made by the Ford Motor Company back in the 70s. A poorly designed automobile named the "Pinto" had a severe weakness in the fuel tank, which greatly increased the chances of explosion on impact. Although the design itself could be seen as a significant mistake, an even bigger mistake was the company's decision to move forward with the production and sales of the Pinto regardless of the obvious danger to human lives. Why? A cost/benefit study was done which suggested that it would be "cheaper" for Ford to pay liability for burn deaths and injuries rather than modify the fuel tank to prevent the fires in the first place. This mistake not only cost hundreds of millions of dollars, but led to over 500 serious burn injuries and deaths, as well [Source: motherjones.com]. Needless to say, this mistake was not handled in the best way and the legal, ethical, and financial repercussions continue even today.

Hopefully, my sharing this horrible mistake in history at least helped you put your mistakes in perspective. We all make mistakes; some more serious than others. A balance must exist between trying to avoid mistakes and giving it your all. It should go without saying that mistakes that can result in death or injury to others should be avoided at all costs, but other mistakes that are less serious should be seen as setbacks and learning experiences. We all make mistakes, but it is how we recover from those mistakes that separate the winners from the losers.

When you make a mistake, your goal should be to better your situation. Very often, if handled correctly, a graceful recovery from a mistake can put you in a better situation than before the mistake was made. As always, look for the positives in the situation and use your persuasive speaking skills to convince others of those benefits if necessary.

Here are some suggestions on how to best handle mistakes you make, or mistakes made by those for whom you are responsible.

- **Take action to better the situation quickly.** You may not always be able to correct the mistake right away, but almost always you can do something to better the situation. The key is to act quickly.
- **Do not call attention to your mistake unless it is necessary.** Some mistakes do require public attention—as in the Ford incident. However, most mistakes can and do go unnoticed unless the one who makes the mistake calls attention to it. A good example of this is in public speaking. While giving speeches, I sometimes lose my place or skip some content, but the audience does not know it because I never say "Whoops... I lost my place"—I simply continue on like no mistake was made.
- **Don't play the blame game.** If you made the mistake, or if someone for whom you are responsible made the mistake, take responsibility for the mistake. Admit your error and assure others that you are taking action to improve the situation. Trying to avoid responsibility for a mistake for which you are responsible does not say much for your character.
- **Apologize.** If your mistake negatively affects others, apologize, especially if they bring the mistake to your attention. Do not try to justify or explain your mistake, simply apologize.
- **Use humor.** When appropriate, use humor to draw attention away from your mistake and lighten up the situation. It is especially important to be able to laugh at your own mistakes.

It takes a person of character to gracefully and effectively deal with their own mistakes. This process is another one to which many people attribute their success. We all make mistakes and we can all recover from our mistakes with a little effort, character, and positive mental attitude.

ACTION STEP(S):

---

1) Think back to a few mistakes you have made recently.   How could you have handled those mistakes better?

"A life spent making mistakes is not only more honorable, but more useful than a life spent doing nothing."

- George Bernard Shaw

Day 355: Fulfill a Need

A brief refresher in Economics 101: most of us were introduced to the *law of supply and demand* in grade school but most people fail to make the connection between this principle and success. The law of supply and demand is one of the most basic economic concepts as well as the foundation of all financial success.* In terms of success, the law states that wherever there is demand there is an opportunity for supply. This opportunity exists until supply exceeds demand. In short, the law of supply and demand, as well as financial success, is all about fulfilling needs.

The world is not, or never will be, a place where everyone is completely content—there will always be needs, wants, and desires (or simply "needs"). These needs create an opportunity for a product or service. Generally speaking, the greater the need, the greater the opportunity.

To be successful in business you must fulfill a need. Those who start businesses in a market where there is little or no demand for their product or service, or already too much supply, ultimately meet with failure. Existing businesses that launch new products or services into a market where no need exists ultimately end up discontinuing the product or service and suffer a financial loss. Employees whose position no longer fulfills a need eventually find themselves without a job.

Recognizing needs is a talent and like most talents can be improved with practice. You can practice by

- **Reviewing Abraham Maslow's Hierarchy of Needs (Day 61).** These needs are physiological needs, safety needs, love needs, esteem needs, and self-actualization needs.
- **Making it a habit of jotting down unfulfilled needs.** This is a specific form of seeking opportunity.

- **Being inquisitive.** Look for needs that are not being met. Listen to people who complain and ask others questions about needs, wants, and desires.

In addition to having the talent for recognizing needs, there are more methodical, but costly ways, specifically any of the many forms of market research, which can include surveys, focus groups, polls, and more.

Once you recognize a need, determine the marketability of fulfilling the need. You can do this by asking yourself one question: is the anticipated investment required, both monetary and non-monetary, to fulfill this need worth the anticipated reward? If you feel that the investment is worth the reward, then go for it.

Fulfilling needs of others is a major part of all success in life. In the business world, where financial success is viewed by most as the top priority, fulfilling needs is a must. You must not only be able to recognize needs and see opportunity, but you must also be able determine if fulfilling the needs are worth the rewards. Get in the habit of thinking of the needs of others and you will certainly help yourself in the process.

* The law of supply and demand is the foundation for all financial success, but not necessarily all wealth. Lottery winners, heirs to fortunes, and bank robbers may have an abundance of money that has nothing to do with supply and demand or true success.

ACTION STEP(S):

---

1) Write down at least 5 needs that you currently see being unfulfilled. For each need, ask yourself, "is the anticipated investment—both monetary and non-monetary—required to fulfill this need worth the anticipated reward?" If the answer is yes, consider taking action.

"There are realities we all share, regardless of our nationality, language, or individual tastes. As we need food, so do we need emotional nourishment: love, kindness, appreciation, and support from others. We need to understand our environment and our relationship to it. We need to fulfill certain inner hungers: the need for happiness, for peace of mind—for wisdom."

- J. Donald Walters

Days 356 and 357 are for "R&R"—review and reflection. Spend these days reviewing the last five articles and reflecting on the information and how it relates to your life. Now is also a good time to make sure all the action steps for the previous days have been completed.

Day 358: Make a Lasting Impression

Throughout life, the average person meets thousands of people and is exposed to even more ideas, concepts, and beliefs. The content of conversation, or the words used to convey a message, quickly fade, but the impression remains.

An impression is an effect, feeling, or image retained as a consequence of experience. However, like a footprint in the sand at a beach, impressions eventually fade away; a lasting impression is one that does not. When we refer to making a lasting impression in terms of success, we are referring to a positive impression.

Those who know how to, and are capable of making lasting impressions on others, have a level of influence over others that is most useful in the pursuit of success. Consider the following situations:

- A contractor bidding for a job who makes a lasting impression on the client is more likely to get the job
- An applicant going through the interview process who makes a lasting impression on the hiring manager is more likely to get selected for the position
- A person who is courting another who makes a lasting impression on the other person is likely to gain the interest of that person.
- An employee of a large organization who makes a lasting impression on the right people is more likely to advance within the organization
- A salesperson selling a similar product or service as other salespeople who makes a lasting impression on the prospect is more likely to sell that prospect his or her product
- A business marketing a similar product or service as other businesses that makes a lasting impression on the market is more likely to have success marketing their product or service

- A parent who makes a lasting impression on a child can change that child's life for the better.

How can you make a lasting impression? Think back to your own experiences in life and think of the impressions that were made on you. What were the circumstances? If you carefully think about this, you will discover three key circumstances:

1. **Strong emotion.** The stronger the emotion, the stronger the impression. It is easy for us to recall events in our lives where we were feeling strong emotion, both positive and negative. However, we generally cannot recall everyday events like what we had for lunch last Tuesday (unless the meal was exceptionally good or exceptionally horrible).

   To make a lasting impression on someone, get them to feel some kind of emotion. The anti-smoking commercials use ex-smokers with holes in their throats to get the public to feel fear. Beer commercials use half-naked people to make us feel good while seeing their product. Of course, your approach to getting others to feel strong emotion can be less gruesome and should certainly be less manipulative.

2. **Use of imagery.** People remember best in pictures, not words. This is why the use of imagery is so important in both memory and creating a lasting impression. For example, one of the most effective techniques for remembering numbers is to convert the numbers into words, then convert the words into mental pictures. The more outrageous the imagery, the more memorable it becomes.

   A great use of imagery is the use of dramatization. Effective communicators use this frequently in presentations, meetings, lectures, speeches, lessons, and in everyday conversation. For example, instead of just telling someone they are wasting money, take a handful of change and throw it in the garbage coin by coin (I would say burn a dollar bill but I think that's illegal, and I do not want to promote illegal activities). At one of our spring conferences for our salesteam, I presented a $1000 bonus to our top producer. The $1000 was in brand-new, crisp, $100 bills that I counted out one at a time with the help of the audience as I presented them to the winner.

3. **Differentiation.** The law of contrast states that which is different or unique makes a greater impression than that which is ordinary. We notice the one light bulb that is burned out more than we notice all the light bulbs that are not. It is the unique and the different that makes a lasting impression.

   Never be afraid to be different or take the road less traveled. Do not be afraid to do or say something others will not (diplomacy and tact take precedence here). Be creative and stand out from the crowd in a positive way.

The impression is what is left over when the words and details have faded. Practice leaving people with positive lasting impressions and when the time comes, they will remember you, your advice, and/or your product.

ACTION STEP(S):

1) Do your best to make a positive lasting impression on someone today.

"The happiest conversation is that of which nothing is distinctly remembered, but a general effect of pleasing impression."

- Samuel Johnson

Day 359: How Marketable Are You?

Imagine a huge retail store where instead of products on the shelves, there were people. This is a store where hiring managers go to "buy" employees for their business or organization. The shoppers think like all shoppers do when buying products. They may ask questions such as, "Do I need this product? How will I benefit from using this product? Is this product outdated or replaced by a better product? Is it reliable? Is it priced right? Do I have a choice of many similar products or is this one unique? Now think of yourself as a product on a shelf in this store. Are you a hot item that is consistently out of stock? Or are you one of those items that sit on the table in the front of the store marked "damaged goods - price reduced"?

When it comes to selling our labor in the form of employment, sometimes it helps to think of ourselves as products. This helps us to better understand the needs of employers. A product that is considered "marketable" is one that can be exchanged fairly easily for something else of value. When people are considered marketable, they can exchange their labor for something else of value, such as a satisfying career.

So the question is, how marketable are you? More important, what can you do to become more marketable? Here are some suggestions.

- **Define the ideal skill sets desired for your industry.** Before you can work on your skills, you must know what skills you need to be working on. Do not make assumptions here. Don't think the skills you learned back in the 60s while attending college are the same skills required today. Talk to your manager, mentor, or any industry expert. Read the trade magazines and keep on top of the industry.
- **Be involved in continual education.** Remember that "formal education" is not the only kind of education. There

are many ways to educate yourself in addition to enrolling in more formal classes. Once you know the skills that will help you to become more marketable, you can begin to develop and/or improve on those skills. Being marketable is about being competitive and desired.

- **Be a leader.** Being good at what you do is fine, but when you are good at what you do as well as being an excellent leader, you stand above the crowd. Having leadership qualities can make you a "hot item"!
- **Promote yourself.** Become a master of self-promotion. When someone says your name, you want the response to be "I heard of [him/her]... [he/she]'s that [guy/lady] who [insert great quality here]". Don't expect anybody to promote you for you (unless you are paying for it)—you must do it yourself.

Now what if you define the skill sets needed for your industry and realize that you have no desire to acquire the skills needed to be seen as marketable? Consider changing vocations. What are your skills? What skills would you enjoy learning? In which industry would you enjoy being? Ski equipment may not sell very well on Miami Beach, but it will sell in Vermont. If you are unwilling to change your product, then change where you are selling it.

Don't be the product that ends up in the "price reduced" bin. Know what it takes to be marketable in your chosen profession and make the effort to not only stay ahead of the curve, but make an effort to lead the pack. Educate, promote, and lead and you will be the hot item that never sits on the shelf for very long.

ACTION STEP(S):

---

1) How marketable are you? Take some kind of action to become more marketable than you are now.

Day 360: Inspiration from Bo Bennett

If you have not figured it out by now, Bo Bennett (1972–) is the author of this book you have been reading for the past year. Bo is also President and CEO of Archieboy Holdings, LLC, holding company to over 30 Internet properties.

Success begins with the desire for success. My fascination/obsession with success began at age 10, while listening to success author Denis Waitley's "Seeds of Greatness" audio program. From that day on, I would read and listen to any book or program I could get my hands on related to personal or business success.

Success is learning from others. Growing up, I learned so much from my family. From my mother I learned sales and how to conquer fear. From my father I learned creative thinking and independence. From my sister I learned about the entrepreneurial spirit. And from my brother I learned about the power of the human spirit and the incredible positive changes of which people are capable.

Success is taking your own path. From my performances of the "Mr. Bill Show" with clay figures for my second grade classmates, to my high school and college days where I chose to abstain completely from drugs and alcohol, I have always been seen by my peers as "different"; but being different is something that has never bothered me.

Success is acting on opportunity. I immediately glimpsed the future when I was first introduced to the Internet. My wife, Kim, and I sold our graphic design business, and the secure income that went with it, to pursue web hosting. Starting with a single customer and revenue of $10 per month, I ended up selling my first web hosting business seven years later for 20 million dollars.

Success is being passionate about life. I love life. I wake up at 4:00 am with a fire in my belly and ideas in my head. I love my work as well as my time away from work. I love my wife Kim, my daughter Annabelle, my son Trebor, and my dog Archie. I just love life.

Success is living a healthy lifestyle. I am a big advocate of health and fitness. Since age 14, I have been exercising on a regular basis while constantly improving my diet. Our bodies are the vessels that carry our minds through life. When we fail to take care of our bodies, our minds suffer as well. The mind can only focus on one thing at any given time. When the mind is focusing on illness or poor health, it is impossible to focus on success and achievement. Take care of yourself, so you can take care of those whom you love and focus on making a difference in the world.

Success is having good relationships with others. For me, a significant portion of my success can be attributed to my relationships: my relationships with my Creator, family, friends, business associates, customers and acquaintances. I hold no grudges, hate no one, and have learned to focus on the good in others rather than their faults.

Success is happiness. While I cannot say I consider myself one of the most successful people alive today, I do consider myself one of the happiest people alive today. To me, happiness is watching my 4-year-old daughter ski down an intermediate slope. It is cuddling with with my son while watching a movie, spending quality time with my wife, eating, writing, programming, designing, creating, reading, learning, and helping others. For me, happiness is found in the little things that I do every day.

Success is being grateful for what you have, and not resentful for what you don't have. I live a blessed life and I am grateful for all that I have and all with which I was born. I am grateful for the fortunate events that led me to my wife and I thank God for the miracle of my two healthy children. I am grateful to live in a country, during a time, of such tremendous opportunity. I am grateful for my ability to not let adversity affect my happiness.

Most of all, I am grateful for having the clarity to see life for what it really is—an amazing gift.

Success is sharing. Writing *Year To Success* has been one of the greatest experiences of my life. The idea of sharing my success philosophy with people all around the globe, and helping others to discover their own gifts, is greater than any financial compensation. It is a dream come true for me.

[Source: me]

"When it comes to success, there are no shortcuts."

- Bo Bennett

Day 361: Job Security

Today, the traditional idea of "job security" is virtually non-existent. No longer does getting hired mean getting hired for life. Mergers, layoffs, downsizing, corporate restructuring, focus shifting, bankruptcy—the list of terms that are synonymous with "you're fired" goes on. It seems as if your job security is completely out of your control... or is it?

Security is number two on Maslow's hierarchy of needs, second only to our physiological needs. It is no wonder that job security is such a pressing and controversial issue today. People traditionally think of job security as the choice of keeping the same job for as long as desired. This is done in the form of tenure or other long-term contract. Finding this kind of job security is extremely rare. However, if job security is viewed as the ability to keep a desired job, not necessarily the same job, and certainly not necessarily for the same organization, then job security is both readily available and within your control.

While you cannot completely prevent being "let go" by an organization, you can reduce your chances. Here are a few ways.

- **Do your job the best you can.** Don't just go through the motions. If you were a manager having to choose only a handful of employees to stay on and the rest would be let go, would you choose those who do the bare minimum or those who give it their all? Even if your best is not good enough, your dedication and commitment may be.
- **Make yourself a key player.** Take on additional responsibilities without necessarily taking on more work. Make yourself indispensible. Be proactive in sharing ideas and play an active role in your organization's success.
- **Never rest on your laurels.** The fact that you once were an important part of an organization does not mean much when it comes to cutbacks. What have you done lately? What are you working on now? Just like success, your

value to an organization is based on what you do on a regular basis, not just what you have done in the past.

- **Keep up with the times.** If you were to re-apply for your job today, would you be hired? As the requirements and expectations for positions change, those filling the positions must change as well. Ask for the requirements of someone applying for your position regularly just to make sure you are still a good candidate.

No job security? Don't get mad, get smart. Who or what is to blame for lack of job security? Do we blame automation? Management? Owners and stockholders? Do we blame the younger people with fewer financial responsibilities that are willing to work for less, or foreigners in other countries who can work for much less? Or perhaps we don't blame anyone or anything; we accept these as standard business practices in a modern economy and focus on creating our own job security by becoming less dependent on the organization for which we work and more dependent on our own resources. Here are a few ways.

- **Be marketable.** Always be working to improve your abilities, talents, and skills.
- **Have a backup plan.** Why spend your valuable time worrying about losing your job when we can spend that time focusing on your success? Be prepared for a sudden loss of your job by having a plan of action, then put it out of your mind. This will help your self-confidence, allow you to perform better at your current job, and reduce your chances of being let go.
- **Create multiple streams of income.** Even with a full-time job, you can create additional streams of income by making your money or creativity work for you. Real estate or financial investments can be a good source of extra funds that require very little time and energy. Side businesses can require very little money and produce unlimited rewards. When you have multiple streams of income, you have a kind of "job security" that is more solid than any tenure or long-term contract.

- **Change your attitude.** Job security can be a great thing, but so can the opportunity to start over and do something you've always wanted to do—something about which you are passionate. People who give too much weight to security tend to ignore their self-actualization needs and never truly live the best parts of life. Job security is not everything.

While traditional job security, or guaranteed employment with a single organization, is virtually non-existent these days, you can increase the chances of your job being more secure. From a non-traditional point of view, one can have the ultimate job security by not focusing on a particular job with a particular organization, but rather by focusing on a reliable income. Job security is within our reach, we just need to be sure we are reaching for the right kind of job security.

ACTION STEP(S):

1) What would you do if you lost your job or primary source of income? Have a plan of action ready so you can eliminate the worry associated with losing your job and spend your mental energy focusing on your success, not your possible losses.

"We have gone completely overboard on security. Everything has to be secured, jobs, wages, hours- although the ultimate in security is jail, the slave labor camp and the salt mine."

- Cola Parker

Day 362: Credit the Other Person for the Idea

Early in my web hosting career, I was interviewed by a journalist for a local paper for my first web hosting business. It turned out to be a great article promoting my business locally while making me look very good. The truth is, during the interview I was a bumbling idiot, not yet skilled in the art of effective communication. The journalist knew this and used a great communication technique to create a win-win situation by making me look good and by creating a great article for her paper. The journalist knew what I wanted to say as well as the kind of information that would make a great article. She would ask the right questions then rephrase my answers while shaking her head up and down looking for a positive response from me, which she did get. The result: an article full of eloquent quotes that I believed came from me. The fact was, the journalist, through her excellent communication skills, was able to get me to say what she wanted me to say while making me think they were all my ideas.

Sounds a little manipulative, doesn't it? Let's remember the difference between manipulation and persuasion—intent. The journalist's intent was not to discredit me nor make me look bad, but to make me look good. She helped me to say the things the readers wanted to read while leaving out the other facts that I liked to talk about, but which no one but me would be interested in. She created a win-win situation while not deviating from the truth and facts.

When people believe the thought or idea is theirs, they are much more likely to accept the thought or idea. By crediting the other person with a thought or idea, you are greatly increasing the chances that they will accept it. This can be an extremely effective technique to use in many different situations. For example, trying to get your boss to accept an idea, making a proposal to a committee, or helping a teenage child to take the right path.

To understand why this technique works so well, we must make some general assumptions about people as a group: they are normally defensive, they like to feel important, and they like to show leadership, superiority, and power when possible. For any one of these reasons, people accept their own ideas over equally as good or better ideas of another person. Once we understand this, we just need to practice techniques that allow us to credit the other person for ideas.

Here are three techniques you can use to give the other person credit for an idea or thought. Use them individually or in conjunction with each other.

- **Credit.** Directly give the other person credit for the idea by saying that they were inspiration for the idea. This technique is only suggested if it is true. It is not hard to see how something or someone could have easily helped inspire an idea. For example, "Mr. Jones, last week at the meeting you spoke about the need to increase productivity. You also mentioned that I would make an excellent manager. I do agree that having me manage this new team would help with overall productivity."
- **Generalize.** Rather than approaching someone with an idea that has all the details worked out, leave something for them to decide, thereby giving them part ownership. This way, they will feel as if it was at least partially their idea, or that they are in control. Add in the "assumptive close", and you have a winner. For example, "Mr. Jones, I suggest we move the meeting to next Thursday. What time do you think would work best?"
- **Rephrase.** This has also been known as "putting words in other people's mouths" and a favorite of lawyers. The key is to not overdo it. You want to use this technique to help people say what they mean, not trick people into saying what they don't mean. Use phrases such as "So what you're saying is...", "If I understand you correctly, you're saying..." or similar phrases. For example,

Mr. Jones: "I need everyone to be more focused on this

project."

Mr. Smith: "So you're suggesting we put our side projects on hold for now?"

When it is more important that an idea be accepted than who gets credit for it, give the person or persons who need to accept the idea credit for the idea. This is a great persuasion technique as well as a great way to create a win-win situation.

ACTION STEP(S):

1) Try this technique.

"Let the other person feel that the idea is his or hers."

- Dale Carnegie

Days 363 and 364 are for "R&R"—review and reflection. Spend these days reviewing the last five articles and reflecting on the information and how it relates to your life. Now is also a good time to make sure all the action steps for the previous days have been completed.

Day 365: Position Yourself for Success

I will admit, I am one of the fortunate people who was in a good position for success. The year was 1994 and I had recently graduated from college. With access to many credit cards and a few bucks from odd jobs here and there, I had enough money to meet the few financial obligations I did have. I was single and technically unemployed. In a nutshell, I had plenty of time, some money, little responsibility, and absolutely no fear of risk. Without knowing it, I managed to position myself for success.

The first element is time. Without committing the proper time to any endeavor, there is little chance that it will succeed. This does not mean that you need a lot of time on your hands, you just need enough time. Before I started my first web hosting company, I knew that I needed to know more than I currently did about the Internet. I devoted just an hour a day to programming, Internet marketing and web design. That one hour a day was all I needed to get me started. Had I committed only 15 minutes a day for those first couple of months, I would have been six months behind and may have missed the Internet "wave".

The second element is money. I am not a believer in the saying "it takes money to make money". I firmly believe that it takes ideas, persistence, and patience, among other things, to make money. However, if you do not have enough money to keep your endeavor growing, the chances for success decrease. Whatever your endeavor may be, make sure that the money you can commit to it is enough to at least keep it going. Do not open a pet store if you don't have enough money to feed the animals.

The third element is responsibility. As we approach middle age, we tend to take on more responsibilities. These responsibilities often take up both our time and money, as well as occupy our minds with "more important" things. Responsibility is the feeling of being responsible for something or someone. Spending time and money on an endeavor that may or may not pay off seems "irresponsible" to most people. If it is not possible to delegate some of your responsibilities, then at least have enough faith in your own ability to do more than you are currently doing. The human spirit is an amazing thing when pushed past the comfort zone.

Finally, we have the element of risk. Generally speaking, one's tolerance for risk is based on the first three elements of time, money, and responsibility. Someone with plenty of time is more likely to risk investing their time. Someone with plenty of money is more likely to risk investing their money. And someone with little responsibility is more likely to takes risks than someone with more responsibilities. It is important to remember that risk can be controlled; a sound idea, backed by a solid business plan, with ample financing, and a leader with enough faith and passion to see the plan through, is a sure formula for success.

Although it is not possible for all of us to go back to when we just finished school, or to another time when we were better positioned for success, we can alter our current position and attitude. There is always something that you can do today, right now, that will put you in a better position for success. Figure out what that something is, and do it.

ACTION STEP(S):

---

1) How can you better position yourself for success? What time can you allocate? How much money? Can you delegate some of your responsibilities? Can you increase your tolerance for risk? Do what you can.

"In whatever position you find yourself determine first your objective."

- Marshal Ferdinand Foch

Day 366: Closing Advice

Over the past year, you have been introduced to hundreds of success principles. My success philosophy detailed in *Year To Success* is based on personal experiences, observations, and proven principles—some of which seem as old as time itself. Rather than trying to sum up every principle contained within this course, I will conclude with some new advice.

Maintain your success. Success is not something to achieve and then forget about. Once you achieve success it is your responsibility to maintain success. People who have small successes in life often get blinded by temporary success and end up only worsening their situation. Great success in life is usually a result of many successes. Forge ahead. Remember that success is a way of life.

Become a farmer of success. Plant the "seeds of success" in your everyday life and you will reap the benefits. When you put these principles into practice, you serve as a role model and inspiration to others. Everyone deserves to be successful, so share these principles with others.

Use your success wisely. With success comes power and with power comes responsibility. There have been some people throughout history who were very successful at doing some terrible things. Your ethics, morals, and values determine your ultimate success in life. Remember that it is never too late to seek spiritual guidance.

The success formula used in *Year To Success* is education + inspiration + action = success. *Year To Success* has provided you with the education, as well as the inspiration, but when it comes to taking action, it is up to you. Have faith in your ability to succeed at anything you do and you will succeed at anything you do. Believe in yourself and start living your dreams!

ACTION STEP(S):

---

1) Take time to congratulate yourself! Not many people have the perseverance to complete this course. You have shown commitment and dedication to your own success and if you have not experienced a significant level of success by now, be patient... it will come your way.

"Grant me the serenity to accept the things I cannot change, the courage to change the things I can, and the wisdom to know the difference."

- The Serenity Prayer

YEAR TO SUCCESS

Written By

BO BENNETT

Since 1995, Bo has been motivating and inspiring his own staff through semi-annual conferences and seminars. He has since formalized several presentations that focus on just about any area of success all audiences.

Bo has a unique style of speaking that is both motivating and entertaining. He is a strong believer in audience participation using several exercises that have been best described as a "whole lot of fun". Bo's presentations follow the 20-minute rule of keeping an audiences attention, which means he does not speak for much more than 20 minutes at a time without involving the audience in some way.

If you are interested in having Bo speak at your school, business, or organization, please visit http://www.yeartosuccess.com/speaking.php.

Notes...